The *Cursus Honorum*

Patristic Studies

Gerald Bray
General Editor

Vol. 3

PETER LANG
New York • Washington, D.C./Baltimore • Boston • Bern
Frankfurt am Main • Berlin • Brussels • Vienna • Oxford

John St. H. Gibaut

The *Cursus Honorum*

A Study of the Origins and Evolution of Sequential Ordination

PETER LANG
New York • Washington, D.C./Baltimore • Boston • Bern
Frankfurt am Main • Berlin • Brussels • Vienna • Oxford

BV
664.5
, G53
2000

Library of Congress Cataloging-in-Publication Data

Gibaut, John St. H.
The cursus honorum: a study of the origins
and evolution of sequential ordination / John St. H. Gibaut.
p. cm. — (Patristic studies; vol. 3)
Includes bibliographical references.
1. Ordination—History of doctrines. I. Title. II. Series:
Patristic studies (Peter Lang Publishing); vol. 3.
BV664.5.G53   264'.14'09—dc21   99-36835
ISBN 0-8204-4592-4
ISSN 1094-6217

Die Deutsche Bibliothek-CIP-Einheitsaufnahme

Gibaut, John St. H.:
The cursus honorum: a study of the origins
and evolution of sequential ordination / John St. H. Gibaut.
–New York; Washington, D.C./Baltimore; Boston; Bern;
Frankfurt am Main; Berlin; Brussels; Vienna; Oxford: Lang.
(Patristic studies; Vol. 3)
ISBN 0-8204-4592-4

*Grateful acknowledgment is hereby made to copyright holders
for permission to use the following copyrighted material:*
John St. H. Gibaut, "The *Cursus Honorum* and the Western Case against Photius." *Logos* 37
(1996), pp. 36–73. Reprinted by permission of the editor. All rights reserved.
John St. H. Gibaut, "The Clerical Cursus of Constantine of Nepi." *Ecclesia Orans* 12 (1995),
pp. 195–205. Reprinted by permission of the editor. All rights reserved.
Norman P. Tanner, ed. and trans., *Decrees of the Ecumenical Councils.* Vol. 2.
Georgetown: Georgetown University Press © 1990.
Reprinted by permission of the publisher. All rights reserved.
José Vives, ed., *Concillios Visigóticos e Hispano-Romanos.* Madrid:
Consejo Superior de Investigaciones científicas, Instituto Enrique Florez © 1963.
Reprinted by permission of the publisher. All rights reserved.

This book was published with the financial support of Saint Paul University, Canada,
and the Anglican Foundation of Canada.

The paper in this book meets the guidelines for permanence and durability
of the Committee on Production Guidelines for Book Longevity
of the Council of Library Resources.

© 2000 Peter Lang Publishing, Inc., New York

Printed in the United States of America

For my son

Peter

CONTENTS

I. SEQUENTIAL ORDINATION
IN THE FIRST THREE CENTURIES

II. THE *CURSUS HONORUM*
IN THE "GOLDEN AGE" OF THE FATHERS

III. The *Cursus Honorum*
from the Eighth Century
to the End of the Tenth

c. Conclusion 245

IV. THE *CURSUS HONORUM*

IN THE ELEVENTH AND TWELFTH CENTURIES

1. Introduction...247

2. The *Cursus Honorum* in Conciliar Legislation.............................248

3. Papal Letters and Decretals...254

4. Canonistic Collections Prior to the Gregorian Reform...................258

    a. Burchard of Worms 258

    b. *Collectio canonum in V libris* 261

5. Canonistic Collections from the Mid-Eleventh Century.................264

    a. The *Diversorum patrum sententiae* 265

    b. Anselm of Lucca..267

    c. Deusdedit 271

    d. Bonizo of Sutri..272

    e. Ivo of Chartres 273

    f. Gratian 276

6. Ordination Liturgies..282

    a. OR XXXV "B"..282

    b. *Pontificale romanum saeculi XII* 283

7. Medieval Literature on Holy Orders..287

    a. Gerard of Cambrai 288

    b. Ivo of Chartres 289

    c. Hugh of St. Victor...291

    d. Peter Lombard..293

8. Biographical Material 296

    a. The Roman Church...296

    b. Italy, France, England...298

V. CONCLUSION:
THE *CURSUS HONORUM* PAST AND FUTURE

ABBREVIATIONS

(For bibliographic information, please consult the Bibliography.)

AT	*Apostolic Tradition.*
COUSTANT	P. Coustant, ed., *Epistolae Romanorum Pontificum.*
CCSL	*Corpus Christianorum Series Latina.*
CCCM	*Corpus Christianorum Continuatio Mediaevalis.*
CSEL	*Corpus Scriptorum Ecclesiasticorum Latinorum.*
DDG	*De distantia graduum.*
DEO	Isidore, *De ecclesiasticis officiis.*
D7OE	Ps.-Jerome, *De septem ordinibus ecclesiae.*
DO7G	Ps.-Isidore, *De officiis VII graduum.*
EL	*Epistula beati Ysidori iunioris episcopi Spalensis ecclesiae ad Leudefredum aepiscopum Cordobensis aecclesiae directa.*
EOMIA	C. H. Turner, ed., *Ecclesiae Occidentalis Monumenta Iuris Antiquissima*
GCS	*Die Griechischen Christlichen Schriftsteller der ersten drei Jahrhunderts.*
Jaffé	P. Jaffé, *Regesta pontificum Romanorum ab condita ecclesia ad annum post Christum natum MCXCVIII.*
LO	M. Férotin, ed., *Le Liber ordinum en usage dans l'église Wisigothique et Mozarabe d'Espagne.*
LP	Louis Duchesne, ed., *Le Liber Pontificalis: Texte, Introduction, et Commentaire.*
MAASSEN	F. Maassen, *Die Geschichte der Quellen und der Literatur des canonischen Rechts im Abendlande bis zum Ausgange deMittelalters. Vol I.*

MANSI	J. D. Mansi, ed., *Sacrorum Conciliorum Novi et Amplissima Collectio.*
MGH	*Monumenta Germaniae Historica.*
	Concilia Concilia aevi Karolini.
	Epp. Epistolae.
	SRM Scriptores Rerum Merovingicarum.
NRSV	*New Revised Standard Version.*
OR	*Ordo Romanus*
PG	J.-P. Migne, ed., *Patrologia Graeca.*
PL	J.-P. Migne, ed., *Patrologia Latina.*
PRG	*Pontificale romano-germanicum.*
PR12	*Pontificale romanum saeculi XII.*
SC	*Sources Chrétiennes.*
SEA	*Statuta ecclesiae antiqua.*
THIEL	A. Thiel, ed., *Epistolae Romanorum Pontificum Genuinae.*
74T	J. Gilchrist, ed., *Diversorum patrum sententiae sive Collectio in LXXIV titulos digesta.*

INTRODUCTION

Every year the church celebrates the ordination of deacons. While some candidates will remain deacons for many years—if not for life—others will be ordained presbyters within twelve months. The ordination of this second group to the diaconate, i.e. those destined to the presbyterate, begs a question. What does it mean to ordain a person to one order as a requirement for ordination to another? The texts of the older ordination liturgies clearly reflected the situation in which the diaconate was a step towards the presbyterate.[1] Similarly, the older rites for the ordination of presbyters assumed that candidates were already deacons.[2] The newer rites for the ordination of both deacons and presbyters, however, reflect no such assumption that the diaconate is a step towards the presbyterate or that candidates for the presbyterate are deacons.[3] On the contrary, there is nothing in the current rite which suggests anything less than the conferral of a permanent office. Although the terminology of "promotion", "inferior" and "higher rank" has been eliminated in the liturgical texts, canon law

---

[1]   E.g. the final petition in the ordination prayer of the *Pontificale Romanum*: "*In moribus eorum praecepta tua fulgeant; ut suae castitatis exemplo imitationem sanctam plebs acquirat: et, bonum conscientiae testimonium praeferentes, in Christo firmi stabiles perseverent; dignisque successibus de inferiori gradu per gratiam tuam capere potiora mereantur.*" *Pontificale Romanum,* vol. I (Torino: Marietti, 1961/62), p. 27. *Cf.* The Ordering of Deacons in the *Book of Common Prayer*: ". . . that they. . . may so well behave themselves in this inferior office, that they may be found worthy to be called unto the higher ministries in thy Church; through the same thy Son. . ." The Church of England in the Dominion of Canada, *The Book of Common Prayer* (Cambridge: The University Press, 1918), p. 622.

[2]   At the presentation of the candidates, e.g. the archdeacon said: "*Reverendissime Pater, postulat sancta mater Ecclesia catholica, ut hos praesentes diaconos ad onus Presbyterii ordinetis.*" *Pontificale Romanum,* vol. I, p. 29.

[3]   *The Rites of the Catholic Church,* vol. 2 (New York: Pueblo Publishing, 1980), pp. 49–69. For the current Anglican rites, see the Church of England, *The Alternative Service Book, 1980* (London: Hodder and Stoughton, 1980), pp. 339–364; The Anglican Church of Canada, *The Book of Alternative Services* (Toronto: Anglican Book Centre, 1985), pp. 643–658.

preserves the practice that all presbyters pass through the diaconate.[4] This apparent incongruity between liturgical and canonical texts reflects the issue in question. When both the candidate and the church "intend" presbyteral ministry, why prior ordination as a deacon? At another level one might ask why in the selection and election of candidates for episcopal ordination, only presbyters (above a certain age and of so many years service) are canonically eligible, while deacons and lay people cannot be considered?[5] These are the questions which this study will address in its consideration of the emergence and development of the process of sequential ordination, known classically as the *cursus honorum*.

The history of the church, particularly in the early centuries, abounds with examples of Christian ministers whose careers did not follow the pattern of the *cursus honorum*. For example, there are cases of lay people and those in minor orders ordained directly to the presbyterate and even to the episcopate; there are numerous examples of deacons ordained to the episcopate without anterior ordination as presbyters. While the diaconate, presbyterate and episcopate are unquestionably related to one another, there was no prescriptive use or understanding of these ministries as serial ranks or grades to be passed through sequentially until well into the fourth century. By analogy, the positions of nurse, physician, and administrator in modern health care institutions, are in the same fashion closely related. Yet one would hardly prescribe sequential promotion through these professions either, though it happens that some nurses do become doctors or administrators, and some doctors do enter the field of administration.

Despite the long association with the clerical grades, the terminology and practice of the *cursus honorum* are not inherently ecclesiastical. Rather, the nomenclature of *cursus honorum*, meaning "career of honour", initially belonged to the military and civil services of the Roman Empire. Members of the senatorial and equestrian orders ascended sequentially from the lowest to the highest ranks of the military and civil services according to a prescribed *cursus honorum* (or *cursus publicus*). In the Republican period the Roman army was a volunteer force in which rank was largely determined by wealth. Thus, if one could afford a horse, one served in the cavalry. The higher military ranks, like the higher offices of state, were similarly dependent on the amount of property owned. In the

---

[4] Canons 1031–§1, 1032–§1,–§2. *Code of Canon Law: Latin and English* (Washington: Canon Law Society of America, 1983), pp. 374/375.

[5] *Code of Canon Law*, canons 377–§2, §4; 378–§1, pp. 138/139, 140/141.

late-first century B.C.E., Augustus implemented the practice of the *cursus honorum* in the reform of the army and navy. He initiated the process by which members of the equestrian and senatorial ranks would embark upon a series or sequence of alternating military and civilian offices to ensure both political and military competence in the higher offices. A typical *cursus honorum* for a member of the equestrian order would commence at the rank of prefect of a cohort, followed by a period as prefect of a squadron, and end up as a legionary tribune.[6] The *cursus honorum* for a senator of patrician rank might begin with service as a tribune. After a few years he would serve in a minor civilian post in Rome, followed by appointment as a legate of a legion for three years. The senator would then be eligible for election to the higher civilian offices, such as consul. Lastly, a consul would be eligible for appointment as a proconsular legate of a province.[7]

From the fourth century the church began to follow the practice of the *cursus honorum* with respect to its ordered ministry. Although movement from one order of ministry to another was not unknown in the first three centuries, there is no evidence of a prescribed clerical *cursus* prior to the fourth century. But from the fourth and fifth centuries conciliar and papal legislation increasingly insisted that candidates for the major orders—especially the episcopate—progress sequentially from the lowest to the highest grades of the ministry, and this within specified intervals known as "interstices." Thus, the ecclesiastical *cursus* was similar to the *cursus honorum* (or *publicus*) of the imperial military and civil services. By the eleventh and twelfth centuries in the medieval church, it had become theologically, canonically and liturgically impossible for candidates for the episcopate to be ordained without passing through the *cursus honorum*; sequential ordination had become an assumed part of catholic order. Although the term *cursus honorum* has fallen into desuetude,[8] the practice remains an established feature of ordination procedure in virtually all

---

[6] James L. Jones, "The Roman Army", *Early Church History: The Roman Empire as the Setting of Primitive Christianity*, eds. Stephen Benko and John O'Rourke (London: Oliphants, 1971), p. 197.

[7] Jones, "The Roman Army", p. 201.

[8] This is easily seen by a glance at *The Oxford Dictionary of the Christian Church*, 2nd ed., rev., F. L. Cross and E. A. Livingstone (Oxford: Oxford University Press, 1983) which contains entries for the "interstices" (p. 709) and "*per saltum*" ordination (p. 1065), but no entry for "*cursus honorum*."

churches that retain the threefold ministries of bishop, presbyter, and deacon (as well as the minor ministries).

In recent years there has been a proliferation of literature on the ordained ministry, much of which is highly critical of received practices and traditions. Such literature seldom, if ever, raises the *cursus honorum* as an issue as the following examples illustrate.

A fairly prolific critic of traditional patterns of ministry is theologian Hans Küng. In his 1971 work, *Why Priests?*, Küng refers to a variety of ministries and to the "institutionalizing" of the church's ministry, yet refers to sequential ordination only in passing and offers no proposals for its reformation. He does, however, criticize clerical celibacy, advocate the ordination of women, and question the place of university education for candidates for the priesthood. In the chapter "Development of the Traditional Conception of Office" he notes that in the second century "[t]he structure of ecclesiastical service was (significantly) adjusted to that of the Roman civil services, with its *'ordines'*; services arranged as finely gradated *'offices'*."[9] While he seems to acknowledge sequential ordination at least implicity, Küng is reticent to critique the practice or offer an alternative. Later he acknowledges that the diaconate has become no more than a liturgical step to the priesthood, but offers no further comment.[10] He also notes that the minor orders have also "degenerated to the condition of contemporary liturgical stages on the way to the priesthood," and adds that they "need not be renewed."[11] In a more recent collection of essays, Küng again takes issue with many aspects of the traditional patterns of ordained ministry, but does not challenge the *cursus honorum*. In a chapter entitled "Church from Above—Church from Below"[12] Küng is highly critical of any hierarchical understanding of the church, and even likens bishops to generals.[13] But once again he does not mention or critique the practice of sequential ordination, or associate it with a hierarchical understanding of the church.

---

[9] Hans Küng, *Why Priests?* (Glasgow: Collins, 1971), p. 37.

[10] Küng, *Why Priests?*, p. 70.

[11] Küng, *Why Priests?*, p. 71.

[12] Hans Küng, *Reforming the Church Today: Keeping Hope Alive*, trans. Peter Heinegg *et al.* (New York: Crossroad, 1990), pp. 52–63.

[13] Küng, *Reforming*, p. 58.

Edward Schillebeeckx has contributed much to the rethinking of ordained ministry in recent years. Yet in his two major works on ministry
Schillebeeckx, too, says little about sequential ordination. While his earlier
book, *Ministry*, makes no reference to the *cursus honorum*,[14] the subsequent *Church with a Human Face* only says little. In the detailed and thor-
ough historical section in the second book, Schillebeeckx points out that as
the church became "institutionalized" it took over the imperial structures
of its environment.[15] The clerical *cursus*, however, is never explicitly cited
by Schillebeeckx as an instance of this phenomenon.[16] The only reference
he makes to the practice of sequential ordination appears in a paragraph on
the late fifth-century (or early sixth-century) theologian, Pseudo-Dionysius the Areopagite. Schillebeeckx suggests that the hierarchical structure
of the church was inspired not only by Graeco-Roman institutions, but
from the sixth century by the works of Pseudo-Dionysius. Under the influence of the works of Pseudo-Dionysius (such as the *De ecclesiastica hierarchia*) the various ministries which arose historically to meet the pastoral
needs of the church were understood theologically to correspond to a hierarchical Neoplatonist world-view. Accordingly, the higher orders of the
church's hierarchy possess to an elevated degree what the lower orders to
an smaller degree: all power comes "from above." "In the end," Schillebeeckx concludes, "the so-called 'lower consecrations' were one step towards the 'higher consecrations'."[17] The appeal to Pseudo-Dionysius is
interesting. Regardless of any legacy of Pseudo-Dionysius for the theology
of holy orders, the linking of his hierarchial world-view to the practice of
sequential ordination is open to criticism, as will be seen. Yet it is curious
that Schillebeeckx mentions sequential ordination in the first place, and
secondly associates it with the theological system of Pseudo-Dionysius.
For in spite of Schillebeeckx' repeated attacks on "the pyramidal hierarchical structure of the church," he does not revisit questions around the

[14] Edward Schillebeeckx, *Ministry: Leadership in the Community of Jesus Christ* (New
York: Crossroad, 1985).

[15] E.g., "From the fourth century, the time of Constantine, we see that the local organization of the church deliberately followed civil models of the empire." Edward Schillebeeckx, *The Church with a Human Face: a New and Expanded Theology of Ministry*
(New York: Crossroads, 1985), p. 147.

[16] Schillebeeckx, *Church*, p. 132.

[17] Schillebeeckx, *Church*, p. 158.

theology, practice, and consequences of sequential ordination raised in this section.

In *Priesthood*, a truly comprehensive and ecumenical work, Kenan Osborne simply refers to the *cursus honorum* in an *excursus* on the minor orders.[18] Similarly, Mary Schaefer and Frank Henderson in *The Catholic Priesthood* refer only briefly to the clerical *cursus* as part of a new organization arising in the fourth century. They describe it as an ecclesiastical parallel to the ranks of the Roman civil service, a form of preparation for the higher offices.[19] Daniel Donovan does not even mention the issue in his overview of contemporary Roman Catholic theologians on ministry, *What Are They Saying About the Ministerial Priesthood.*[20]

The significant lack of attention that sequential ordination has received would seem to suggest that, like the existence of major orders themselves, the *cursus honorum* has been so long assumed that it is past the point of comment. Notwithstanding, the practice of the clerical *cursus* is not completely without comment or critique. The one place it tends to be treated as an identifiable issue is within the body of literature written during the past thirty years on the restoration of the diaconate. For instance, in his study on the diaconate Edward Echlin sees the historic rivalry with the presbyterate as the reason for the decline of the diaconate. The canonical insistence that all presbyters pass through the diaconate is a consequence of deacons having lost the struggle. Echlin asserts: "Gradually the diaconate receded in importance until the diaconal order became merely a preliminary and ceremonial step to the sacralized priesthood."[21] Nonetheless, in his final chapter on the future of the diaconate, Echlin does not question the inherited practice of sequential ordination, regardless of its association with the decline of the diaconate.[22]

---

[18] Kenan Osborne, *Priesthood: A History of the Ordained Ministry in the Roman Catholic Church* (New York: Paulist Press, 1988), pp. 197–199.

[19] Mary M. Schaefer and J. Frank Henderson, *The Catholic Priesthood: A Liturgically Based Theology of the Presbyteral Office*, Canadian Studies in Liturgy, No. 4 (Ottawa: Canadian Conference of Catholic Bishops, 1990), p. 41.

[20] Daniel Donovan, *What Are They Saying About the Ministerial Priesthood* (New York: Paulist Press, 1992).

[21] Edward P. Echlin, S.J., *The Deacon in the Church: Past and Future* (New York: Society of St. Paul, 1971), p. 61.

[22] Echlin, *Deacon*, pp. 127–136.

Norbert Brockman's important ecumenical study on the permanent diaconate is more critical of the use of the diaconate as a "stepping stone" to the presbyterate.[23] Yet for all his reservations about the use of the diaconate (as well as the minor ministries) as a ritual preparation for the presbyterate, Brockman as well does not question the transitional diaconate, nor the practice of sequential ordination.

A direct challenge to the practice of sequential ordination appears in Patrick McCaslin and Michael Lawler's *Sacrament of Service*. Like Echlin, McCaslin and Lawler associate the decline of the diaconate with the power-struggle between deacons and presbyter; they, however, associate the struggle with the rise of sacerdotalism in the ninth century.[24] Early in their study they pose the question: "Does every priest need to approach priesthood through diaconate?" They suggest that there is a groundswell among proponents of the restored diaconate who say no, and who would argue for the abolition of a transitional diaconate to remove the anomaly of trying to restore the diaconate as a permanent order while retaining it as a transitional order.[25] Towards the end of their study McCaslin and Lawler return to the question about sequential ordination from the diaconate to the presbyterate. Throughout the book they argue that the diaconate and presbyterate are different ministries, with different symbolic functions. "We are saying that we see a need for a serious reassessment of the policy of ordaining transitional deacons, because the policy is perpetuating the institutionalization of contradictory symbols."[26] If the diaconate is currently a preparation for the presbyterate, they advocate some other form of "internship" which need not be ordained or institutionalized. If, as the argument goes, a lay person can do almost anything that a deacon can do, then the diaconate need not be a transitional internship for the presbyterate.[27] In short, they argue against the canonical insistence on sequential ordination.

An earlier study of the restored diaconate, *The Diaconate: A Full and Equal Order*, by James Barnett (an Anglican) is one of the most comprehensive and influential studies on the diaconate to date—especially

---

[23] Norbert Brockman, S.M., *Ordained to Service: A Theology of the Permanent Diaconate* (Hicksville, New York: Exposition Press, 1976), pp. 19–20, 27, 61.

[24] Patrick McCaslin and Michael G. Lawler, *Sacrament of Service: A Vision of the Permanent Diaconate Today* (New York: Paulist Press, 1986), p. 14.

[25] McCaslin and Lawler, *Sacrament*, p. 14.

[26] McCaslin and Lawler, *Sacrament*, p. 124.

[27] McCaslin and Lawler, *Sacrament*, pp. 123–124.

in its historical account—as noted by McCaslin and Lawler.[28] Barnett identifies the *cursus honorum* as being the greatest single contributor to the decline of the order of deacon,[29] and insists that as long as the diaconate remains a stepping-stone to the presbyterate it will remain an "inferior" office. Accordingly, he commends ordination directly to the presbyterate to those called to that office: ". . . nothing would help restore its [i.e. the diaconate] integrity more than a return to the original practice of the pre-Nicene church by ordaining only those to the diaconate who intend to make it a permanent vocation."[30] In addition, Barnett commends direct ordination even for the episcopate, leaving baptism as the only essential *sacramental* prerequisite for ordination to any office in the church.[31] In short he rejects the *cursus honorum*: "A necessary part of any profound renewal of the ministry must include abandoning all requirements of passing through successive orders or offices."[32] Barnett does not deny that those who are to be chosen for office must first have demonstrated their competence by service in the church. But, he does not ground this testing of people in a succession or series of offices.[33]

An interesting debate is underway between Anglican scholars on the place of the *cursus honorum*. If Barnett represents one side of the debate, J. Robert Wright represents the other. In "Sequential or Cumulative Orders vs. Direct Ordination" Wright unequivocally defends the inherited pattern.[34] While he acknowledges that no mention is made of the doctrine of cumulative or sequential orders in the first two centuries, he locates its beginnings in the mid-third century, associated with the letters of Cyprian of Carthage (especially *Epistle* 55.8). Wright deduces that it ". . . soon becomes standard consensus of the church catholic."[35] Wright argues that the doctrine of cumulative orders affirms that ordination is

---

[28] McCaslin and Lawler, *Sacrament*, p. 13.

[29] James M. Barnett, *The Diaconate: A Full and Equal Order* (New York: Seabury, 1981), p. 156.

[30] Barnett, *Diaconate*, p. 156.

[31] Barnett, *Diaconate*, p. 156.

[32] Barnett, *Diaconate*, p. 145.

[33] Barnett, *Diaconate*, p. 146.

[34] J. Robert Wright, "Sequential or Cumulative Orders vs. Direct Ordination," *Anglican Theological Review*, 75.2 (1993).

[35] Wright, "Sequential Orders", p. 248.

the particular vocation of the bishop since the episcopate contains both the diaconate and the presbyterate. If sequential ordination were to be abolished, he wonders if ordinands in the future will want to be ordained deacon or priest by a bishop who is neither?[36] Wright fears that "[s]uch an episcopate would certainly have less claim to be 'historic'. It would certainly be difficult to retain the concept of "Holy Order" as *one* sacramental ministry related to, summarized by, and focused in the norm of the Historic Episcopate . . . if the orders of deacon and priest were by direct ordination split apart from it."[37] Thus for Wright the "doctrine of cumulative orders" appears as something of a sacramental priority.

The questions raised by Echlin, Brockman, McCaslin and Lawler, Barnett, Wright and others on the restored diaconate point to the need for a reappraisal of the *cursus honorum*, the tradition of sequential ordination. An appraisal of any tradition must take into account its origins and evolution. What Robert Taft has written of the liturgy in general, may be applied to the study of the *cursus honorum* in particular:

> As a historian of Christian liturgical traditions, it is my unshakeable conviction that a tradition can only be understood genetically, with reference to its origins and evolution. Those ignorant of history are prisoners of the latest cliché, for they have nothing against which to test it. That is what a knowledge of the past can give us. A knowledge of the future would serve us equally well, but unfortunately that is not yet available to us.
>
> This does not mean that our ignorance of the future leaves us enslaved by our past. For we do know the present; and in the present the past is always instructive, but not necessarily normative. What we do today is ruled not by the past but by the adaptation of the tradition to the needs of the present. History can only help us decide what the essentials of that tradition are, and the parameters of its adaptation.[38]

Despite the excellent modern studies on the origins of the *cursus honorum*, the work needs to be continued. Paul-Henri Lafontaine, in a book written in the early 1950s and published posthumously a decade later, not only considers the *cursus honorum* and the interstices, but also explores other areas in the emerging legislation on clerical grades.[39] Yet the narrow

---

[36] Wright, "Sequential Orders", p. 250

[37] Wright, "Sequential Orders", p. 250.

[38] Robert Taft, S.J., *The Liturgy of the Hours in East and West* (Collegeville: The Liturgical Press, 1986), pp. xiv–xv.

[39] Paul-Henri Lafontaine, *Les Conditions positives de l'accession aux ordres dans la première législation ecclésiastique (300–492)*, (Ottawa: Éditions de l'Université d'Ottawa, 1963).

scope of this work—a study of canonical sources of the fourth and fifth centuries—is both its strength and limitation. Another critical study, by Alexandre Faivre, focusses on the emergence and development of the minor rather than the major orders.[40] While Faivre's time-line is broader than Lafontaine's (third to sixth centuries), it remains very much a patristic study. Nevertheless, his attention to the clerical *cursus* and his use of "*le modèle canonico-liturgique*" is significant.

Building on the work of Lafontaine, Faivre and others, this study expands the historical account of sequential ordination by tracing its evolution in the pre-Nicene church and the patristic period, as well as the early and later medieval stages. Lastly, developments from the Reformation and Counter-Reformation to the present will be outlined. Current questions about sequential ordination are largely Western, having arisen in regard to the restored permanent diaconate. Accordingly, this study will deal with the *cursus honorum* chiefly as it developed in the Western church though it will make necessary references to the Eastern churches, particularly in the early centuries. Furthermore, beyond considering patristic and medieval canonical sources (conciliar and papal legislation), it includes canonistic collections, liturgical texts, literature on holy orders, and biographical information. The underlying questions of this study are: what are the stages of the development of the *cursus honorum*? and what were the underlying motives for its emergence and evolution? In responding to these questions, the following pages, beyond extending the research already begun in this area, attempts to round out the sparse picture drawn of the *cursus honorum* in the more general works on ordained ministry and on the restored diaconate, and to encourage a fresh appreciation of its role in the history of ordered ministry. Lastly, it is my hope that this account of the "origins and evolution" of sequential ordination may contribute to further reflection on the "essentials of that tradition. . . and the parameters of its adaptation"[41] for the church of our own day.

---

[40] Alexandre Faivre, *Naissance d'une hiérarchie: les premières étapes du cursus clérical* *Théologie historique* 40 (Paris: Éditions Beauchesne, 1977).

[41] *Cf.* Taft, *Liturgy*, p. xv

I

SEQUENTIAL ORDINATION

IN THE FIRST THREE CENTURIES

1. Introduction

In the midst of upheaval, division, and persecution, the church in the first three centuries experienced tremendous growth and development. During this period the books of the New Testament were written and the canon established; Christian theology was first articulated and the liturgical life of the church achieved its early shape. It was also in this epoch that the ordered ministry of the church emerged into the three-fold pattern of bishops, presbyters, and deacons, as well as a variety of minor ministries.

It is generally assumed that the collective presbytery was characteristic of the Jewish-Christian churches, whereas the ministry of bishops and deacons was a feature of the Hellenistic or Pauline churches.[1] Towards the end of the first century the resident ministries of presbyters, and of bishops and deacons, assumed more prominence, taking over many of the functions previously exercised by the declining itinerant ministers (apostles, prophets, evangelists, and teachers). The increased prominence of the resident ministers reflects the change in the churches from missionary to permanent communities.

---

[1] *Cf.*, Douglas Powell, "Ordo Presbyterii," *Journal of Theological Studies*, 26 (1975), p. 306; Joseph T. Lienhard, *Ministry, Message of the Fathers of the Church* vol. 8 (Wilmington, Delaware: Michael Glazier, Inc., 1984), pp. 14–15; Kenan B. Osborne, *Priesthood: A History of Ordained Ministry in the Roman Catholic Church* (New York: Paulist Press, 1988), pp. 45, 47. For an alternative view, *cf.* Schillebeeckx, *Church with a Human Face*, pp. 125–128.

As the resident ministers began to assume more responsibility, another important development occurred: the Jewish-Christian and the Hellenistic structures were beginning to merge into a three-fold ministry of bishop, presbyter, and deacon, though the process which led to this amalgamation remains a mystery. By the time of the Ignatian epistles, (*ca.* 110) the amalgamation of the Jewish and Hellenistic Christian structures and the emergence of the three-fold ministry had been achieved, at least in Asia Minor. None of the surviving documents of the post-apostolic period provide sufficient evidence to account for the emergence of the three-fold ministry as it is revealed in the Ignatian Epistles. Towards the end of the second century, the three-fold structure became universal.

This chapter will examine evidence of sequential movement from one ministry to another in the church of the first three centuries. In comparison with other epochs in the life of the church there is a paucity of material on this topic; there are few liturgical texts, and no conciliar or canonical texts on which to draw. Evidence will be examined from the New Testament, sub-apostolic and early patristic authors, the liturgical rites of the *Apostolic Tradition*, and biographical data.

2. The New Testament

The New Testament is a indispensable source of information on the early developments of the church's ordered ministry. The books of the New Testament reflect different types of ministries. There are the ministries of the Twelve and the Seventy(-two), appointed directly by Jesus, and the ministry of the Seven appointed by the Twelve, as well as a variety of ecclesial offices such as the itinerant ministries mentioned by Paul in the letter to the Ephesians:

> The gifts he gave were that some would be apostles, some prophets, some evangelists, some pastors and teachers, to equip the saints for the work of ministry, for building up the body of Christ. (Eph. 4.11–12, NRSV).

The resident ministries of the presbyters, and bishops and deacons are represented in the Pastoral epistles and elsewhere.

a. The Twelve, the Seventy(-two), and the Seven

The ministries of the "Twelve" (Mt. 10.1; Mk.3.1; Lk. 9.1; Jn. 6.70; 1 Cor. 15.5; Rev. 21.14), the "Seventy(-two)" (Lk. 10.1), and the "Seven" (Acts 6) were closely associated with the ministry of Jesus and the early apostolic community. The Twelve, the Seventy, and the Seven were construed by patristic and medieval commentators as models for the episcopate, presbyterate, and the diaconate respectively.[2]

The association of the Seven and the diaconate dates from the late second century in the writings of Irenaeus.[3] According to Osborne, the association between the Twelve and the Seventy with bishops and presbyters was made popular by Bede;[4] the association probably dates from at least the seventh century.[5] The association of the Seventy(-two) with the presbyterate became important in the ninth century following the attack on the chorbishops in the Western Church. The chorbishops had earlier been

---

[2] E.g., Jerome, *Epistle* 146.2, *Ad Evangelum Presbyterum*, ed. I. Hilberg, CSEL 56, p. 312.

[3] Irenaeus, *Adversus Haereses* III.12.10; IV.15.1; *SC* 211, pp. 224–225, *SC* 100, pp. 550–551; Jerome, *Ep.* 146, *Ad Evangelum Presbyterum*, I. Hilberg, ed., CSEL 56.308; Pseudo-Jerome, *Ep.* 11, *De septem ordinibus ecclesiae*, *PL* 30.153; Isidore of Seville, *De ecclesiasticis officiis*, Bk II.8, *PL* 83.788; Amalarius of Metz, *Liber Officialis* II.11, ed., J. Hanssens, *Amalarii episcopi Opera liturgica omnia* vol. 2, *Liber officialis* (Studi e Testi 139) (Vatican: Biblioteca Apostolica Vaticana, 1984), p. 223; Gerard of Cambrai, *Acta synodi Atrebatensis* VI, *PL* 142.1292; Ivo of Chartres, *Sermo II*, *PL* 162.516; Hugh of St. Victor, *De sacramentis*, Bk II.3.11, *PL* 176.426; Peter Lombard, *Libri IV sententiarium* IV.24.10, ed., PP Collegii S. Bonaventurae, *Magistri Petri Lombardi Parisiensis episcopi Sententiae in IV libris distinctae* 2 (Grottaferrata: 1981), p. 402.

[4] Osborne, *Priesthood*, p. 62.

[5] Bede, *De Tabernaculo*, Bk III, ed., D. Hurst, *Baedae Venerabilis Opera*, CCSL 199a, p. 112; Pseudo-Isidore, *Epistola Anacleti Tertia*, Paul Hinschius,ed., *Decretales Pseudo-Isidoriane*, (Leipzig: Bernhard Tauchnitz, 1896), p. 82; During the ninth century Photian controversy, Pope Nicholas I cited the example of Matthias who was made an apostle after the death of Judas. Nicholas claimed that Matthias had been a member of the seventy-two disciples, and that his election as an apostle had been in accordance with the *cursus honorum*. "The Letter of Nicholas to Michael, Emperor of the Greeks," 28 September, 865, MANSI XVI, cols. 59–60. Gerard of Cambrai, *Acta synodi Atrebatensis* VI, *PL* 142.1292–1294; Ivo of Chartres, *Sermo II*, *PL* 162.518; Hugh of St. Victor, *De sacramentis* Bk II.3.12, *PL* 176.428; Peter Lombard, *Libri IV sententiarium* Bk IV.11, ed., PP Collegii S Bonaventurae, *Magistri Petri Lombardi Parisiensis episcopi Sententiae in IV libris distinctae* 2 (Grottaferrata: 1981), p. 404.

associated with the Seventy(-two), at least from the promulgation of Canon XIII of the Council of Neocaesarea (*ca.* 314–325).[6]

Within the New Testament itself, however, there is nothing to associate bishops with the Twelve, presbyters with the Seventy-two, or deacons with the Seven. Furthermore, there is no evidence to suggest any movement from one of the "numerical" ministries to another. Chronologically the "Twelve" antedate the "Seventy" who antedate the "Seven". Each of these three ministries emerged out of the general body of Jesus' disciples.

b. The Acts of the Apostles

The Acts of the Apostles reflects a variety of ministries in the apostolic church. After the appointment of the Seven, the Book of Acts does not refer to the "Twelve" again, but rather to "apostles". Paul's defense of his "apostleship", according to the author of the Acts of the Apostles , indicates that the scope of the term was much wider than simply the "Twelve".

Acts 15.4–6 refers to the gathering of the apostles and the presbyters (*ton apostolon kai ton presbyteron*) presided over by James. This appears to be the Christian counterpart, in Jerusalem, of the Jewish sanhedrin. Although the New Testament does not record the establishment of the Christian presbyterate, it is likely that it was modelled after the Jerusalem sanhedrin and local Jewish presbyteries. The Jewish presbyterate was not a liturgical ministry, though the presbyters had places of honour in the synagogue; they were a committee of presbyters which constituted an "advisory board".

Paul's discourse to the Ephesian presbyters, in Acts 20, uses the terms *presbyteros* and *episkopos* synonymously:

> From Miletus he [i.e. Paul] sent a message to Ephesus, asking the elders of the church to meet him. When they came to him, he [i.e. Paul] said to them.... Keep watch over yourselves and over all the flock, of which the Holy Spirit has made you overseers, to shepherd the church of God.... (Acts 20.17–18; 28, NRSV).

---

[6] (from the *Prisca* version:) "De praesbyteris locorum. De aliquibus locis praesbyteri in dominico civitatis offere non possunt praesente episcopo aut praesbytero civitatis, neque panem dare in oratione neque calicem. si autem absentes sint et oratione vocatus fuerit qui de locis est solus dat. quia corepiscopi sunt quidem de forma septuaginta, et sicut comministrantes propter curam pauperum offerent, honorantes eos." C. H. Turner, ed., *Ecclesiae Occidentalis Monumenta Iuris Antiquissima* 2 (Oxford: Clarendon Press, 1899), p. 31.

Joseph Sultana notes that many scholars believe that in this instance Luke was probably reflecting the structure of the church in the 80s (when the Acts of the Apostles was written) rather than the structure of the 40s and 50s.[7]

Although presbyters are mentioned in the Book of Acts, virtually nothing is said about them or their function. Elsewhere in the New Testament, the Pastoral and Catholic epistles portray presbyters as exercising a ministry of leadership and pastoral responsibility in local Christian communities (1 Peter 5.1–4; James 5:14; the Johannine epistles).

c. Pauline Epistles

The Pauline epistles reflect a variety of ministries in the life of the church, such as the enumeration in Ephesians 4.11–12. While the author of the Acts of the Apostles indicates that Paul (and Barnabas) appointed presbyters in Asia minor (Acts 14.23), the ministry of the presbyters is not mentioned in the Pauline literature itself.

There is only one instance where Paul refers specifically to the ministries of bishops and deacons. In the opening greeting in the letter to the church at Philippi Paul writes:

> Paul and Timothy, servants of Christ Jesus, To all the saints in Christ Jesus who are at Philippi, with the bishops and deacons (Phil. 1.1, NRSV).

While this early use of the terms *episkopoi* and *diakonoi* is significant, these offices cannot be understood in the later sense of the terms bishop and deacon. The word *episkopos*, for instance designates the function of inspector or overseer. As Brendan Byrne has commented: "While remote from the use of those terms in the later church, their mention here marks the dawn of a permanent ministry".[8]

The terms *episkopoi* and *diakonoi* were widely used in the ancient world. The term *episkopoi* was applied to everything from the gods to building financiers; *diakonoi* encompassed a variety of functions from community officers to table servants. Both terms were used by religious

---

[7] Joseph M. Sultana, "The Authenticity of the Mono-Episcopate in the Ignatian Letters vis-à-vis Recent Critics", diss., USMC, 1983, p. 14.

[8] Brendan Byrne, "The Letter to the Philippians", in Raymond E. Brown *et al.*, eds., *The New Jerome Biblical Commentary* (Englewood Cliffs, New Jersey: Prentice Hall, 1990), p. 793; *Cf.* Joseph A. Fitzmeyer, "The Letter to the Philippians", in *The Jerome Biblical Commentary* (1968), p. 249.

societies to refer to those with administrative and practical responsibilities.[9] Byrne identifies the term "bishop" in Philippians 1.1 with the presbyters of the post-Pauline churches.[10] Hans Lietzmann suggests that *episkopoi* and *diakonoi* are names freely given to the model of a leading Christian community, perhaps Antioch, which were adopted by the rest of the Hellenistic churches.[11] Harry Maier concludes that the titles bishop and deacon are too general here to identify their specific function. He suggests that bishops may have been the wealthy members, or householders, of the Christian community.[12]

It is not clear whether in Philippians 1.1 *episkopoi kai diakonoi* refers to two distinct offices or to one. Some commentators on the letter to the Philippians identify *episkopoi kai diakonoi* with two groups of office holders,[13] while others imply that the terms refer globally to the leaders ("guardians and assistants") of the Philippian church.[14]

While Philippians 1.1 is an important piece of evidence in tracing the development of ordered ministry, it neither suggests nor supports sequential movement from the diaconate to the episcopate.

d. The Pastoral Epistles

Scholars have dated the Pastoral epistles (I and II Timothy, Titus) anywhere from 60–160, though a likely estimate of the date of their

---

[9] G. R. Beasley-Murray, "Philippians" in Matthew Black, ed., *Peake's Commentary on the Bible* (London: Thomas Nelson and Sons, 1962), p. 985.

[10] Byrne, "Philippians", p. 793.

[11] Hans Lietzmann, *A History of the Early Church*, Vol. I (London: Lutterworth Press, 1961), p. 145.

[12] Harry O. Maier, *The Social Setting of the Ministry as Reflected in the Writings of Hermas, Clement and Ignatius* (Waterloo: Wilfrid Laurier Press, 1991), p. 38.

[13] *Cf.* Byrne, "Philippians", p. 793; John J. Greehy, "Philippians", in Reginald Fuller, ed., *A New Catholic Commentary on Holy Scripture* (New York: Thomas Nelson Publishers, 1969), p. 910a.

[14] *Cf.* G. R. Beasley-Murray, "Philippians", in Matthew Black, ed., *Peake's Commentary on the Bible* (London: Thomas Nelson and Sons, 1962), p. 985; Powell, "Ordo Presbyterii", p. 306. Powell compares this passage to I Corinthian 16: "In the Pauline tradition we find bishops and deacons. The term appears in Phil. i.I, though with no indication that they as yet imply two distinct offices—I Cor xvi would suggest rather that men [who] 'bishop' because they 'deacon', are great among you because they serve." p. 306.

composition is *ca.* 100.[15] They reflect the period of transition between the two-fold ministries of bishop and deacon, and the presbyters on the one hand, and the three-fold ministry of bishop, presbyter, and deacon, on the other.

The Pastoral epistles reflect the prominence of the ministries of bishop and deacon. They also testify to the use of Jewish and Hellenistic-Christian terminology to describe the same office holders. For example, the terms "bishops and deacons" and "presbyters" are applied to the same people, suggesting a merger of the Hellenistic and Jewish-Christian structures of leadership beginning by the end of the first century.

The First Letter to Timothy highlights the offices of bishop and deacon (1 Tim 3). Yet the term "presbyter" also appears:

> Let the elders (*presbyteroi*) who rule well be considered worthy of double honour, especially those who labour in preaching and teaching (1 Tim.5.17, NRSV).

In this instance the terms "presbyter" (*presbyteros*) and "bishop" (*episkopos*) are again used synonymously.[16] The same feature is found elsewhere in the Pastoral epistles:

> I left you in Crete for this reason, so that you should put in order what remained to be done, and should appoint elders [*presbyterous*] in every town, as I directed you: someone who is blameless, married only once, whose children are believers, not accused of debauchery and not rebellious. For a bishop, as God's steward, must be blameless. (Titus 1.5–7, NRSV)

The third chapter of I Timothy describes the characteristics sought in candidates for the offices of bishop and deacon. Here the terms bishop and deacon clearly describe two separate offices.[17] The author treats them in the descending sequence of bishop and deacon. Yet there is nothing in the texts which suggests or prescribes movement or promotion from the office of deacon to that of bishop. Some confusion, however, has arisen from a sentence at the end of the discourse on deacons:

---

[15] Robert A. Wild, "The Pastoral Letters" in *The New Jerome Biblical Commentary*, p. 893.

[16] J. C. Beker, "Pastoral letters", *The Interpreter's Dictionary of the Bible* Vol. III (Nashville: Abingdon Press, 1986), p. 674; George A. Denzer, "The Pastoral Letters", in *The Jerome Biblical Commentary*, (Englewood Cliffs, New Jersey: Prentice Hall, 1968) p. 354. Powell suggests that the term presbyter is a "status" title which comprises both bishops and deacons. Powell, "Ordo Presbyterii", p. 306.

[17] *Cf.* Powell, "Ordo Presbyterii", p. 306.

....for those who serve well as deacons gain a good standing for themselves and great boldness in the faith that is in Christ Jesus. (I Timothy 3.13, NRSV)[18]

Not surprisingly, later generations would understand this as a reference to promotion to a higher office, suggesting sequential movement from one grade to another. This sentence would appear in ordination prayers for the diaconate from the *Apostolic Tradition* of Hippolytus in the early third century, to the Leonine Sacramentary in the fifth century, through the medieval pontificals to the ordinals of the early Anglican Prayer Books.

It is unlikely, however, that the author of I Timothy was referring to promotion within the ministries of the church. He probably intended to say that deacons who are competent and fervent will win the respect and gratitude of the church.[19] Moreover, the descriptions of the two ministries in the sequence of bishop then deacon appear to suggest precedence within the Christian community, rather than the sequence of hierarchical grades with promotion from the lower to the higher. Maier suggests that both bishops and deacons were drawn from the ranks of the wealthy householders.[20]

A significant verse from I Timothy which appears with great frequency in the later patristic and medieval church is also from chapter three. In the discussion on the qualifications for the office of bishop, the author of the epistle states:

---

[18] *Cf.* Vulgate: "Qui enim bene ministraverint, gradum bonum sibi acquirent"; *cf.* King James: "For they that have used the office of deacon well purchase to themselves a good degree, and great boldness of faith in Christ Jesus."

[19] George A. Denzer, "The Pastoral Epistles", in *The Jerome Biblical Commentary*, (Englewood Cliffs, New Jersey: Prentice Hall, 1968) p. 355.

Cf. Robert A. Wild, "The Pastoral Epistles" in *The New Jerome Biblical Commentary*, p. 897, asserts that the sentence explains why "overseership" is a good work; H. Wansbrough, "The Pastoral Epistles" in *A New Catholic Commentary on Holy Scripture* (Hong Kong: Thomas Nelson Publishers, 1984), p. 1213, understands the reference in terms of the earthly or heavenly standing as a promised reward; W.K. Lowther Clarke, *The Concise Bible Commentary*, (London: SPCK, 1952), p. 895, sees no necessary thought of promotion to higher office; F.F. Bruce, *The International Bible Commentary*, (Grand Rapids Mich.: Marshall Pickering/Zondervan, 1986) says that the passage is to ensure that those not called to leadership will not view the work of a deacon with disdain; Ralph P. Martin, "1,2 Timothy & Titus", in *Harper's Bible Commentary*, (San Francisco: Harper & Row, Publishers, 1988) p. 1239, however, says that the phrase refers to promotion to office of bishop.

[20] Maier, *Social Setting*, pp. 38, 45–47.

He must not be a recent convert, or he may be puffed up with conceit and fall into the condemnation of the devil. (I Tim.3.6, NRSV)

The admonition against the appointment of neophytes to the episcopate would become a significant theme in support of the *cursus honorum* in conciliar and papal legislation in subsequent centuries.

3. Early Christian Literature

A variety of sub-apostolic writers and early patristic texts reflect the emergence of an ordered ministry in the primitive church. None of the documents arising from the first two centuries of this period reveal any movement or promotion from one ministry to another; the sub-apostolic literature provides only clues as to whether or not the practice was known. The sources to be examined from the first century are the *Didache* and the *First Epistle of Clement*; second-century sources to be surveyed are the Ignatian Epistles, the *Apologies* of Justin Martyr, and the writings of Irenaeus. The third century offers more documentation of sequential ordination on which to draw. Third-century evidence will be taken from the writings of Tertullian, Cyprian, Cornelius of Rome, and the *Didascalia apostolorum*.

a. The *Didache*

The *Didache*, or the "Teaching of the Apostles", is a Syrian document, possibly from Antioch, written in the late first century,[21] *ca.* 100.[22] In the history of ordered ministry the *Didache* witnesses to the period of transition from the itinerant ministries of apostles, prophets, and teachers, to the resident ministries of bishops and deacons. The ministry of the prophet is the most prominent in the *Didache*; the prophets are likened to the

---

[21] On the history of the scholarly debate on the date of the *Didache*, see Clayton N. Jefford, *The Sayings of Jesus in the Teaching of the Twelve Apostles* (Leiden: E. J. Brill, 1989), pp. 3–17; *Cf.* Paul F. Bradshaw, *The Search for the Origins of Christian Worship* (New York: Oxford University Press, 1992), pp. 85–86.

[22] Georg Schöllgen, *Didache: Zwölf-Apostel-Lehre* (Freiburg: Herder, 1991), p. 13.

"high-priest".[23] Further, they are to preside at the eucharist,[24] and they are not to be judged.[25]

Of the local ministers, only the bishops and the deacons are mentioned; no mention of the presbyterate is made in the *Didache*. Perhaps presbyters were unknown to the community which produced the *Didache*. Unfamiliarity with the presbyterate, however, would be somewhat anomalous, since the *Didache* appears to have been written in a Jewish-Christian context. K. Niederwimmer suggests that the absence of any mention of the presbyterate is indicative of the lack of Jewish influence in the community of the *Didache*.[26] Clayton Jefford suggests that the reason the presbyters are not mentioned is because the *Didache* was addressed to those who aspired to the office of presbyter.[27] While this is a alluring proposal, there is nothing to support it in the text itself. G. Schöllgen assumes that the community of the *Didache* did not know of the presbyterate, but acknowledges Jefford's hypothesis.[28]

Bishops and deacons are mentioned only once in the *Didache*. In chapter 15 the *Didache* directs:

> Appoint for yourselves, then, bishops and deacons who are worthy of the Lord—men who are unassuming and not greedy, who are honest and have been proved.

> For they also are performing for you the task of the prophets and teachers. Therefore do not hold them in contempt, for they are honourable men among you, along with the prophets and teachers.[29]

---

[23] *Didache* 13, Willy Rordorf & André Tuillier, *La Doctrine des Douze Apôtres (Didaché)*, *SC* 248, (Paris: Éditions du Cerf, 1978), p. 190. This section of the *Didache* directs that first-fruits are to be offered to the prophet as if to the high priest. In the absence of a prophet, the first fruits are to be given to the poor. According to Daniel Donovan, the emphasis here is more on the act of offering by the community and serves to minimize the idea that prophets are in any way "priestly". Daniel Donovan, *The Levitical Priesthood and the Ministry of the New Testament*, diss., Münster, 1970, pp. 272–273.

[24] *Didache* 11, *SC* 248, p. 186.

[25] *Didache* 11, *SC* 248, p. 186.

[26] Kurt Niederwimmer, *Die Didache* (Göttingen: Vanderhoek & Ruprecht, 1989), p. 241.

[27] Clayton N. Jefford, "Presbyters in the Community of the *Didache*", *Studia Patristica* 21 (1989), pp. 126–128.

[28] Schöllgen, *Didache*, p. 73, note 191.

[29] *Didache* 15.1–2, *SC* 248, p. 192; R. A. Kraft, trans. & comm., *Barnabas and the Didache, The Apostolic Fathers*, vol. 3 (New York: Thomas Nelson & Sons, 1965), p. 174.

Like Paul's letter to the Philippians and the Pastoral epistles, the author of the *Didache* has coupled the terms *episkopoi kai diakonoi*. Once again it is difficult to understand what the terms mean in the original context. Audet recalls that at the time of the *Didache* the terms "bishops and deacons" were general. *Episkopos* could refer to a foreman, a caretaker, or a moderator; *diaconos* could refer to any type of service.[30] Again, like Philippians 1.1, it is not clear in the *Didache* whether the terms refer to one group or to two distinct groups of leaders; scholars are divided on the question. Jefford suggests that there are three groups of ministers: the bishops, deacons, and, implicitly, the presbyters.[31]

There are those who argue that bishops and deacons are the same individuals. Sultana, in his "state of the question" thesis, notes that most modern scholars maintain that the expression *episkopoi kai diakonoi* is used globally to signify the leaders of a community.[32] André Lemaire, for example, argues that "bishops and deacons" is a global expression which refers to the local leaders.[33] This position is held by R. A. Kraft in his commentary on the *Didache*.[34]

André Tuillier suggests that since the bishops and deacons fulfil the functions of the prophets and teachers, there is therefore a distinction between them.[35] In his analysis of the *Didache*, W. Rordorf says that the *episkopoi kai diakonoi* are not the respective substitutes for prophets and teachers, although they exercise their liturgical functions. He notes, however, that the text does not indicate any distinctions between the liturgical functions of the two groups. While acknowledging the difficulty in being precise about the ministries of bishops and deacons in the *Didache*, Rordorf finds it is hard to believe with Lemaire that *episkopoi kai diakonoi* refer to the same people. He concludes that the bishops presided at the eucharist, and the deacons served the bishops. In addition, he submits that

---

[30] Jean-Paul Audet, *La Didaché: Instructions des Apôtres* (Paris: Librairie LeCoffre, 1958), p. 465.

[31] Jefford, "Presbyters", p. 128.

[32] Sultana, "Authenticity of the Mono-Episcopate", p. 24.

[33] André Lemaire, *Les Ministères aux origines de l'église* (Paris: Éditions du Cerf, 1971), p. 142.

[34] Kraft, *Apostolic Fathers* 3, p. 174.

[35] André Tuillier, "La Doctrine des Apôtres et la Hiérarchie dans l'Eglise Primitive", *Studia Patristica* 18.3 (1989), p. 232.

in general the difference between bishops and deacons was one of seniority, either in age or standing in the community.[36]

More recent scholarship understands the term "bishops and deacons"
as a reference to two groups. For instance, Niederwimmer sees two ministries in the *episkopoi kai diakonoi*, though he concedes that the terms are
unclear and vague.[37] Schöllgen likewise understands that the term "bishops and deacons" refers to two distinct groups, though he acknowledges
that it is difficult to discern the differences in function between them; in
the *Didache* both exercised ministries of leadership.[38]

If Rordorf is correct (i.e. the difference between bishops and deacons is
a matter of age and seniority), then it is not impossible that some deacons
might eventually have become bishops, and that some bishops might have
been deacons. There is, however, no evidence in the text of the *Didache*
itself to suggest any sequential movement between the offices. Moreover,
in chapter 15 the bishops and deacons are said to share in the tasks and honour of the prophets and teachers. There is no suggestion in the *Didache*
of promotion or movement from the office of teacher to that of the prophet.
Given the lack of clarity on the meaning of the term *episkopoi kai diakonoi*, the *Didache* cannot be used as a evidence for sequential movement
from one office to another in the primitive period.

b. *First Clement*

The *First Epistle of Clement* to the Corinthians (I Clement) is a document
of the primitive Roman church. Scholarly opinion generally assigns a late-
first-century date, *ca.*95.[39] Thomas J. Herron, however, argues
convincingly on the basis on internal evidence, such as the "pro-Temple"
stance of the letter, that I Clement was written earlier, *ca.* 70.[40]

I Clement reflects the "institutionalization" of the ministry of the early
church. Barbara Bowe notes that interpreters of I Clement have focused on

---

[36] Rordorf and Tuillier, *La Doctrine*, pp. 73–74.

[37] Niederwimmer, *Didache*, p. 241.

[38] Schöllgen, *Didache*, pp. 71–72.

[39] On the history of the dating of I Clement, see Thomas J. Herron, "The Most Probable
Date of the First Epistle of Clement to the Corinthians," *Studia Patristica* 21 (1989), pp.
106–107.

[40] Herron, "Probable date", pp. 120–121.

questions about ministry more than on any other issue.[41] I Clement uses the terms "bishop" and "deacon", as well as "presbyter". Comparable to the letter to the Philippians and the *Didache*, I Clement couples the terms "bishops and deacons". For instance, in chapter 42 the author writes:

> So as they preached from country to country and from city to city, they appointed their first converts, after testing them by the Spirit, to be the bishops and deacons of the future believers. Nor was this an innovation; since bishops and deacons had been written of long before. For thus says the Scripture somewhere, "I will appoint their bishops in righteousness and their deacons in faith".[42]

Like the use of the term *episkopoi kai diakonoi* in the letter to the Philippians and in the *Didache*, it is not clear whether or not in I Clement it refers to two distinct offices or to one, since the titles are not clearly distinguished from one another. Sultana, for instance, argues (from the secondary sources which he summarizes) that in I Clement *episkopoi kai diakonoi* is a global term referring to the churches' leaders in Rome and in Corinth.[43] J. Jeffers understands from the reference to deacons in 42.4–5 that the offices of bishop and deacon are distinct, though he acknowledges that I Clement does not explain the difference between them.[44]

It is likely that the terms bishop and presbyter refer to the same people in I Clement. In I Clement the titles bishop and presbyter appear to be interchangeable. For example, in chapter 44 the author writes:

> Surely we will be guilty of no small sin if we thrust out of the office of bishop those who have offered the gifts in a blameless and holy fashion. Blessed indeed are the presbyters who have already passed on, who had a fruitful and perfect departure, for they need not be concerned lest someone remove them from the place established for them.[45]

---

[41] Barbara Bowe, *A Church in Crisis: Ecclesiology and Paraenesis in Clement of Rome* (Minneapolis: Fortress Press, 1988), p. 144.

[42] I Clement, 42.4–5, Annie Jaubert, trans. & comm., *Clément de Rome, Épître aux Corinthiens*, SC 167 (Paris: Éditions du Cerf, 1971), pp. 168, 170; R. M. Grant & H. H. Graham, trans. and comm., *The Apostolic Fathers* 2 (New York: Thomas Nelson & Sons, 1965), pp. 71–72.

[43] Sultana, "Authenticity of the Mono-episcopate", p. 20.

[44] James S. Jeffers, *Conflict at Rome: Social Order and Hierarchy in Early Christianity* (Minneapolis: Fortress Press, 1991), p. 176.

[45] I Clement 44.4–5, SC 167, p. 172; Grant and Graham, trans., *Apostolic Fathers* 2, p. 74.

In this passage the activity of the bishops' office is associated with that of the presbyters.[46] Bowe says that the presbyters and bishops in I Clement are the same office holders.[47] Jeffers claims that I Clement uses the terms "presbyter" and "bishop" synonymously.[48] Powell, however, suggests that in I Clement the bishops *and* the deacons are the presbyters.[49]

A quite different position is outlined by Maier. Although he speaks of the "presbyter-bishops" of the Corinthian church,[50] he states that "[t]erms such as *episkopoi, presbyteroi,* and *diaconi* are used by Clement to refer to distinct groups whom he assumes the Corinthians recognize".[51] Although Maier grants that there is no information regarding a hierarchy of leadership or the relations between the presbyters, bishops, and deacon,[52] he suggests that a bishop was the patron of a household church who exercised authority over the other presbyters and deacons. Moreover, Maier suggests that the presbyters, as the senior members of the community in either age or faith, were a group from whose membership the bishops and even deacons were selected. Not all presbyters, however, would have been householders.[53]

In I Clement there is no suggestion of movement or promotion from one ministry to another. Furthermore, scholarly opinion does not agree on the nature of the offices, and the relationships between them. If, for instance, the terms "bishops and deacons" and "presbyters" all refer to the same people, or if the presbyterate was a seniority group (of age or faith) from which bishops and deacon emerged, then any discussion of sequential movement within these grades in Rome and Corinth at the time of I Clement is senseless. At any rate, it is not possible to use the First Letter of Clement as a witness to sequential movement from one ministry to another.

---

[46] *Cf.* I Clement 47, 57, *SC* 167, pp. 178, 190.

[47] Bowe, *Church in Crisis*, p. 149.

[48] Jeffers, *Conflict at Rome*, p. 176.

[49] Powell, "Ordo Presbyterii", p. 306.

[50] Maier, *Social Setting*, pp. 93–94.

[51] Maier, *Social Setting*, p. 103.

[52] Maier, *Social Setting*, p. 104.

[53] Maier, *Social Setting*, p. 105.

One final point can be made in connection with I Clement. In one instance the "army" is offered as a model for discipline and obedience in the church. In chapter 37, the author writes:

> Let us consider those who serve under our military commanders, with what good discipline, subordination, and obedience they carry out orders. Not all are prefects or tribunes or centurions, or captains of fifty and so on, but "each in his own rank" carries out orders under the emperor and the commanding officers.[54]

Jaubert assumes that this reference is to the Jewish army;[55] Grant and Graham concur,[56] since the rank of one "in charge of fifty" was a term used in the Jewish army, not the Roman.

Conversely, Jeffers argues convincingly that the army in question was not the Jewish but the Roman army.[57] His argument, however, depends on the late date of I Clement, *ca.* 95, at a time when the Jewish army no longer existed. Jeffers' suggestion is noteworthy; if he is correct, then I Clement is a first-century witness to a phenomenon associated with the fourth century, specifically the use of the Roman army and its officers (with its system of the *cursus honorum*) as a model for the church and its leaders.

c. Ignatius of Antioch

The first unequivocal evidence of the three-fold ministry of bishop, presbyter, and deacon appears in the letters of Ignatius of Antioch (*ca.* 35–*ca.* 113). The Ignatian epistles, written *ca.* 110,[58] witness to a stage of development beyond the Pastoral epistles and I Clement. Ignatius reflects the existence of the three-fold ministry in the communities of Asia Minor such as Antioch, Ephesus, Magnesia, Tralles, Philadelphia, and Smyrna.

The Ignatian epistles reflect the emergence of "monepiscopacy", i.e., a single bishop presiding, with presbyters and deacons, over a local church. This structure marks a shift from the more collective leadership of the "bishops and deacons"/"presbyters" in the Pastorals and I Clement. Moreover, in the Ignatian epistles the offices of bishop, presbyter, and deacon

---

[54] I Clement 37.2–3, *SC* 167, p. 160; Grant and Graham, trans., *Apostolic Fathers* 2, p. 64.

[55] Jaubert, *Clément de Rome*, *SC* 167, p. 80.

[56] Grant and Graham, *Apostolic Fathers* 2, pp. 64–65.

[57] Jeffers, *Conflict at Rome*, pp. 139–141.

[58] Maier, *Social Setting*, p. 147.

are clearly distinguished from one another, although they often appear together as a triad.[59]

A notable feature of the Ignatian epistles is the typologies used to describe the ministers. According to Maier, the purpose of these typologies was to "legitimize" and support the existing or latent structure of leadership.[60] For instance, the bishop is likened to God the Father, the presbyters to the Apostles, and the deacons to Jesus Christ. In the letter to the Magnesians Ignatius writes:

> Since, then, in the persons already mentioned I have beheld the whole congregation in faith and have loved it, I exhort you: be eager to do everything in God's harmony, with the bishop presiding in the place of God and the presbytery in the place of the council of the apostles and the deacons, most sweet to me, entrusted with the service of Jesus Christ—who before the ages was with the Father and was made manifest at the end.[61]

The same typologies are found in the letter to the Trallians, where Ignatius writes:

> Similarly all are to respect the deacons as Jesus Christ and the bishop as the copy of the Father and the presbyters as the council of God and the band of the apostles. For apart from these no group can be called a church.[62]

A similar correlation is found in the letter to the Smyrnaens: "All of you are to follow the bishop as Jesus Christ follows the Father, and the presbytery as the apostles. Respect the deacons as the command of God."[63]

In the letters to the Magnesians and the Smyrnaens, Ignatius describes the ministers in the sequence of bishop, presbyter and deacon; to the Trallians the sequences are deacon, bishop, presbyter, as well as bishop,

---

[59] E.g., *Mag.* 2, 6, 13; *Tral.* 2, 3, 7; *Phil.* 4, 7, 10; *Smyrn.* 8, 12; *Polycarp.* 6. *SC* 10, pp. 68, 72, 78; 82–84, 84, 88; 110, 114, 118; 126–128, 130; 140.

[60] Maier, *Social Setting*, pp. 182, ff.

[61] Ignatius, *Epistle to the Magnesians*, 6.1, P. Th. Camelot, ed. & comm., *Ignace D'Antioche, Lettres, SC* 10 (Paris: Éditions du Cerf, 1944), pp. 70, 72; Robert M. Grant, trans., *The Apostolic Fathers* vol. 4 (Camden, New Jersey: Thomas Nelson & Sons, 1966), pp. 60–61.

[62] Ignatius, *Epistle to the Trallians*, 3.1, *SC* 10, p. 84; Grant, trans., *Apostolic Fathers* 4, p. 73.

[63] Ignatius, *Epistle to the Smyrnaens* 8, *SC* 10, pp. 126, 128; Grant, trans., *Apostolic Fathers* 4, p. 120.

presbyter, and deacon.[64] These sequences of ministries do not necessarily correspond to their importance for Ignatius. The deacon, though third in the enumeration in the Letter to the Magnesians, is equated with Christ. The bishop corresponds to God the Father. By comparison, the presbyters, equated with the college of apostles, appear much less significant.

Following an early tradition, Ignatius frequently preserves the coupling of the bishop and the deacons;[65] deacons are often referred to as Ignatius' "fellow-servants".[66] Although Ignatius says that the bishop and the deacon are as inter-related to one another as the Father is to the Son, they are clearly two distinct offices. In the Letter to the Ephesians, Ignatius refers to Burrhus as the deacon of that church, rather than of its bishop.[67] Elsewhere, however, the deacon appears to be the minister of the bishop rather than more generally of the church. And so there is some ambiguity as to whether the deacon was the minister of a church or of its bishop. The typology of Father and Son applied to bishop and deacon associate these two office much more closely to one another than either one to the presbyterate, which is likened to the apostolic college. And yet, Ignatius often couples the presbyters with the bishop,[68] though little is said about the ministry of the presbyters. The presbyters appear to exercise a collective ministry, and are described as the counsellors of the bishop.[69] Ignatius often compares the presbyters to the college of the apostles.[70] Maier finds the association of the presbyters with the apostles "difficult" and complex, but maintains a lofty significance for the presbyters in the Ignatian Epistles.[71]

Ignatius uses the word synedrion in reference to the collegiality of the presbyters.[72] A. Vilela suggests that this collegial term, together with the analogy to the college of Apostles, may have been used by Ignatius in deference to Jewish-Christians; the use of the word *synedrion* would make the sanhedrin of Jerusalem around the high priest analogous to the college of

---

[64] Ignatius, *Epistle to the Trallians*, 2.2, *SC* 10, pp. 82, 84.

[65] E.g., *Eph.* 2; *Tral.* 3; *Phil.* 11. *SC* 10, pp. 48; 84; 118.

[66] E.g., *Mag.* 2; *Phil.* 4; *Smyrn.* 12. *SC* 10, pp. 68; 110; 130.

[67] *Eph.* 2.1, *SC* 10, p. 48; *cf. Tral.* 2. *SC* 10, p. 84.

[68] E.g., *Eph.* 2, 4, 20; *Mag.* 3, 7; *Tral.* 12, 13. *SC* 10, pp. 50, 50, 56; 70, 72; 90, 92.

[69] *Mag.* 6.1; *Trall.* 3.1. *SC* 10 pp. 70, 72; 84.

[70] E.g., *Mag.* 6; *Tral.* 3; *Smyrn.* 8. *SC* 10, pp. 70–72; 84; 126–128.

[71] Maier, *Social Setting*, p. 185.

[72] *Mag.* 6.1; Trall. 3.1. *SC* 10 pp. 70, 72; 84.

presbyters around the bishop.[73] Ignatius says that the bishop and the presbyters are as related to one another as a lyre is to its strings.[74] Further, in the absence of a bishop, the most likely person to have presided at the eucharist as his representative [75] would have been a presbyter.[76]

Although three distinguishable offices are reflected in the Ignatian epistles, there is no evidence of sequential movement between the ministries of bishop, presbyter and deacon. Moreover, the different sequences of the offices described by Ignatius (bishop, presbyter, deacon; deacon, bishop, presbyter), with the theological weight attached to the offices,[77] seem to make sequential appointment from the diaconate to the presbyterate to the episcopate unlikely. If sequential movement was known at all in the Ignatian communities, one might expect promotion from the diaconate to the episcopate, or from the presbyterate to the episcopate, but not from the diaconate to the presbyterate. After all, the diaconate and the presbyterate both appear more related to the episcopate than either to the other. The Ignatian epistles themselves, however, offer no evidence or suggestion of such sequential ordination.

d. Justin Martyr

A significant mid-second-century witness to the history of Christian ministry is the *First Apology* (*ca.* 155) of Justin Martyr (*ca.* 100–*ca.* 165). Justin wrote 1 *Apol.* in order to explain Christian doctrine and practice to the Roman world in response to charges of immorality against the church.

Although Justin remarks on the ministers of the church, nowhere does he use the terms bishop or presbyter. There are two descriptions of the eucharist in 1 *Apol.*: a normal Sunday celebration and the eucharist at

---

[73] Albano Vilela, "Le Presbytérium selon S. Ignace D'Antioche", *Bulletin de littérature ecclésiastique* 74 (1973), p. 175.

[74] *Eph.* 4.1–2, *SC* 10, p. 50.

[75] *Cf. Smyrn.* 8, *SC* 10, pp. 126, 128.

[76] William R. Schoedel, *Ignatius of Antioch: A Commentary on the Letters of Ignatius of Antioch* (Philadelphia: Fortress Press, 1985), p. 243; Maier, *Social Setting*, p. 154.

[77] *Cf.* Schoedel does not assign much weight to the typologies used by Ignatius. He asserts that it is unlikely that Ignatius meant to say that God the Father, the apostles, and Jesus are mystically present in the episcopate, presbyterate, and diaconate. Schoedel, *Ignatius*, p. 114.

baptism. The minister who presides at the eucharist is simply described by a present participle, *proestos*, that is, "the one who presides":

> And when he who presides has celebrated the Eucharist, they whom we call deacons permit each one present to partake of the Eucharistic bread, and wine and water; and they carry it also to the absentees.[78]

> Then, when the reader has finished, the president of the assembly verbally admonishes and invites all to imitate such examples of virtue. Then we all stand up together and offer up our prayers, and, as we said before, after we finish our prayers, bread and wine are presented. He who presides likewise offers up prayers and thanksgivings, to the best of his ability, and the people express their approval by saying 'Amen.'[79]

Justin's omission of any title more precise than *proestos* has aroused some curiosity. Since Justin was writing to a non-Christian audience, it is possible that he chose a simple term to describe the *function* rather than the title of the leader of the eucharistic community. It is also possible that since Justin knew that some communities were lead by presbyters, and others by bishops, he chose to use more inclusive terminology. L. W. Barnard understands Justin's *proestos* as a permanent officer of the church whose function includes liturgical and administrative leadership. Barnard argues that since the *title* applied to this officer, though not the functions, varied from church to church in Justin's time, he uses a non-specific term in order to describe a Christian leader to a non-Christian readership. Accordingly, the *proestos* might refer to either bishop or presbyter.[80] P. J. Fedwick, on the other hand, suggests that Justin uses the term *proestos* because "[a]s Paul, Justin Martyr knows nothing of a Christian presbyter or an office of the bishop".[81] Fedwick suggests that the *proestos* was a "charismatic" office holder in the Pauline sense; the office was not permanent and was shared amongst the members of the community.[82] A. Faivre notes that Justin uses neither the terms bishop or presbyter, but does refer to the lector and the deacon. Faivre asks if the *proestos* was simply included among the

---

[78] Justin Martyr, *First Apology* 65.3, in Louis Pautigny, ed., *Apologies* (Paris: Alphonse Picard et Fils, 1904), p. 138; trans., Thomas B. Falls, *Writings of Justin Martyr*, The Fathers of the Church, vol. 6 (New York: Christian Heritage, 1948), p. 105.

[79] 1 *Apology* 67.5, Pautigny, *Apologies*, p. 142; Falls, trans., *Justin Martyr*, pp. 106–107.

[80] L. W. Barnard, *Justin Martyr: His Life and Thought* (Cambridge: The University Press, 1967), pp. 132–133.

[81] P. J. Fedwick, "The Function of the *proestos* in the Earliest Christian *koinonia*", *Recherches de théologie ancienne et médiévale* 48 (1981), p. 7.

[82] Fedwick, "Function of the *proestos*", p. 8.

deacons. Is the diaconate a global terms referring to all Christian ministers? Is the *proestos*, he wonders, a "deacon-*episkopos*?"[83]

In brief, the absence of any mention of bishop or presbyter, combined with the confusion over the term *proestos*, make it impossible to use Justin Martyr as a witness to sequential movement from one ministry to another in the mid-second century.

e. Irenaeus

The *Adversus haereses* (*ca.* 180) of Irenaeus of Lyons (*ca.* 130–*ca.* 200) is an extremely valuable late-second-century source for the history of ordered ministry. Osborne notes that Irenaeus' description of the bishop in *Ad. haer.* marks "a sort of closure and opening as regards Christian ministry."[84] *Ad. haer.* reveals that by *ca.* 180 the names of Christian ministers, specifically bishops, presbyters, and deacons, had become stabilized. Further, monepiscopacy had become the universal structure of leadership in the church. As noted above, Irenaeus provides the first written evidence associating Stephen and the "Seven" of Acts 6 with the diaconate.[85]

Ad. haer. also reveals a close relationship between bishop and presbyter. Irenaeus often seems to use the terms "bishop" and "presbyter" interchangeably. For instance, Irenaeus speaks of the apostolic tradition which is guarded by presbyteral succession[86] and also by episcopal succession.[87] In referring to Acts 20.17,28, where the distinctions between "bishop" and "presbyter" are not clear, Irenaeus writes:

---

[83] Alexandre Faivre, *The Emergence of the Laity in the Early Church*, trans. David Smith (New York: Paulist Press, 1990), pp. 32–33.

[84] Osborne, *Priesthood*, p. 109.

[85] Irenaeus of Lyons, *Ad. haer.*, III.12.10. A. Rousseau & L. Doutreleau, eds. and trans., *Irénée de Lyon, Contre les Hérésies, Livre III, SC* 211.2 (Paris: Éditions du Cerf, 1974), pp. 224–225. *Ad. haer.* IV.15.1. A. Rousseau *et al.*, eds. and trans., *Irénée de Lyon, Contre les Hérésies Livre IV, SC* 100.2 (Paris: Cerf, 1965), pp. 550–551.

[86] *Ad. haer.* III.2.2, *SC* 211.2, pp. 26–27. *Cf. Ad. haer.* IV.26.2, *SC* 100.2, pp. 718–719. *Cf.* the letter from Irenaeus to Victor of Rome in Eusebius' *The History of the Church*, V.24, in which Victor's predecessors are called presbyters. It is not certain whether the letter is genuine. Eduard Schwartz, ed., *Die Kirkengeschichte, Eusebius Werke* 2.1, Die griechischen christlichen Schriftsteller der ersten drei Jahrhunderts (hereafter: *GCS*) (Leipzig: J. C. Hinrichs'sche Buchhandlung, 1903), p. 494.

[87] *Ad. haer.* III.3.3, *SC* 211.2, pp. 32–35, 38–39.

> For when the bishops and presbyters who came from Ephesus and the other cities adjoining had assembled in Melitus, since he [i.e. Paul] was himself hastening to Jerusalem to observe Pentecost....[88]

It is difficult to ascertain the precise distinction between the episcopate and the presbyterate in Irenaeus. For instance, in his article "Ordo Presbyterii" Powell argues that for Irenaeus there is a distinction between bishops and presbyters. He writes that for Irenaeus not all presbyters are bishops, nor are bishops "still presbyters" or "one of the presbyters". Rather, the bishop is *the* presbyter in continuing succession to the original presbyters, that is, the apostles. Powell states:

> Implicit therefore in the language of Irenaeus is the assumption that the bishop stands in the succession as The Presbyter, by virtue of the *primatus* rather than of *episkope*; implicit also is the assumption that from him stems all other presbyterate in that particular church.[89]

This position is supported by R. Berthouzoz who also argues that presbyters and bishops are not synonymous; bishops are *the* presbyters, but not all presbyters are bishops.[90]

Lastly, nothing in *Adversus haereses* specifies movement from the presbyterate to the episcopate. Such movement was known in the church of Gaul in the second half of the second century. Irenaeus, for instance, had been a presbyter before he was made a bishop (*ca.* 178) after the martyrdom of his predecessor. Although Irenaeus provides no clues as to how bishops were appointed, or by whom, it seems likely that candidates for the episcopal office in Lyons would have been drawn from the presbyterate.

f. Tertullian

The works of Tertullian (*ca.* 160–*ca.* 220) are important sources for the history of ordered ministry. With the *Apostolic Tradition* of Hippolytus, Tertullian is one of the earliest witnesses of a sacerdotal understanding of

---

[88] *Ad. haer.* III.14.2, *SC* 211.2, pp. 264–267; A. Roberts & W. H. Rambaut, trans., *The Writings of Irenaeus*, Vol. I, in *The Ante-Nicene Christian Library*, Vol. 5 (Edinburgh: T. & T. Clark, 1884), p. 317.

[89] Powell, "Ordo Presbyterii", p. 327.

[90] Roger Berthouzoz, *Liberté et Grâce suivant la théologie d'Irénée de Lyon* (Fribourg: Éditions Universitaires, 1980), pp. 27–28, n. 49.

the episcopate. For example, in *De baptismo* Tertullian refers to the bishop as "high-priest".[91]

An interesting comment on movement from one ministry to another appears in *De praescriptione haereticorum*, written *ca.* 198–200,[92] in Tertullian's earlier catholic phase. In chapter 41 he defends the need for order in the church by deriding the disorder among the heretics:

> Ordinationes eorum temerariae, leves, inconstantes. Nunc neophytos conlocant, nunc saeculo obstrictos, nunc apostatas nostros, ut gloria eos obligent, quia veritate non possunt. Nusquam facilius proficitur quam in castris rebellium, ubi ipsum esse illic promereri est. Itaque alius hodie episcopus, cras alius, hodie diaconus qui cras lector, hodie presbyter qui cras laicus. Nam et laicus sacerdotalia munera iniungunt.[93]

In this section, which is most likely directed against the Marcionites,[94] Tertullian complains that the ordinations performed by the heretics are hasty, irresponsible, and unstable. He complains that in the "rebels' camp" efforts to win believers are made by promotions: neophytes, those "bound to the world", and catholic apostates are appointed to ministries. Furthermore, appointment to ministries among the heretics was erratic: Tertullian relates that today one person is bishop, the next day another is bishop instead; an individual is a deacon one day and a lector on the next; one is a presbyter today and a lay person tomorrow. Lastly, he complains that sacerdotal functions are imposed on lay people. Commenting on this passage M. Bévenot writes:

> This public attack on the goings on of heretics would have been impossible if the same practices were current in the Church which he himself was defending.[95]

---

[91] "Dandi quidem habet ius summus sacerdos, qui est episcopus; de hinc presbyteri et diaconi, non tamen sine episcopi auctoritate, propter ecclesiae honorem, quo saluo salva pax est." *Liber de baptismo* XVII, *CSEL* 20.1, p. 214; Maurice Bévenot notes that this is the only instance where Tertullian uses sacerdotal language in his early phase. "Tertullian's Thought about 'Priesthood'", in *Corona Gratiarum* I (Brugges: Sint Pietersabdij, 1975), p. 134.

[92] Ian S. L. Balfour, "The Relationship of Man to God, from Conception to Conversion, in the Writings of Tertullian," diss., U of Edinburgh, 1980, p. xv; Lienhard, *Ministry*, p. 122.

[93] Tertullian, *De praescriptione haereticorum*, 41, *CSEL* 70, p. 53.

[94] R. F. Refoulé & P. de Labriolle, eds. & comm., *Tertullian: Traité de la prescription contre les Hérétiques*, *SC* 46 (Paris: Éditions du Cerf, 1957), p. 147.

[95] Bévenot, *Priesthood*, p. 130.

Chapter 41 of *De praescript.* is not evidence of sequential movement or promotion from one ministry to another. Tertullian's invective is directed against the hasty, irresponsible, and unstable nature of appointment to ecclesiastical ministries among the heretics, and the ensuing confusion between the lay and ordained members of the Marcionite communities. And so, remarking on the same passage Faivre notes:

> Tertullian does not tell us whether we ought to be presbyters, or deacons or bishops for life, but he calls for a serious approach to the choice of ministers, a certain constancy in the exercise of ministries and functions.[96]

It is significant that Tertullian uses the word *proficitur:*"nowhere," he says "is it easier to be *advanced* than in the rebel camp". Can one conclude that advancement was more difficult in the catholic church? If so, is this a hint or intimation of promotion within the ministries of catholic Christianity in North Africa in the late second or early third centuries? One notes that in two of Tertullian's complaints there is descending movement between the ministries among the heretics: deacons become lectors, and presbyters become lay people. Could it be that in the catholic church there was an ascending sequence of ministries, that is, lectors normally became deacons, and lay people became presbyters?

De praescript. is an example of the extent to which words such as *exorcismos, neophytus, laicus, lector, diaconus, presbyter*, and *episcopus* had assumed a technical sense in the church. It is one of the earliest Western texts where the lectorate is mentioned,[97] as well as being an instance where sacerdotal language (*sacerdotalia munera*) is used to describe a function of the ordained.

Tertullian's use of the word *ordinationes* is notable; *De praescript.* is often cited as one of the earliest examples of the use of terminology associated with *ordo* and *ordinationes*.[98] In the Roman world the term *ordo* was used to describes specific social classes, in particular the senatorial and equestrian "orders". People who belonged to these orders were placed in positions of leadership in the civil and military services of the Empire. As P. M. Gy has noted:

---

[96] Faivre, *Emergence*, p. 48.

[97] Refoulé & Labriolle, *Tertullian*, p. 148, note d.

[98] E.g. Osborne, *Priesthood*, pp. 114–115.

> With the emergence of Christian Latin in Tertullian we see that the analogy of the
> *ordo* and the people of the city of Rome was taken up to describe the relationship
> of the clergy to the people of God.[99]

While Tertullian does not indicate sequential movement in the orders of
the clergy parallel to the *cursus honorum* of the senatorial and equestrian
orders, it is not insignificant that he uses the terminology of *ordo*, thus
making an analogy between the church and the imperial institutions which
did know sequential movement within the "orders".

Lastly, one of the great ironies is the fact that later in life, *ca.* 207, Tertullian joined the Montanist sect, where he would have repudiated much of
what he had written in *De praescript.*, in particular the lack of order he denounced among the Marcionites.

g. Cyprian

By the mid-third century there are indications of a new relationship
between the orders of ministry, that is, unequivocal evidence of sequential
ordination or promotion from one ministry to another (or others). A principal witness to this phenomenon is Cyprian of Carthage (d. 258).

In *Epistle* 38, written *ca.* 250,[100] Cyprian writes to the clergy and people of Carthage to explain why he ordained a young man, Aurelius, a confessor, to the lectorate without having consulted them:

> In ordinationibus clericis, fratres carissimi, solemus vos ante consulere et mores ac
> merita singulorum communi consilio ponderare. sed expectanda non sunt testimo-
> nia humana cum praecedunt divina suffragia. Aurelius frater noster inlustris adule-
> scens a Domino iam probatus et Deo carus est, in annis adhuc novellis, sed in
> virtutis ac fidei laude provectus, minor in aetatis suae indole, sed maior in honore....
>
> Merebatur talis clericae ordinationis ulteriores gradus et incrementa maiora, non de
> annis suis sed de meritis aestimandus. sed interim placuit ut ab officio lectionis in-
> cipiat....[101]

In the first section Cyprian alludes to what would have been the normal
way of selecting candidates for ecclesiastical ministry: the bishop consults
the presbyters, deacons, and people about the morals and merits of a

---

[99] P. M. Gy, "Notes on the Early Terminology of Christian Priesthood," *The Sacrament of
Holy Orders* (Collegeville: The Liturgical Press, 1962), p. 99.

[100] Lienhard, *Ministry*, p. 129.

[101] Cyprian, Epistle 38.1–2, *Cyprianus presbyteris et diaconibus item plebi universae s.*,
CSEL 3.2, pp. 579–580.

candidate. This consultation would have provided the means for testing a candidate. In the case of the young confessor Aurelius, however, the candidate was considered to have already been tested—*probatus*—by God. In the second section, Cyprian explains that Aurelius is worthy of the "higher grades"—*ulteriores gradus et incrementa maiora*—but that in the meantime he will "begin" at the lectorate.

Cyprian's use of language is noteworthy, in particular, his use of the term "grade"—*gradus*—to describe ecclesiastical ministry. The term *gradus* is associated with the civil and military *cursus honorum*.[102] It conveys a sense of movement through the grades. While the term *gradus* would appear with greater frequency from the fourth century, it is significant that a mid-third-century Christian writer would employ it as well.

Clearly Cyprian intended to promote Aurelius to the "higher ranks" at a later date. The lectorate appears not so much as a ministry with an integrity of its own, but rather as the first rung on the way up the ecclesiastical ladder. One ministry is in fact being used as a preparatory and probationary stage before promotion to another.

A perhaps more significant text from the letters of Cyprian with regard to sequential movement through the offices is *Epistle* 55.8, concerning the ecclesiastical career of Cornelius, bishop of Rome (251–253).

> Venio iam nunc, frater carissime, ad personam Corneli collegae nostri.... nam quod Cornelium carissimum nostrum Deo et Christo et ecclesiae eius, item consacerdotibus cunctis laudabili praedicatione commendat, non iste ad episcopatum subito pervenit, sed per omnia ecclesiastica officia promotus et in divinis administrationibus Dominum saepe promeritus ad sacerdotii sublime fastigium cunctis religionis gradibus ascendit.[103]

Cyprian declares that Cornelius was not made a bishop suddenly, but "was promoted through all the ecclesiastical offices"; he "ascended through all the grades of religion to the exalted pinnacle of the priesthood." This text will be examined again below in regard to Cornelius and the history of the Roman church regarding the clerical *cursus*.

Taken with *Epistle* 38, *Epistle* 55.8 indicates that by the mid-third century, at least in Rome and North Africa, one ministry could be used as a preparatory stage prior to promotion to another. Moreover, an individual might well serve sequentially in "all the ecclesiastical offices".

---

[102] David Power, *Ministers of Christ and his Church* (London: Geoffrey Chapman, 1963), pp. 63–64.

[103] Cyprian, Epistle 55.8, *Cyprianum Antoniano fratri s.*, CSEL 3.2, p. 629.

h. *Didascalia apostolorum*

The *Didascalia apostolorum*, a Northern Syrian document, *ca.* 230,[104] discusses the ordained ministry at great length, offering a valuable Eastern testimony to the ordered ministry. The fourth chapter deals with the appointment of a new bishop: "the shepherd who is appointed bishop and head among the presbyterate in the church in every congregation".[105] It is specified that candidates for the episcopate must be at least fifty years old, and the husband of one wife. While much is said about the moral qualities sought in a bishop, no suggestion is made that episcopal candidates will have been either presbyters or deacons. By the same token, no intimation is made of presbyters ever having been deacons prior to election and consecration. In short, there is no indication of sequential movement or promotion from one ministry to another in the *Didascalia*.

And yet hints within the work itself suggest that if sequential ordination was practised in the community which produced the *Didascalia*, the more likely sequence would have been from the diaconate to the episcopate. Although the bishop is associated with the presbyterate in the *Didascalia apostolorum*, greater emphasis is placed on the association between the bishop and the deacon. For instance, the *Didascalia* warns: "What hope, indeed, is there, even a little, for him who speaks evil against the bishop, or against a deacon."[106] The order of precedence in ministers in the *Didascalia* resembles that of Ignatius of Antioch, two centuries earlier:

> But let him [i.e. the bishop] be honoured by you as [is] God, because the bishop sits
> for you in the place of God Almighty. But the deacon stands in the place of Christ,
> and you should love him. The deaconess, however, shall be honoured by you in the
> place of the Holy Spirit. But the presbyters shall be to you in the likeness of the
> apostles, and the orphans and widows shall be reckoned by you in the likeness of
> the altar.[107]

The presbyterate is modestly honoured through its association with the bishop. Unlike the episcopate and the diaconate, the presbyterate does not have a divine parallel; its stature within the structure of ordered ministry is

---

[104] Bradshaw, *The Search*, p. 88.

[105] Arthur Vööbus, ed. & trans., *The Didascalia Apostolorum in Syriac*, Corpus Scriptorum Christianorum Orientalium 176, vol. 1 (Louvain: 1979), p. 43.

[106] *Didascalia*, Vol.I.IX, p. 103.

[107] *Didascalia*, Vol.I.IX, p. 100.

well below that of episcopate and diaconate. For example, the author of the *Didascalia* writes:

> But if anyone wished to honor the presbyter also, let him give him a double [por-tion], as to the deacons, for it is required for them that they should be honoured as the apostles, and as the counsellors of the bishop, and as the crown of the church, for they are fashioners and counsellors of the church. But if there be a lector, let him also receive with the presbyter.[108]

While the presbyters have a teaching role,[109] it is the deacons and the bishop who are the pastoral and liturgical leaders of the community. The presbyters appear to function as an "advisory board" to the bishop, not as a "career-stream" order of ministry such as the diaconate.

In summary, as a document of a Semitic Christianity of the third century, the *Didascalia apostolorum* may well reflect a much earlier portrait of church order. Yet as Osborne notes, "[a]ll in all, the picture we receive from the *Didascalia apostolorum* is consistent with the picture we find in most of the other material for the third century".[110] In this discussion on the *cursus honorum*, the *Didascalia* is significant in that it neither prescribes nor implies any movement or promotion from one order to another. Like the churches described in the Ignatian epistles, if there were sequential movement in the church of the *Didascalia*, it is unlikely that it would have been from deacon to presbyter, or from presbyter to bishop. The presbyterate does not share in the precedence and honour which link the diaconate and the episcopate. Again, like the Ignatian epistles, the more likely sequence is between the diaconate and the episcopate.

i. Cornelius of Rome

An important witness to the development of the clerical grades is preserved in Eusebius of Caesarea's *Ecclesiastical History*. Eusebius has preserved a letter from Cornelius, bishop of Rome (251–253) to Fabius of Antioch, against the schismatic Novatian:

> Thus the vindicator of the gospel was unaware that there can only be one bishop in a Catholic church, in which, as he knew perfectly well, there are forty-six

---

[108] *Didascalia*, Vol.I.IX, p. 101.

[109] "Let, however, the teaching of the presbyter be fitting and suitable, gentle and temperate, mingled with reverence and trembling, in the likeness also of that of the bishop." *Didascalia*, Vol.I.III, p. 28.

[110] Osborne, *Priesthood*, p. 119.

presbyters, seven deacons, seven subdeacons, forty-two acolytes, fifty-two exorcists, readers, and doorkeepers, and more than fifteen hundred widows and dis-
tressed persons.[111]

This passage is said to describe the organization of the church of Rome in
the mid-third century, around the year 251.[112] Cornelius lists the ordered
ministries of the Roman church in the descending sequence of bishop,
presbyter, deacon, subdeacon, acolyte, exorcist, lector, and doorkeeper.
There is nothing, however, to suggest prescribed sequential promotion
through the orders of ministers mentioned by Cornelius. Yet the hierarchical sequence in which ministries are listed is remarkable. The sequence
corresponds to the fifth-century *Statuta ecclesiae antiqua*, the *Orationes
solemnes* of the Good Friday rite, and ultimately the full *cursus honorum*
of the western medieval church. Faivre indicates that there are no grounds
to suspect the affirmations of Eusebius on this point.[113]

The fact that Cornelius mentions only seven deacons, each with an as-
sisting subdeacon, reveals the importance and prominence that the deacons
enjoyed at this time.[114] The fact that there were so many more presbyters
than deacons (46/7) would imply that not all of the presbyters, if any, had
ever been deacons; in fact, most, if not all presbyters were ordained directly to that office, as was Novatian himself. Moreover, surely not all the acolytes and exorcists were waiting to become one of the seven subdeacons.

Cornelius describes briefly the ordination of Novatian to the presbyterate in the same letter to Fabius:

This fine fellow left the Church of God, in which after becoming a believer he was
accepted for the presbyterate, by favour of the bishop who ordained him to presbyter's orders. The whole clerical body, and many laymen too, objected that the rules
did not permit anyone baptized in bed by affusion owing to illness, as in the present
case, to receive any orders, so the bishop asked leave to lay hands on this man
only.[115]

---

[111] Eusebius, *History*, VI.43; Eduard Schwartz, ed., *Die Kirchengeschichte Eusebius Werke*,
GCS 2.2 (Leipzig: J. C. Hinrichs'sche, 1908), p. 618; G. A. Williamson, trans., *Euse-
bius: the History of the Church from Christ to Constantine*, 2nd ed. (London: Penguin
Books, 1989), p. 216.

[112] Faivre, *Naissance d'une Hiérarchie*, p. 301.

[113] Faivre, *Naissance*, p. 301.

[114] R. P. Symonds, "Deacons in the Early Church", *Theology*, Vol. 58 (1955), p. 409.

[115] Eusebius, *History*, VI.43, GCS 2.2, p. 620; Trans. Williamson, *Eusebius*, p. 217.

Cornelius' objection to Novatian's ordination to the presbyterate is on the grounds that he had been baptized in illness, not that he had never served in any other order. That Cornelius does not comment on the omission of any orders below the presbyterate stands in contrast to the view that the ministries mentioned by Cornelius in the letter to Fabius were to be received sequentially, or that Cornelius' own *cursus* through the grades was a standard practice.

4. Liturgical Rites: *The Apostolic Tradition*

The *Apostolic Tradition (AT)*, a reconstructed text of the early third century, is regarded by the majority of (though not all) scholars to be a church order from Rome, *ca.* 215.[116] The *AT* is usually ascribed to Hippolytus of Rome, though its Hippolytan authorship is questionable.[117] Furthermore, it is not clear which Hippolytus is supposed to have composed the *AT:* the presbyter Hippolytus of Rome (d. *ca.* 235), or the bishop Hippolytus of Portus Romanus (d. *ca.* 253).[118]

At any rate, the *AT* contains a number of liturgical rites, including the earliest known ordination rites extant.[119] While the *AT* claims to describe the rites known in Rome in the early third century, it remains the only account of any ordination rite prior to the fourth century.[120] Nonetheless, as Bradshaw warns, caution is needed in using the *AT*:

> This church order ...deserves to be treated with greater circumspection than has generally been the case, and one ought not automatically assume that it provides reliable information about the life and liturgical activity of the church in Rome in the early third century.[121]

The *AT* treats the ordinations of bishops, presbyters, and deacons separately, since only these three receive appointment though the imposition

---

[116] Bradshaw, *The Search*, p. 91.

[117] Bradshaw, *The Search*, p. 91.

[118] Bradshaw, *The Search*, p. 91.

[119] Dom Bernard Botte, ed., *La Tradition Apostolique de Saint Hippolyte* (Münster/Westfalen: Aschendorffshe Verlagsbuchhandlung, 1963).

[120] Paul Bradshaw, *Ordination Rites of the Ancient Church of East and West* (New York: Pueblo, 1990), p. 3.

[121] Bradshaw, *The Search*, p. 92.

of hands. According to the reconstructed text and to the Arabic and Ethiopic versions of the *AT*,[122] the ministries are treated in the descending sequence of bishop,[123] presbyter,[124] deacon,[125] confessor,[126] widow,[127] lector,[128] virgin,[129] subdeacon,[130] and one with the gifts of healing.[131] In the Sahidic text the minor ministries appear in a different sequence,[132] that is, lector, subdeacon, widow, virgin, one with the gifts of healing.

There is no mention of the ministries of acolyte and doorkeeper which appear in the mid-third-century letter of Cornelius to Fabius. Widows and virgins appear in the list of ministries; they too are absent in the letter to Fabius. Given the distinctly women's ministries in the sequence(s), the minor ministries cannot be said to appear in a hierarchical sequence suggestive of sequential movement through the grades. It is interesting to note, however, that in the sequences of the reconstructed text and the Sahidic version, the lector appears above the subdeacon.

The *AT* witnesses to a parallel, but distinct, relationship between the bishop and the presbyters on the one hand, and the bishop and the deacon on the other. In the prayer for the ordination of a presbyter (from the Latin version; the Ethiopic is analogous), the bishop prays that the new presbyter might receive the "spirit of counsel":

> .... respice super seruum tuum istum et inpartire sp[iritu]m gratiae et consilii praesbyteris ut adiubet et gubernet plebem tuam in corde mundo....[133]

While Bradshaw understands that the "spirit of counsel" directs the presbyter to the people,[134] Donovan argues that this expression relates the

---

[122] *Cf.* Faivre, *Naissance*, p. 57.

[123] Botte, *Tradition*, II, pp. 2–10.

[124] Botte, *Tradition*, VII, pp. 20–22.

[125] Botte, *Tradition*, VIII, pp. 22–27.

[126] Botte, *Tradition*, IX, pp. 28–29.

[127] Botte, *Tradition*, X, pp. 30–31.

[128] Botte, *Tradition*, XI, pp. 30–31.

[129] Botte, *Tradition*, XII, pp. 32–33.

[130] Botte, *Tradition*, XIII, pp. 32–33.

[131] Botte, *Tradition*, XIV, pp. 32–33.

[132] *Cf.* Faivre, *Naissance*, p. 57.

[133] Botte, *Tradition*, VII, p. 20.

[134] Paul Bradshaw, "Ordination," *Essays on Hippolytus*, Grove Liturgical Study No. 15, ed. C. J. Cuming (Bramcote Notts.: Grove Books, 1978), p. 38.

presbyterate to the bishop as his *synedrion*, that is, the presbyters assist the bishop in his task of leadership.[135] Yet the presbyters are much more than an "advisory board" to the bishop in the *AT*; they impose hands on candidates for the presbyterate with the bishop[136] and associated with the bishop at the eucharist where they impose hands together on the eucharistic elements.[137] In fact, the *AT* describes the presbyters as participating in the sacerdotal ministry of the bishop.[138] Though Tertullian's *De baptismo* is one of the earliest texts to describe the episcopate as sacerdotal,[139] the *AT* is the earliest to associate the presbyterate with the priesthood of the bishop.

At the same time, the *AT* also reflects the primitive association of bishop and deacon. For instance, only the bishop imposes hands in the ordination of a deacon, because the deacon is ordained to the service of the bishop:

> In diacono ordinando solus episcopus inponat manus, propterea quia non in sacerdotio ordinatur, sed in ministerio episcopi, ut faciat ea quae ab ipso iubentur.[140]

The deacon in the *AT* is clearly described as the servant of the bishop. The liturgical functions mentioned in the ordination prayers of the *AT* are associated with the bishop and deacon,[141] though not with the presbyterate which is described in terms of governing.[142] Levitical language is used to describe the bishop and the deacon in their respective ordination prayers, but not the presbyterate. In addition, Dix asserts that at the time of the *AT*, bishops and deacons were paid officials of the church, while the presbyters

---

[135] Donovan, *Levitical Priesthood*, p. 437.

[136] Botte, *Tradition*, VII, p. 20.

[137] Botte, *Tradition*, IV, p. 10.

[138] Botte, *Tradition*, VIII, p. 22. *Cf.* Gerard Luttenberger, "The Priest as a Member of a Ministerial College," *Recherches de théologie ancienne et médiévale* 43 (1976), p. 38; August Jilek, "Bischof und Presbyterium," *Zeitschrift für katholische Theologie* 106 (1984), pp. 383–384.

[139] Tertullian, *Liber de baptismo* XVII, *CSEL* 20.1, p. 214.

[140] Botte, *Tradition*, VIII, p. 22; According to the Latin version. The Sahidic, Arabic, and Ethiopic versions are analogous.

[141] Botte, *Tradition*, III, pp. 6,8,10; VIII, p. 26.

[142] Botte, *Tradition*, VII, p. 20.

earned their living elsewhere.[143] Osborne notes that the relationship between the deacon and the bishop in the *AT* is similar to that in the *Didascalia apostolorum*.[144]

There is no mention of the qualifications needed to be admitted to any of the major orders in the *AT*, and thus no clear indication of sequential movement or promotion within the grades. Although the sequence of the ordination rites in the *AT* is bishop, presbyter, and deacon, if there were any movement from one ministry to another, the natural alliance would be between deacon and bishop. Sequential movement or promotion from the diaconate to the episcopate might be suggested by the petition in the ordination prayer in the deacons' rite which asks that "he [the new deacon] may attain the rank of higher order":

> in sancto sanctorum tuo quod tibi offertur a constituto principe sacerdotum tuo ad gloriam nominis tui, ut sine reprehensione et puro more ministrans, gradum maioris ordinis assequatur, et laudet te et glorificet te per filium tuum....[145]

The source of this petition is undoubtedly 1 Timothy 3.13. E. Segelberg remarks that a petition for the deacon to accede to higher office is strange, since deacons only occasionally succeeded bishops in office.[146] W. Geerlings notes that from the text it is not clear to what the words *gradum maioris ordinis assequator* refer: they could imply promotion in the clerical career, or they could be a figurative reference to the heavenly reward. For Geerlings, the latter interpretation makes more sense from the point of view of the text, since it renders an easier transition to the doxology which concludes the ordination prayer.[147]

Bradshaw insists that bishops at the time of the *AT* would have been chosen from among the laity. He argues that "since each office was conferred for life and there could be no movement to a higher order,"[148]

---

[143] Dom Gregory Dix, "The Ministry in the Early Church, c. A.D. 90–410", in ed. Kenneth E. Kirk, *The Apostolic Ministry*, (London: Hodder & Stoughton, 1957) p. 226. *Cf.* Karl Baus, *From the Apostolic Community to Constantine*, Vol. I, eds. H. Jedin and J. Dolan, *The History of the Church* (New York: Crossroad, 1986), p. 351.

[144] Osborne, *Priesthood*, p. 20.

[145] Botte, *Tradition*, VIII, Ethiopic version, p. 26.

[146] E. Segelberg, "The Ordination Prayers in Hippolytus", in *Studia Patristica*, 13 (1975), p. 405.

[147] Wilhelm Geerlings, *Traditio Apostolica Apostolische Überlieferung*, Fontes Christiani, vol. 1 (Freiburg: Herder, 1989), pp. 170–171.

[148] Bradshaw, "Ordination," *Essays on Hippolytus*, p. 33.

deacons and presbyters would have been ineligible for election to the episcopate at the time of the *AT*. Moreover, he notes that the *AT* directs confessors to be counted within either the presbyterate *or* diaconate, on
account of their suffering. And yet if a confessor were to be elected bishop,
he would receive the imposition of hands:

> Confessor autem, si fuit in vinculis propter nomen domini, non imponetur manus
> super eum ad diaconatum vel presbyteratum. Habet enim honorem presbyteratus
> per suam confessionem. Si autem instituitur episcopus, imponetur ei manus.[149]

It is arguable that since a sequence or series of offices was unnecessary for
confessors, it would not have been required of other candidates for holy
orders. For example, as late as 236, Fabian was a lay person at the time of
his election and ordination as bishop of Rome, without having served in
any other order.[150]

Bradshaw concludes that the petition for the new deacon, that he "may
attain the rank of a higher order", is a later adaptation of the text when the
situation had changed. Furthermore, it is found only in the Ethiopic version
of the *AT*. He suggests that the original text was similar to the parallel text
in the later fourth (or fifth)-century *Testamentum Domini*,[151] that "he may
be worthy of this high and exalted rank" (Book I.38):

> .... Illumina, Domine, quem dilexisti et elegisti ad ministrandum ecclesiae tuae, of-
> ferendumque in sanctitate sanctuario tuo, quae tibi offeruntur ab haereditate prin-
> cipatus sacerdotii tui, ut ministerio fungens sine reprehensione et pure et sancte et
> mente candida, dignus fiat ordine hoc magno et excelso per voluntatem tuam et te
> laudet indesinenter per Filium tuum....[152]

Bradshaw's view accords with some of the interpretations of 1 Timothy
3.13 noted above. If he is correct, then the *Apostolic Tradition* is evidence
of a developed three-fold ministry which neither required nor permitted
sequential movement between the orders.

---

[149] Botte, *Tradition*, IX, p. 28; after the Sahidic, Arabic, and Ethiopic versions.

[150] Eusebius records that as the Roman church was preparing to elect a new bishop, a dove
landed upon the head of Fabian, who had recently arrived from the country. As this was
understood to be a sign from God, Fabian was forthwith elected bishop of Rome. Eusebius, *History*, VI.29, GCS 2.2, pp. 582, 584. See below.

[151] Bradshaw, "Ordination", p. 38. *Cf.* Bradshaw, *Ordination Rites of the Ancient
Churches*, p. 73.

[152] I. E. Rahmani, ed., *Testamentum Domini Nostri Jesu Christi* XXXVIII (Hildescheim:
Georg Olms, 1968), p. 93.

E. C. Ratcliffe argues a similar point of view. Ratcliffe understands the "charismata" of the Spirit given to deacons and presbyters to be final, "[t]here can be no movement to a higher order."[153] Accordingly, a "bishop cannot be taken from among the deacons or the presbyters; he must be taken from the *laos* or *pleithos*."[154]

If the *Apostolic Tradition* represents not early-third century, but mid-second-century practice, then Bradshaw's and Ratcliffe's point is well taken. If, however, the *AT* simply reflects late-second-century/early-third-century practice, then their theory needs to be reassessed, since from the late-second and early-third centuries deacons were candidates for the episcopate in the church of Rome. For instance, Eleutherus (175–189) and possibility Callistus (217–222) were deacons prior to their appointments to the episcopate. In addition, sequential movement from the presbyterate to the episcopate was known in the West in the late second century; Irenaeus, as noted, was a presbyter before being made a bishop in the church of Lyons. In Rome itself presbyters were episcopal candidates in the third century. One such example is Hippolytus the presbyter of Rome, one of the possible authors of the *AT*, who became a schismatic bishop in Rome after the election of Callistus in 217.

In brief, while there was clearly movement from one order to another in the West and in Rome in the early third century, such movement, however, was neither prescribed nor implied within the ordination rites of the *Apostolic Tradition*.

5. Biographical Material

Both the silence on the *cursus honorum* and the allusions to sequential movement or promotion from one ministry to another suggested in the *Apostolic Tradition* and in the literature of the pre-Nicene church need to be measured against the historical and biographical information available from the period. Such information will be drawn from the careers of the bishops of Rome, various historical figures, and the ordination practice of

---

[153] E. C. Ratcliffe, "'Apostolic Tradition': Questions Concerning the Appointment of the Bishop", in A. H. Couratin & D. H. Tripp, eds., *Liturgical Studies* (London: SPCK, 1976), p. 159.

[154] Ratcliffe, "Apostolic Tradition", p. 159.

the church of Alexandria. This biographical evidence is intended as illustrative rather than as an exhaustive list.

a. Rome

i.

The *Apostolic Tradition* became more influential in subsequent Eastern Church Orders and ordination rites than in the West, yet it remains a document of the early third-century Roman church. While the *AT* describes the rites of ordination to the various orders, and is an important witness to the development of holy orders, the actual history of the Roman church at the same period is equally important, for it reveals ordination from the lay state directly to the episcopate, as well as sequential movement from both the diaconate and the presbyterate to the episcopate.

For example, in the *Ecclesiastical History*, Eusebius relates that Fabian (236–250) in the mid-third century was a lay person when he became bishop of Rome:

> Gordian having succeeded Maximin as Roman emperor, Pontian, after six years as bishop of the Roman church, was succeeded by Anteros, and he, after filling the office for a month, by Fabian. It is said that after Anteros's death Fabian came with a party from the country and paid a visit to Rome, where by a miracle of divine and heavenly grace he was chosen to fill the place. When the brethren had all assembled with the intention of electing a successor to the bishopric, and a large number of eminent and distinguished men were in the thoughts of most, Fabian, who was present, came into no one's mind. But suddenly out of the blue a dove fluttered down and perched on his head (the story goes on), plainly following the example of the descent upon the Saviour of the Holy Spirit in the form of a dove. At this, as if moved by one divine inspiration, with the utmost enthusiasm and complete unanimity the whole meeting shouted that he was the man, and then and there they seized him and set him upon the bishop's throne.[155]

This sort of appointment appears to have been extremely rare in the early Roman church.

Deacons appear to have been candidates for the episcopate in Rome from the second half of the second century. In many churches the number of deacons was adjusted to meet the needs of the local communities. In Rome, however, the number was fixed at seven, in fidelity to the "seven"

---

[155] Eusebius, *History*, VI.29, *GCS* 2.2, pp. 582, 584; Williamson, trans., *Eusebius*, pp. 203–204.

appointed in Acts 6.[156] Bishop Fabian divided the city of Rome into seven ecclesiastical districts, each administered by a deacon. Fabian decreed that each region would have a subdeacon to assist the deacon. Moreover, the subdeacon would succeed to the deacon's office when it became vacant. Thus, there was an easy and effective transition from one deacon to another in a given district.[157] In the Roman church the college of deacons worked closely with the bishop in the daily administration of the church. In consequence, deacons were logical candidates for the episcopate; the bishop's office entailed much administration, with which the deacons were already familiar.[158] As Dix writes:

> In the second and third centuries it was as often as not the archdeacon[159] who was elected to succeed to a dead bishop's throne, and not one of the presbyters, because of his grasp of the affairs of the Church as his predecessor's right hand man marked him out as the best person to succeed him.[160]

For example, Eleutherus (175–189) was a deacon before being elected bishop of Rome in the late second century. Eusebius includes a section from the works of Hegesippus identifying Eleutherus as the deacon of Anicetus (*ca.* 155–*ca.* 166).[161] Callistus (217–222) likely was a deacon,[162]

---

[156] This was common in many churches in Asia Minor as well in the third and fourth centuries.

[157] Lietzmann, *Early Church*, vol 2, p. 249.

[158] Bo Reicke, "Deacons in the New Testament and the Early Church", in *The Ministry of Deacons*, (Geneva: WCC, 1965) p. 12.

[159] The title "archdeacon" does not appear until the early fourth century, in the North African Church. Chadwick, *Early Church*, p. 48.

[160] Dix, "The Ministry in the Early Church", p. 283.

[161] Eusebius, *History*, IV.22, *GCS* 2.1, p. 370.

[162] Some uncertainty surrounds Callistus' status at the time of his election and consecration to the episcopate. George H. Williams in "The Ministry of the Ante-Nicene Church", p. 37, claims that he was a confessor. Chadwick identifies him as a deacon in *The Early Church*, p. 82. Dix in "Ministry in the Early Church", p. 225, identifies him (anachronistically) as archdeacon of Rome. Faivre says that he was a confessor, *Emergence of the Laity*, pp. 82–84. While noting that the few documents which deal with Callistus do not explicitly identify him as a deacon, Andrieu contends that there are some hints in the *Philosophumena* that Callistus was a deacon; "La carrière des papes", p. 91. Andrieu's evidence is based on the description of Callistus in the *Philosophumena* (*Origensis Philosophumena sive omnium hæresium refutatio*) IX, PG 16/III, 3369–3379. The author's (probably not Hippolytus; definitely not Origen) unfavourable account of Callistus (associating with the heretic Noetus) portrays him as a colleague of his predecessor Zephyrinus (198–217). The role he played in Zephyrinus's episcopate corresponds to that of senior deacon.

as were Stephen I (254–257)[163] and Sixtus II (257–258).[164]

Presbyters were also likely candidates for the episcopate in the Roman church throughout the third century, and perhaps even earlier.[165] For example, the presbyters Hippolytus (*ca.*170–*ca.*236) and Novatian (d. 257) both aspired to the episcopate of Rome; Novatian, at least, became a schismatic bishop of Rome.

ii.

After the martyrdom of Fabian in 250, the Roman church was not able to elect a new bishop for over a year. In the interim, the presbyter Novatian, a rigorist, showed great leadership, and expected to be elected bishop. However, when Cornelius was elected in April, 251, Novatian established a schismatic church and became its bishop. Novatian appealed to the North African church for support. Cyprian of Carthage, however, supported Cornelius. In retaliation, in 252, Fortunatus, a presbyter, was elected as the Novatian bishop of Carthage in opposition to Cyprian.

Not only was Cornelius a presbyter when he became bishop of Rome (251–253), but had apparently served in *all* the ecclesiastical offices. In *Epistle* 55.8, an anti-Novatian letter to Antonianus, a wavering North African bishop, Cyprian defends Cornelius's election:

> Venio iam nunc, frater carissime, ad personam Corneli collegae nostri, ut Cornelium nobiscum verius noveris, non de malignorum et detrahentium mendacio, sed de Dei iudicio qui episcopum eum fecit et coepiscoporum testimonio quorum numerus universus per totum mundum concordi unanimitate consensit. nam quod Cornelium carissimum nostrum Deo et Christo et ecclesiae eius, item consacerdotibus cunctis laudabili praedicatione commendat, non iste ad episcopatum subito pervenit, sed per omnia ecclesiastica officia promotus et in divinis administrationibus

---

[163] In the later biography of Lucius (253–254) Stephen is identified as his archdeacon: "Hic potestatum dedit omni ecclesiae Stephano archdiacono suo, dum ad passionem pergeret". L. Duchesne, ed., *Le Liber Pontificalis: Texte, Introduction, & Commentaire*, 2nd ed. vol. 1 (Paris: Ernest Thorin, 1886), p. 153.

[164] Sixtus (or Xystus) is mentioned in the later biography of Stephen in the *Liber pontificalis* as having been his archdeacon: "Ibidem in carcerem ad arcum stellae fecit synodo et omnia vas aecclesiae archdiacono suo Xysto in potestatem dedit vel arcam pecuniae." LP I, p.154.

[165] The sixth century *Liber pontificalis* records that Pope Anacletus (*ca.* 79–*ca.* 91) was a presbyter before he became bishop. Apparently he was ordained a presbyter by St. Peter himself! LP I, p. 125.

Dominum saepe promeritus ad sacerdotii sublime fastigium cunctis religionis gradibus ascendit.[166]

Cyprian explains that Cornelius did not attain the episcopal rank suddenly, but was "promoted through all the ecclesiastical offices"; he "rose through all the grades of religion to the exalted pinnacle of the priesthood." One recalls the letter of Cornelius to Fabius of Antioch, preserved by Eusebius, in which Cornelius mentions, in sequence, the ministries of presbyter, deacon, subdeacon, acolyte, exorcist, lector, and doorkeeper. One can only conjecture that these grades are synonymous with "all the ecclesiastical offices" and "all the grades of religion."

Although there are instances prior to the mid-third century of deacons becoming bishops, and of presbyters becoming bishops, the example of Cornelius is generally regarded as the first evidence of a person having been promoted through all the orders,[167] a century before the first canonical legislation enjoining the clerical *cursus* appeared. Again, one can only infer that the list of ministries Cornelius mentions to Fabius of Antioch is synonymous with the series of offices to which Cyprian alludes by *omnia ecclesiastica officia*.

As noted earlier, J. Robert Wright cites the letters of Cyprian, especially *Epistle* 55.8, as the earliest appearance of the "doctrine of cumulative orders".[168] Yet in *Epistle* 55.8, as well as in *Epistle* 38, there is no suggestion that Cyprian understood the example of Cornelius' ecclesiastical career as normative or prescriptive. Nor does Cyprian attach any theological significance to such sequential movement. Hence, it is not possible to use *Epistle* 55.8 as a theological source for the "doctrine of cumulative orders"; it merely describes the career of one bishop.

Nevertheless, there are commentators who regard Cyprian's letter to Antonianus as evidence of the existence of *cursus honorum* in the third century. For example, G.W. Clarke in his commentary on the epistles of Cyprian states that *Epistle* 55.8 is a remarkable testimony to the extent to which the clerical *cursus* was established in the mid-third century.[169] Clarke suggests that for Cyprian to have produced such a reference to

---

[166] Cyprian, Epistle 55.8, *Cyprianum Antoniano fratri s.*, CSEL 3.2, p. 629.

[167] E.g., Chadwick, *Early Church*, p. 48, n.1.

[168] Wright, "Sequential Orders," p. 248.

[169] G. W. Clarke, trans. & comm., *The Letters of St. Cyprian of Carthage*, vol. 3 Ancient Christian Writers 46 (New York: Newman Press, 1986), p. 173.

Cornelius' career as his evidence of his qualification to be bishop of Rome, Cornelius must have been a well established figure among the Roman clergy. Clarke suggests that Cornelius must have been the senior presbyter, adding that it is "not without irony that Cyprian himself would have been poorly qualified for office on the criterion he provides in Cornelius' eulogy as would Cornelius' predecessor Fabian."[170]

Since there are third-century Roman instances of laity becoming presbyters or bishops, and of deacons becoming bishops, it is difficult to concur with Clarke that the *cursus* of Cornelius' career was typical in the mid-third-century Western church. In addition, it does not seem possible, as Clarke asserts, that Cornelius was the senior Roman presbyter during the period after Fabian's death when Rome was without a bishop (*ca.* 250); it was Novatian, not Cornelius, who assumed that role. Moreover, there is nothing to suggest that in the third-century Roman church episcopal candidates needed to be presbyters prior to election or consecration. Deacons were as likely as presbyters to be elected bishop of Rome at this time (e.g., Callistus, Stephen I, and Sixtus II). One recalls again Cornelius's letter to Fabius, regarding the ministers at Rome during his episcopate: the fact that there were so many more presbyters than deacons (46/7) would imply that not all the presbyters had ever been deacons. A more likely suggestion regarding Cornelius' career comes from W.H. Frere, who submits that Cyprian made mention of Cornelius' movement through the orders because it was such an exceptional incident.[171]

iii.

There were other Roman bishops in the pre-Nicene period who had been presbyters prior to episcopal election. Eusebius records that Dionysius (260–268) was a presbyter before he became bishop of Rome in July, 260.[172] For two years after the martyrdom of Sixtus II in 258, the Roman church was governed by a council of presbyters; even the seven deacons

---

[170] Clarke, *Letters of Cyprian*, p. 173.

[171] W. H. Frere, "Early Forms of Ordination in the Early Church", *Essays on the Early History of the Church and the Ministry*, ed. H. B. Swete (London: MacMIllan, 1918), p. 306.

[172] Referring to a letter by Dionysius, bishop of Alexandria, Eusebius writes: "The fourth of his letters on baptism was written to Dionysius of Rome, who had recently been ordained presbyter and was shortly to be ordained bishop of the diocese." Eusebius, *History* VII.7 *GCS* 2.2 pp. 642, 644. Williamson, trans., *Eusebius*, p. 224.

had been martyred. Dionysius had been one of those presbyters. According to the *Liber pontificalis*, in the early fourth century Marcellus (306-308) had been a presbyter under his predecessor, Marcellinus (296–304).[173]

In summary, the Roman church in the second and third centuries knew bishops who had been either deacons or presbyters. In addition, there is at least one instance of a lay person becoming bishop, and at least one instance of a bishop who had risen through all the grades.

b. Irenaeus

Although little is known about the life of Irenaeus of Lyons (*ca.* 130–*ca.* 200), it is known that he was a presbyter before he became a bishop (*ca.* 178) after the martyrdom of his predecessor Pothinus in 177. Furthermore, it is likely Irenaeus was ordained to the episcopate by the presbyters of Lyons. Einar Molland in his article "Irenaeus of Lugdunum and the Apostolic Succession" draws attention to the fact that no evidence of Irenaeus having been ordained to the episcopate by a bishop exists, for the only city in Gaul with a bishop was Lyons, which was without a bishop after the death of Pothinus. Given the speed with which Irenaeus was ordained a bishop, Molland concludes that the simplest solution is that he was ordained by his own presbyters. Such an ordination, Molland suggests, would not have been uncommon elsewhere in the early church.[174]

Both Irenaeus' writings and career reflect the close association between the presbyterate and the episcopate. This association led to a natural sequence from the presbyterate to the episcopate—at least in Gaul in the second half of the second century.

c. Origen

The Alexandrian teacher and theologian Origen (*ca.*185–254) was a lay person at the time of his controversial ordination to the presbyterate in 229. He is noted as one of the great lay teachers of the pre-Nicene period.[175] Eusebius refers to the ordination in Book VI of the *Ecclesiastical*

---

[173] LP I, p. 162.

[174] Einar Molland, "Irenaeus of Lugdunum and the Apostolic Succession," *Journal of Ecclesiastical History*, vol. 1 (1950), p. 28.

[175] E.g., Faivre, *Emergence*, pp. 63–64.

History.[176] During a voyage from Alexandria to Athens, Origen was ordained a presbyter by two admiring bishops in Caesarea. "This", Eusebius records, "made him the subject of agitation on which the prelates of the church passed judgement".[177] Demetrius, the bishop of Alexandria, contested the ordination on the grounds that it had been performed without his permission; as bishop of Alexandria only he had the authority to ordain a member of his church. Furthermore, Origen had left Alexandria without the permission of his bishop. In addition, Demetrius also opposed Origen's ordination on the grounds that he was a eunuch. Incidentally, Duchesne speculates that Alexandrian usage prohibited the ordination of eunuchs, a century before it was forbidden by the Council of Nicaea.[178] Finally, in 232 a synod of the clergy of Alexandria deposed Origen from the presbyterate. As a result of the incident, Origen spent the rest of his life in Caesarea.

Historians, ancient and modern, point to the personalities of Origen and Demetrius as the source of the conflict.[179] Nowhere is it suggested that Origen's ordination to the presbyterate was irregular and controversial because he had not served in any other grade of ministry, including the diaconate.

d. Cyprian

Commenting on Cyprian's Letter 55.8, regarding the clerical career of Cornelius, G. W. Clarke notes that "Cyprian himself would have been poorly qualified for office on the criterion he provides in Cornelius' eulogy...."[180] Unlike his contemporary Cornelius of Rome, it is unlikely that Cyprian of Carthage (d. 258) served in any ecclesiastical office, other than possibly the presbyterate for a short while, prior to his election and ordination as bishop of Carthage (*ca.* 248).

Scholars disagree concerning Cyprian's status before his consecration. For example, Duchesne says that he was "admitted to the bench of

---

[176] Eusebius, *History*, VI.23, *GCS* 2.2, p. 570.

[177] Eusebius, *History* VI. 23, *GCS* 2.2 p. 570; Williamson, trans., *Eusebius*, p. 199.

[178] Duchesne, *Early*, p. 88.

[179] E.g., Duchesne, *Early*, p. 88; Frend, *Early*, p. 88.

[180] Clarke, *Letters of Cyprian*, vol. 3, p. 173.

presbyters" shortly after his baptism in 246.[181] R. P. Symonds records that while he thought Cyprian was a presbyter before he was a bishop, E. W. Benson thought he was a deacon.[182] W. H. Frere says that Cyprian was a presbyter, though never a deacon, before he was a bishop.[183] Dix, however, says he was a lay person.[184] More recently, G. W. Clarke speaks of Cyprian's "conversion, baptism, renunciation of his worldly estate, and advancement to clerical office" prior to his episcopal election and consecration.[185] Robert Sider asserts that Cyprian was made a presbyter shortly after his baptism;[186] this position is also held by Ekkehard Mühlenberg.[187]

Actually, very little is known about the early life of Cyprian. His own writings provide few details about his career prior to his episcopal ministry.[188] Much depends on the outline of his career given by his biographer Pontius in the *Vita Cypriani*. The confusion regarding Cyprian's status at the time of his episcopal election can be traced to the *Vita Cypriani*. Chapter 3.3–4 of the *Vita* describes Cyprian's election to episcopal office. Pontius writes:

> 3.3. Mora denique circa gratiam Dei nulla, nulla dilatio; parum dixi: presbyterium vel sacerdotium statim; quis enim non omnes honoris gradus crederet tali mente credenti? 4. Multa sunt quae adhuc plebeius, multa quae iam presbyter fecerit, multa quae ad veterum exempla iustorum imitatione consimili persecutus promerendo Deo totius religionis obsequia praestiterit.[189]

"Finally there is no delay concerning the grace of God, no postponement," writes Pontius, "I have said but little: [he received] the presbyterate and [*vel*] the episcopate immediately". The confusion surrounds the words

---

[181] Duchesne, *Early History*, p. 289.

[182] R. P. Symonds, "Deacons in the Early Church", *Theology*, Vol. 58 (1955), p. 412.

[183] W. H. Frere, "Early Forms of Ordination," *Essays on the Early History of the Church and the Ministry*, ed. H. B. Swete (London: MacMillan, 1918), p. 306.

[184] Dix, "The Ministry of the Early Church", p. 284.

[185] G. W. Clarke, *The Letters of St. Cyprian of Carthage* vol. 1, Ancient Christian Writers, vol. 44 (New York: Newman Press, 1984), introduction, p. 16.

[186] Robert D. Sider, "Cyprian," *Encyclopedia of Early Christianity*, ed. Everett Ferguson (New York: Garland Publishing Inc., 1990), p. 247.

[187] Ekkehard Mühlenberg, "Les Débuts de la Biographie Chrétienne," *Revue de Théologie et de Philosophie*, vol. 122 (1990), p. 528.

[188] Sider, "Cyprian", p. 246.

[189] A. A. R. Bastiaensen, ed., *Vita Di Cipriano, Vite Dei Santi*, vol. 3 (Verona: Fondazione Lorenzo Valla Arnoldo Mondadori Editore, 1975), p. 10.

presbyterium vel sacerdotium; here *sacerdotium* is likely synonymous with the word *episcopate*.[190] It is difficult to ascertain whether the *Vita* is referring to promotion to the presbyterate and the episcopate in general, or whether it is referring to the promotion of Cyprian in particular. Pontius also speaks of the deeds Cyprian did as a lay person then later as a presbyter: *Multa sunt quae adhuc plebeius, multa quae iam presbyter fecerit....* This sentence strongly suggests that he was at one time a presbyter.

The confusion resumes in chapter 5, which describes the controversy over Cyprian's election. The *Vita* says:

> 5.1. Ad probationem bonorum operum solum hoc arbitror satis esse, quod iudicio Dei et plebis favore ad officium sacerdotii et episcopatus gradum adhuc neophytus et ut putabatur novellus electus est, quamvis in primis fidei suae adhuc diebus et rudi vitae spiritalis aetate sic generosa indoles reluceret, ut, etsi nondum officii, spei tamen fulgore resplendens, inminentis sacerdotii totam fiduciam polliceretur.[191]

After Cyprian's consecration, *ca.* 248, there were objections raised by some of the Carthaginian presbyters on the grounds that he had been too recently baptised. Pontius speaks of the "neophyte" who by the judgement of God and the favour of the people was considered for the priestly and episcopal office—*ad officium sacerdotii et episcopatus gradum*. Here again *sacerdotium* refers to the episcopate and not to the presbyterate. As well, Pontius makes no mention of objection to Cyprian's election to the presbyterate on the grounds that he was a neophyte. This passage, on its own, might suggest that Cyprian was a lay person at the time of his election and consecration.

Lastly, there is no suggestion that Cyprian served in any other order, such as the diaconate, before he was a (presbyter or) bishop. Regardless of whether Cyprian was a presbyter or a lay person at the time of his election and consecration, his ecclesiastical career does not correspond to that of Cornelius of Rome, or in fact to the later *cursus honorum* of the church. As Clarke says, "Cyprian himself would have been poorly qualified for office on the criterion he provides in Cornelius' eulogy...."[192]

---

[190] From the Italian translation of Bastiaensen, *Cipriano*, p. 11.

[191] Pontius, *Vita S. Cypriani* 5.1; Bastiaensen, *Cipriano*, p. 14.

[192] Clarke, *Letters of Cyprian*, vol. 3, p. 173.

e. Alexandria

The church of Alexandria was governed by a council of twelve presbyters. The bishop was normally elected from among the presbyters, and ordained by them without episcopal ordination from neighbouring bishops.[193] While this procedure is similar to that by which Irenaeus of Lyons was ordained in the late second century, it is in marked contrast to the practice of most churches in the third century. Writers such as Ambrosiaster and Jerome noted the Alexandrian practice a century later. For example, in *Epistle* 146 to Evangelus the presbyter, Jerome writes:

> nam et Alexandria a Marco evangelista usque ad Heraclam et Dionysium episcopos presbyteri semper unum de se electum et in excelsiori gradu conlocatum epis-copum nominabant....[194]

In an effort to curb the power of the Roman deacons Jerome argues for the original identity of presbyters with bishops. He cites the example of the Church at Alexandria which from the time of St. Mark to the bishops Her-aclas and Dionysius had elected its bishops from among the presbyters. Jerome recounts that the Alexandrian presbyters themselves elected the bishop, placed him in the higher rank, and named him bishop. According to Telfer, this practice lasted in the Alexandrian church until the Council of Nicaea in 325:

> The probability is that the old custom was undisturbed until Nicaea, that Alexander was the last Alexandrian pope to take office without the imposition of living epis-copal hands, and that the new order came in with Athanasius.[195]

By comparison, Gerard Luttenberger notes that Jerome witnesses only to the election of bishops by presbyters, not to the presbyteral ordination of bishops. And yet, Luttenberger recognizes that there is no indication that such an election was followed by episcopal ordination. Thus, it is unclear whether election was sufficient to install a new bishop, or whether it was simply the preliminary stage to episcopal ordination.[196]

---

[193] See W. Telfer, "Episcopal Succession in Egypt", *Journal of Ecclesiastical History*, 3.1, 1952, pp. 1–13. Telfer writes: "It is probable that a majority of scholars hold the opinion that the early bishops of Alexandria received their episcopal office at the hands of their fellow-presbyters." p. 1.

[194] *CSEL* 56, p. 310; *Cf.* Ambrosiaster, *Ad Efesios* IV.11, *CSEL* 81/3, p. 100.

[195] Telfer, "Episcopal Succession in Egypt", pp. 10–11.

[196] Gerard H. Luttenberger, "The Decline of Presbyteral Collegiality and the Growth of the Individualization of the Priesthood (4th–5th Centuries)", *Recherches de théologie ancienne et médiévale*, vol. 48 (1981), p. 45.

Now in terms of the *cursus honorum*, the Alexandrian model provides a significant contrast to the practice of the Roman church (and others). At Rome, in the third century, bishops were drawn from the ranks of the laity and the diaconate as well as the presbyterate. In Alexandria, bishops seem to have been drawn exclusively from the presbyterate. Yet, like the church in Gaul in the second century, this practice was not a reflection of the imperial *cursus honorum*, but rather a consequence of the close affinity between the episcopate and the presbyterate in the early Egyptian church.

Presbyteral consecration of bishops was forbidden after Canon IV of the Council of Nicaea in 325 directed that all bishops must be ordained by at least three other bishops.[197] The Egyptian church complied with the universal custom. The effect of the fourth Canon of the Council of Nicaea was two-fold. First, Alexandrian bishops were henceforth to be ordained by other bishops. Second, candidature for the episcopal office was no longer restricted to the presbyterate. The initial consequence of this was the election of the deacon Athanasius to succeed (the presbyterally installed) Alexander as bishop of Alexandria in 328. It is interesting to note that neither the "validity" of those bishops who received presbyteral consecration (such as Athanasius' predecessor, Alexander who was present at Nicaea) nor those who were consecrated by them (the entire Egyptian episcopate) was ever questioned.

6. Summary

This chapter has examined evidence of sequential movement through the orders of ministry in the first three centuries. The sources have been the New Testament, early Christian literature, ordination rites, and biographical information. In the New Testament there is no evidence of the later *cursus honorum*. However, since there is also little evidence of the later major and minor "orders" associated with the *cursus honorum*, it is perhaps prudent to say that the New Testament evidence is inconclusive in the debate on whether or not to retain the *cursus honorum*.

Correspondingly, evidence from the post-apostolic period seems equally inconclusive. The *Didache*, I Clement, and Justin Martyr, despite their

---

[197] Turner, *EOMIA*, vol. 1, p. 116.

value in the history of holy orders, cannot be used as evidence of sequential ordination. If, as some commentators have suggested, the terms "bishops and deacons" and "presbyters" refer to the same group of church leaders, then it becomes impossible to speak of promotion through these ministries. Moreover, like the New Testament sources, there is little evidence of the major and minor orders associated with the later *cursus honorum*, except in an embryonic form.

Similarly, evidence from the second century is indecisive in the modern debate over the retention or abolition of the *cursus honorum*. A variety of patterns is evident in the evolving relationship between the episcopate, the presbyterate, and the diaconate. For instance, although in the Ignatian epistles there is no evidence of movement from one ministry to another in the communities of Asia Minor at the beginning of the second century, it is doubtful that presbyters would have succeeded the bishop in office, or that deacons would have succeeded the presbyters. On the other hand, it seems that presbyters may well have normally succeeded bishops in office in Gaul in the mid-second century (as well as in Alexandria until the early fourth century), leading one to assume the same was true in the Roman church, given its presbyteral foundation. By the late second century, however, there is evidence of deacons becoming bishops in Rome. The series or succession of offices (either of presbyters who became bishops, or deacons who became bishops) in the second century is not so much a parallel to the imperial *cursus honorum* as much as it is a reflection of the relationship between the presbyterate and the episcopate (Lyons), or the close association of the diaconate and the episcopate (Ignatian churches, Rome).

From the third century there is evidence of an emerging hierarchical and ranked understanding of holy orders. The letter of Cornelius to Fabius of Antioch is significant because of its list of ministers who appear in the sequence of the later clerical *cursus honorum*. Yet a well established hierarchical precedence does not in itself imply sequential movement or promotion from one ministry to the next. Cyprian's *Epistle* 38 indicates that the lectorate could be used as a preparatory office. In Cyprian's letter regarding Cornelius (*Epistle* 55.8), who had "advanced through all the ecclesiastical offices", the later clerical *cursus* is certainly embryonic. Particular ministries were no longer exclusively life-long vocations; individuals could and did "advance" from one grade of ministry to another. Yet, as noted above, in the mid-third century, it was probably Cornelius' career which was the exception. As noted above, it is impossible to find in this letter any underlying doctrinal implications for sequential ordination or cumulative orders.

In other communities, where the association was closer between the bishop and the diaconate, deacons were the likely candidates for the episcopal office. In the church of Rome deacons were natural, though not exclusive, candidates for the episcopacy. From the third century, Roman presbyters clearly became bishops as well. Some clerics are said to have been "advanced through all the ecclesiastical offices"; Cornelius, according to Cyprian, is one such example. Given the varied sequences, or lack thereof, it becomes difficult to conclude with Wright, that in the mid-third century the doctrine of cumulative or sequential orders "soon becomes a standard consensus of the church catholic."[198]

Christians in the first three centuries seem to have enjoyed considerable flexibility and diversity in choosing those they considered to be most suited to ordered ministry. An episcopal candidate might have been a deacon who had helped the previous bishop in the administration of a church, or a presbyter who had shown leadership during a time of persecution, or an obviously gifted lay person. As Dix has said:

> If a man were chosen to be bishop, then he was ordained bishop, regardless if he were already an acolyte or a presbyter or a simple layman; if a deacon were elected then he was ordained bishop without first being ordained presbyter, and so on.[199]

There are no examples (extant) of candidates for the minor orders, or for the diaconate or the presbyterate in the pre-Nicene period who appear to have anticipated Wright's fears about being ordained by a bishop who had never served in the minor orders, or in the diaconate or the presbyterate.[200] Nor is there any suggestion that early patristic bishops (e.g., Irenaeus, Eleutherus, Fabian, Cyprian, Stephen I, Sixtus II....) , who had not served in all or any of the lower orders were in any way regarded as having "less claim to be 'historic'", as some might fear would be the case today.

Examples have been noted of members of the laity who were made presbyters, deacons who were made bishops, presbyters who became bishops, and of members of the laity who became bishops. The relationship which seems to have been by-passed, for which there is very little evidence, is sequential ordination from the diaconate to the presbyterate.

---

[198] Wright, "Sequential Orders," p. 248.

[199] Dix, "The Ministry of the Early Church", p. 284.

[200] *Cf*. Wright, "Sequential Orders," p. 250

Perhaps the reason for this is that diaconate and the presbyterate were un-related; they were related more to the episcopate and to the laity, than they were to one another. Since it is sequential ordination between the diacon-ate and the presbyterate which has raised questions regarding the value of retaining the *cursus honorum* today, the paucity of evidence regarding se-quential movement between these two orders in the primitive church is sig-nificant.

Evidence from the third century does reveal instances of sequential movement (or promotion) from one ministry to another; possibly this mo-bility is the embryo of the later ecclesiastical *cursus honorum*. At the same time evidence also exists of direct ordination, that is, lay people becoming bishops, deacons becoming bishops, and lay people becoming presbyters as well. Clearly progression from one office to another was neither pre-scriptive nor normative in this period.

II

THE *CURSUS HONORUM*

IN THE "GOLDEN AGE" OF THE FATHERS

1. Introduction

This chapter will examine the development of the *cursus honorum* and the related issues of the ages of clerics and the interstices in the patristic period from the time of Constantine in the early fourth century to the death of the Venerable Bede in the early eighth century. As noted in the previous chapter, the hierarchical ordering of the church's ministry was well established by the third century. While sequential ordination was practised in the pre-Constantinian Church, there is no evidence that such movement was either prescriptive or normative. In contrast, from the time of the Peace of the Church in the early fourth century sequential movement from one grade to another, the *cursus honorum*, became a prescribed and increasingly normative feature of the church's ordered ministry.

In the current debate on the value of sequential ordination, negative judgements are often made on the emergence of the *cursus honorum* in the patristic period on the basis of the present situation. This chapter will seek to understand the development of the *cursus honorum* in the light of the needs and challenges of the Constantinian and late patristic church. Evidence will be examined from conciliar and papal legislation, early canonical collections, liturgical sources, and lastly from the biographical evidence available in this period.

2. The Church of the Empire

After the conversion of Constantine in 312, imperial policy brought Christianity from a position of persecution to one of equality, and eventually of preëminence within the Roman Empire. In fact, the church of the fourth century is often referred to as the "Church of the Empire."[1]

The church experienced tremendous growth, becoming a popular movement by the mid-fourth century, as the legal restrictions against the Church were removed and as it became the recipient of imperial favour. For example, the state conferred various privileges upon the church which enhanced the positions of its leaders in public life. In 313, for instance, Constantine exempted catholic clergy from the obligation to contribute to municipal taxes; in 349 clergy and their children were exempted from financial responsibilities in their respective municipalities. The church began to receive a share of the general taxes. Clergy became eligible to receive special apportionments of food. In 343 clergy were relieved from the responsibility of billeting soldiers and were soon exempted from military service altogether. These privileges were not exceptional; they were the marks of the middle classes in the late Roman Empire.

The church became prosperous in the fourth century. After the Edict of Milan in 313, Constantine enacted a series of laws which restored property to Christians (and others) who had lost them in the persecutions. In 321 Constantine gave the church permission to receive bequests. At ordination the clergy were required to hand over their property to the church which they served.[2] As a result, the estates of the church became large and wealthy. The new found wealth and holdings of the church led to a new quality sought in candidates for the episcopate: administrative ability. Further, it led to ecclesiastical leadership becoming the object of envy and ambition.

A helpful monetary comparison between the imperial bishop of the fourth century and his third-century counterpart is provided by historian W. H. C. Frend. In *The Rise of Christianity* Frend notes that the earliest

---

[1] E.g. Karl Baus, *et. al.*, *The Imperial Church from Constantine to the Early Middle Ages*, eds. H. Jedin and J. Dolan, History of the Church, vol. II (New York: Crossroad, 1986), p. 78.

[2] *Cf.* Canon XLIX, Council of 397, Charles Munier, ed., *Concilia Africae A. 345–A. 525*, CCSL 149 (1973), p. 341.

mention of a bishop's salary is supplied by Eusebius in the *Ecclesiastical History* (Bk. V 28.10).[3] Eusebius records that in Rome *ca.* 200, the sum of 105 denarii a month was paid by a heretical group, the Theodotian Monarchians, to the confessor Natalius while he was their bishop. This amount was not a great deal of money: it amounted to 7,200 sesterces a year compared to 100,000 paid to a middle grade imperial official. Frend comments that "Bishops had a long way to go before their pay was equated to that of provincial governors."[4] In *The Early Church*, Frend points out that during the fourth and fifth centuries, the bishop of a large see was paid 720 solidi a year, an amount equivalent to that paid to senior imperial officers such as provincial governors.[5]

In short, growth in terms of numbers, wealth, and civic status effected change in every aspect of the church's life, including its ordered ministry. Consequently, ecclesiastical offices, particularly the episcopate, became enviable positions and the objects of considerable ambition. The office of bishop was particularly attractive to the middle classes; ecclesiastical office, along with the imperial administration, had become one of the few career outlets in the stratified society of the Empire. Moreover, the size, position, and resources of the church required well-trained, capable administrators. Hence, there was a tendency to select former lawyers and those trained in administration. The complexity of liturgy and theology required a clergy well trained in these areas as well.

From the early fourth century onwards it became increasingly evident that the older, unprescribed and variable method of electing leaders in the Christian community (especially presbyters and bishops) was unsuited to the new circumstances, and was often open to abuse. From the documents of the fourth, fifth, and sixth centuries, it is patent that all too often candidates were appointed to episcopal office who were thoroughly unsuited, untested, and unprepared.

It is in this context that the patristic documents also reveal the church's solution to this predicament: the ecclesiastical *cursus honorum*. Though the actual term "*cursus honorum*" is seldom found in the patristic texts, the custom was familiar enough to Christians of the fourth and fifth centuries; for centuries the imperial civil and military services had used such

---

[3] W. H. C. Frend, *The Rise of Christianity* (Philadelphia: Fortress, 1984), p. 405.

[4] Frend, *The Rise*, p. 405.

[5] W. H. C. Frend, *The Early Church*, (Philadelphia: Fortress Press, 1987) p. 238.

progression through the grades or ranks as a means of selection, training, and testing. In conjunction with the *cursus honorum*, one notes legislation determining the ages of candidates for various offices, and the "interstices" or the prescribed intervals spent in one office before proceeding to the next. The term *"interstitia"*, like *cursus honorum*, is seldom found in the patristic texts; an equivalent term, *tempora*, however, is frequently used.[6] The clerical *cursus* and the interstices emerged as part of the church's effort to select, train, and test its leaders.

3. The *Cursus Honorum* in Patristic Conciliar Legislation

Along with the papal decretals, the patristic councils are major sources in the development of the *cursus honorum*. This section will examine the pre-Nicene Councils of Neocaesarea and Ancyra, as well as the Council of Nicaea, the Council of Sardica, the Council of Laodicea, and the patristic Gallican and Hispanic councils. In addition, note will be made of the transmission of the particular canons surveyed in the later patristic and medieval canonistic collections. The canonistic collections are both the vehicles for the transmission of the conciliar statements, and also gauges of the general significance of the canons in question. The canonists arranged their material either historically (i.e. according to chronology) or systematically. The systematic collections are perhaps a better gauge of the overall significance of a particular canon, since the choices of canons in these collections were deliberate and intentional.

a. The Pre-Nicene Councils

One of the earliest councils after the Peace of the Church is the Council of Neocaesarea, held in Cappadocia some time between 314 and 325. Its fifteen canons were concerned with questions of ecclesiastical discipline, including ordered ministry. While there is no explicit evidence of a prescribed *cursus*, canons from the council do reflect sequential movement between the ministries. Canons IX and X (*Interpretatio Gallica*) state:

---

6 P.-H. Lafontaine, *Les Conditions positives de l'Accession aux Ordres* (Ottawa: Éditions de l'Université d'Ottawa, 1963), pp. 321–322.

IX. Presbiter si carnale peccatum habeat et promoveatur et confessus fuerit quia peccavit antequam ordinatus est, non offerat: si autem alteri, peccata dixerunt penitus manus inpositione dimitti.

X. Similiter autem et diaconus si in ipso peccato inventus fuerit, subdiaconi ordinem accipiat.[7]

The two canons deal with the situation of presbyters and deacons whose sins committed prior to ordination have been discovered. A presbyter in such a predicament is inhibited from celebrating the eucharist. The presbyter retains his office, though not the function. A deacon is demoted to the subdiaconate. Movement in the grades is usually ascending. Such a movement downwards is unusual.

A significant canon from the Council of Neocaesarea, Canon XI (*Interpretatio Gallica*), deals with the ages of clerics:

Presbiter ante XXX annos non ordinetur: etsi satis sapiens fuerit, sub oculis custodiatur. Dominus enim noster in XXX anno baptizatus est, et sic coepit docere.[8]

This canon establishes thirty as the minimal age for the presbyterate, despite of the wisdom and maturity of the candidate. This is the earliest fourth-century evidence of a prescribed age for any office holder in the church. The grounds for the age of thirty years is in deference to the age of Jesus when he was baptised and began to teach.[9]

Another important pre-Nicene council is the Council of Ancyra, held in 314. Meeting in what is today the city of Ankara, Turkey, the council was attended by between twelve and eighteen bishops from Syria and Asia Minor. The council is best known for its treatment of the *lapsi*. In the history of ordered ministry, Canon XIII is often cited since it seems to reflect ordination by presbyters.[10] For the purpose of charting the development of the clerical *cursus*, Canon XVII (*Prisca*) is the most valuable witness:

---

[7]   C. H. Turner, ed., *Ecclesiae Occidentalis Monumenta Iuris Antiquissima*, vol. 2 (Oxford: Clarendon Press, 1899), p. 13.

[8]   Turner, *EOMIA*, vol. 2, p. 14.

[9]   Canon XI is cited frequently in the subsequent canonical collections. Of the systematic collections, it is found in the *Breviatio canonum* of Ferrandus, the *Concordia canonum* of Cresconius, the *Collectio Dacheriana*, the Pseudo-Isidorian Decretals, the *Collectio Anselmo dedicata*, the collection of Regino of Prüm, the *Collectio in V libris*, the collections of Anselm of Lucca, Deusdedit, and Gratian.

[10]   E.g., Charles Gore, *The Church and the Ministry* (London: Longman, Green, & Co., 1919), pp. 327–330.

XVII. De his qui in episcopatu sunt probati et non suscepti.

Qui in episcopatum consecrati sunt et non suscepti a parrocias [*sic.*] in quibus sunt nominati, et in aliis voluerint ire parociis et per vim obprimere ibidem constitutos et lites contra eos... [*sic.*]: ipsos perpelli et alienari. Si autem voluerint in praesbyterium in quo fuerunt primum sedere ordine ut praesbyteri, non eos pelli. Si enim voluerint resultare eis qui ibidem sunt constituti episcopi, expelli eos censemus et de ordine praesbyterii, et fieri expraedicatos.[11]

This canon deals with the situation of those who have been appointed bishops, but have not been received by the communities which nominated them. Thus, in order to avoid conflict and litigation with the installed bishop of the "parish", the canon offers bishops without a parish two options: they may either be deposed, or they may sit among the presbyters: *Si autem voluerint in praesbyterium in quo fuerunt primum sedere ordine ut praesbyteri, non eos pelli.* The second option does not suggest that such bishops reverted to the rank of presbyter. Noteworthy are the words: "in which order they were in first"—*in praesbyterium in quo fuerunt primum.* Thus, the bishops of the Council of Ancyra assumed that bishops were at one time presbyters. This canon is an early fourth-century confirmation of a customary sequential ordination from the presbyterate to the episcopate, at least in Asia Minor.[12]

b. Council of Nicaea

The first ecumenical council was convened by Constantine at Nicaea in 325, ostensibly to deal with the Arian controversy. Along with the creed and the synodal letter, a collection of twenty canons are all that remain from the proceedings of the council. The twenty canons deal with various issues of church law and discipline. A number of canons deal with the ordered ministry of the church. For instance, Canon I deals with the promotion of castrated men to the ranks of the clergy; canons IX and X deal with the ordination of candidates to the presbyterate without examination, and ordination of the *lapsi* to any order. Canon IV prescribes the imposition of hands by at least three bishops in episcopal ordinations.

Canon II (*Caeciliani*) of the Council of Nicaea is significant in the development of the clerical interstices and the *cursus honorum*, and well as

---

[11] Turner, *EOMIA*, vol. 2, pp. 25–26.

[12] Of the systematic collections, Canon XVII of the Council of Ancyra is found in the *Breviatio canonum*, the *Concordia canonum*, the Pseudo-Isidorian Decretals, the *Collectio Anselmo dedicata*, and the collection of Burchard of Worms.

enlightening regarding aspects of church life at the time of the council
which made the *cursus honorum* necessary:

II De neophitis.

> Quoniam multa sepe sive necessitate sive cogentibus quisbusdam facta sunt extra
> ecclesiasticum canonem, ut homines venientes de gentili vita simul accesserint ad
> fidem, et in brevi tempore postquam baptismum fuerint consecuti ad sacerdotium
> vel presviterii [*sic.*] vel episcopatus promoveantur; placuit nihil fieri tale de cetero,
> quia et longiore tempore ut diucius caticizentur est opus antequam baptizentur, et
> posteaquam fuerint baptizati diu sunt conprobandi: manifestum est enim apostoli-
> cum dictum NON NEOPHITUM NE INFLATUS IN IUDICIUM CADAT ET LA-
> QUEUM DIABOLI. quod si procedente tempore peccatum aliquod quod animae
> noceat inveniatur circa personas huiusmodi et a duobus vel tribus testibus arguan-
> tur, recedant de clero. qui autem extra haec fecerit, velut audacter contrarius magne
> synodo, ipse clericatus periculum sustinebit.[13]

Canon II is evidence that in the early fourth century neophytes were admitted to the presbyterate and to the episcopate immediately after their baptism. It acknowledges that such a practice is a breach of the church's
canon—*extra ecclesiasticum canonem*—and that such things have
occurred either through necessity, or through the "importunate demands of
certain individuals." Although there is no evidence of any previous legislation against the ordination of neophytes, the reference to a canonical precedent reveals the church's instinct that such a practice is illegitimate. The
canon denounces such ordinations, citing biblical support from the first letter to Timothy condemning the appointment of recent converts to the
office of "bishop" (1 Tim. 3.6–7).

The canon is also evidence that in the early fourth century candidates
could be, and were, ordained to the presbyterate and the episcopate without
having received *any* of the intervening clerical ministries. The canon does
not call into doubt the validity of such ordinations, indeed some were performed out of "necessity". The canon simply calls for an end to the practice
of conferring the presbyterate and episcopate on neophytes. Such legislation puts into relief subsequent legislation which not only requires intervening orders, but specifies the times to be spent within them.

A variety of circumstances could be covered under the term "necessity". Lafontaine in *Les Conditions positives de l'Accession aux Ordres* recalls that at the time of the Council of Nicaea, the ranks of the clergy had

---

[13] Turner, *EOMIA*, vol. 1, p. 114. *Cf.* Norman P. Tanner, trans. & ed., *Decrees of the Ecumenical Councils*, vol. 1 (Georgetown: Sheed and Ward, 1990), p. 6.

been greatly diminished in the recent persecutions. In order to replace the bishops, presbyters, and deacons who had died, it became necessary to appoint new leaders without sufficient preparation. After the Peace of the Church this practice could have continued.[14]

Canon II also alludes to other motivations behind the promotion of neophytes: the *cogentibus quibusdam facta sunt extra ecclesiasticum canonem*. Here the pride and greed of those ambitious for ecclesiastical leadership is the intended target. Pride and greed as motives for seeking ecclesiastical office are frequently cited in patristic canons prohibiting the ordinations of the untested and unprepared.

Despite the reference within the canon itself to "the breaches of *ecclesiasticum canonem*," this canon is the earliest example of the policy of councils and popes requiring a lengthy period of testing and probation for candidates for the higher offices. The immediate effect of Canon II of the Council of Nicaea cannot have been great, since throughout the fourth, fifth, and sixth centuries councils and popes continue to condemn the practice of ordaining neophytes. Canon II is significant in that it marks the first (extant) effort of a council to limit access to ecclesiastical office. It identifies one of the primary reasons for a long period between baptism and admission to the clerical ranks: the need for testing. The process initiated at Nicaea would culminate in the later interstices canons and those requiring a succession of offices. The canons of the Council of Nicaea were transmitted through a number of Latin versions in the early medieval church: for example, the *Caeciliani*, *Prisca*, *Isidoriana*, and Gallican-Hispanic versions. Canon II of the Council of Nicaea marks a significant step towards the development of the clerical *cursus* and the interstices.[15]

In addition, two other canons from the Council of Nicaea are noteworthy with regards to the development of the clerical interstices and the *cursus honorum*. Canon IX (from the *versio Caeciliani*) deals with those who have been made presbyters or bishops without examination. If such men have been found to be sinners after investigation, they are not to be admitted to office. Similarly, Canon X (*Caeciliani*) orders the deposition from

---

[14] Lafontaine, *Les Conditions*, p. 258.

[15] Canon II of the Council of Nicaea reappears in many of the major canonistic collections. Of the systematic collections cited in this study, it is found in the *Breviatio canonum*, the *Concordia canonum*, the Pseudo-Isidorian Decretals, the *Collectio Anselmo dedicata*, and Gratian's *Decretum*.

office of those who have been promoted to ordination from among the
lapsed through the ignorance of the "promoters" in time of persecution:

> IX. De his qui ad sacerdotium sine examinatione promoventur.
>
> Si quis inexaminate ad presbyterium vel episcopatum promoveantur et examinati
> consisteantur crimina sua aut ab aliis fuerint revicti, abiciantur: etsi incitate quidam
> non circumspecte manus eis inponant, huiusmodi canon respuit nec admittit. inrep-
> rehensibilem enim requirit catholica ecclesia.
>
> X. De his qui negaverunt in persecutione et postea ad clericatum promoti sunt.
>
> Quicumque ordinati sunt per ignorantiam aut dissimulationem ordinantium de his
> qui in persecutione sunt lapsi, nullum ecclesiastico canoni preiudicium faciunt;
> cogniti enim cum fuerint deponuntur.[16]

Both canons IX and X reflect the growing requirements of examination of
candidates in the early fourth century.[17]

c. The Council of Sardica

A decisive step towards establishing the clerical *cursus* was taken by the
Council of Sardica. The council was convened by the emperors Constans
and Constantine II in the autumn of 342 or 343.[18] Sardica, the present-day
Sofia, is on the western side of the boundary between the Eastern and
Western halves of the Empire. Unlike the Council of Nicaea, the western
bishops outnumbered the eastern bishops (ninety-six to seventy). In many
ways the council was a failure. The Eastern bishops left *en masse* for Phil-
ippolis before the conclusion of the council, where they condemned Athanasius, as well as Julius, the bishop of Rome.

The purpose of the council was primarily theological; it was anti-Arian
and had as its goal the vindication of Athanasius and the re-affirmation of
the creed promulgated by the Council of Nicaea. The council also dealt
with matters of discipline. The twenty-one canons of the Council of Sardica deal with issues such as the translation of bishops, the reception of excommunicate clergy, rights of appeal, and episcopal journeys to the

---

[16] Turner, *EOMIA*, vol. 1, p. 11. *Cf.* Tanner, *Decrees*, pp. 10–11.

[17] Of the systematic collections, Canons IX and X of the Council of Nicaea are both found
in the *Concordia canonum* of Cresconius; Canon IX appears in the Pseudo-Isidorian
Decretals, the collection of Burchard of Worms, and in the *Decretum* of Ivo of Chartres.

[18] On the date of the Council of Sardica, *cf.* Hamilton Hess, *The Canons of the Council of
Sardica, A.D. 343* (Oxford: Clarendon Press, 1958), Appendix I, pp. 140 ff.

imperial court. Canon XIII[19] (from the *versio Caeciliani*) of the council deals with the testing of candidates for the episcopate. It is perhaps the classic patristic conciliar text on the *cursus honorum*:

Canon XIII [VIII]

Ossius episcopus dixit: Et hoc necessarium arbitror ut diligentissime tractetis: si forte aut dives, aut scolasticus de foro, aut ex administratore, episcopus postulatus fuerit, non prius ordinetur nisi ante et lectoris munere et officio diaconii et ministerio praesbyterii fuerit perfunctus; ut per singulos gradus (si dignus fuerit) ascendat ad culmen episcopatus. Potest enim per has promotiones, quae habebunt utique prolixum tempus, probari qua fide sit, qua modestia, qua gravitate et verecundia: et si dignus fuerit probatus, divino sacerdotio inlustretur. Nec conveniens est nec rationis disciplina patitur ut temere aut leviter ordinetur aut episcopus aut praesbyter aut diaconus—maxime qui sit neofitus, cum beatissimus apostolus magister gentium ne hoc fieret denuntiasse et prohibuisse videatur; quia longi temporis examinatio merita eius probabit. Universi dixerunt placere sibi haec.[20]

The canon decrees that if a rich man, public advocate, or civil official aspires to be a bishop, he shall not be ordained until he has served sequentially in the offices of lector, deacon and presbyter.

As noted in the previous chapter, in the third century there were notable examples of bishops being chosen from among the ranks of the laity, such as Fabian of Rome and Cyprian of Carthage. Candidates for the episcopate commonly arose from the ranks of the presbyterate, as in the church at Alexandria and in Gaul, or from the diaconate, as in Rome. There is also evidence of at least one bishop who proceeded through all the grades: Cornelius of Rome. Canon XIII of the Council of Sardica marks the first instance where progression through the orders is actually mandated. It is the earliest text of a prescribed *cursus* through the grades of ministry.

The express purpose of the canon is to assure that worthy candidates be chosen for office. The emphasis is upon testing or probation: *ut per singulos gradus (si dignus fuerit) ascendat ad culmen episcopatus*. It is the intent of the canon that by means of service in successive offices, candidates will have been proved worthy in terms of faith, modesty, seriousness, and reverence. Moreover, although the time to be spent in the various offices is not mentioned, the process will be lengthy—*prolixum tempus*. One

---

[19] Canon VIII according to Turner's own enumeration; it is generally referred to as canon XIII in the western Church according to the enumeration of the Council of Sardica in the *Dionysiana* and *Prisca* canonical collections. *Cf.* Hess, *Sardica*, Table A, p. 136.

[20] Turner, *EOMIA*, vol. 1, pp. 472–474.

notes the use of the word *gradus*—grade or step—in the text of the canon. This term has a particular connection with the *cursus honorum* in the civil and military services of the empire.[21]

Canon XIII, following the First Epistle to Timothy and the Council of Nicaea, condemns the ordination of neophytes to the major offices. Hess regards this canon as a continuation of what was initiated in Canons II and IX of the Council of Nicaea.[22]

From the first line of the canon, it is clear that one of the problems faced by the fourth-century church was the election of unsuitable candidates for the episcopate. Evidently worthiness for office was not the only criterion for promotion; rather, candidates were appointed to the episcopate because they were rich, public advocates, or civil servants. The wealthy, who were also well-connected in secular and political life, were often sought-after in the hopes that they would provide strength and leadership for the church, and that they would attract the favour of the state in the construction of new cathedrals, or pay for them themselves.[23] In short, the bishops of the Council of Sardica were eager to move away from this sort of thing.

It is interesting to note the sequence of offices listed in Canon XIII: lector, deacon, presbyter, bishop. There is no mention of the subdeacon, lector, acolyte, exorcist, or doorkeeper, though these offices were clearly in existence in some parts of the church.[24]

The canons of the Council of Sardica appeared in many versions in the Western church. Canon XIII of the Council of Sardica was of great significance in the development of the *cursus honorum*. Its themes are repeated in later conciliar legislation, as well as in various papal writings.[25]

---

[21] David Power, *Ministers of Christ and his Church* (London: Geoffrey Chapman, 1963), p. 63.

[22] Hess, *Sardica*, p. 69.

[23] Ramsay MacMullen, *Christianizing the Roman Empire (AD 100–400)* (New Haven: Yale University Press, 1984), p. 53.

[24] E.g., the list of offices provided by Cornelius from the Roman church in the third century, as preserved by Eusebius: bishop, presbyter, deacon, subdeacon, acolyte, exorcist, lector, doorkeeper; Eusebius, *Ecclesiastical History*, VI.43. , *GCS* 2.2, p. 618.

[25] Of the systematic collections, Canon XIII appears in the *Breviatio canonum* (partially), the *Concordia canonum*, the *Collectio vetus gallica*, the *Dacheriana*, the Pseudo-Isidorian Decretals, the *Collectio Anselmo dedicata*, the collection of Burchard of Worms, the *Collectio in V libris*, the *Decretum* of Ivo, and Gratian's *Decretum*.

An important canonistic source is the fifth- or sixth-century Roman collection, the *Dionysiana*. The Dionysian recension of Canon XIII differs from the original in one respect. The words "*et officio diaconii et ministerio presbyterii*" have been modified to read "*et officio diaconii aut presbyterii*." The reasons for this modification will be discussed below. Western canonistic collections repeated this modification, with the exception of the *Collectio hispana* and the Pseudo-Isidorian Decretals which were faithful to the original.

From the fourth century to the sixth, the Roman Church regarded the canons of the Council of Sardica as those of the Council of Nicaea. Hess points out that the Roman synod of 485 assumed that the Sardican canons were Nicene. Zosimus quotes them as Nicene canons in a letter sent to the Council of Carthage in 418. Leo the Great likewise identified them as Nicene. It was not until the publication of the *Dionysiana* in the early sixth century, that the canons of the Council of Sardica were recognised as such in Rome.[26]

d. Council of Laodicea

Sometime in the second half of the fourth century, *ca.* 341–381,[27] the Council of Laodicea issued sixty canons on various aspects of church life. Canon IV (from the *versio Dionysii*) of the council reiterated Canon II of the Council of Nicaea against the ordination of neophytes:

> IV. Quod non oporteat ad clerum quemquam mox post baptismum promovere.[28]

Such a fresh restatement of the ban on the ordination of neophytes illustrates the continuance of the practice.[29]

Another important canon from the Council of Laodicea is Canon XII (from the *versio Dionysii*):

---

[26] Hess, *Sardica*, pp. 49–55.

[27] *Cf.* C. J. Hefele, *Histoire des Conciles*, vol. 16 (Paris: Letouzay et Ané, 1907), p. 989.

[28] Turner, *EOMIA*, vol. 2, p. 327.

[29] Of the systematic collections cited in this study, Canon IV is found in the *Breviatio canonum* of Ferrandus and the *Concordia canonum* of Cresconius.

XII. De episcopalibus ordinationibus.

Ut episcopi iudicio metropolitanorum et eorum episcoporum qui circumcirca sunt provehantur ad aecclesiasticam potestam, hi videlicet qui plurimo tempore probantur tam verbo fidei quam rectae conversationis exemplo.[30]

The canon directs metropolitans that those to be made bishops are to be tested for a long time.[31]

e. Council of Carthage III

An early source dealing with the ages of clerics is the *Breviarium Hipponense* promulgated by the third Council of Carthage, 397.[32] Canon IV establishes twenty-five as the minimum age for deacons and virgins:

IV. Ut levitae et virginis ante viginti quinque annos non consecrentur.

Item placuit, ut ante viginti quinque annos aetatis nec diacones ordinentur, nec virgines consecrentur, et ut lectores populum non salutent.[33]

The designation of twenty-five as the minimum age for deacons would appear again and again in the patristic and medieval periods.[34]

f. Gallican Councils

There was much conciliar activity in Gaul from the fourth to the seventh century. Material relating to the clerical interstices and the *cursus honorum* began to appear in the fifth century. Here evidence will be examined from the councils of Orange (441), Agde (506), Arles (524), and Orleans (549).

The Council of Orange, which met in 441, dealt with questions concerning clerical chastity. Canons XXI–XXIII of the council also provide evidence of the clerical *cursus* in Gaul in the mid-fifth century:

---

[30] Turner, *EOMIA*, vol. 2, p. 353.

[31] Of the systematic collections in this study, Canon XII appears in the *Concordia canonum* of Cresconius.

[32] Hefele, *Conciles*, vol. 2.1, p. 98.

[33] *PL* 84.189; J. D. Mansi. *Sacrorum Conciliorum Novi et Amplissima Collectio*, vol. 3 (Venice, Expensis Antonii Zatta, 1759), col. 880.

[34] Of the systematic collections cited in this study, Canon IV of the Council of Carthage III is found in the *Breviatio canonum* of Ferrandus, the *Collectio Dacheriana*, the collection of Burchard of Worms, the *Collectio in V libris*, Ivo's *Panormia* and *Decretum*, and the *Decretum* of Gratian.

XXI. Sedit praeterea ut deinceps non ordinentur diacones coniugati nisi qui prius conversionis proposito professi fuerint castitatem.

XXII. Si quis autem post acceptam benedictionem leviticam cum uxore sua incontinens invenitur ab officio abiciatur.

XXIII. De his autem qui prius ordinati hoc ipsum inciderunt, Taurinatis synodi sequendam esse sententiam, qua iubentur non ulterius promoveri.[35]

These canons, while dealing the clerical chastity, are important in the history of the clerical *cursus*. Deacons who are sexually active with their wives, according to Canon XXIII (and its source, the Synod of "Taurinatis"), are not to be promoted any higher; presumably, had they remained continent such deacons could have been promoted to the presbyterate and the episcopate. The assumption of Canon XXIII is that one could expect to be promoted from the diaconate to other offices.

Canon XVII of the Council of Agde in 506 legislated the minimum age for ordination to the diaconate, presbyterate, and the episcopate:

XVI. Episcopus vero benedictionem diaconatus minoribus a viginti et quinque annorum penitus non committat. Sane si coniugari iuvenes consenserint ordinari, etiam uxorum voluntas ita requiranda est, ut sequestato mansionis cubiculo, religione praemissa, posteaquam pariter conversi fuerint, ordinentur.[36]

XVII. Presbyterum vero vel episcopum ante triginta annos, idest antequam ad viri perfecti aetatem veniant, nullus metropolitanorum ordinare praesumat: ne per aetatem, quo aliquoties evenit, aliquo errore culpentur.[37]

Canon XVI, in terms of the ages of clerics, sets twenty-five as the minimum age for ordination to the diaconate, recalling Canon IV of Carthage III. Canon XVII directs metropolitans not to ordain a bishop or a presbyter under thirty years of age. The age of thirty for presbyters recalls Canon IX of the Council of Neocaesarea, though the Council of Agde extended the same age to bishops. Unlike the Neocaesarian canon, the reason given is not deference to the age when Jesus began his ministry, but concern for the maturity of candidates for the presbyterate and the episcopate.[38]

---

[35] Charles Munier, ed., *Concilia Galliae A. 314–A. 506*, CCSL 148, p. 84.

[36] Munier, *Concilia Galliae*, p. 201.

[37] Munier, *Concilia Galliae*, p. 201.

[38] Canons XVI and XVII often appear together in the canonistic collections. Of the systematic collections cited in this study they are found in the *Collectio Anselmo dedicata*, the collection of Burchard of Worms, both the *Panormia* and *Decretum* of Ivo of Chartres, and the *Decretum* of Gratian.

The first two canons of the Council of Arles, held in 524, deal with the *cursus honorum* and the interstices:

> I. Et quia in ordinandis clerecis antiquorum patrum statuta non ad integrum, sicut expedit, observata esse cognoscitur, ne forte quorumcumque importunis et inordinatis praecibus sacerdotis Domini fatigentur et ea, quae toties sunt praecepta, transgredi compellantur, hoc inter se observandum esse definiunt, ut nullus episcoporum diaconum, antequam viginti et quinque annus impleat, ordinare praesumat, episcopatus vero vel presbyterii honore nullus laicus ante praemissa conversatione vel ante triginta aetatis annus accipiat.[39]

> II. Et licet de laici prolixiora tempora antiqui patris ordinaverint observanda, tamen quia crescente ecclesiarum numiro necesse est nobis plures clericos ordinare, hoc inter nos sine praeiudicio dumtaxat canonum constitit antiquorum, ut nullus metropolitanorum cuicumque laico dignitatem episcopatus tribuat, sed nec reliqui pontifices presbyterii vel diaconatus honorem conferre praesumant, nisi anno intigro fuerit ab eis praemissa conversio.[40]

Canon I forbids ordination to the diaconate of any one under twenty-five years of age. No one is to receive the honour of the episcopate or the presbyterate before an approved manner of living, or (*vel*) before he has reached thirty years of age. Yet like canons XVI and XVII of Agde, the reason for the minimum of ages of thirty and twenty-five have nothing to do with the age of Jesus when he began his ministry nor to the levitical prescriptions for the ages of levites. The first part of Canon I speaks of the "unsuitable and disordered prayers of the priest". Setting minimum age restrictions for bishops, presbyters, and deacons was part of the solution of this problem. In the case of bishops and presbyters, a proved manner of living is also requisite.[41]

Canon II of the Council of Arles deals primarily with the question of the ordination of the laity to the episcopate, and secondarily with the ordination of laity to the presbyterate and the diaconate as well. From the text of the canon, it is clear that because of the large number of churches the Gallican bishops found it necessary to ordain members of the laity directly to the major orders, including the episcopate. And yet, the canon acknowledges that this practice is without precedence in the ancient canons. The solution is that metropolitans are to refrain from ordaining laymen to the

---

[39] Charles de Clercq, ed., *Concilia Galliae A. 511–A. 695*, CCSL 148a, p. 43.

[40] de Clercq, *Concilia Galliae*, CCSL 148a, pp. 43–44.

[41] Canon I of the Council of Arles is found in the *Collectio vetus gallica*, the Pseudo-Isidorian Decretals, the collection of Burchard of Worms and the *Decretum* of Ivo of Chartres.

higher grades unless they have been tested for a full year as to their manner of life. Once again, the emphasis is on testing.[42]

The same concern and solution are repeated in Canon IX of the Council of Orleans in 549:

> IX. Ut nullus ex laicis absque anni conversione praemissa episcopus ordinetur, ita ut intra anni ipsius spatium a doctis et probatis viris et disciplinis et regolis spiritalibus plenius instruatur. Quod si hoc quisque episcoporum transcendere quacumque conditione praesumserit ordinandum, anno integro ab officio vel a caritate fratrum habeatur extraneus.[43]

Once again, laity are forbidden to be ordained directly to the episcopate. Lay people called to the office of bishop must spend a year in preparation with "learned and tested men," so that by discipline and spiritual examples they might be prepared for episcopal ministry. The expressed concern for delaying ordination by a year is the need for preparation.

In Canons I and II of the Council of Arles, and in Canon IX of the Council of Orleans, no suggestion is made of using the minor orders as a vehicle for training and testing for episcopal office.

g. Hispanic Councils

From the end of the fourth century to the early eighth century a great deal of conciliar activity took place in the Hispanic church as well. Consequently, much evidence, direct and indirect, of the development of the *cursus honorum* can be culled from the legislation of these councils. Here evidence will be examined from the Councils of Toledo I (*ca.* 397–400), Toledo II (527), Braga I (561), Braga II (572), Barcelona II (599), and Toledo IV (633).

The first Council of Toledo met between the years 397 and 400. The first, third, and fourth canons of the council, while ostensibly concerned with clerical continence, are evidence of the developing *cursus honorum*:

> I. De presbyteris et diaconibus si post ordinationem filios genuerint.

> Placuit, ut diacones vel integri vel casti sint et continentes vitae, etiam si uxores habeant, in ministerio constituantur, ita tamen ut si qui etiam ante interdictum, quod per Lusitanos episcopos constitutum est, incontinenter cum uxoribus suis vixerint,

[42] In this study, Canon II of the Council of Arles appears only in the *Decretorum Libri XX* of Burchard of Worms.

[43] de Clercq, *Concilia Galliae*, CCSL 148a, p. 151.

presbyteri[i] honore non comulentur. Si quis vero ex presbyteris ante interdictum filios susceperit, de presbyterio ad episcopatum non admittatur.[44]

III. De his qui viduas acceperint ne diacones efficiantur.

Item constituit sancta synodus, ut lector fidelis, si viduam alterius uxorem acceperit, amplius nicil sit, sed semper lector habeatur aut forte subdiaconus.[45]

IV. Ut si diaconus, si defuncta uxore aliam duxerit, ostiarius fiat.

Subdiaconus autem defuncta uxore si aliam duxerit, et ab officio in quo ordinatus fuerat removeatur, et habeatur inter ostiarios vel inter lectores, ita ut evangelium et Apostolum non legat, propterea ne qui ecclesiae servierit publicis officiis servire videatur. Qui vero tertiam, quod nec dicendum aud audiendum est, acceperit, abstentus biennio, postea inter laicos reconciliatus per poenitentiam communicet.[46]

While these three canons are perhaps of more value in the history of clerical celibacy, they do have some bearing upon the *cursus honorum*. Canon I directs that a deacon who is "incontinent" with his wife shall "not accrue the honour of the presbyterate." Like canons XXII–XXIII of the Gallican Council of Orange dealing with incontinent deacons, a presbyter who is likewise sexually active with his wife, and, who furthermore "will have recognised a child as his own shall not be admitted from the presbyterate to the episcopate." This reference is evidence, most likely, of a customary *cursus* from the diaconate to the presbyterate, and from the presbyterate to the episcopate.

It is difficult to ascertain from this canon whether all deacons would have proceeded to the presbyterate; certainly not all presbyters would have acceded to the episcopate. Even so, an assumed sequential movement through these orders is evident, only to be disrupted by incontinence. The canon assumes that diaconate leads to the presbyterate, and it is the presbyterate which leads to the episcopate; there is no reflection of direct movement from diaconate to the episcopate.

Canon III directs that lectors who marry widows will not proceed to the diaconate. At the least, they will remain in the lectorate; at most, they may become subdeacons. From the title of the canons it would appear as though the lectorate normally leads to the diaconate. The lectorate also can lead to the subdiaconate by default.

---

[44] José Vives, ed., *Concilios Visigóticos e Hispano-Romanos* (Barcelona-Madrid: Consejo superior de Investigaciones Científicas Instituto Enrique Flórez, 1963), p. 20.

[45] Vives, *Concilios Visigóticos*, p. 20.

[46] Vives, *Concilios Visigóticos*, pp. 20–21.

The title of Canon IV indicates that if a widowed deacon marries again he is to be demoted to the doorkeepers. The body of the canon, however, refers to widowed subdeacons. The subdeacon who marries again is to be demoted to the doorkeepers or lectors. This canon reflects demotion within the orders of ministry, at least with the minor orders. It also reflects the place of the subdiaconate as a minor order.

The canons from the Council of Toledo indicate no explicit sequence of grades. One can, however, construct the following sequence of grades from the internal evidence: doorkeeper, lector, subdeacon, deacon, presbyter, bishop.[47]

Over a century later, the second Council of Toledo in 527 reflects not only the *cursus honorum*, but also a well established series of intervals, or interstices, between the grades. Canon I of the council deals with the careers of boys who have been dedicated to the ordered ministry as lectors:

> I. De his quos parentes ab infantia in clericatus officio manciparunt, si post eam volumtatem habent nbendi.
>
> De his quos volumtas parentum a primis infantiae annis clericatus officio manciparit hoc statuimus observandum: ut mox detonsi vel ministerio electorum contraditi fuerint in domo ecclesiae sub episcopali praesentia a praeposito sibi, debeant erudiri; at ubi octavum decimum aetatis suae compleverint annum, coram totius cleri plebisque conspectu volumtas eorum de expectendo coniugio ab episcopo prescrutetur. Quibus si gratia castitatis Deo inspirante placuerit et professionem castimoniae suae absque coniugali necessitate sponderint servaturos, hii tamquam adpetitores artissimae vitae lenissimo Domini iugo subdantur, ac primum subdiaconatus ministerium habita probatione professionis suae a vicesimo anno suscipiant; quod si inculpabiliter ac inoffense vicesimum et quintum annum aetatius suae peregerint, ad diaconatus officium, si scienter implere posse ab episcopo conprobantur, promoveri.[48]

The canon directs that young boys offered to the clerical state by their parents are to be educated at the bishop's house. When they have reached the eighteenth year, they will publicly choose between marriage or celibacy. Those who choose to remain celibate, after a period of testing, are to receive the subdiaconate at twenty years. If they remain blameless and inoffensive, they are to be promoted to the office of deacon when they are twenty-five years old. While the lectorate is not mentioned, it is likely that the boys would have been lectors prior to reception of the subdiaconate.[49]

---

[47] In this study, Canon IV of Toledo I is found in the Pseudo-Isidorian Decretals.

[48] Vives, *Concilios Visigóticos*, pp. 42–43.

[49] Canon I of Toledo II appears in the Pseudo-Isidorian Decretals, the *Collectio Anselmo dedicata*, and the *Collectio canonum* of Anselm of Lucca.

Canon XX of the first Council of Braga in 561 deals the *cursus honorum* and the clerical interstices:

XX. De laicorum gradu. [Quod de laicis nemo ad sacerdotium venire permittitur nisi per statuta.]

Item placuit, ut ex laico ad gradum sacerdotii ante non veniat, nisi prius anno integro in officio lectorati vel subdiaconati disciplinam ecclesiasticam discat, et sic per singulos gradus eruditus ad sacerdotium veniat; nam satis reprehensibile est ut qui necdum didicit iam docere praesumat, dum et antiquis hoc patrum institutionibus interdictum sit.[50]

Although of all the canonistic collections cited in this study, Canon XX appears only in the Pseudo-Isidorian Decretals, it is nonetheless significant. The canon is concerned with members of the laity who are elected to the "priesthood" (*ad gradum sacerdotii*). It is not clear whether "priesthood" here refers to the presbyterate or the episcopate. At any rate, following fourth and fifth-century conciliar and papal legislation, no one is to be ordained to the "priesthood" directly from the laity. Braga I directs that a candidate for the sacerdotal office spend a preparatory year in either the lectorate or the subdiaconate, in order that he might learn the "ecclesiastical discipline". Thus, "through a single learned grade let him come to the priesthood." One notes for the first time in this survey of the Hispanic councils the use of the word *gradus* in the canon, and its close association with the *cursus honorum*.

Canon XX prescribes a *cursus* of sorts, with a specified length of time to be spent in the minor orders of either the lectorate or the subdiaconate. No other intervening orders, in specific the diaconate, are mentioned. The intent of this canon is preparation: "it is completely disgraceful that whoever has not yet learned presume to teach." This reason is similar to the two Gallican examples already noted: Canon II of the Council of Arles (525) and Canon IX of the Council of Orleans (549).

The second Council of Braga in 572 reiterates much of the earlier conciliar materials with regards to the *cursus*. For instance, Canon XX repeats Canon XI of the Council of Neocaesarea, directing that presbyters be at least thirty years at the time of ordination.[51] The injunction of Canon II of the Council of Nicaea is reiterated in Canon XXII, forbidding the ordination of neophytes.[52] Canon XXIII recapitulates Canon IX of the Council

---

[50] Vives, *Concilios Visigóticos*, p. 75.

[51] Vives, *Concilios Visigóticos*, p. 92.

[52] Vives, *Concilios Visigóticos*, pp. 92–93.

of Nicaea, on the question of examining of candidates for the presbyterate. Braga II expands the canon by referring to the examination of deacons as well.[53] A repetition of the injunction of Canon III of Toledo I, Canon XLVIII forbids lectors who marry widows to proceed any higher than the subdiaconate.[54] Canon XXV is a conflation of canons VIII, IX and X of the Council of Neocaesarea:

> XXV. De presbyteris vel diaconibus qui post ordinationem denotantur.
>
> Si quis presbyter ante ordinationem peccaverit et post ordinationem confessus fuerit quia ante erravit, non offerat sed tantum pro religione nomen presbyteri portet. Si autem non ipse confessus sed ab alio publice fuerit convictus, nec ad hoc ipsud habeat potestatem ut nomen presbyteri portet. Similiter et de diaconibus observandum est, ut si ipse confessus fuerit ordinem subdiaconatus accipiat.[55]

Like Canon IX of Neocaesarea, Canon XXV of Braga II inhibits presbyters from the functions of their office if they are found to have sinned prior to ordination. It makes it clear, though, that such presbyters retain the name of presbyter. Sinful deacons continue to be demoted to the subdiaconate. In this instance there appears to be "sequential demotion" within the orders.

Canon III of the second Council of Barcelona (599) contains a specific reference to the *cursus honorum* and to the interstices:

> III. Hunc etiam innovandum custodiendumve in omnibus sancta statuit synodus, ut secumdum priscorum canonum constituta vel synodalium epistolas praes[u]llun [*sic*] praemonentes, nulli deinceps laicorum liceat ad ecclesiasticos ordines praetermissas canonum prefixa tempora aut per sacra regalia aut per consensionem cleri vel plebis vel per electionem asse[n]sionemque [*sic*] pontificum ad summum sacerdotium adspirare vel provehi, set cum per canonum conscripta tempora ecclesiasticos per ordinem spirituali opere desudando, probatae vitae adminiculo comitante conscenderit grados, ad summum sacerdotium, si dignitati vita responderit, au[c]tore [*sic*] domino provehatur: ita tamen aut duobus aut tribus quos consensus cleri et plebis selegerit metropolitani iudicio eiusque quoepiscopis praesentatis, quem sors praeeunte episcoporum ieiunio, Christo domino terminante monstraverit, benedictio consecrationis adcumulet; aliter deinceps, quod absit praesumptum, et ordinatores et ordinato[s] proprii honoris depositio subsequatur.[56]

The canon restates the prohibition against ordaining laity directly to the episcopate—*ad summum sacerdotium*—without having previously passed

---

53 Vives, *Concilios Visigóticos*, p. 93.

54 Vives, *Concilios Visigóticos*, p. 98.

55 Vives, *Concilios Visigóticos*, pp. 93–94.

56 Vives, *Concilios Visigóticos*, pp. 159–160.

through the ecclesiastical offices at the designated times. This is the first Hispanic canon noted which enjoins both the clerical interstices and the *cursus honorum*. The canon prohibits ordination to the episcopate based upon the "grace of right and privilege, or through the agreement of the clergy and people, or through the election and assent of the pontiff." Yet, since these three situations are noted, it would appear that the ordination of laity to the episcopate was still a fact of life. The expressed purpose for following the *cursus* is that the candidates for the episcopate "will have ascended the grades accompanied by the support of a tested life" which will have been shown equal to the dignity of episcopal office. The sequence of grades intended by the canon is not mentioned, nor is the length of time to be spent in them. Since they are referred to as the "ecclesiastical offices appointed at the canonical times", however, and later on as the "prescribed times of the ecclesiastical canon" one can assume that the pattern of the *cursus honorum* and the interstices was well known, though not necessarily observed.

The fourth Council of Toledo, held in 633, contains two canons which touch upon the *cursus honorum* and the interstices. A portion of Canon XIX outlines the conditions which prohibit a person from ordination to the "priesthood", such as infamy, public penance, heresy, heretical baptism, natural defects, a second wife, ignorance, being a neophyte, and being members of the laity:

> XIX. ....Praeteritis omissis, deinceps qui non promoveantur ad sacerdotium ex regulis canonum necessario credimus inserendum: id est.... qui neofyti vel laici sunt, qui seculari militiae dediti sunt, qui curiae nexibus obligati sunt, qui inscii litterarum sunt, qui nondum ad XXXX [*sic*.][57] annos pervenerunt, qui per gradus ecclesiasticos non accesserunt, qui ambitu honorem quaerunt, qui muneribus honorem obtinere moliuntur, qui a decessoribus in sacerdotio eliguntur.... Si quis autem deinceps contra praedicta vetita canonum ad gradum sacerdotii indignus adspirare contenderit, cum ordinatoribus suis adepti honoris periculo subiacebet.[58]

The canon establishes forty [or thirty] as the minimum age for admission to the priesthood. Laity and neophytes are restricted from ordination to the priesthood, as well as those who "will not have arrived [at the episcopate] through the ecclesiastical grades." Although the clerical *cursus* is treated as normative, one can glean from the canon that it was not always

---

[57] The spanish translation of Vives states the number as thirty, not forty.

[58] Vives, *Concilios Visigóticos*, p. 199.

the practice in the Hispanic church, even as late as the early seventh century. One again notes the use of the term *gradus*.[59]

Canon XX of the Council of Toledo IV deals with the ages of clerics, in particular deacons and presbyters:

> XX. [De numero annorum quo sacerdotes et levitae ordinentur.]
>
> In vetere lege ab anno vicesimo et quinto levitae tabernaculo servire mandantur, cuius auctoritatem in canonibus et sancti patres sequuti sunt. Nos et divinae legis et conciliorum praeceptis inmemores infantes / et pueros levitas facimus ante legitimam aetatem, ante experientiam vitae: ideoque ne ulterius fiat a nobis et divinae legis et canonicis admonemus sententiis, sed a viginti quinque annis aetatis levitae consecrentur, et a XXX presbyteres ordinentur, ita ut secundum apostolicum praeceptum probentur primum, et sic ministrent nullum crimen habentes.[60]

The canon fixes the age for deacons at twenty-five, and the minimum age for presbyters at thirty, an interval of five years. What is surprising is the admission within the canon that infants and boys were being made deacons before the lawful age. The difficulty is that such candidates lack an experience or testing of life.[61]

4. Papal Letters and Decretals

The papal documents of the late patristic period reveal bishops of Rome taking an active interest in the ordering and development of the church's ministry, including the *cursus honorum* and the interstices.[62] This section will survey the papal statements on sequential ordination from the pontificates of Damasus (366–384), Siricius (384–399), Innocent I (401–417), Zosimus (417–418), Celestine (422–432), Leo I (440–461), Gelasius (492–496), Hormisdas (514–523), Pelagius (555–560), and Gregory I (590–604).

---

[59] In this study, Canon XIX of Toledo IV is found in the Pseudo-Isidorian Decretals.

[60] Vives, *Concilios Visigóticos*, p. 200.

[61] Canon XX of Toledo IV is found in the Decretals of Pseudo-Isidore, the *Collectio Anselmo dedicata*, the collection of Burchard of Worms, both the *Panormia* and *Decretum* Ivo of Chartres, and in the *Decretum* of Gratian.

[62] According to the *Liber pontificalis* the first bishop of Rome to advocate the clerical *cursus* was Gaius (282–296). LP I, p. 161. This ascription, however, is simply a fabrication, more reflective of the sixth than the third century.

a. Damasus

The earliest evidence of papal endorsement for the clerical *cursus* is from an anonymous decretal contained in an ancient series of papal letters transmitted under the title *Canones Romanorum* or *Canones Romanorum ad Gallos episcopos*. Although the decretal is often attributed to Siricius,[63] E. Ch. Babut has argued convincingly on the basis of internal evidence that the decretal comes from the pontificate of Damasus (366–84).[64] In the letter to the Gallican bishops, of unknown date, Damasus writes:

Cap. II

> X. ....Nicaenum concilium, divino Spiritu anuenti, dum fidei confessio fuisset jure firmata, etiam apostolicas traditiones episcopi in unum congregati ad omnium notitiam prevenire voluerunt, definientes inter cetera, neque abscissis clericum fieri, quoniam abscissus et mollis non introibunt sanctuarium Dei. Deinde post baptismi gratiam, post indulgentiam peccatorum, cum quis saeculi militia fuerit gloriatus, vel illum qui purpura et fascibus fuerit delectatus, ad sacerdotium aliqua irruptione minime admitti jusserunt. Meritis enim et observatione legis ad istiusmodi dignitatis culmen accedunt, non Simonis pecunia vel gratia quis poterit pervenire, aut favore populari: non enim quid populus velit, sed quid evangelica disciplina perquiritur. Plebs tunc habet testimonium, quoties ad digni alicujus meritum reprehendens auram favoris impertit.[65]

> XII. De ordinationibus maxime observandum est, ut semper clerici fiant episcopi. Sic enim scriptum est: Et hi primo probentur, et sic ministrent. Qui non ut probatur tempore praecedenti in minori officio ministrasse, quomodo praeponitur clero? Non est auditum necdum tironem militum imperium suscepisse. Is ergo debet fieri quem aetas tempus, meritum commendat, et vita. Aut quare apostolus neophytum prohibet, et cito manus alicui imponi non permitti.[66]

Recalling the Council of Nicaea, Damasus condemns hasty ordinations of neophytes on the basis of greed and ambition. This reference to Nicaea is actually a reference to the Council of Sardica, and is an example of how

---

[63] E.g., Friedrich Maassen, *Geschichte der Quellen und der Literatur des canonischen Rechts im Abendlande bis zum Ausgange de Mittelalters* (Graz: Verlag von Leuschner & Lubensky, 1870), p. 242.

[64] "Je regarde les *Canons aux Gaulois* comme la plus ancienne décrétale qui nous ait été conservée, et comme l'oeuvre du pape Damase." E. Ch. Babut, *La Plus Ancienne Décrétale*, diss., Faculté des Lettres de l'Université de Paris, 1904 (Paris: Société Nouvelle de Librairie et d'Édition, 1904), p. 39.

[65] *Canones Romanorum*, MANSI III.1137–1138.

[66] MANSI III.1138.

the Sardican canons were regarded in Rome in the fourth century as Nicene.[67]

Drawing on the injunctions of the First Letter to Timothy, Damasus stresses the need for testing, forbids the ordination of neophytes, and warns against hasty ordinations. His concern for testing is met by service in the minor offices. Damasus draws the analogy between service in the minor offices prior to ordination to the higher offices and the Roman army: "it is unheard of, at least for now, that a recruit has received military command". Damasus emphasises the minor offices as the means of testing. It is not clear what the minor orders were preparatory for: the episcopate, presbyterate, or diaconate? There is no implication here that the higher orders were in any way preparatory to one another. Interestingly, Damasus was a deacon prior to election as bishop of Rome.

b. Siricius

Siricius was bishop of Rome towards the end of the fourth century (384–399). The decretal of Siricius to Himerius of Tarragona (*Epistle* 1; 10 Feb. 385) is significant in a number of respects. It is usually regarded as the earliest surviving papal "decretal": that is, a letter in the style of the chancery of the imperial Roman Curia.[68] The sending of decretals was a means by which Roman emperors gave authoritative answers to questions posed by lower imperial officials. Evidently, Himerius, bishop of Tarragona, a city in Spain, had requested of Siricius answers to various questions about church life, including the ordered ministry.

The decretal of Siricius contains directives about clerical celibacy, the ordination of monks, as well as the clerical interstices and the *cursus honorum*:

> IX.13. Quicumque itaque se Ecclesiae vovit obsequiis a sua infantia, ante pubertatis annos baptizari, et lectorum debet ministerio sociari. Qui [ab] accessu adolescentiae usque ad tricesimum aetatis annum, si probabiliter vixerit, una tantum, et ea, quam virginem communi per sacerdotem benedictione perceperit, uxore contentus, acolythus et subdiaconus esse debebit; postque ad diaconii gradum, si se ipse primitus continentia praeeunte dignum probarit, accedat. Ubi si ultra quinque annos laudabiliter ministrarit, congrue presbyterium conseqatur. Exinde post

---

[67] Lafontaine, *Les Conditions*, p. 284.

[68] E.g., Lienhard, *Ministry*, pp. 171–172. *Cf.* Babut argues that the earliest decretal extant was written by Damasus. Furthermore, Babut argues that *Epistle* 1 of Siricius was based on the *Canones Romanorum ad Gallos episcopos*. Babut, *La plus ancienne*, pp. 18 ff.

decennium, episcopalem cathedram poterit adipisci, si tamen per haec tempora integritas vitae ac fidei ejus fuerit approbata.[69]

X.14. Qui vero jam aetate grandaevus, melioris propositi conversione provocatus, ex laico ad sacram militiam pervenire festinat, desiderii sui fructum non aliter obtinebit, nisi eo quo baptizatur tempore, statim lectorum aut exorcistarum numero societur, si tamen eum unam habuisse vel habere, et hanc virginem accepisse, constet uxorem. Qui dum initiatus fuerit, expleto bienno, per quinquennium aliud acolythus et subdiaconus fiat, et sic ad diaconium, si per haec tempora dignus judicatus fuerit, provehatur. Exinde jam accessis temporum, presbyterium vel episcopatum, si eum cleri ac plebis edecumarit electio, non immerito sortietur.[70]

XIII.17. Monachos quoque quos tamen morum gravitas et vitae ac fidei institutio sancta commendat, clericorum officiis aggregari et optamus et volumus; ita ut qui intra tricesimum aetatis annum sunt, in minoribus per gradus singulos, crescente tempore, promoveantur ordinibus: et sic ad diaconatus vel presbyterii insignia, maturae aetatis consecratione, perveniant. Nec saltu ad episcopatus culmen ascendant, nisi in his eadem quae singulis dignitatibus superius praefiximus, tempora fuerint custodita.[71]

This text is an important piece of evidence regarding the status of the *cursus honorum* and the interstices at the end of the fourth century in the Western church. The tenor of Siricius' decretal makes it clear that his answers are not pastoral responses to a particular situation, but are authoritative legislation directed to a broad constituency. As Lafontaine has observed: "Les décrets de Sirice sur les ordinations revêtent ce caractère universel et impérieux".[72]

In IX.13 Siricius states that boys who have been dedicated to the ministry of the church ought to be baptised before they reach puberty, and admitted to the lectorate. If a boy has lived "honourably" from adolescence to the thirtieth (or twentieth) year, and has later married within the discipline of the church, he may be admitted as an acolyte and as a subdeacon. If he is able to live continently, he then may be advanced to the diaconate. After five years as a deacon, if he will "have served well", he may be ordained to the presbyterate. After ten years as a presbyter, if the integrity of his life and faith are proven, he may "attain the episcopal chair."

Section X.14 of the decretal deals with the ordination of older men. When an older man is baptised and is eager to advance to the "sacred

---

[69] *PL* 13.1142–1143.

[70] *PL* 13.1143.

[71] *PL* 13.1144–1145.

[72] Lafontaine, *Les Conditions*, p. 290.

service", if he lives within the marriage discipline of the church, he is to be admitted immediately to the office of lector or (*aut*) exorcist. After an interval of two years such an older man will serve as "an acolyte and subdeacon" for a period of five years. If he is judged worthy throughout this time, he is to be made a deacon. Thereupon, he is as likely to be ordained a presbyter or bishop as any other cleric.

In XIII.17 Siricius deals with the question of the ordination of monks. He directs that monks who are less than thirty years old be advanced through the minor orders, through the appointed times, until they reach the diaconate and the presbyterate. Siricius directs that monks not ascend to the "height of the episcopate" in a "leap"—*nec saltus*—but in their case also the same times for each rank shall be observed.

The sequence of *cursus* as outlined by Siricius is as follows: lector/exorcist, acolyte/subdeacon, deacon, presbyter, and bishop. Except for the omission of the doorkeeper, these are the same grades as outlined by Cornelius in Rome a century and a half earlier. Siricius couples the orders of lector and exorcist, and acolyte and subdeacon. And yet it is not clear from the text whether one receives both orders within the coupling, or only one.

The intervals, or interstices, reflected in the decretal are: the lectorate (and the office of exorcist for older men) until thirty years of age (or for a period of two years for older men), the offices of acolyte and subdeacon for five years (explicitly for older men), the diaconate for five years, the presbyterate for ten years, then the episcopate. No one, not even a monk, is to be ordained to the episcopate by a leap.

The terminology used is noteworthy, for instance, the use of the term *gradus*. This decretal is one of the earliest examples of the language of *per saltum*. Later, direct ordinations to the higher offices without the intervening orders would be referred to as "*per saltum* ordinations".

With regards to the *cursus honorum* and the interstices, Siricius' underlying considerations are testing and worthiness. Promotion from one office to the next is always conditional: "*si probabiliter vixerit.... si ultra quinque annos laudabiliter minstrarit.... si tamen per haec tempora integritas vitae ac fidei ejus fuerit approbata....*" Unlike Damasus' letter to the Gallican bishops, Siricius includes the diaconate and presbyterate as part of the *cursus*. Like the minor orders, they too serve as vehicles of testing and preparation. Incidentally, Siricius had never been a presbyter himself.

The decretal is evidence of the fact that by the end of the fourth century the lectorate had become an order for boys and young men preparing for a clerical career in the church. There is also provision in the decretal for the ordination of older men, the recently baptised men as well as monks.[73]

Another text from the pontificate of Siricius dealing with the *cursus honorum* is *Epistle 6, Ad diversos episcopos*, of uncertain date:

III.

> 5. Certe etiam illud non fuit praetermttendum, ut quod semel aut secundo necessitas haereticorum intulit contra apostolica praecepta velut lege licitum coepisse praesumi, neophytum vel laicum, qui nullo ecclesiastico functus fuerit officio, inconsiderate vel presbyterum vel diaconum ordinare: quasi meliores Apostolis sint, quorum audeant mutare praeceptum. Et qui non didicit, jam docere compellitur. Ita nullus reperitur idoneus clericorum? Nec inter diaconos, nec inter alios clericos invenitur, qui sacerdotio dignus habeatur; sed ad condemnationem Ecclesiae laicus postulatur? Quod ne fiat ultra, admoneo....[74]

While the decretal to Himerius was prescriptive, the epistle *Ad diversos episcopos* is proscriptive. Siricius complains that neophytes and lay people have been ordained deacons and presbyters, a practice he associates with heretics and contrary to apostolic precept. In the letter he laments that no one among the clergy or among the deacons is chosen to the "priestly dignity," but instead lay people are chosen. "What I advise," he closes, "is that this practice go on no further."

The negative tone indicates a number of things. First, at the end of the fourth century members of the laity were still being ordained directly to the diaconate, the presbyterate, and to the episcopate. Second, the epistle reveals Siricius' concern that candidates for the "priesthood" be drawn from the diaconate, or at least from the minor offices. Though the *cursus*

---

[73] The decretal of Siricius to Himerius is one of the most important patristic texts dealing the *cursus honorum* and the interstices. It is found in at least fifteen of the early historically arranged canonical collections (MAASSEN, p.240). Not surprisingly, the decretal of Siricius to Himerius is included in most of the systematic collections; it is found in the *Concordia canonum* of Cresconius, the *Collectio hibernensis*, the *Dacheriana*, the Pseudo-Isidorian Decretals, the *Collectio Anselmo dedicata*, the *Collectio in V libris*, the *Decretum* of Ivo, and the *Decretum* of Gratian.

[74] *PL* 13.1166.

honorum was strongly commended, it was far from being a universal practice.[75]

c. Innocent I

Innocent I (401–417) supported the *cursus honorum* in *Epistle* 37 to Felix of Nocera (near Perugia), of uncertain date:

V

> 6. Ita sane, ut in eos tempora a majoribus constituta serventur. Nec cito quilibet lector, cito acolythus, cito diaconus, cito sacerdos fiat: quia in minoribus officiis si diu perdurent, et vita eorum pariter et obsequia comprobantur, ut ad sacerdotium postea emensis stipendiorium meritis veniant, nec praeripiant quod vita probata meretur accipere.[76]

In the decretal Innocent urges that the constituted times—the interstices—be observed in the ordination of candidates through the grades. The decretal contains the sequence of grades of the *cursus*: lector, acolyte, deacon, "priest". Here *sacerdos* means either presbyter or bishop; presumably the diaconate could lead to either sacerdotal office. Interestingly, there is no mention of the doorkeeper, the exorcist, or the subdeacon in this list.

The letter of Innocent to Felix of Nocera is significant in what it says about the observation of the interstices. Innocent speaks of the appointed times—the *tempora constituta*—which are to be observed in the reception of offices. Innocent prohibits hasty (*cito*) ordinations to the lectorate, the office of acolyte, the diaconate, and to the "priesthood". Given the sequence, and the repetition of the word *cito*, it would seem that Innocent is denouncing an actual practice of "rushing" people through the orders.

It would appear that by the early fifth century, at least in Nocera, the problem of ordaining members of the laity directly to the higher offices was being compounded by another problem: ignoring the interstices. In the end, the result was the same, namely, untested candidates were appointed to the major offices. And so, Innocent stresses the importance of time spent

---

[75] *Ad diversos episcopos* is not cited as frequently as the decretal of Siricius to Himerius in the later canonistic collections. It appears in only one historically arranged canonical collection, the *Hispana* (MAASSEN, p. 242). Of the systematic collections cited in this study, it is found in the Pseudo-Isidorian Decretals, the Collection in Seventy-four Titles, and the *Collectio canonum* of Anselm of Lucca.

[76] *PL* 20.604–605.

in the minor offices on the grounds that the lives and obedience of candidates for the higher offices might be proved and tested.[77]

d. Zosimus

The brief (and ignominious) pontificate of Zosimus (417–418) contains a number of important documents relating to the development of the clerical *cursus* and interstices. For instance, in *Epistle* 7 to Patroclus of Arles (*Quid de proculi*; 26 Sept. 417) Zosimus wrote:

> 2. Et quia nonulli es quacumque militia se ad Ecclesiam conferentes, statim saltu quodam summatem locum religionis affectant, qui gradatim per ecclesiastica stipendia venientibus explorata solet discussione differri: idcirco quoniam in nonnullis factum infirmare non possumus, si qui jam ordinati sunt, in eo gradu, ad quem saltu subito pervenerunt, perdurare debebunt. Si enim Apostolus neophytum sacerdotio non statim cumulari jubet, et hoc idem canonum statuta sanxerunt; hoc addimus nostra sententia, ut quisquis de caetero vel summo sacerdotio, vel presbyterii gradu vel diaconatus crediderit cumulandum, sciat et se gradus sui subire jacturam, nec in illum valitura esse quae contulit: ut saltem ab ordinatione praecipiti metus iste summoveat, quos examinata discussio coercere debuisset....[78]

This decretal provides an insight into the state of ecclesiastical life in Gaul in the early fifth century. Zosimus complains that members of the laity, in this case soldiers, have been ordained directly to the episcopate: "they have immediately seized by a certain leap the highest place in religion." Such offices, Zosimus says, ought to be conferred on those who have come through the ecclesiastical service step by step, by careful examination. Zosimus repeats the injunction against the ordination of neophytes to the diaconate, presbyterate, and the episcopate. Once again, the purpose of service in a succession of offices is testing and examination. One notes Zosimus' use of *gradus* and *saltus* terminology.[79]

A more notable text from the pontificate of Zosimus is *Epistle* 9, to Hesychius of Salone (21 Feb. 418):

---

[77] *Epistle* 37 appears in only two historically arranged canonical collections (MAASSEN, p.247). Section V.6 of the letter appears in systematic collections such as the *Concordia canonum* of Cresconius, the *Dacheriana*, Pseudo-Isidorian Decretals, the *Collectio in V libris*, the *Collectio canonum* of Anselm of Lucca, and the *Decretum* of Gratian.

[78] *PL* 20.668–669; P. Coustant, ed., *Epistolae Romanorum Pontificum*, vol. 1 (Paris: 1721), p. 961.

[79] *Epistle* 7 does not seem to have been attributed later significance, for it is found in only one historical collection (MAASSEN, p.249), and in this study appears only in Decretals of Ivo of Chartres and Gratian.

I

1. Exigit dilectio tua praeceptum apostolicae sedis, in quo Patrum decreta consentiunt, et significas nonnullos ex monachorum populari coetu, quorum solitudo quavis frequentia major est, sed et laicos ad sacerdotium festinare. Hoc autem specialiter et sub praedecessoribus nostris, et nuper a nobis interdictum constat, litteris ad Gallias Hispaniasque transmissis, in quibus regionibus familiaris est ista praesumptio, quamvis nec Africa super hac admonitione nostra habeatur aliena ne quis penitus contra patrum praecepta, qui ecclesiasticis disciplinis per ordinem non fuisset imbutus, et temporis approbatione divinis stipendiis eruditus, nequaquam ad summum Ecclesiae sacerdotium aspirare praesumeret: et non solum in eo ambitio inefficax haberetur, verum etiam in ordinatores ejus, ut carerent eo ordine, quem sine ordine contra praecepta Patrum crediderant praesumendum. Unde miramur ad dilectionem tuam statuta apostolicae sedis non fuisse perlata. Laudamus igitur constantiam propositi tui, frater charissime, nec aliud de pontificii tui vetere censura auctoritatis genus expectandum fuit, quam ut talibus ambitionibus, pro praeceptis Patrum, in procinctu fidei constitutus occurreres.[80]

2. Igitur si quid auctoritati tuae, quod nos non opinamur, aestimas defuisse, supplemus. Obsiste talibus ordinationibus, obsiste superbiae et arrogantiae venienti. Tecum faciunt praecepta Patrum, tecum apostolicae sedis auctoritas. Si enim officia saecularia principem locum, non vestibulum actionis ingressis, sed per plurimos gradus examinatio temporibus deferunt, quis ille tam arrogans, tam impudens invenitur, ut in coelesti militia, quae pensius ponderanda est, et sicut aurum repetitis ignibus exploranda, statim dux esse desideret, cum tyro ante non fuerit, et prius velit docere, quam discere? Assuescat in Domini castris, in lectorum primitus gradu rudimenta servitii; nec illi vile sit exorcistam, acolythum, subdiaconum, diaconum per ordinem fieri: nec hoc saltu, sed statutis majorum ordinatione temporibus. Jam vero ad presbyterii fastigium talis accedat, ut et nomen aetas impleat, et meritum probitatis stipendia anteacta testentur. Jure inde summi pontificis locum sperare debebit.[81]

III

5. Haec autem singulis gradibus observanda sunt tempora. Si ab infantia ecclesiasticis ministeriis nomen dederit, inter lectores usque ad vicesimum aetatis annum continuata observatione perduret. Si major jam et grandaevus accesserit, ita tamen, ut post baptismum statim, si divinae militiae desiderat mancipari, sive inter lectores, sive inter exorcistas quinquennio teneatur: exinde acolythus vel subdiaconus quatuor annis; et sic ad benedictionem diaconatus, si meretur, accedat; in quo ordine quinque annis, si inculpate se gesserit, haerere debebit. Exinde suffragantibus stipendiis, per tot gradus datis propriae fidei documentis, presbyterii sacerdotium poterit promereri. De quo loco, si eo illum exactior ad bonos mores vita produxerit, summum pontificatum sperare debebit....[82]

---

[80] *PL* 20.670.

[81] *PL* 20.670–671.

[82] *PL* 20.672–673; COUSTANT, I.968–971.

Zosimus begins by confirming the prohibition against the ordination of lay people directly to the episcopate. He censures Hesychius' colleagues for condoning such ordinations. The reason given (other than it is against the "decrees of the fathers" and his papal predecessors) is that such an ordination precludes the possibility for the candidate to be "educated in divine service". Zosimus identifies the motivation for such ordinations as ambition.

In the second section Zosimus exhorts Hesychius to forbid the ordinations of lay people to the presbyterate and the episcopate. By drawing an analogy between the grades of the church and secular office, Zosimus notes that it is through the testing of time in the many grades that one comes to the higher offices. Though the principal reason for such a *cursus* remains testing, Zosimus emphasises education and training as well.

The last selection from the letter to Hesychius is very much like the decretal of Siricius to Himerius of Tarragona, for it deals with the clerical *cursus* and the interstices in some detail. For instance, Zosimus states that those who have been dedicated to the ecclesiastical offices from infancy are to be enrolled in the lectorate until they reach twenty years of age. Likewise, older men who are destined to ecclesiastical office are to spend a five year period in the lectorate. After the time in the lectorate, candidates are to spend the next four years as acolytes or as subdeacons. If found worthy, they may then receive the "diaconal blessing". If a man is found blameless after five years as a deacon, he may be "promoted to the priesthood of the presbyterate" from which office he may one day "assume the highest pontificate". In sum, the sequence of the clerical *cursus* according to Zosimus is: lector, (lector *sive* exorcist for adults), acolyte or (*vel*) subdeacon, deacon, presbyter, then "high priest", according to the times or intervals determined by the fathers.

There are both similarities and differences between the arrangements of Zosimus and Siricius a generation earlier. In like manner, both place boys destined for ecclesiastical office among the lectors; for Siricius the lectorate might have been until either twenty or thirty years of age, for Zosimus the age is twenty years. Siricius keeps older men in the lectorate for two years; Zosimus for a five year period. Siricius maintains an interstice of five years for acolytes and subdeacons; Zosimus for four years. Both specify a five-year interval between the diaconate and the presbyterate, though only Siricius mentions the ten-year interval between the presbyterate and the episcopate. Lastly, both stress the conditional nature of promotion from one office to the next.

In similar fashion Siricius and Zosimus use the language of *per saltum* ordination. Lafontaine identifies Zosimus' use of expressions such as *statim saltu quodam* and *ad quem saltu subito pervenerunt* as being one the earliest examples of *saltum* terminology.[83] And yet, as noted above, Siricius used this terminology in the letter to Himerius thirty-three years earlier.

Lafontaine argues that in fourth- and fifth-century legislation, *per saltum* has two senses: omission of the lower orders, as well as omission of the interstices:

> Mais aux IVe et Ve siècles, c'est plutôt l'omission des interstices qui est ainsi désignée. D'ailleurs, le mot «saltus» n'est pas encore employé dans un sens technique. Mais là où on le rencontre, c'est en relation avec l'omission des interstices, surtout avec l'ordination immédiate à l'épiscopat.[84]

For Lafontaine, the textual support for this position is the letter of Zosimus to Hesychius, in particular the expression: *nec illi sit exorcistam, acolytum, subdiaconum, diaconum fieri: nec hoc saltu, sed statutis majorum ordinatione temporis* (I.2).

Innocent, too, addressed the problem of ignoring the interstices, that is, of candidates "rushing through the grades." Yet *per saltum* language was not used in this instance. Clearly in the letter to Patroclus, Zosimus uses the term *saltus* in criticising not the omission of the interstices, but omission of any one or more orders by certain bishops. Could this not also be implied in I.2 of the letter to Hesychius?

Both Siricius and Zosimus couple the minor orders of lector and exorcist, and acolyte and subdeacon together, making two classes of minor orders. In the letter of Innocent to Felix a similar structure is found within the minor orders: lector and acolyte, with no mention of the exorcist or subdeacon. Again, it is not clear if both minor orders within a coupling were received together, or if only one was received?

In *Les Conditions positives de l'Accession aux Ordres* Lafontaine concludes that only one order within a coupling would have been received.

---

[83] Lafontaine, *Les Conditions*, p. 237, n.3.

[84] Lafontaine, *Les Conditions*, p. 237. This is also the opinion expressed by Henri Leclerq in "Ordinations irrégulières", *Dictionnaire d'Archéologie Chrétienne et de Liturgie* vol. 12.2 (Paris: Librairie Letouzey et Ané, 1936), col. 2391.

Drawing on earlier scholarly treatments of the question (particularly Tho-massin), Lafontaine concludes that there was a choice between the orders which might have been determined by the needs of the "diocese" (or rather *parrocia* at this time).[85] Incidentally, there is no indication that boys en-rolled as lectors would become exorcists, as did older men.

The emphasis within the texts of both Siricius and Zosimus is on the in-tervals spent within the lectorate/exorcistate and the office of acolyte/sub-diaconate, rather than on the precise sequence of grades of the *cursus*. The incongruities and similarities between the letters of Siricius and Zosimus, thirty-three years apart, witness to both a considerable consensus on the *cursus honorum* and the interstices, as well as to a noteworthy degree of flexibility, particularly with regards to the interstices.[86]

e. Celestine

Epistle 4 of Celestine I (422–432) to the bishops of Vienne and Narbonne in southern France (26 July 428) is a valuable source of information on the *cursus honorum* and the interstices in the early fifth century:

> 4. Ordinatos vero quosdam, fratres charissimi, coepiscopos, qui nullis ecclesiasticis ordinibus ad tantae dignitatis fastigium fuerint instituti, contra Patrum decreta, hu-jus usurpatione qui se hoc recognoscit fecisse, didicimus: cum ad episcopatum his gradibus, quibus frequentissime cautum est, debeat perveniri, ut minoribus initiati officiis, ad majora firmentur. Debet enim ante esse discipulus quisquis doctor esse desiderat, ut possit docere quod didicit. Omnis vitae institutio, hac ad id quo tendit, se ratione confirmat. Qui minime litteris operam dederit, praeceptor non potest esse litterarum. Qui non per singula stipendia creverit, ad emeritum stipendii ordinem non potest pervenire. Solum sacerdotium inter ista, rogo, vilius est, quod facilius

[85] Lafontaine, *Les Conditions*, pp. 345–349. *Cf.* Duchesne also argues for the reception of only one order within a coupling, in particular that adults had the choice of entering either the exorcistate or the lectorate. *Christian Worship: Its Origins and Evolution*, (London, SPCK, 1949) p. 347, n.2. In "Les ordres mineurs dans l'ancien rit romain", *Revue des sciences réligieuse* 5 (1925), p. 271, Andrieu also indicates that one could be ordained a subdeacon without having been an acolyte.

[86] The letter of Zosimus to Hesychius was one of the most widely transmitted patristic papal sources of the *cursus honorum* and the interstices. It is found in at least fifteen early medieval historically arranged canonical sources (MAASSEN, pp.249–50). Of the systematic collections it is found in the *Concordia canonum*, the *Collectio vetus gallica*, the *Hibernensis*, the *Collectio Dacheriana*, the Pseudo-Isidorian Decretals, the *Collectio Anselmo dedicata*, the *Collectio in V libris*, the *Collectio canonum* of Anselm of Lucca, and in Gratian's *Decretum*. Chapter III.5 of the letter is reproduced as the intro-duction to the ordination rites in the Gelasian sacramentaries.

tribuatur, cum difficilius impleatur? Sed jam non satis est laicos ordinare quos nullus fieri ordo permittit, sed etiam quorum crimina longe lateque per omnes pene
sunt nota provincias, ordinantur.[87]

Celestine laments the fact that certain bishops have reached the episcopate without having served in any of the lower ecclesiastical offices,
which, he notes is contrary to the decrees of the fathers. Furthermore,
Celestine complains that not only are lay people being ordained to the episcopate, but specifically those "whose sins are noted far and wide throughout almost all the provinces". In addition, Celestine commends the minor
offices as a means of strengthening and preparation for the major offices:
"For whoever desires to be a teacher ought to have been first a student, so
that he might teach what he has learned." By comparison to the military
ranks, one who has not served in successive offices cannot be a veteran.
"Is the priesthood, I ask, alone among such a kind, because it is more easily
conferred, though it is more difficult to fulfil?" Here the purpose of the
cursus honorum is clearly training and preparation.[88]

In *Epistle* 5, written to the bishops of Apulia and Calabria in southern
Italy (429), Celestine again condemns the ordination of laity to the episcopate:

2. Audivimus quasdam propriis destitutas rectoribus civitates episcopos petere sibi
velle de laicis, tantumque fastigium tam vile credere, ut hoc iis qui non Deo, sed
saeculo militaverint, aestiment nos posse conferre, non solum male de suis clericis,
in quorum contemtum hoc faciunt, judicantes, sed de nobis pessime, quos credunt
hoc posse facere, sentientes. Quod numquam auderent, si non quorumdam illic his
consentiens sententia conniveret. Ita nihil quae frequentius sunt decreta proficiunt,
ut hoc, quasi numquam de hac parte scriptum fuerit, ignoretur.

Quid proderit per singula clericos stipendia militasse, et omnem egisse in Dominicis castris aetatem, si qui his praefuturi sunt, ex laicis requiruntur, qui vacantes
saeculo, et omnem ecclesiasticum ordinem nescientes, saltu praepropero in alienum honorem ambiunt immoderata cupiditate transscendere [*sic*.], et in aliud vitae
genus, calcata reverentia ecclesiasticae disciplinae, transire? Talibus itaque, fratres
carissimi, qui juris nostri, id est, canonum gubernacula custodimus, necesse est ob-
viemus: hisque fraternitatem vestram epistolis commonemus, ne quis laicum ad

---

[87] *PL* 56.578; COUSTANT, vol. 1, pp. 1069–1070.

[88] *Epistle* 4 of Celestine appears in thirteen historically arranged canonical collections
(MAASSEN, p. 252). Of the systematic collections in this study, section 4.4–5 is found
in the *Concordia canonum*, the *Dacheriana*, the Pseudo-Isidorian Decretals, the *Collectio Anselmo dedicata*, the *Decretum* of Burchard of Worms, the *Collectio in V libris*, the
Collection canonum of Anselm of Lucca, Bonizo's *Liber de vita christiani*, Ivo's *Decretum*, as well as Gratian's *Decretum*.

ordinem clericatus admittat; et sinat fiere unde et illum decipiat, et sibi causas ge-
neret, quibus reus constitutis decretalibus fiat.[89]

Celestine asks what it profits clerics to have served in every office, if prelates are chosen from the laity, having no knowledge of any ecclesiastical
order. Celestine notes that such candidates aspire to episcopal office from
immoderate ambition and ignorance of the nature of church office: "This
type of person, most beloved brothers, we must oppose." Celestine once
again demonstrates that while the ordination of lay people to the episcopate was undesirable, it was a reality in the fifth century.

Like Siricius and Zosimus, Celestine too uses per saltum language.
Lafontaine cites the words *saltu praepropero* (very hasty leap) as an instance where what is omitted is not the minor orders, but the interstices.[90]
What this terminology implies is that those whom Celestine censures for
coming to the episcopate from the laity, have been, in effect, "rushed
through the orders". While this practice is known to have occurred later,
there is little indication that it was known in the early fifth century, or that
it was in any way a regular (albeit illicit) practice.[91]

f. Leo I

A century after the Council of Sardica, the epistles from the pontificate of
Leo the Great (440–461) reveal the papacy still pressing for an observance
of the *cursus honorum* and the interstices. For instance, in *Epistle* 6 to
Anastasius of Thessalonica (12 Jan. 444) Leo writes:

> 6. ....Cognovimus sane, quod non potuimus silentio praeterire, a quibusdam fratri-
> bus solos episcopus tantum diebus dominicis ordinari; presbyteros vero et dia-
> conos, circa quos par consecratio [fieri] debet, passim quolibet die dignitatem
> officii sacerdotalis accipere; quod contra canones et traditionem Patrum usurpatio
> corrigenda committit, cum mos quibus est traditus, circa omnes sacros ordines
> debeat omnimodis custodiri; ita ut per longa temporum curricula, qui sacerdos vel

---

[89] COUSTANT, vol. 1. cols. 1072–1073.

[90] Lafontaine, *Les Conditions*, p. 237.

[91] The letter of Celestine to the bishops of Apulia and Calabria was frequently reproduced
in the canonistic collections. It appears in sixteen historically arranged collections
(MAASSEN, pp. 252–53). Of the systematic collections, it appears in the *Concordia
canonum* of Cresconius, the *Collectio Anselmo dedicata,* the Collection in Seventy-four
Titles, the collections of Anselm of Lucca, and Gratian.

> levita ordinandus est, per omnes clericalis officii ordines provehatur: ut diuturno discat tempore, cujus et doctor ipse futurus est.[92]

Leo complains that bishops, presbyters, and deacons are not being ordained according to the proper intervals of time. The rationale identified by Leo for the interstices is testing and training: "so that in this manner, through a long career of time, whoever is to be ordained a priest or a levite will have been tested through all the orders of the clerical offices; so that over a long period of time, whoever is to become a teacher might himself learn about the things [he is to teach]", recalling the words of Celestine (*Epistle* 4.4).

In a subsequent letter to Anastasius, *Epistle* 14 (*ca.* 446), Leo reiterates the prohibition against the ordination of members of the laity and neophytes, as well as others:

> 3. In civitatibus quarum rectores obierint, de substituendis episcopis haec forma servetur: ut is qui ordinandus est, etiamsi bonae vitae testimonium habeat, non laicus, non neophytus, nec secundae conjugis sit maritus, aut qui unam quidem habeat, vel habuerit, sed quam sibi viduam copularit. Sacerdotum enim tam excellens est electio, ut haec quae in aliis Ecclesiae membris non vocantur ad culpam, in illis tamen habeantur illicita.[93]

Here Leo directs that when a bishop has died, he may not be replaced by a lay person or a neophyte, even if he is supported by the evidence of a good life. Likewise, those married a second time or those married to widows are barred from episcopal office.[94]

A more extensive treatment of the *cursus* and the interstices is dealt with in Leo's *Epistle* 12 to the north African bishops of Mauritania Caesariensis (10 Aug. 446), in present day Algeria:

> 2. Quod si quibuslibet Ecclesia gradibus providenter scienterque curandum est ut in Domini domo nihil sit inordinatum nihilque praeposterum, quanto magis elaborandum est ut in electione ejus qui supra omnes gradus constituitur non erretur? Nam totius familiae Domini status et ordo nutabit, si quod requiritur in corpore, non inveniatur in capite. Ubi est illa beati Pauli apostoli per Spiritum Dei emissa praeceptio, qua in persona Timothei omnium Christi sacerdotum numerus eruditur,

---

[92] *PL* 54.620.

[93] *PL* 54.672.

[94] *Epistle* 6 appears in nine historical collections (MAASSEN, p. 259). Of the systematic collections, the letter of Leo to Anastasius is found in the *Concordia canonum*, the Pseudo-Isidorian Decretals, the *Collectio Anselmo dedicata*, the Collection in Seventy-four Titles, the collection of Burchard of Worms, the *Collectio canonum* of Anselm of Lucca, and the Decretals of Ivo and Gratian.

et unicuique nostrum dicitur: Manus cito nemini imposureris, neque communices peccatis alienis? Quid est cito manus imponere, nisi ante aetatem maturitatis, ante tempus examinis, ante meritum obedientiae, ante experimentiam disciplinae sacerdotalem honorem tribuere non probatis? Et quid est communicare peccatis alienis, nisi et talem effici ordinantem, qualis est ille qui non meruit ordinari? Sicut enim boni operis sibi comparat fructum qui rectum tenet in eligendo sacerdote judicium, ita gravi semetipsum afficit damno qui in suum collegium assumit indignum. Non ergo in cujusquam persona praetermittendum est quod institutis generalibus continetur, nec putandus est honor ille legitimus qui fuerit contra divinae legis praecepta collatus.[95]

4. Monente vero Apostolo, atque dicente: Et hi autem probentur primum, et sic ministrent, quid aliud intelligendum putamus, nisi ut in his provectionibus non solum matrimoniorum castimoniam sed etiam laborum merita cogitemus, ne aut a baptismo novellis, aut a saeculari actu repente conversis officium pastorale credatur; cum per omnes gradus militiae Christianae de incrementis profectuum debeat aestimari an possint cuiquam majora committi?

Merito beatorum Patrum venerabiles sanctiones cum de sacerdotum electione loquerentur, eosdem ut idoneos sacris administrationibus censuerunt, qui multo tempore per singulos officiorum gradus provecti, experimentum sui probabile praebuissent, ut unicuique testimonium vitae suae actuum suorum ratio perhiberet. Si enim ad honores mundi sine suffragio temporis, sine merito laboris indignum est pervenire, et notari ambitus solent, quos probitatis documenta non adjuvant; quam diligens et quam prudens habenda est dispensatio divinorum munerum et coelestium dignitatum? Ne in aliquo apostolica et canonica decreta violentur, et his Ecclesia Domini regenda credatur, qui legitimarum institutionum nescii, et totius humilitatis ignari, non ab infinis sumere incrementum, sed a summis volunt habere principium; cum valde iniquum sit et absurdum, ut imperiti magistris, novi antiquis, et rudes praeferantur emeritis.

In domo quidem magna sicut Apostolus disserit, necesse est ut vasa diversa sint, quaedam aurea et argentea, quaedam vero lignea et fictilia; sed horum ministerium pro materiae qualitate decernitur, nec idem est pretiosorum usus et vilium. Nam inordinata erunt omnia, si fictilia aureis, et lignea praeferantur argenteis. Sicut autem in ligneis et fictilibus eorum hominum species figurantur qui nullis adhuc virtutibus nitent; ita in aureis et argenteis hi sine dubio declarantur qui per longae eruditionis ignem, et per fornacem diuturni laboris excocti, aurum probatum et argentum purum esse meruerunt. Quibus si merces pro devotione non redditur, omnis ecclesiastica disciplina resolvitur, omnis ordo turbatur, dum in Ecclesia, qui nullum subierunt ministerium, perverso eligentium judicio indebitum obtinent principatum.[96]

5. ....Caeteros vero, quorum provectio hoc tantum reprehensionis incurrit, quod ex laicis ad officium episcopale electi sunt, neque ex hoc quod uxores habent, possunt

---

[95] *PL* 54.647–648.

[96] *PL* 54.649–651.

esse culpabiles, susceptum sacerdotium tenere permittimus, non praejudicantes apostolicae sedis statutis, nec beatorum Patrum regulas resolventes, quibus salubriter constitutum est, ne primum, aut secundum, aut tertium in Ecclesia gradum quisquam laicorum quibuslibet suffragiis suffultus ascendat, priusquam ad hoc meritum per legitima augmenta perveniat. Quod enim nunc utcumque patimur esse veniale, inultum postmodum esse non poterit, si quisquam id quod omnino interdicimus usurparit: quia remissio peccati non dat licentiam deliquendi, neque quod potuit aliqua ratione concedi, fas erit amplius impune committi.[97]

This lengthy selection discloses much about the value Leo the Great placed on the *cursus honorum* and the interstices in terms of the training and testing of candidates for ecclesiastical office. In chapter 2, after citing the injunction against imposing hands suddenly (1 Tim. 5.22), Leo asks "what is it to impose hands suddenly, unless [it means] before the age of maturity, before a period of examination, before the service of obedience, to give the priestly honour to those untested before the experience of discipline". Leo's reasons for supporting the *cursus* are training, maturity, examination, and experience. Elsewhere in the letter Leo refers to the apostolic precepts against the ordination of laity and neophytes, as well as the decrees of the Fathers. Here Leo describes such ordinations as also being "contrary to the precepts of divine law."

In chapter 4, Leo continues to promote advancement through the grades, stressing the merits of experience and testing. He discourages the practice of ordaining men directly to the offices of leadership: "We have decreed that the apostolic and canonical decrees be not violated in any way and the Lord's church not be entrusted to be ruled by those who, ignorant of its lawful institutions and lacking in all humility, do not want to rise up from the lowest [estates], but desire to start at the top, since it is unfair and absurd that the inexperienced and the unskilled are given preference over the teachers, the masters, and the seasoned, [that is] the new over the old." Such ordinations, however, must have been common in north Africa.

By way of analogy, Leo likens preparation for ministry to the analogy of the vessels of gold and silver, wood and earthenware, from the second Epistle to Timothy (2 Tim. 2.20). He compares the testing of the *cursus* to the trying of gold and silver: "therefore these men are proven without doubt in gold and silver, which, refined through the fire of a long education, and the furnace of long hardened labour, deserved to be as tried gold

---

[97] *PL* 54.652–653.

and silver." The emphasis, again, is on the selection and preparation of the church's leaders.

In the fifth chapter Leo condemns the election of both the laity and those who are married to the episcopate. Members of the laity who would be bishops must first come to this "reward" through legitimate enrichment.[98]

g. Gelasius

At the end of the fifth century, encouragement for the clerical *cursus* and the interstices was still on the papal agenda, as evidenced in the writings of Gelasius I (492–496). Yet Gelasius displays extraordinary flexibility with regards to both the interstices and the *cursus honorum*. In a letter to a bishop Victor (*Fragmentum* 10), which first appeared in the canonical collections of the eleventh century, Gelasius commends the *cursus honorum*:

> Consuluit dilectio tua de suorum promotione clericorum perhibens, quod diaconi ad presbyterii gradum, quo ecclesiam tuam memoras indigere, venire detrectant. Quapropter quia invitos fieri ecclesiastica moderatio gravitasque non patitur, ut ex nolentibus fiant volentes, ordinatio illa potest perficere: scilicet si quos habes vel in acolythis vel in subdiaconibus maturioris aetatis et quorum sit vita probabilis, hos in presbyteratum studeas promovere: ut qui in suis ordinibus proficere noluerint, reddantur suis inferioribus post minores; ipsaque commoda presbyteri propensius quam diacones consequantur, ut hac saltem ratione constricti, et honorem, quem refugerant, appetere nitantur et quaestum.[99]

Gelasius writes to Victor concerning the promotion of clergy in his church, particularly promotion between the diaconate and the presbyterate. Evidently deacons in Victor's church were avoiding promotion to the presbyterate. Gelasius suggests a virtual "end-run" on Victor's deacons. He proposes that if Victor has acolytes or subdeacons of mature years and tested lives, he should be eager to promote them to the presbyterate. This text suggests that normally in Victor's church, there was a customary *cursus* between the diaconate and the presbyterate.

---

[98] This letter appears in eleven historically arranged collections (MAASSEN, p.258). Of the systematic collections in this study, *Epistle* 12 of Leo to the bishops of Mauritania Caesariensis is found in the Pseudo-Isidorian Decretals, the *Collectio in V libris*, the Collection in Seventy-four titles, the *Collectio canonum* of Anselm of Lucca, and in Gratian's *Decretum*.

[99] Andreas Thiel, *Epistolae Romanorum Pontificum Genuinae*, vol. 1 (Braunsberg: Edward Peter, 1896), pp. 488–489.

And yet the text of Gelasius' letter to Victor demonstrates that while the *cursus* was certainly advisable, it was not so resolved that in difficult situations, such as a shortage of presbyters, it could not be circumvented. And so he permits the ordination of acolytes and subdeacons directly to the presbyterate. There is no mention in the text of any intervening ordination to the diaconate. Here it is primarily the *cursus*, and not the interstices, which is abrogated. At the same time, the principle behind the *cursus honorum*—testing—must be maintained.[100]

A second example from the pontificate of Gelasius is *Epistle* 14 (494) to the bishops throughout Lucania, Brutium, and Sicily in southern Italy. Gelasius writes:

> 2. Priscis igitur pro sui reverentia manentibus constitutis, quae, ubi nulla vel rerum vel temporum perurgeat angustia, regulariter convenit custodiri, eatenus ecclesiis, quae vel cunctis sunt privatae ministris vel sufficientibus usque adeo dispoliatae servitiis, ut plebibus ad se pertinentibus divina munera supplere non valeant, tam instituendi quam promovendi clericalis obsequii sic spatia dispensanda concedimus: ut si quis, etiam de religioso proposito et disciplinis monasterialibus eruditis, ad clericale munus accedit, imprimis ejus vita praeteritis acta temporibus inquiratur: si nullo gravi facinore probatur infectus, si secundam non habuit fortassis uxorem, nec a marito relictam sortitus ostenditur; si poenitentiam publicam fortasse non gessit, nec ulla corporis parte vitiatus apparet; si servilis aut originariae non est conditionis obnoxis; si curiae jam probatur nexibus absolutus; si assecutus est litteras, sine quibus vix fortassis ostiarium possit implere: ut si his omnibus quae sunt praedicta fulcitur, continuo lector vel notarius aut certe defensor effectus, post tres menses exsistat acolythus, maxime si huic aetas etiam suffragatur, sexto mense subdiaconi nomen accipiat, ac si modestae conversationis honestaeque voluntatis exsistit, nono mense diaconus completoque anno sit presbyter: cui tamen, quod annorum fuerant interstitia collatura, sancti propositi sponte suscepta doceatur praetitisse devotio.[101]

Epistle 14.2 is an example of a pastoral adaptation of an ordination practice to meet two exceptional situations. In this instance it is the interstices, not the *cursus*, which is modified. The first situation is a church deprived of the sacraments because the clergy have "withdrawn" (*privatiae*), perhaps as Lafontaine suggests, because of the barbarian invasions.[102] The second

---

[100] Of the systematic collections cited in this study, the letter of Gelasius to Victor is found in the *Collectio canonum* of Anselm of Lucca, the *Collectio canonum* of Deusdedit, Ivo's *Decretum* and the *Decretum* of Gratian.

[101] *PL* 84.798–799; THIEL I.362–363.

[102] Lafontaine, *Les Conditions*, p. 259. Southern Italy and Sicily, however, seem too far south to have been affected by barbarian invasions at this date.

situation envisaged by Gelasius is one in which the clergy have been despoiled to such a degree that they are not willing to provide their people with the *divina munera*.

In both predicaments Gelasius allows a dispensation, though not in terms of the *cursus*, which must be observed, but in terms of the interstices which may be significantly reduced. Gelasius directs that where there are suitable candidates, monks in particular, whose lives have been investigated and tested, and who live according to the requisite marriage discipline, such men are to be admitted as doorkeepers. They are to continue as lectors (or "notaries" or "defensors"). After three months they are to be made acolytes. In the sixth month they are to be made subdeacons; in the ninth month deacons; at the end of one year, they are to be ordained presbyters.

This text is significant in many respects. The doorkeeper is part of the *cursus*. The diaconate is requisite for reception of the presbyterate. The ten year period from lectorate to presbyterate as evidenced in the decretals of Siricius and Zosimus has been reduced by Gelasius to twelve months. It is significant that the *cursus* has remained while the interstices have changed.

The phenomenon of a one year period of training is reflected in some of the Gallican canons examined from the early sixth century.[103] It is also reflected in the twentieth canon of the Council of Braga I (561) which directs that lay men destined to the "priesthood" spend a year in the office of lector or the subdiaconate; the similarity is of a year of preparation. The difference is that Gelasius sees progression through all the orders as providing that preparation, the Gallican and Hispanic councils do not.

It is interesting to note that what Gelasius commends here, i.e. hasty ordination from one grade to another, Innocent (a century earlier) and Leo (only a generation earlier still) both rejected. When the expressed purpose of moving through the grades has been training and preparation, one wonders what the reason for keeping a candidate for the presbyterate among the acolytes, subdeacons, and deacons for sequential three month periods was intended to achieve. Such an abrogation of the interstices illustrates the extent to which the *cursus honorum* has been reduced to the level of *pro forma* convention, rather than as being a viable means of selection and training. *Epistle* 14.2 epitomizes the extent to which the *cursus* has been altered. Gelasius seems to defeat completely the logic of imposing a *cursus* on the clerical orders. Once it is possible to distort the

---

[103] The Gallican Councils of Arles (525) and Orleans (549).

interstices to the degree Gelasius has, the primary purpose for the *cursus honorum*—testing and preparation—has disappeared.

One notes two contemporary solutions to a similar exceptional circumstances faced by Gallican and Hispanic bishops. Both the Councils of Arles (524) and Orleans (549) provide a year in which a lay man is tested and trained prior to ordination to the major orders. One notes a similar provision made by the Council of Braga (561), though it is specified that such a candidate for the "priesthood" will spend the year in either the office of lector or subdeacon. These Gallican and Hispanic canons also abrogate the interstices as well as the *cursus honorum*. They reflect, however, a certain logic that seems to have eluded Gelasius, namely that simply spending three months in each order serves little purpose. Gelasius' letter to the bishops throughout Lucania, Brutium and Sicily is an early sign that the *cursus honorum* is shifting from being a means to an end, to being an end in itself.[104]

h. Hormisdas

In *Epistle* 25 to the Hispanic bishops (*Ad universos episcopos Hispaniae, 517*), Hormisdas (514–523) reveals that in the early sixth century the practice of ordaining members of the laity directly to the episcopate was still a feature of ecclesiastical life:

> I.2 Ut in sacerdotibus ordinandis, quae sunt a patribus praescripta et definita, cogitetis: quia sicut caput est Ecclesiae Christus, Christi autem vicarii sacerdotes, sic et in eligendus his curam oportet esse praecipuam. Irreprehensibiles enim esse convenit, quos praeesse necesse est corrigendis: nec quidquam illi deesse personae, penes quam est religionis summa et substantia disciplinae. Aestimet quis pretium dominici gregis, ut sciat quod meritum constituendi deceat esse pastoris. Hoc ita fiet, si non ad sacerdotii gradus saltu quodam passim laici transferantur. Longa debet vitam suam probatione monstrare, cui gubernacula committuntur Ecclesiae. Non negamus in laicis Deo placitos mores; sed milites suos probatos sibi quaerunt instituta fidelia. Discere quis debet ante, quod doceat, et exemplum religiosae conversationis de se potius aliis praestare quam sumere. Emendatiorem esse convenit populo, quem necesse est orare pro populo. Longa observatione religiosi cultus teratur, ut luceat, et diu clericalibus obsequiis erudiendus inserviat, ut ad venerandi gradus summa perductus, qui sit fructus humilitatis, ostendat. Non leve non

---

[104] Gelasius' *Epistle* 14.2 appears in ten historically arranged canonical collections (MAASSEN, p.281). Of the systematic collections cited in this study, the letter is found in the *Concordia canonum* of Cresconius, the Pseudo-Isidorian Decretals, the *Collection Anselmo dedicata*, the *Collectio in V libris*, and in Gratian's *Decretum*.

vacuum fuit, quod nec apud veteres quidem nisi Levitici generis viri ad sancta ad-
mittebantur altaria, ne passim, meritis aut pretio aut praesumptione contemptis, ad
sacros cultus impar accederet. Migravit illa praerogativa familiarum ad instituta
cultorum. Nunc est doctrina pro genere: quod illis fuit nasci, hoc nobis imbui; illos
tabernaculo dabat natura, nos altaribus parturit disciplina.[105]

Hormisdas cautions the Hispanic bishops against ordaining members of
the laity to the episcopate by in a leap (*saltu*); whoever would govern the
church must demonstrate the worthiness of his life by a lengthy testing.
Hormisdas acknowledges that there are many among the laity whose lives
are pleasing to God, "but their worthy institutions seek as their servants
men tested to themselves." Hormisdas reiterates that a person must learn
before he teaches. While there is no explicit reference made to either the
cursus or interstices in this text, the pope recalls the motives for both:
training and selection.

The letter further reveals that the early sixth-century Hispanic Church
knew the practice of ordaining members of the laity to the episcopate.
Even though such candidates may have been worthy, Hormisdas recalls
the Hispanic church to the practice advocated by the Council of Sardica
two centuries earlier, namely that no lay person be ordained to the "priesthood".[106]

i. Pelagius

Two letters from the pontificate of Pelagius (555–560) in the mid-sixth
century are worth noting. The first example is from part of *Epistle* 5 to
Sapaudus, bishop of Arles (*ca.* 558–560), preserved in the *Collectio Bri-
tannica*. Pelagius writes:

Quis autem ex vobis de eo, quod illic fieri comperimus, redditurus est rationem, vel
in quibus canonibus invenitur, ut uno eodem die laicus homo et clericus et acolitus

---

[105] *PL* 63.423; THIEL I, pp. 789–790.

[106] The letter of Hormisdas to the Hispanic bishops appears in at least two historically
arranged collections (MAASSEN, p.289). Of the systematic collections, *Epistle* 25.I.2
(with some alterations) is found in the Pseudo-Isidorian Decretals, the *Collectio
canonum* Anselm of Lucca, the Collection in Seventy-four Titles, and the *Decretum* of
Gratian.

et subdiaconus et diaconus et presbyter et episcopus fiat et subito quasi teathrali spectaculo mutato habitu missas faciat...[107]

Here Pelagius complains about the sudden ordination of a lay person to the clerical state, through the orders of acolyte, [subdeacon,] deacon, and presbyter, to the episcopate "on one and the same day", as though "changed in some sort of theatrical spectacle." This is a startling mid-sixth-century instance of the practice of "rushing" a candidate through four or five offices in the space of a day. It demonstrates the fixity of the *cursus* in the sixth century, and the extent to which the interstices could be abused.

In the second example, *Epistle* 23, a letter found first in the collections of the eleventh century, Pelagius writes to a bishop, Bonus of Vescovio (north-east of Rome) regarding a monk who is to be ordained a presbyter:

....Et quia praefatus filius noster nobis retulit invenisse Rufinum quemdam monachum olim sibi vita et moribus comprobatum, et hunc postulat ibi presbyterum consecrari, quod subito fieri nos praerogata observantia non acquievimus. Ideoque dilectio tua, his acceptis, sabbato veniente faciat eum subdiaconum et, si Deus voluerit et vixerimus, mediana hebdomada presbyterum faciemus: quatenus superveniente festivate paschali sacra mysteria in memorata basilica a persona competenti valeant adimpleri.[108]

In this letter Pelagius responds to a request by a lay person, Theodore, that the monk Rufinus be ordained a presbyter to serve in a basilica built by Theodore on his property. Since the basilica was within Bonus's diocese, Pelagius directs Bonus to ordain Rufinus to the subdiaconate, and then to send him to Rome to be ordained to the presbyterate during the *mediana* week (most likely on the Saturday before Passion Sunday),[109] so that he might be ready to celebrate the eucharist at Easter. It is noteworthy that there is no mention of any ordination to the diaconate. The interval spent

---

[107] MGH *Epistolae* vol. 3, *Merowingici & Karolini*, vol. 1 (Berlin: Weidmann, 1892), pp. 444–445; A. Theiner, *Disquisitiones Criticae in Praecipuas Canonem et Decretalium* (Rome: in Collegio Urbano, 1836), p. 202. *Cf.* Paul Ewald, ed., *Neus Archiv, Gesellschaft für ältere deutsche Geschickskunde*, vol. 5 (Hannover: Hahn'sche Buchhandlung, 1880), pp. 538–539. Ewald's edition, which enumerates the letter as *Epistle* 6, does not include the subdeacon between the acolyte and the deacon.

[108] THIEL, vol. 1, p. 454. Jaffé (433) and Thiel attribute this letter to Gelasius (*Epistle* 41). According to M. Andrieu, *Les Ordines Romani du haut moyen age*, vol. 3 (Louvain: Spicileum Sacrum Lovaniensis, 1951), p. 565, the letter must be attributed to Pelagius. Ewald, *Neus Archiv*, vol. 5, p. 546, n. 1, also argues for a Pelagian authorship.

[109] *Cf.* G. G. Willis, "What is *Mediana* Week?," *Essays in Early Roman Liturgy* (London: SPCK, 1964), pp. 101–104.

in the subdiaconate is reduced, making the subdiaconate in this instance a *pro forma* grade on the way to the presbyterate.

j. Gregory the Great

The last patristic bishop of Rome whose writings on the *cursus honorum* and the interstices are to be considered is Gregory the Great (590–604). The letters to be considered are directed towards the Gallican church. They reveal the general state of disarray and turmoil in the current Gallican church, especially in the appointments of bishops and other clergy. These letters complement the description of the Gallican church provided by Gregory of Tours in the *Historia francorum*.

From all accounts, the Gallican church at this time, like the rest of Frankish society, was in a state of chaos, decadent, and full of abuses. As Homes Dudden has summarised: ".... as a whole, the Gallican clergy, both high and low, were as brutal and degraded as the abandoned princes and nobles among whom they served."[110] Bishops were drawn into political intrigue, war, and rebellion. Episcopal sees were often bought or given away as royal favours. One of the abuses frequently cited is the ordination of members of the laity directly to the episcopate with no prior ecclesiastical probation or preparation.

Gregory the Great had much to say about pastoral office in the church. His *Liber regulae pastoralis* is one of the great patristic treatises on the episcopal office. In it he says nothing about the selection and training of candidates in terms of the *cursus honorum* and the interstices. His interests and concerns in this aspect of pastoral offices are reflected in his correspondence with the royal and episcopal leaders of the Gallican church. Moreover, it is these letters which reappear in the later canonistic collections.

In a portion of a letter to Brunhilda (*Reg.* 8.4), Queen of the Franks, (Sept. 597) Gregory writes:

---

[110] F. Homes Dudden, *Gregory the Great: His Place in History and Thought*, vol. 2 (London: Longman's, Green, and Co., 1905), p. 54. Katherine Scherman offers a more positive evaluation: "The scoundrels were a small minority: most of the Gallic clergy were well-intentioned men, hard-working and reasonably pious." Katherine Scherman, *The Birth of France: Warriors, Bishops and Long-haired Kings* (New York: Random House, 1987), p. 208.

....Sed et hoc vobis curae sit, ut, quia, sicut nostis, neophytum egregius praedicator ad sacerdotii regimen omnino vetat accedere, nullum ex laico patiamini episcopum consecrari. Nam qualis magister erit, qui discipulus non fuit? Aut quemadmodum ducatum gregi dominico praebeat, qui disciplinae pastoris subditus ante non fuerit? Si cuius ergo talis vita constiterit, ut ad hunc dignus sit ordinem promoveri, prius ministerio debet ecclesiae deservire, quatenus longae exercitationis usu videat, quod imitetur, et discat, quod doceat, ne forte onus regiminis conversionis novitas non ferat, et ruinae occasio de provectus inmaturitate consurgat.....[111]

Here Gregory forbids the ordination of neophytes and the laity to the episcopate, evidence that the practice was current in the Gallican church at the end of the sixth century. He recalls the reasoning of Celestine, Leo, Hormisdas and other papal predecessors that whoever would teach, must first have been a student. He emphasises the need for proven worthiness of life, and a long period of discipline.[112]

In a portion from another letter to Brunhilda (*Reg.* 9.213; July, 599), Gregory again condemns the practice of ordaining members of the laity to the episcopate:

.... Quorum officium in tanta illic, sicut didicimus, ambitione perductum est, ut sacerdotes subito, quod grave nimis est, ex laicis ordinentur. Sed quid isti acturi, quid populo praestaturi sunt, qui non ad utilitatem, sed fieri ad honorem episcopi concupiscunt? Hi igitur quia necdum quod docere debeant didicerunt, quid aliud agitur, nisi ut paucorum provectus inlicitus fiat multis interitus et in confusionem ecclesiasticae moderationis observantia deducatur, quippe ubi nullus regularis ordo servatur? Nam qui ad eius regimen improvidus et praecipitatus accedit, qua ammonitione subiectos aedificet, cuius exemplum non rationem docuit, sed errorem? Pudet profecto, pudet aliis imperare, quod ipse nescit custodire.

Nec illud quidem, quod similiter emendationi tradendum est, praeterimus, sed omnino execrabile et esse gravissimum detestamur, quod sacri illic ordines per simoniacam heresem, quae prima contra ecclesiam orta et districta maledictione damnata est, conferantur. Hinc ergo agitur, ut sacerdotis dignitas in dispectu et sanctus sit honor in crimine. Perit utique reverentia, adimitur disciplina, quia qui culpas debuit emendare committit, et nefaria ambitione honorabilis sacerdotii ducitur in depravatione censura. Nam quis denuo veneretur quod venditur, aut quis non vile putet esse quod emitur? Unde valde contristor et terrae illi condoleo; quia, dum sanctum spiritum, quem per manus impositionem omnipotens Deus hominibus largiri dignatur, divino munere habere dispiciunt, sed praemiis assequuntur, sacerdotium illic substistere diu non arbitror. Nam ubi dona supernae gratiae

[111] L. M. Hartmann, ed., *Gregorii I Papae: Registrum Epistularum* vol. 2, *Monumenta Germaniae Historica, Epistolarum Tomus II* (Berlin: Weidmann, 1899), pp. 6–7.

[112] Oddly, of the systematic collections cited in this study, this portion of Gregory's letter to Brunhilda (*Reg.* 8.4) is found only in the *Collectio in V libris*.

venalia iudicantur, ad Dei servitium non vita quaeritur, sed magis contra Deum pecuniae venerantur.....[113]

Gregory complains that not only are ambitious lay men being promoted directly to the episcopate, but that the episcopal office is being bought. The disregard for the *cursus honorum* and the interstices is compounded with the practice of simony; from Gregory's language, the latter is by far the more serious offense. Gregory complains that these ambitious men desire to be bishops not for the service but for the honour it brings. He notes that the "illicit promotion of the few" is becoming the ruin of many, through the lack of respect for the governance of the church.[114]

In a concurrent letter (July 599) to the Frankish kings Theodoric and Theodobert (*Reg.* 9.215), Gregory again censures the practice of simony, that "terrible disease". The simoniacal bishops are those who through greed and ambition have also been ordained *per saltum* to the episcopate. This practice Gregory also condemns:

.... Nec hoc quoque malum sollicitudo nostra patitur neglegenter omittere, quod quidam instinctu gloriae inanis inlecti ex laico repente habitu sacerdotii honorem arripiunt et, quod dicere pudet et grave tacere est, regendi rectores et qui docendi sunt doctores nec erubescunt videri nec metuunt. Ducatum animarum impudenter adsumunt, quibus via omnis ignota ductoris est et, quo vel ipsi gradiantur, ignari sunt. Quod quam pravum quamve sit temerarium, saeculari etiam ordine et disciplina monstratur. Nam dum dux exercitus non nisi labore et sollicitudine expertus eligitur, quales animarum duces esse debeant, qui episcopatus culmen inmatura cupiunt festinatione conscendere, huius saltem rei comparatione considerent et adgredi repente inexpertos labores abstineant, ne caeca honoris ambitio et ipsis in poena sit et aliis pestifera erroris semina iaciat, quippe qui non didicere, quod doceant. Proinde paterno salutantes affectu petimus, praecellentissimi filii, ut hoc tam detestabile malum de regni vestri studeatis finibus prohiberi, et nulla apud vos excustio, nulla contra animam vestram suggestio locum inveniat, quia facientis procul dubio culpam habet, qui quod potest corrigere neglegit emendare.....[115]

Here Gregory refers to the practice of ordaining the laity to the episcopate an "evil". Gregory denounces such ordinations as an absurdity, the result of vainglory, impudence and blind ambition. Gregory urges Theodoric and

---

[113] MGH *Epp* 2. pp. 198–199.

[114] This letter of Gregory to Brunhilda appears in at least two historically arranged canonical collections (MAASSEN, p. 303). Of the systematic collections, this portion of Gregory's letter to Brunhilda (*Reg.* 9.213) appears in the *Collectio Anselmo dedicata*, the Collection in Seventy-four Titles, the *Collectio canonum* of Anselm of Lucca, and in Gratian's *Decretum*.

[115] MGH *Epp*. 2. p.202.

Theodobert to correct this abuse; otherwise they will share in the guilt of those who perpetrate such an evil. Gregory also mentions the concern for preparedness for office: "they impudently assume the rule of souls when they do not know the whole way of the teacher and do not know the way they ought to progress". He draws an analogy to military office: an army leader is chosen only if he is proficient in his duties.[116] Similar concerns are expressed by Gregory in another concurrent letter to the Gallican bishops Syagrius, Etherius, and Desiderius (*Reg.* 9.218; July 599):

> .... Hoc quoque ad nos pervenisse non dissimili dignum detestatione complectimur, quod quidam desiderio honoris inflati defunctis episcopis tonsorantur et fiunt repente ex laicis sacerdotes atque inverecunde religiosi propositi ducatum arripiunt, qui nec esse adhuc milites didicerunt. Quid putamus, quid isti subiectis praestaturi sunt, qui, antequam discipulatus limen attingant, tenere locum magisterii non formidant? Qua de re necesse est, ut, etsi quamvis inculpati quisque sit meriti, ante tamen per distinctos ordines ecclesiasticis exerceatur officiis. Videat quod imitetur, discat quod doceat, informetur quod teneat, ut postea non debeat errare, qui eligitur viam errantibus demonstrare. Diu ergo religiosa meditatione poliatur, ut placeat, et sic lucerna super candelabram posita luceat, ut adversa ventorum vis inruens conceptam eruditionis flamman non extinguat, sed augeat. Nam cum scriptum sit: 'Ut prius quis probetur, et sic ministret', multo amplius ante probandus est, qui populi intercessor adsumitur, ne fiant causa ruinae populi sacerdotes mali. Nulla igitur contra hoc excusatio, nulla potest esse defensio, quia cunctis liquido notum est, quae sit in huius rei diligentia sancta egregii sollicitudo doctoris, qua neophitum ad ordines vetat sacros accedere. Sicut autem tunc neophitus dicebatur, qui initio in sanctae fidei erat conversatione plantatus, sic modo neophitus habendus est, qui repente in religionis habitu plantatus ad ambiendos honores sacros inrepserit. Ordinate ergo ad ordines accedendum est; nam casum appetit, qui ad summa loci fastiga postpositis gradibus per abrupta quaerit ascensum. Et cum idem apostolus doceat inter alia sacri ordinis instituta discipulum manum non esse cuiquam citius imponendam, quid hoc celerius quidve praecipitantius, quam ut exoriatur a summitate principium et ante esse incipiat episcopus quam minister? Quisquis igitur sacerdotium non ad elationis pompam, sed ad utilitatem adipisci desiderat, prius vires suas cum eo quo est subiturus onere metiatur, ut et inpar abstineat et ad id cum metu, etiam qui se sufficere existimat, accedat....[117]

> .... De his itaque quae superius dicta sunt fraternitatem vestram auctore Deo volumus synodum congregare atque in ea reverentissimo fratre nostro Aregio episcopo et dilectissimo filio nostro Cyriaco abbate mediantibus omnia, quae sanctis canonibus, sicut praediximus, sunt adversa, districte sub anathematis interpositione

---

[116] This portion of the letter of Gregory to Theodoric and Theodobert (*Reg.* 9.215) is found in the *Collection Anselmo dedicata*, the Collection in Seventy-four Titles, and the *Collectio canonum* of Anselm of Lucca.

[117] MGH *Epp.* 2, pp. 207–208.

damnentur, id est, ut nullus pro adipiscendis ecclesiasticis ordinibus dare aliquod commodum praesumat vel pro datis accipere, neque ex laico habitu quisquam repente audeat ad locum sacri regiminis pervenire, neque ut aliae mulieres cum sacerdotibus habitent, nisi hae [*sic.*], quae sacris, ut praedictum est, canonibus sunt permisssae.[118]

Gregory disparages the fact that members of the laity have been ordained to the episcopate out of greed and ambition for office. Even in a situation where a lay person of blameless merit is chosen to be a bishop, Gregory advocates the *cursus* through the various offices of the ecclesiastical order. The reasons given are formation, instruction, and testing, for what could be more inordinate, he argues, than beginning at the top as master before one has been a disciple? Though recalling the long standing prohibition against the ordination of neophytes, Gregory shifts the meaning of neophyte from one newly baptised to one who has recently received the religious habit. He again stresses that candidates must rise through the orders in regular succession: *Ordinate ergo ad ordines accedendum est.*

Gregory concludes the letter to the Gallican bishops by calling for a synod to oppose simony, clergy living with women (except mothers, sisters, aunts, etc.), and the ordination of the laity directly to the major orders. Finally, those who oppose the sacred canons are to be anathematized.[119]

In the four letters surveyed, Gregory the Great indicates little about the structure or sequence of the *cursus* or the lengths of the interstices to be observed. And yet of all the popes noted thus far, Gregory is by far the most emphatic in opposing the ordination of members of the laity to the episcopate. While Gregory's denunciation of *per saltum* ordination (in conjunction with simony) needs to be seen within the context of the sixth-century Frankish church, the texts from his pontificate demonstrate the weight of the *cursus honorum* at the end of the sixth century: to abrogate them is to invoke an anathema.

---

[118] MGH, *Epp.* 2. pp. 209–210.

[119] The letter of Gregory to Syagrius, Etherius, and Desiderius (*Reg.* 9.218) appears in at least one historical collection (MAASSEN, p. 303). Of the systematic collections, it is included in the *Collectio vetus gallica*, the *Collectio Anselmo dedicata*, the *Collectio in V libris*, the Collection in Seventy-four Titles, the collection of Anselm of Lucca, and in Gratian's Decretals.

5. Canonistic Collections

While conciliar and papal legislation enjoining the *cursus honorum* were essential to the introduction and promotion of the clerical *cursus* and the interstices, equally important were the canonistic collections, the intermediate sources by which the canons of popes and councils were transmitted to the church.[120] The early medieval canonistic sources were arranged either historically or systematically. The historically arranged collections present the canonical sources as they appeared chronologically in conciliar or papal legislation. The compilers of the systematically arranged collections, however, displayed conscious choice in the material they chose to include in their collections. Hence, while the historical collections are not unimportant, the systematically arranged collections are more significant in the transmission of the canons dealing with the *cursus honorum* and the interstices.

There are many patristic canon law collections which could be examined. This section will survey three examples: the *Breviatio canonum* of Fulgentius Ferrandus of Carthage, the *Concordia canonum* of Cresconius, and the *Collectio vetus gallica*.

a. The *Breviatio canonum*

The *Breviatio canonum*[121] was compiled by Fulgentius Ferrandus, a deacon of the church at Carthage (a. 520–547), *ca.* 546/547. It consists of 232 capitula from Eastern and African councils, arranged systematically on an assortment of topics including holy orders. The full texts are not provided; the *Breviatio canonum* contains only the introductions (rather than simply the incipits) to the canons.[122]

The *Breviatio canonum* contains five canons which deal with the *cursus honorum* and the interstices. Canon I of the collection, based on Canon II of the Council of Nicaea, Canon XIII of Sardica, and Canon III of Laodicea, states that neophytes are not to be ordained.[123]

---

[120] Roger E. Reynolds, "Law, Canon: to Gratian", *The Dictionary of the Middle Ages*, vol. 7, ed. Joseph R. Strayer (New York: Charles Scribner's Sons, 1986), p. 395.

[121] Charles Munier, ed., *Concilia Africae A. 345–A. 525*, CCSL 149, pp. 287–306.

[122] Reynolds, "Law, Canon", p. 400.

[123] Munier, *Concilia Africae*, p. 287.

Canon II is from a Council of Sufutela, the present day city of Sbeitla, in the province of Byzacena in North Africa; the date of the council is unknown, though was likely after 416.[124]. Canon II states that members of the laity elected to the episcopate must pass through all the ecclesiastical grades of the ministry in a year:

> Ut quicumque laicus ad episcopatum eligitur prius annum in ministerio ecclesiastico per omnes gradus transeat.[125]

There is no account of a Council of Sufutela (if one ever existed) extant; the *Breviatio canonum* is the earliest mention of the canon from the council,[126] which was later ascribed to Innocent I. Interestingly, Cresconius makes no mention of it in the *Concordia canonum*. Canon II shares much in common with the fifth-century letter to Victor (*Fragmentum* 10) of Gelasius, and the sixth-century Canon XX of Braga I.

Canon VIII reiterates Canon XVII of the Council of Ancyra, directing that bishops who are not received shall not take up another church, but will sit with the presbyters.[127] Canon LXXXV, from Canon XI of the Council of Neocaesarea, states that presbyters shall not be ordained before thirty years of age.[128] Canon CXXI of the collection, based on Canon IX (really Canon IV) of the third Council of Carthage, states that no clergy or virgins are to be consecrated before twenty-five years of age.[129]

While some legislative sources of the *cursus* and the interstices are included in the *Breviatio canonum*, what is perhaps more significant are the sources that are not included, especially Canon XIII of the Council of Sardica. The *Breviatio canonum* of Ferrandus is significant because it had such a widespread circulation in Europe in the early medieval period.[130]

b. The *Concordia canonum*

A much more important patristic canonical collection is the *Crisconii episcopi Africani Breviarium canonicum*, also known as the *Concordia*

---

[124] *Cf.* Munier, *Concilia Africae*, p. xxxvii.

[125] Munier, *Concilia Africae*, p. 287.

[126] MAASSEN, p. 184.

[127] Munier, *Concilia Africae*, p. 287.

[128] Munier, *Concilia Africae*, p. 294.

[129] Munier, *Concilia Africae*, p. 297.

[130] Reynolds, "Law, Canon", p. 400.

canonum,[131] compiled in the sixth or seventh century.[132] Attributed to Cresconius, the collection is said to have been drawn up by an African bishop as a supplement to the *Breviatio canonum* of Ferrandus. The canons are arranged systematically. The *Concordia canonum* appears to be based on the Roman *Collectio Dionysiana*; some have speculated that it could have been drawn up by Dionysius Exiguus himself.[133] Reynolds refers to the *Concordia canonum* as the "systematized version" of the *Collectio Dionysiana*.[134] Hence, in examining the *Concordia canonum* of Cresconius, two major canonistic collections are being surveyed, which were widely distributed in Europe and Italy. Moreover, because of the close identification with the *Dionysiana*, a Roman collection, the *Concordia canonum* is a sample of both a late patristic Roman and Italian canonistic collection.

The *Concordia canonum* includes not only conciliar statements, but papal letters and decretals as well. It contains much material about the church's ministry, including texts relating to the *cursus honorum* and the interstices. For instance, the *Concordia canonum* includes the letter of Innocent (*Epistle* 37) enjoining a time of testing, clearly against the hasty ordination of lectors, acolytes, deacons, and "priests,"[135] as well as his directions concerning the ordination of monks.[136] The decretal of Siricius (*Epistle* 1) on the *cursus* and the interstices is included,[137] as well as the parallel decretals of Zosimus (*Epistle* 9),[138] Celestine (*Epistle* 4.5),[139] and Gelasius (*Epistle* 14.2).[140] The decretal of Celestine against the ordination of lay men is incorporated (*Epistle* 5.2).[141]

---

[131] *PL* 88.829–942.

[132] Reynolds, "Law, Canon", p. 400.

[133] Reynolds, "Law, Canon", p. 400.

[134] Reynolds, "Law, Canon", p. 400.

[135] *PL* 88.834–835.

[136] *PL* 88.836.

[137] *PL* 88.835,836.

[138] *PL* 88.835.

[139] *PL* 88.836.

[140] *PL* 88.837–838.

[141] *PL* 88.895–896.

From the conciliar sources, the *Concordia canonum* reproduces Canon II of the Council of Nicaea[142] as well as canons IX and X dealing with testing and suitability for ordination.[143] Canon III (IV) of the Council of Laodicea which also prohibits the ordination of neophytes,[144] and Canon XII of the Council of Laodicea which enjoins a time of testing for those to be promoted to the episcopate[145] are also included.

Canon XIII from the Council of Sardica appears in the *Concordia canonum*.[146] The text of the Sardican canon had been subtly, though significantly, modified in the *Breviarium canonicum*. Instead of saying that candidates for the episcopate must have first served as lectors, *et officii diaconii et ministerio presbyterii*, the text has been altered to read: *et officii diaconii aut ministerio presbyterii*. Instead of serving in the diaconate *and* the presbyterate, the modified canon says diaconate *or* the presbyterate. The source of this change is undoubtedly the Roman *Dionysiana* of the early sixth century. Andrieu asks:

> Pourquoi donc Denys a-t-il modifié son modèle?—L'explication la plus simple serait qu'il a voulu éviter de le mettre en contradiction avec les usages qu'il voyait régner à Rome.[147]

The omissions of reference to the diaconate as a step in the *cursus* have already been noted in the letter of Gelasius to Victor and in the letter of Pelagius to Bonus. The omission of the diaconate is apparent in the papal biographies as well.[148]

Canon XVII of the Council of Ancyra regarding bishops who are not accepted in the churches is included in the *Concordia canonum*.[149] Canon XI of the Council of Neocaesarea limiting the age of presbyters to thirty is incorporated as well.[150]

The *Concordia canonum* of Cresconius is an important collection for two reasons. First, all the major papal and conciliar texts dealing with the

---

[142] *PL* 88.838–839.
[143] *PL* 88.873.
[144] *PL* 88.839.
[145] *PL* 88.833.
[146] *PL* 88.839.
[147] Andrieu, *Les Ordines Romani*, vol. 3, p. 564.
[148] See below.
[149] *PL* 88.857.
[150] *PL* 88.875.

cursus and the interstices are represented in it. Second, since it was so widely distributed, like the *Breviatio canonum* of Ferrandus, the *Concordia canonum* became an important vehicle for the transmission of papal and conciliar texts concerning the *cursus honorum* and the interstices throughout the medieval church.

c. The *Collectio vetus gallica*

The third canonical collection in this period to be examined is the *Collectio vetus gallica.*[151] Formerly known as the *Collectio Andegavensis II*, it is the most important of the many early Gallican canon law collections. The collection was compiled between 585 and 626/627, somewhere in Burgundy, probably Lyons; its most likely author is Etherius of Lyons.[152] There was a wide distribution of the *Vetus gallica*, which underwent many recensions and redactions, becoming an important source for many later canonistic collections.

The author of the collection was a reformer concerned with the structure and administration of the church and its properties. One of his concerns was ordination. Cap. IV.13 of the *Vetus gallica* includes Canon XIII of the Council of Sardica, albeit in a much truncated form:

> Si forte aut dives aut scolasticus de foro aut aministracione episcopus fuerit postulatus, ut non prius ordinetur nisi et lectores munere et officio diaconi aut presbyteri perfunctus, ut per singulos gradus, si dignus fuerit, ascendat ad culmen episcopatus.[153]

Nonetheless, all the ingredients of the *cursus honorum* are present in this recension of Sardica XIII; what is omitted is any rationale for the *cursus*.

A portion from the letter of Zosimus to Hesychius (*Epistle* 9.III.5) outlining the *cursus* and the interstices is incorporated in cap. V.4a, under the heading of the third Council of Arles (a. 538).[154] Cap. IV.10, ascribed to Canon VI of the Council of Arles III, though actually it is Canon I of the Council of Arles, 524), directs that deacons be at least twenty-five years old, and that presbyters be at least thirty years of age at the time of

---

[151] H. Mordek, ed., *Kirchenrecht und Reform im Frankenreich: Die Collectio Vetus Gallica, dei Älteste systematische Kanonessammlung des fränkischen Gallien*, Beitrage zur Geschichte und Quellenkunde des Mittelaters, vol. 1 (Berlin: Walter de Gruyter, 1975).

[152] Reynolds, "Law, Canon", p. 402.

[153] *Vetus gallica*, pp. 373–374.

[154] *Vetus gallica*, pp. 386–388.

ordination.[155] The ordination rubrics from the *Statuta ecclesiae antiqua*, with its sequence of grades, is also included in cap. V.4c-l.[156] The letters of Gregory I to Syagrius *et al.* (*Reg.* 9.218) appears in cap. IV.13b.[157]

The *Collectio vetus gallica* included significant conciliar and papal statements on the interstices and the *cursus honorum*, and was an important vehicle for their transmission to the Gallican church in the late patristic period and well into the Middle Ages.

6. Ordination Liturgies

While sequential ordination and the interstices are clearly reflected in the papal, conciliar, and canonical texts, patristic liturgical texts are also valuable sources in tracing the development of the *cursus honorum*. This section will consider the so-called Leonine Sacramentary of the Roman Church, the Gallican *Statuta ecclesiae antiqua*, and the Hispanic *Liber ordinum*.

a. The Leonine Sacramentary

After the *Apostolic Tradition* of Hippolytus from the early third century, the next evidence of the Roman liturgy, including ordination rites, is the Leonine Sacramentary.[158] Questions arise over the nomenclature of this book, since it is neither a sacramentary nor is it from the pontificate of Leo the Great. It is not a complete liturgical book, thus no celebrant could ever have used it liturgically. Rather, the Leonine Sacramentary is based upon a series of *libelli* that have been assembled chronologically by month, rather than topically. The work is often referred to as the Sacramentary of Verona, after the city where the library which preserves the manuscript is found; for example, L. C. Mohlberg has named his edition the *Sacramentarium Veronense*. On the other hand, since there is another manuscript

---

[155] *Vetus gallica*, pp. 371-372.

[156] *Vetus gallica*, pp. 388-390.

[157] *Vetus gallica*, p. 375.

[158] L. C. Mohlberg *et al.*, eds., *Sacramentarium Veronense*, Rerum Ecclesiasticarum Documenta, Series Major Fontes I (Rome: Herder, 1956), pp. 118–122; C. L. Feltoe, ed., *Sacramentarium Leonianum*, (Cambridge: 1896) pp. 119–123.

called the "Sacramentary of Verona" (a Gregorian type: MS LXXXVI) in the same city, J. Deshusses recommends keeping the older title, the Leonine, despite the problems associated with it, for reasons of clarity.[159]

From the year 1735, when F. Biachini attributed the collection to Leo the Great, there has been much scholarly debate over the date of the *Leonensis*.[160] For instance, Cyril Vogel locates its date of origin between 558–590.[161] In contrast, Paul Bradshaw dates the collection as seventh century.[162] In either case, the *Leonensis* is an example of Roman ordination prayers within the patristic era. The ordination texts are located in the material for the month of September. The *Leonensis* contains ordination prayers for a bishop, deacon, and presbyter in that sequence; there are no provisions for appointments of subdeacons or any of the other minor offices in the manuscript. Only the ordination prayers for the major orders are extant. Rubrical directions and other liturgical material are not included.

Since normally the sequence of ordination rites corresponds to the hierarchical sequence of the grades, i.e., bishop, presbyter, and deacon (or deacon, presbyter, bishop), it is significant that the sequence of prayers in the Leonine is: *consecratio episcoporum, benedictio super diaconos,* and *consecratio presbyteri.* Is this a reflection of a *cursus* where the presbyterate does not always follow from the diaconate and does not necessarily lead to the episcopate? This situation would accord with the modifications to Canon XIII of the Council of Sardica already noted in the *Dionysiana.* Later, when the biographical details of the bishops of Rome will be examined, it will be seen that many popes during the patristic age (especially the Byzantine period) had never been presbyters. In this case, the ordering of the ministries in the Leonine Sacramentary would be an accurate reflection of the Roman *cursus* in the late patristic period. Conversely, the ordering may simply reflect the close collaboration between the bishop and the deacons in the church of Rome.

[159] J. Deshusses, "Les Sacramentaires: Etat actuel de la recherche," *Archiv für Liturgiewissenschaft* 24 (1982), pp. 24–25.

[160] For a summary of the debate, see C. Vogel, *Medieval Liturgy: An Introduction to the sources,* trans. & eds. William Story and Neils Rasmussen (Washington: The Pastoral Press, 1986), pp. 38–43.

[161] Vogel, *Medieval Liturgy,* p. 40.

[162] Paul Bradshaw, *Ordination Rites of the Ancient Churches of East and West* (New York: Pueblo Publishing Co., 1990), p. 14.

Within the prayers themselves, there is no evidence of movement from one office to another, with one exception, the prayer of blessing over deacons. The final petition contains the words:

.... In moribus eorum praecepta tua fulgeant, ut suae castitatis exemplo imitationem sancte plebis adquira[n]t, et bonum conscientiae testimonium praeferentes in Christo firmi et stabiles perseverent, dignisque successibus de inferiori gradu per gratiam tuam capere potiora mereantur: per....[163]

The bishop prays that the new deacons may reflect God's commandments in their conduct so that by the example of their chastity they might win the imitation of the people, *and* that by displaying the testimony of a good conscience they may be strong and stable in Christ. Finally the bishop prays that ".... by fitting advancements from a lower rank [they] may be worthy through your grace to take up higher things; through..."[164] The final words are an allusion to the First Letter to Timothy (1 Tim. 3.13). It was found in the *Apostolic Tradition*,[165] and is reflected in Western liturgies, and through them to the ordinals of the Prayer Book tradition.[166]

While there is no explicit *ita ut* structure to the final petition, it seems clear that advancement from the lower grade to the "higher things," i.e. the presbyterate or the episcopate, is conditional upon the deacons' conduct, chastity, testimony of a good conscience, and strength and stability in Christ. These interests reflect the classical purpose behind the *cursus honorum*, namely, testing and examination.

What is indisputable in the prayer is that the diaconate at the time of the composition of this prayer was no longer perceived as a permanent office; it was a transitional office, that is, a step or grade of the *cursus honorum*. What may be asked, though, is to which office or offices does "higher things" refer: the presbyterate or the episcopate, or both? From what is

---

[163] Mohlberg, *Sacramentarium Veronense*, p. 121.

[164] trans. Bradshaw, *Ordination Rites*, p. 217.

[165] ".... ut sine reprehensione et puro more ministrans, gradum maioris ordinis assequator...." Botte, *La Tradition Apostolique*, VIII, p. 26.

[166] ".... to have a ready will to observe all spiritual disciple; that they having always the testimony of a good conscience, and continuing stable and strong in thy Son Christ, may so well behave themselves in this inferior office, that they may be found worthy to be called unto the higher ministries in the Church; through..." *Book of Common Prayer*, Canada, 1921, p. 622.

known of the history of the Roman church in this period[167] it most likely refers to both. As David Power has commented on this text:

> The prayer for the ordination of deacons sees ecclesiastical office as a hierarchical ascent from the lowest ranks to the highest, within the body of the clergy. It is taken for granted that the newly ordained deacons should aspire to higher office, and so the prayer asks that as a result of the way they fulfil their office, they might be deemed worthy of advancement to a higher one. This higher grade would have been either the episcopate or the presbyterate.[168]

H.B. Porter commenting on the same text, offers a slightly different perspective:

> The diaconate had greater prestige in Rome than the presbyterate, and was not normally viewed as a preliminary to the latter. The final clause in the deacon's prayer, therefore, can hardly refer to advancement to the priesthood (as is often supposed nowadays), but either to the weighty responsibilities of the "cardinal deacons" themselves, or to the possibility of advancement to the episcopate. It was from the college of Roman deacons that the bishop of that city was normally chosen, and consecrated to the episcopate without passage through the presbyterate.[169]

There are two instances in the text where the language of *gradus* is used. In the blessing over the deacon, the prayer includes a reference to the threefold ministry: ....*sacri muneris servitutem trinis gradibus ministrorum nomini tuo militare constituens....*[170] The word *gradus* also appears in the prayer over the presbyter, whose office is referred to as the second dignity—*secundi meriti*.[171] The close association between the word *gradus* and the *cursus honorum* has already been noted. It is significant that this language appears in a liturgical text.

b. The *Statuta ecclesiae antiqua*

One of the most influential documents in the history of medieval ordination rites is found within the *Statuta ecclesiae antiqua* (SEA), which

---

[167] *Cf.* M. Andrieu "La carrière ecclésiastique des papes et les documents liturgiques de Moyen Age," *Révue des sciences réligieuses*, 21 (1947).

[168] Power, *Ministers of Christ*, p. 72.

[169] H. B. Porter Jr., *The Ordination Prayers of the Ancient Western Churches* (London: SPCK, 1967), p. 13.

[170] Mohlberg, *Sacramentarium Veronense*, p. 120.

[171] Mohlberg, *Sacramentarium Veronense*, p. 122.

is technically a canonical collection.[172] The SEA is a small book for ordinations; it contains a profession of faith, disciplinary canons, and a series of rubrical directions for ordination rituals. In the *Collectio hispana*, the SEA is identified as the decrees of the fourth Council of Carthage (398); it is sometimes referred to as the Council of Valence (374). The SEA was composed in Gaul in the late fifth century (*ca.* 475), probably by Gennadius of Marseilles. Its usages are reflected in the Gelasian sacramentaries, the *Ordines*, and the *Pontificale Romanum.* Its ordination rubrics were found in the ordination rites of the Roman Catholic Church until the Pontifical of Paul VI (1972); many of its directions are reflected (with modifications) in the Ordinal attached to the *Book of Common Prayer* from the time of the Reformation to the present.

The introduction to the SEA deals with the qualifications for episcopal ordination in terms of character and faith:

> I. Qui episcopus ordinandus est, ante examinetur si natura prudens est, si docilibus, si moribus temperatus, si vita castus, si sobrius, si semper sui negotii, si humilibus affabilis, si misericors, si litteratus, si in lege Domini instructus, si in scripturarum sensibus cautus, si in dogmatibus ecclesiasticis exercitatus, et ante omnia si fidei documenta verbis simplicibus asserat, idest Patrem et Filium et Spiritum sanctum unum Deum esse confirmans....
>
> .... Cum in his omnibus examinatus inventus fuerit plene instructus, tunc consensu clericorum et laicorum et conventu totius provinciae episcoporum, maximeque metropolitani vel auctoritate vel praesentia ordinetur episcopus, suscepto in nomine Christi episcopatu, non suae delectationi nec suis motibus, sed his patrum definitionibus adquiescat.[173]

This particular text from the SEA is significant because there is no indication of, or reference to, the clerical *cursus*. The list of qualities sought in a bishop is structured like something out the pastoral epistles (e.g. 1 Tim 3.1 ff.), which may well have been the intent of the author.

Although the *cursus honorum* is not mentioned, its underlying concerns are: examination of character, holiness of life, preparation in the law of the Lord, the understanding of Scripture, and the teaching of the church. The dearth of any references to the *cursus* is significant, but not in determining whether it was normative or not. As noted earlier, the *Liber regulae*

---

[172] Munier, *Concilia Galliae*, pp. 164–185.

[173] Munier, *Concilia Galliae*, pp. 164–166; Charles Munier, *Les Statuta Ecclesiae Antiqua* (Paris: Presses Universitaires de France, 1960) , pp. 181–185.

pastoralis of Gregory the Great is similarly lacking in any explicit references to the *cursus honorum* though Gregory himself was an ardent supporter of it.[174]

The canons containing the ordination rituals of the SEA are important in determining the shape of the Gallican *cursus* at the end of the fifth century.[175] The rituals are set out according to this sequence: bishop, presbyter, deacon, subdeacon, acolyte, exorcist, lector, doorkeeper, psalmist; rites for virgins and widows follow.[176] According to Munier, the inclusion of the office of psalmist was anachronistic even in the fifth century.[177]

Many of the ordination rubrics of the SEA reflect those of the *Apostolic Tradition* and other sources, rather than the contemporary Gallican usages.[178] There is reason to question whether the offices mentioned in the SEA, and the sequence in which they appear, are genuinely Gallican. For example, Bradshaw notes that in other early Gallican sources there is no trace of the existence of the offices of acolyte or psalmist, apart from one inscription about an acolyte in Lyons in 517.[179] Munier makes the conjecture that the sequence in the SEA was modelled after the third-century sequence mentioned by Cornelius, or the interstices texts. Munier, with Faivre, also suggests that the sequence could have been based in the sequence found in the *Orationes solemnes* for Good Friday.[180]

No precise indication is given within the SEA texts as to whether or not a cleric would expect to receive all nine orders in succession. From the sixth century sources it is clear that often the *cursus* and the interstices were neglected in the Gallican church, much to the exasperation of Gregory the Great. If a prescribed sequence of grades had been observed, it is not certain that such a sequence would be that of the SEA. In the end, however,

---

[174] The introduction to the SEA became popular with the compilers of the later canonistic collections. It is found in the *Hibernensis*, Pseudo-Isidorian Decretals, the collections of Regino of Prüm and Burchard of Worms, and in the *Collectio in V libris*.

[175] *Cf.* Bernard Botte, "Le Rituel d'ordination des Statuta Ecclesiae Antiqua," *Recherches de théologie ancienne et médiévale* 11 (1939), pp. 223–241.

[176] Munier, *Concilia Galliae*, pp. 181–185; Munier, *Les Statuta*, pp. 95–99.

[177] Munier, *Les Statuta*, p. 175.

[178] Bradshaw, *Ordination Rites*, p. 15.

[179] Bradshaw, *Ordination Rites*, p. 102.

[180] Munier, *Les Statuta*, pp. 170ff; Alexandre Faivre, *Naissance d'une Hiérarchie: Les premières étapes du cursus clerical*, *Théologie Historique*, vol 40 (Paris: Éditions Beauchesne, 1977), p. 182; Reynolds, *Ordinals of Christ*, p. 30.

the sequence of grades in the SEA became universal throughout the Western church.

The ordinatin rubrics of the *Statuta ecclesiae antiqua* were often included in the medieval canonistic collections.[181]

c. The *Liber ordinum*

The liturgical texts of the early Hispanic ordination rites are found in the *Liber ordinum*,[182] the ritual used in Spain before 712. The present manuscript of the *Liber ordinum* (LO), edited by Dom Marius Férotin in 1904, dates from the eleventh century, yet the biddings and ordination prayers themselves date from the sixth century.

The ordination rites begin with various prayers for boys who are entering the service of the church. For example, the LO contains a prayer over children who wish to receive the tonsure, followed by a prayer over a child entering a school, then a prayer for one who has been tonsured for the service of God, followed by a rite for entering the clerical state. These preliminary rites are followed by rites for the ordination of sacristans and of those committed to the care of the library and scriptorium. There is a blessing over one who has reached puberty: *ordo super eum qui barbam tangere cupit.* This prayer is followed by the ordinations of a subdeacon, a deacon, an archdeacon, a *primiclericum*, a presbyter, an archpresbyter, and lastly the blessings of abbots and abbesses.[183] No text for the ordination of a bishop remains in the LO, although there is a eucharistic rite for an episcopal consecration. Other Hispanic liturgical books, such as

---

[181] Of the systematic collections cited, they are found in the *Hibernensis*, the *Dacheriana*, the Pseudo-Isidorian Decretals, the collections of Anselm of Lucca and Bonizo, and in the *Panormia* and *Decretum* of Ivo of Chartres. On the transmission of the SEA, *cf.* M. Coquin, "Le sort des «Statuta Ecclesiae antiqua» dans les Collections canonique jusqu'a la «Concordia» de Gratian", *Recherches de Théologie Ancienne et Médiévale* 28 (1961), pp. 193–224.

[182] Marius Férotin, ed., *Le Liber Ordinum en Usage dans l'Eglise Wisigothique et Mozarabe d'Espagne*, Monumenta Ecclesiae Liturgica, vol. 5 (Paris: Librairies de Firmin- Didot et C., 1904).

[183] Férotin, *Liber Ordinum*, cols. 37–59.

the *Antiphonary of Léon* and the *Liber communicus*, provide other elements of an episcopal ordination rite.[184]

No discernible *cursus* between the grades is evident in this sequence of rites in the LO. At the same time, within the texts themselves evidence can be seen of sequential movement through the grades. For instance, in the ordination of a subdeacon the following petition is found:

> .... respice, quesumus, super hunc famulum tuum Illum, quem ad subdiaconii officium provehimus testimonio seniorum....[185]

This text indicates that the candidate for the subdiaconate has been in a period of training and examination, and has been found worthy to be "promoted" to the subdiaconate. It is difficult to ascertain from which of the offices in the LO the subdeacon might have been promoted; perhaps it was the office of sacristan, or simply the clerical state.[186] In any case, clearly the subdiaconate itself was intended to lead to "higher things" as the *completuria* of the prayer makes clear:

> ....Karitatis in se, te opitulante, conservet premium: ut mortificata vitia virtutibus crescat, et bene conversando ad superiorem gradum, te annuente, perveniat..... Amen.[187]

Here the bishop asks that retaining the reward of chastity, mortification of faults, growth in virtue, and by good behaviour, the new subdeacon may attain to a "higher grade".

The same sort of petition is found in the deacon's ordination rite, in the blessing of the deacon. The bishop prays:

> ....Firmus in Christo perseveret et stabilis, dignoque successu semper a paruo ad maiora provehi mereatur: ut Sancti Spiritus gratia comitante, devotus in iudicio Filii tui Domini nostri, integram sibi rationem gaudeat constitisse. Rogamus gloriam tuam....[188]

---

[184] *Cf.* Roger Reynolds, "The Ordination Rite in Medieval Spain: Hispanic, Roman, and Hybrid," *Santiago, Saint-Denis, and Saint Peter: The Reception of the Roman Liturgy in Léon-Castile in 1080*, ed. Bernard F. Reilly (New York: Fordham University Press, 1985), p. 132.

[185] Férotin, *Liber Ordinum*, col. 47.

[186] From the contemporary works of Isidore, one might posit that it was the lectorate which led to the subdiaconate; *cf. Etymologiae*, DEO, and so forth.

[187] Férotin, *Liber Ordinum*, col. 47.

[188] Férotin, *Liber Ordinum*, col. 49.

The prayer asks that the new deacon may ever merit promotion to greater things, presumably the presbyterate and the episcopate (or possibly the archidiaconate and the archipresbyterate). Like its Roman counterpart, the Leonine Sacramentary, the source for this petition is clearly I Timothy (although the *Liber ordinum* is more faithful to the original sense). By comparison, no similar reference to promotion to "higher things" is found in the ordination of a presbyter.

7. Patristic Literature on Holy Orders

In addition to papal and conciliar documents, there is an abundance of patristic literature on the topic of ordained ministry, much of which contains evidence of the development of the clerical *cursus* and the interstices. This section will examine merely a sampling of the major sources on the topic, principally from Western patristic sources: the writings of Jerome (*ca.* 347–419/420), the pseudo-Hieronymian *De septem ordinibus ecclesiae*, the writings of Isidore of Seville (*ca.* 560–636), and the sixth-century texts of the *Liber pontificalis*. Two Eastern sources will be examined: the *De sacerdotio* of John Chrysostom (*ca.* 347–407) and the sixth-century pseudo-Dionysian *De ecclesiastica hierarchia*.

a. Jerome

The works of Jerome (*ca.* 347–419/420) are important sources for the history of holy orders. Two of Jerome's letters which bear on the *cursus honorum* will be examined: the letter to Evangelus the Presbyter, and the letter to Oceanum.

The Letter of Jerome to Evangelus the Presbyter, *Epistle* 146, is an important historical source for knowledge of ancient Alexandrian ordination practices; the letter is often cited as an instance of patristic "presbyterianism," for Jerome states that "bishop" and "presbyter" were two names for the same office in the early church. The letter testifies to the strained relations between the powerful deacons and the more humble presbyters of the church of Rome. In this letter Jerome also reveals something about the state of the *cursus honorum*:

> 2. ....qui provehitur, de minori ad maius provehitur. aut igitur ex presbytero ordinetur diaconus, ut presbyter minor diacono conprobetur, in quem crescit ex parvo, aut

si ex diacono ordinatur presbyter, noverit se lucris minorem, sacerdotio esse maiorem. et ut sciamus traditiones apostolicas sumptas de veteri testamento: quod Aaron et filii eius atque levitae in templo fuerunt, hoc sibi episcopi et presbyteri et diaconi in ecclesia vindicent.[189]

Thus, Jerome concludes his arguments on the superiority of the presbyterate over the diaconate. He simply states the obvious when he writes: "whoever is promoted, is promoted from the lesser to the greater"; this is indicative of how standard promotions from one grade to another were at the time of this letter. Jerome satirically suggests that presbyters be ordained deacons if the diaconate is in fact a superior grade, or if deacons are ordained presbyters, let them realise that the presbyterate is greater in the "priesthood" (though lower on the pay scale), implying that movement from the diaconate to the presbyterate was fairly normative. Or, Jerome could be simply underlining the hierarchical superiority of the presbyter over the deacon.

On the other hand, by the mere fact that Jerome poses the notion that presbyters might be ordained deacons—a ridiculous thought because such an act would be a demotion—Jerome insinuates that not all presbyters had been deacons. For such a suggestion to be made, even in jest, seems implicitly to suggest that some had been ordained to the presbyterate without prior ordination to the diaconate.

Jerome does not mention a deacon becoming a bishop. While it is known that in Rome many deacons became bishops (at least five during Jerome's own life time), the obvious sequence remains from deacon to presbyter.[190]

A second Hieronymian text is the letter to Oceanum, *Epistle* 69 (*ca.* 395–397), in which Jerome utters the following invective against the practice of ordaining members of the laity (and others) to the episcopate:

9. ....non neophytum, ne in superbiam elatus in iudicium incidat diaboli: mirari satis non queo, quae hominum tanta sit caecitas de uxoribus ante baptismum disputare et rem in baptismate mortuam, immo cum Christo vivificatam, in calumniam trahere, cum tam apertum evidensque praeceptum nemo custodiat. heri

---

[189] I. Hilberg, ed., CSEL 56.311–312.

[190] Curiously, *Epistle* 146.2, to Evangelus the Presbyter, is found in two of the later systematically arranged canonical collections cited in this study: the collections of Anselm of Lucca, and Deusdedit. Reynolds points out that *Epistle* 146 appears in the early medieval canonical collections only five times during five centuries, "again, in rather isolated instances". Roger Reynolds, "Patristic 'Presbyterianism' in the Early Medieval Theology of Sacred Orders", *Mediaeval Studies* 45 (1983), p. 237.

catechumenus, hodie pontifex; heri in amphitheatro, hodie in ecclesia; vespere in circo, mane in altari; dudum fautor strionum, nunc virginum consecrator: num ignorabat apostolus tergiversationes nostras et argumentorum ineptias nesciebat? qui dixit: unius uxoris virum, ipse mandavit inreprehensibilem, sobrium, prudentem, ornatum, hospitalem, doctorem, modestum, non vinolentum, non percussorem, non litigiosum, non neophytum. ad omnia claudimus oculos, solas videmus uxores. quod autem ait: ne in superbiam elatus incidat in iudicium diaboli, quis non exemplo verum probet? ignorat momentaneus sacerdos humilitatem et mansuetudinem rusticorum, ignorat blanditias Christianas, nescit se ipse contemnere, de dignitate transfertur ad dignitatem; non ieiunavit, non flevit, non mores suos saepe reprehendit et adsidua meditatione correxit, non substantiam pauperibus erogavit: de cathedra, quod dicitur, ad cathedram, id est de superbia ad superbiam. iudicium autem et ruina diaboli, nulli dubium, quin adrogantia sit. incidunt in eam, qui in puncto horae necdum discipuli iam magistri sunt....[191]

In this portion of the letter Jerome attacks bishops who rise suddenly from the catechumenate. He complains that "he who is not yet a disciple, is already the master." Jerome pokes fun at a man who yesterday was a catechumen, and today is a *pontifex*; who yesterday was in the amphitheatre, today is in a church; who in the evening is at the race-track, in the morning is at the altar. For Jerome, the "instant priest"—*momentaneus sacerdos*— lacks both the virtue and the necessary preparation for episcopal office.

Epistle 69.9 is significant in two respects. For one thing, the recipient of Jerome's attack is Ambrose of Milan, whom Jerome disliked intensely.[192] As David Wiesen has commented:

> It could only have been petty jealousy of Ambrose's powerful position that led Jerome to mock him as a croaking raven, dressed in coloured feathers of other birds. Jerome could not forgive Ambrose for having reached so high a station while he himself remained a humble monk.[193]

For another thing, the letter reflects Jerome's antipathy to the practice of *per saltum* ordination. Jerome's intense dislike of what was once a common and accepted practice demonstrates the extent to which the *cursus honorum* and the interstices, only half a century after the Council of Sardica, had become valued as preparation and testing for episcopal office, for it is these things which the *momentaneus sacerdos* lacks. The custom of ordaining men immediately to the episcopate must have been common

---

[191] CSEL 54.697–699.

[192] David Wiesen, *St. Jerome as a Satirist: A Study in Christian Latin Thought and Letters* (Ithica, New York: Cornell University Press, 1964), p. 83.

[193] Wiesen, *St. Jerome*, p. 244.

enough for Jerome to have made such an "anonymous" attack on Ambrose. The letter is evidence of the general inappropriateness felt by some in the church of ordaining neophytes, catechumens, and the laity directly to the higher offices.[194]

b. John Chrysostom—*De sacerdotio*

Along with the *Liber regulae pastoralis* of Gregory the Great and *De fuga* of Gregory Nazianzus, *De sacerdotio* of John Chrysostom (*ca.* 347–407) is one of the great patristic treatises on ordained ministry. *De sacerdotio* describes the office and work of a bishop. The fictitious backdrop is the story of two lay men (one of them named Basil) trying to avoid capture and ordination to the episcopate by the people. In the story Basil is betrayed by the narrator of *De sacerdotio* and is ordained directly to the episcopate. The story itself is an important statement about the *cursus*: it would appear that for Chrysostom it was not yet essential and that the ordination of members of the laity to the episcopate was still common practice.

In the third chapter of *De sacerdotio*, Chrysostom deals with the issue of clerical promotion. Chrysostom laments the fact that candidates for the episcopate are often elected on spurious grounds: either they come from distinguished families, or are wealthy, or are simply ambitious. These are the very concerns raised in Canon XIII of the Council of Sardica. Chrysostom notes that even recent converts to catholic Christianity are elected, contrary to the canons of Nicaea and Sardica. This admission also reflects the reality that in the fourth century the clerical *cursus* was not always observed.

Chrysostom argues that only the best qualified, those who have been spiritually tested, ought to be elected. In Book II he complains: "No one will look for the best qualified man or apply any spiritual test".[195] He writes:

> 15. Again, if a man has spent all his life in the lowest order of the ministry and has reached extreme old age, we will not, simply out of respect for his age, promote him to the next order. What if he should still be unsuitable, even after a lifetime? I

---

[194] *Epistle* 69.9 was often included by the canonists; of the systematic collections cited in this study it is found in the *Collectio canonum* of Anselm of Lucca, the Collection in Seventy-four Titles, and Gratian's *Decretum*.

[195] *PG* 48.652; Graham Neville, trans., *Saint John Chrysostom, Six Books on the Priesthood*, (Crestwood, New York: St. Vladimir's Seminary Press, 1984) p. 89.

do not say this out of disrespect for grey hairs, nor am I laying down a rule that we should entirely exclude from such responsibility those who come from the monastic fraternity. It has turned out that many even from that body have shed lustre upon this office. But I am anxious to show that, if neither piety by itself nor old age alone are sufficient to prove a man worthy of the priesthood, the reasons I have mentioned are hardly likely to do so.[196]

Hence, John Chrysostom excludes a *cursus* from one order to another on the grounds of old age or out of respect. He also rejects the *cursus* on the ground of *honoris* as well:

I once used to deride secular rulers because they distributed honours, not on grounds of inherent merit, but of wealth or seniority or worldly rank. But when I heard that this stupidity had swaggered into our own affairs, I no longer reckoned their actions so strange.[197]

If you want to know the reasons for this scandal, you will find they are like those I mentioned before... They have ready to hand all the pretexts they require. Even the number of existing clergy is sufficient argument, when they have no better. Or they argue that it is advisable not to promote a man to this honour suddenly, but gently and by degrees. And they can find as many other reasons as they want.[198]

John Chrysostom insinuates that there is in practice a *cursus*, which, as long as it is based on *honor* and not ability, is highly undesirable. One of the ironies of *De sacerdotio* is the fact that its author was himself a product of the *cursus honorum*, having been ordained sequentially deacon, presbyter, and bishop.

c. Pseudo-Dionysius—*De ecclesiastica hierarchia*

A patristic writer of significance for the development of the theology of ordered ministry, especially for the later medieval and Byzantine theologians, is an anonymous early sixth-century bishop writing under the pseudonym of Dionysius the Areopagite. The *corpus dionysiarum* was composed in the East, most likely in Syria, and is usually dated *ca.* 500.[199] Central to writings of Pseudo-Dionysius is the concept of "hierarchy"; in the medieval church he was known as the *doctor hierarchicus*. The very

---

[196] *PG* 48.652. Neville, trans., *Priesthood*, p. 90.

[197] *PG* 48.653. Neville, trans., *Priesthood*, p. 91.

[198] *PG* 48.653–654. Neville, trans., *Priesthood*, p. 92.

[199] On the date and provenance of the *corpus dionysiarum*, *cf.* Thomas L. Campbell, *Dionysius the Pseudo-Areopagite: The Ecclesiastical Hierarchy* (Washington: University Press of America, 1981), pp. 2–11.

word *hierarchia*—from *heiros* (sacred) and *arche* (source)—is first found in the works of Pseudo-Dionysius, and appears to be his own innovation.[200] Regarding the influence of Pseudo-Dionysius on the theology of hierarchy, Paul Rorem has said:

> The Dionysian writings profoundly shaped the idea of hierarchy in the Christian tradition, whether a churchly hierarchy of clerical officers or a heavenly hierarchy of angelic beings. They also influenced the overall picture of reality, as it was transmitted down through a vertical structure, as "the order which God himself has established", a concept gladly embraced by Christian monarchs of all kinds. Not only did Dionysius influence the evolution of this concept, but he also created the word *hierarchy* itself, which, with cognates (like *hierarchical*) simply did not exist until the anonymous author invented it to express and to crystallize such thoughts about order. Few writers have ever coined a new word with a broader history in Western thought than the Dionysian neologism *hierarchy*. . .[201]

In both *De coelesti hierarchia* and *De ecclesiastica hierarchia* (DEH) the author affirms that an ordered society is ordained by God. For Pseudo-Dionysius, hierarchy is more than simply a question of rank and order, but is part of the process of mystical union with God. Of particular importance for the development of ordained ministry is *De ecclesiastica hierarchia*. Modelled after the earlier *De coelesti hierarchia* dealing with the nine-fold orders of angels in three triads, the DEH treats "our" (i.e. the earthly) hierarchy of the church in a parallel triadic structure: baptism, eucharist, and the consecration of oils (the sacraments); bishops, presbyters and deacons (those who initiate people into the sacraments); monks, the baptised, and catechumens (those initiated by them). Within this framework "priesthood" is not simply a function within the church, but is a different level of being Christian.[202]

The ecclesiastical hierarchy of bishop, presbyter and deacon is dealt with specifically in the fifth chapter of the DEH, entitled "Sacerdotal

---

[200] Andrew Louth, *Denys the Areopagite* (London: Geoffrey Chapman, 1989), p. 38.

[201] Paul Rorem, *Pseudo-Dionysius: A Commentary on the Texts and an Introduction to their Influence* (New York: Oxford University Press, 1993), p. 19. *Cf.* Bernard Cooke: "It is not entirely accurate to single out the Dionysian influence, because much the same notion of a hierarchical universe was contained in the persistent and dominant Augustinian theology. However, in the Middle Ages the influence of Pseudo-Denis was greatly augmented; he was a frequent object of commentaries and because of his supposed apostolic authority a favourite among the *auctores* appealed to by theologians in their treatises." *Ministry to Word and Sacraments: History and Theology* (Philadelphia: Fortress Press, 1976), p. 577.

[202] *Cf.* Cooke, *Ministry,* p. 83.

Consecrations." The three-fold hierarchy of deacon, presbyter, and bishop parallels the process of sanctification in the three-fold movement of purification, illumination, and perfection, reflecting the mode and operation of God. Here, the hierarchical "superiority" is essential in purifying, illuminating, and perfecting those "below." As Bernard Cooke has commented, this "... situation of bishops and priests in a higher "rank" is an ontological ranking which defines their capacity to heal and sanctify and teach."[203]

A feature of the Pseudo-Dionysian system of hierarchy is the notion that the higher "powers" always contain within themselves the lower. This property is seen particularly in the case of the bishop, *the* "hierarch":

> The divine order of the bishops is the first order of those who contemplate God. It is at the same time the highest and the lowest, because every rank of our hierarchy is summed up and completed in it. Just as we see that every hierarchy terminated in Jesus—so each hierarchy has its term in its own godlike bishop. The power of the pontifical order permeates all of the sacred orders, and it accomplishes the mysteries peculiar to its hierarchical rank in every sacred order.[204]

The notion that the higher orders contain within themselves the functions of the lower is further elaborated with respect to the roles of presbyters and deacons:

> We have shown that the order of bishops has the power of perfecting and consecrating, that the order of priests has the power of illuminating and conducting to the light, that the task of the deacons is purifying and discriminating. Clearly, the function of the pontifical order is not only to perfect, but likewise to enlighten and purify. The order of priests has in it the purifying science as well as the illuminating. However, it is impossible for inferiors to leap over to the functions of their superiors; it is not right for them to attempt such audacity as that. Still, the more divine powers possess along with their own sacred sciences those subordinate in perfection to their own.
>
> Nevertheless, since the sacerdotal orders are images of divine operations, and are arranged in hierarchical distinctions that show illuminations (ordered into first, middle, and last) of the harmonious and unconfused order of the divine energies, they manifest in themselves the regulated and distinct character of the divine operations.[205]

---

[203] Cooke, *Ministry*, pp. 356–357.

[204] DEH 5.1.5. *PG* 3.506; Thomas L. Campbell, trans., *Dionysius the Pseudo-Areopagite: The Ecclesiastical Hierarchy* (Washington, University Press of America, 1981), p. 64.

[205] DEH 5.1.7. *PG* 3.507; Campbell, trans., *Dionysius*, pp. 66–67.

The chapter on "Sacred Consecrations" concludes with a brief description and reflection on the rites of ordination for bishops, presbyters, and deacons.

The ranked ordering of bishop, presbyter and deacon is not new to Pseudo-Dionysius, nor the divine origin of these ministries. What is new is the application of the term of hierarchy within the conceptual framework of Pseudo-Dionysius. Within this framework, the theological rationale behind ecclesiastical order is greatly strengthened and further elaborated, particularly the notion that the higher powers contain within themselves the functions of the lower.

As noted earlier, Edward Schillebeeckx understands the process of sequential ordination as a consequence of the hierarchical system of Pseudo-Dionysius: "In the end the so-called 'lower consecrations' were one step towards the 'higher consecrations'."[206] In *Naissance d'une hiérarchie* Alexandre Faivre arrives at a similar conclusion in an excursus on Pseudo-Dionysius:

> La systématisation de l'idée de hiérarchie, poussée à l'extrême par le Pseudo-Denys, nous amène fort près de l'idée d'ordination par degrés. Si chaque ordre doit rester à sa place et s'il n'est aucune raison de renverser l'ordre voulu par Dieu, si les puissances supérieures, outre leur savoir propre, possèdent aussi la science sacrée des rangs inférieurs, et si ce mécanisme hiérarchique transparaît jusque dans las gradation des cérémonies d'ordination, il serait logique de passer dans tous les ordres les uns après les autres, en commençant par les plus bas, pour avoir accès aux plus hauts. Lorsque, plus tard, l'ordination par degrés deviendra la règle, cette sacralisation apportée à l'idée de hiérarchie par le Pseudo-Denys (si l'on peut se permettre le pléonasme), contribuera fortement à renforcer cette loi. En effet, pour le Pseudo-Denys, la hiérarchie n'est pas d'abord une loi de la nature, c'est avant tout la volonté de Dieu.[207]

Yet within the DEH there is no reference or allusion made to sequential ordination; there is nothing like the *ut per singulos gradus (si dignus fuerit) ascendat ad culmen episcopatus* of Canon XIII of the Council of Sardica. The language of "promotion" reflected in the councils of Neocaesarea, Nicaea and Laodicea, and later in the *De sacerdotio* of John Chrysostom is likewise absent. Again, the text of the DEH contains no suggestion that 'lower consecrations' are one step towards the 'higher consecrations', or following Faivre, that the idea of hierarchy leads us close to the idea of "ordination by degree." The text of the DEH never explicitly refers to one

---

[206] Schillebeeckx, *Church*, p. 158.

[207] Faivre, *Naissance*, pp. 178–179.

order leading the next, that is, ordination by degree or that "il serait logique de passer dans tous les ordres les uns après les autres, en commençant par les plus bas, pour avoir accès aux plus hauts." The design of the DEH is not to be a Church Order, but is limited to the explanation of how the celestial hierarchy is continued in the earthly leading to union with God in the triadic process of purification, illumination, and perfection. Thus, one would not necessarily expect to find such canonical prescriptions within this text. At best, evidence of sequential ordination can only be inferred from the text of the DEH.

One could argue that just as catechumens rise to the ranks of the baptised, only the baptised become monks, and the clergy have ascended from the ranks of the baptised (and monks), so deacons would accordingly become presbyters, and presbyters bishops. There is, however, nothing to suggest that members of the angelic hierarchy—the model of the earthly—ascended from one angelic order to another. Moreover, the DEH does not suggest that the path of sanctification is one that leads up the different ranks of the hierarchy, otherwise, everyone would presumably need to become (successively) a deacon, presbyter, and bishop. The hierarchy is not itself the path to purification, illumination, and perfection, but its *means*. Schillebeeckx links the "principle of substitution", that is, the lower functions are contained within the higher, with sequential ordination. Yet there is no suggestion made in the DEH that a bishop contains the functions of presbyters and deacons (i.e. illuminating and purifying) because he was ever ordained sequentially through these orders. Such a suggestion would give rise to an ascending theology of hierarchy, whereas in the DEH hierarchy operates in a descending fashion. Lastly, the hierarchical structure outline by Pseudo-Dionysius appears rather static. For example, the last chapter of the DEH deals with funeral rites. In the description of the rite, the author notes:

> The divine bishop gathers together the holy company. If the deceased was of the priestly rank, he places him lying down in front of the divine altar and offers the prayer of thanksgiving to God. If he was numbered among the pious monks or holy people, he places him near the honorable sanctuary in front of the entrance of the priests.[208]

> We who have perceived the spiritual meaning of what is done, with Jesus as our guiding light, may say that the bishop does not put the deceased in the place apart for his order without reason, but that he shows in a sacred manner that on the re-

---

[208] DEH 7.2. *PG* 3.556; Campbell, trans., *Dionysius*, p. 81.

generation all will obtain those inheritances in accordance with which they directed their life here below.[209]

Even in death there is a stability and permanence in the hierarchy.

Unquestionably, Pseudo-Dionysius contributed greatly to a systematized, hierarchical understanding of the cosmos, the church and its ordered ministry. Yet whatever theological weight the DEH might lend to the notion of the clerical *cursus* for subsequent generations, it is difficult to appeal to it as a evidence of sequential ordination in the patristic period.

d. *De septem ordinibus ecclesiae*

Along with the *Statuta ecclesiae antiqua*, the pseudo-Hieronymian *Epistle* 12, known as the *De septem ordinibus ecclesiae*[210] (D7OE), became one of the major sources for later patristic treatises on holy order, particularly the *De ecclesiasticis officiis* and the *Etymologiae* of Isidore of Seville. It is the first patristic text in Latin to deal exclusively with the grades of the church's ministry. Falsely attributed to Jerome, the D7OE may have been written as early as the first quarter of the fifth century in southern Gaul, or as late as the early seventh century in Spain.[211] It is the first Latin text devoted to the seven orders of the church's ministry.

The author of the D7OE describes a seven-fold ministry in the following sequence: grave-digger, doorkeeper, lector, subdeacon, deacon, presbyter and bishop. This list is an example of the seventh and eighth-century fascination with the number seven.[212] If the D7OE is an early fifth-century Gallican text, then in comparison with other early fifth-century texts,[213] it is curious that missing from the sequence of grades of the D7OE are the acolyte, the exorcist, and the psalmist, while included is the grave-

---

[209] DEH 7.3.1. *PG* 3.558; Campbell, trans., *Dionysius*, p. 82.

[210] *PL* 30.148–162.

[211] On the dating of the D7OE, see Roger Reynolds, "The Pseudo-Hieronymian *De septem ordinibus ecclesiae*: Notes on it Origins, Abridgements, and Use in Early Medieval Canonical Collections", *Revue Bénédictine* 80 (1970), 238–240.

[212] *Cf.* Roger Reynolds, "At Sixes and Sevens—and Eights and Nines: The Sacred Mathematics of Sacred Orders in the Early Middle Ages", *Speculum*, 54.4 (1979), pp. 670–671.

[213] E.g., Zosimus, *Epistle* 9; canon IV of Council of Toledo I, which directs that incontinent [deacons or] subdeacons are demoted to the order of doorkeeper; there is no mention of the gravediggers.

digger. If the D7OE is a seventh-century Hispanic text, it is curious that it does not reflect the grades of the *Liber ordinum*. Nor does it correspond to the sequences of the *Etymologiae* and the *De ecclesiasticis officiis*, which include the exorcist, and the psalmist, but not the grave-digger; the *Etymologiae* includes the acolyte while the DEO does not.

In the D7OE the author reproaches a bishop or an archbishop for intimidating the orders of ministry beneath him. Pseudo-Jerome makes the point that each grade, from gravedigger to presbyter, is as necessary to the bishop as the body is to the head. In outlining the various offices, the author in no way indicates that one office is preparatory to the next. In the description of the grave-digger, it would seem that such an office holder actually did dig graves. Given that boys entering the service of the church entered as lectors, it is difficult to see the office of grave-digger as a regular part of the clerical *cursus*. On the other hand, the author uses the word *gradus*—step—to describe each grade as though one did lead from the lower to the higher.

e. Isidore of Seville

Isidore of Seville (*ca.* 560–636) is commonly regarded as the last of the patristic writers. Along with the Hispanic councils and the *Liber ordinum*, the works of Isidore are valuable sources of information about the late patristic Hispanic church. His works are a source of knowledge for many aspects of church life, including holy orders. Here Isidore's treatment of the *cursus honorum* will be examined as evidenced in the *De ecclesiasticis officiis* (DEO) and the *Etymologiae*.

Between *ca.* 598–615 Isidore wrote his *De ecclesiasticis officiis*, a work which addresses the ordered ministries of the church. Isidore must have had knowledge of the Gallican sequence of grades, since the DEO contains extracts from the SEA. In Book II, chapters 5–15, of the DEO Isidore lists and discusses "priests", presbyters, deacons, sacristans, subdeacons, lectors, psalmists, exorcists, and doorkeepers.[214] With the inclusion of the sacristans (*custodes sacraria*), who are really part of the diaconate, the number of ecclesiastical grades in the DEO is nine. The unusual sequence is typical of the Hispanic *cursus* in which the lector was superior to the exorcist.

---

[214] *De ecclesiasticis officiis*, ed. Christopher M. Lawson, CCSL 113 (Turnhout: Brepols, 1989), pp. 56–73.

Book II, 5.10 directs that "priests" (i.e. bishops) must be at least thirty years old, since Jesus began to preach at this age.[215] The section *De diaconibus* in Book II, 8.2 indicates that deacons must be twenty-five years or older to serve.[216] Drawing on material from First Timothy, in Book VII.8, Isidore says that like bishops, deacons must be tested first before they serve.[217] Interestingly, Isidore does not draw on the author of First Timothy's words about the deacon obtaining the "higher grade".

One of the most important works of Isidore is the *Etymologiarum sive originum libri XX*, finished shortly after the completion of the DEO.[218] It is a virtual encyclopedia of the knowledge of the time, both sacred and secular. In Book VII, chapter 12 of the *Etymologiae*, entitled *De clericis*, Isidore deals with the church's ordered ministry. Here he lists the grades of ministers in the ascending sequence of doorkeeper, psalmist, lector, exorcist, acolyte, subdeacon, deacon, presbyter, and bishop. The order of bishops is further expanded to include patriarchs, archbishops, metropolitans, and simple bishops.[219] The position of the lector and the exorcist in the sequence along with the inclusion of the acolyte reflects the Gallican sequence of grades.

In Isidore's treatment of the grades they are listed in a descending and slightly different sequence: bishop, presbyter, deacon, subdeacon, lector, psalmist, acolyte, exorcist, and doorkeeper.[220] The position of the lector over the exorcist is similar to the sequence of the DEO. The nine-fold order, of both the DEO and the *Etymologiae*, is similar to that of the Gallican *Statuta ecclesiae antiqua* in content, though not in sequence, and may reflect Gallican influence.[221]

---

[215] CCSL 113, p. 59.

[216] CCSL 113, p. 66.

[217] CCSL 113, p. 68.

[218] Roger Reynolds, *The Ordinals of Christ from their Origins to the Twelfth Century, Beiträge zur Geschichte und Quellenkunde de Mittelaters* 7 (New York—Berlin: 1978), p. 34.

[219] *PL* 82.290.

[220] *PL* 82.291–293.

[221] Of the systematic collections cited in this study, Book VII of Isidore's *Etymologiae* is found in the *Collectio in V libris*.

f. The *Liber pontificalis*

The *Liber pontificalis* (LP) is a witness to the early sixth-century Roman practice of the *cursus honorum* and interstices. The composition of the LP began in the first half of the sixth century, the "first edition" composed some time after 530.[222] Although the LP records the lives and accomplishments of bishops of Rome in the first five centuries, much can be gleaned about sixth-century practice.

Two entries in the LP reflect the *cursus honorum* and the interstices canons. The first instance comes from the entry on Pope Gaius (282–295). The author of the LP ascribes the clerical *cursus* to Gaius:

> Hic constituit ut ordines omnes in ecclesia sic ascenderentur: si quis episcopus mereretur, ut esset ostiarius, lector, exorcista, sequens, subdiaconus, diaconus, presbyter, et exinde episcopus ordinaretur.[223]

The sequence of the *cursus* here is doorkeeper, lector, exorcist, acolyte, subdeacon, deacon, presbyter, and bishop. Except for the lack of the psalmist, the sequence is identical to that of the *Statuta ecclesiae antiqua*.[224]

The second example in the LP which includes both the interstices and the clerical *cursus* comes from the entry on the life of Pope Silvester (314–335):

> ....Hic constituit ut si quis desideraret in ecclesia militare aut proficere, ut esset lector annos XXX, exorcista dies XXX, acolitus annos V, subdiaconos annos V, custos martyrum annos X, diaconus annos VII, presbiter annos III, probatus ex omni parte, etiam et a foris qui sunt, testimonium habere bonum, unius uxoris virum, uxorem a sacerdote benedictam, et sic ad ordinem episcopatus accedere....[225]

Silvester is said to have decreed that if anyone wished to assume service in the church he must be a lector for thirty years, an exorcist thirty days, an acolyte for five years, a subdeacon for five years, a "guardian of martyrs" for ten years, a deacon for seven years, and a presbyter for three years before ordination to the episcopate. Missing from this list are the

---

[222] Raymond Davis, *The Book of the Pontiffs* (Oxford: Liverpool University Press, 1989), p. xxxvii.

[223] LP I, p. 161.

[224] The Gaian section of the LP was often incorporated by the canonists; of the systematic collections cited in this study it is found in the Pseudo-Isidorian Decretals, the *Collectio canonum* of Deusdedit, and the *Decretum* of Gratian.

[225] LP I, pp. 171–172.

doorkeeper and the psalmist; added to the list is the office of *custos martyrum*. According to this *cursus*, one would have to be fifty-five years and thirty days old at the time of ordination to the episcopate.[226]

All the biographies in the *Liber pontificalis* for this period list the numbers of ordinations performed by bishops of Rome during their pontificates. They provide an interesting comment on the *cursus honorum*. It would be too lengthy to record the numbers of ordinations performed by all the popes from Constantine to Isidore. This section will examine only the bishops of Rome whose writings have been cited in this study.

According to the *Liber pontificalis*, Damasus ordained thirty-one presbyters and eleven deacons;[227] Siricius ordained thirty-one presbyters and sixteen deacons;[228] Innocent ordained thirty presbyters and twelve deacons;[229] Zosimus ordained ten presbyters and three deacons;[230] Celestine ordained thirty-two presbyters and twelve deacons;[231] Leo ordained eighty-one presbyters and thirty-one deacons;[232] Gelasius ordained thirty-two presbyters and two deacons;[233] Hormisdas ordained twenty-one presbyters and no deacons;[234] Pelagius ordained twenty-six presbyters and nine deacons;[235] Gregory ordained thirty-nine presbyters and five deacons.[236] Theodore (642–649), the bishop of Rome at the time of the death of Isidore, ordained twenty-one presbyters and four deacons.[237] Gregory III (731–741), bishop of Rome at the time of the death of Bede (d. 735), ordained twenty-four presbyters and three deacons.[238]

---

[226] The Silvestrian section of the LP was also included by the canonists: of the systematic collections in this study it is found in the Pseudo-Isidorian Decretals, and partially reproduced in the *Collectio in V libris*.

[227] LP I, p. 213.

[228] LP I, p. 216.

[229] LP I, p. 222.

[230] LP I, p. 225.

[231] LP I, p. 230.

[232] LP I, p. 239.

[233] LP I, p. 255.

[234] LP I, p. 272.

[235] LP I, p 303.

[236] LP I, p. 312.

[237] LP I, p. 333.

[238] LP I, p. 421.

Although the figures vary from pontificate to pontificate, every example from the fourth century to the early eighth indicates that far more presbyters were ordained for the church in Rome than deacons. Whether the *Liber pontificalis* is accurate or not in its ordination figures, clearly it was considered normative that more presbyters be ordained than deacons. It is not unreasonable to assume that very few of those ordained to the presbyterate by bishops of Rome in this period were ever ordained to the diaconate.

8. Biographical Material

As well as the conciliar, papal, canonistic, liturgical, and literary witnesses to the *cursus honorum* and the interstices in the patristic period, one must also examine the vast amount of biographical details from the same time. Details of the clerical careers of many of the well-known bishops and theologians from the fourth to the mid-seventh century reveal a tremendous flexibility in terms of the actual practice of the clerical *cursus* and the interstices. This section will examine the careers of the bishops of Rome, as well as those of Ambrose, Augustine, Nectarius of Constantinople, and other Western and Eastern figures. The list of clerical careers outlined in this section is intended to be illustrative rather than exhaustive.

a. The Roman Church

Thanks to the work of Michel Andrieu, in particular his article "La carrière ecclésiastique des papes et les documents liturgiques du moyen âge", the clerical careers of the bishops of Rome in this period are made easily accessible.

In the patristic period, the regional deacons in the Roman Church were regularly consecrated to the episcopate without prior ordination to the presbyterate. For example, Popes Siricius, Damasus, and Liberius, all seem to have been lectors as youths, then deacons prior to episcopal consecration; none of them appear ever to have been presbyters. While this is a *cursus* of sorts, it is not the *cursus honorum* of a later generation. Neither, ironically, is it the *cursus* commended by Siricius to Himerius, of Zosimus to Hesychius, nor that prescribed by the Council of Sardica.

During the patristic period both deacons (usually archdeacons) and presbyters were eligible for the episcopal office in the Roman church. During the Byzantine period from the sixth to the mid-eighth century, deacons were the customary successors to the bishops of Rome. In the patristic period, the following bishops of Rome were deacons or archdeacons of Rome at the time of their ordination to the episcopate: Liberius (352–366)[239], the schismatic Felix II (355–358),[240] Damasus (366–384),[241] Siricius (384–399),[242] perhaps Innocent (401–417),[243] the schismatic Eulalius (418–419),[244] Celestine (422–427),[245] Leo the Great (440–461)[246], Hilarus[247] (461–468), Felix III (483–492),[248] perhaps Gelasius (492–496),[249] Anastasius II (496–498),[250] Symmachus (498–

---

[239] Andrieu, "La carrière", p. 92, notes that while Liberius does not explicitly bear the title of deacon, there is good reason to suggest that he was. On Liberius' tomb are written the words: "Diaconos hinc factus iuvenis meritoque fedeli qui sic sincere... ac tali iusta conversatione beata dignus qui merito in libatus iure perennis huic tantae sedi Christi spendore serenae electus fidei plenus summusque sacerdos." Cited in Duchesne, *Liber Pontificalis*, vol. 1, pp. 209–210, n. 19.

[240] In *Faustini et Marcellini presbyterorum patris Ursinus adversus Damasum libellus precum ad imperatores, Praefatio*, Felix is identified as archdeacon of Rome. *PL* 13.81.

[241] Both Damasus and his rival Ursinus in the violent struggle for the see of Rome in 366 were deacons, according to *Faustini et Marcellini... Praefatio, PL* 13.81–82.

[242] LP I, p. 217, n. 5: "Liberium lector mox et levita secutus post Damasus, clerus totus quos vixit in annos fonte sacro magnus meruit sedere sacerdos."

[243] According to J. N. D. Kelly, *The Oxford Dictionary of Popes* (Oxford: Oxford University Press, 1988), p. 37.

[244] Eulalius is identified as archdeacon of Rome: "sed quoniam Lateranensem ecclesiam obstrusis paene omnibus ingressibus archidiaconus Eulalius... obsederant." *Collectio avellana*, no. 17 (*Exemplum precum presbyterorum pro Bonifatio*), CSEL 35/1, pp. 63–64.

[245] Kelly, *Popes*, p. 41.

[246] Leo the Great is identified as a deacon before consecration to the episcopate by Prosper of Aquitaine: "Defuncto Xisto episcopo, XL amplius diebus Romanae Ecclesia sine antistite fuit, mirabili pace atque patientia prœsentiam diaconi Leonis exspectans... Igitur Leo diaconus legatione publica accitus et gaudenti patriae praesentatus XLIII Romanae ecclesiae episcopatus ordinatur". *Chronicum integrum, PL* 51.599.

[247] THIEL, vol. 1, pp. 126–130.

[248] LP I, p. 253, n. 2.

[249] Kelly, *Popes*, p. 48.

[250] LP I, p 259, n. 5.

514),[251] Hormisdas (514–523),[252] Boniface II (530–532),[253] Agapitus (535–536),[254] Vigilius (537–555),[255] Pelagius (556–561),[256] Gregory the Great (590–604),[257] Sabinian (604–606),[258] probably Boniface III (607) and Boniface IV (608–615),[259] John IV (640–642),[260] and towards the end of the seventh century, John V (685–686).[261]

There is one instance of a subdeacon being elected and consecrated bishop of Rome: Silverius (536–537) was a subdeacon when elected in 536.[262] This choice was largely instigated by Theodahad, the Ostrogothic king of Italy.

There were also presbyters who were elected bishops of Rome in the patristic period. For instance, Boniface I (418–422),[263] John II (533–535),[264] Benedict II (684–685),[265] Conon (686–687),[266] and Sergius I (687–701) who is said to have arisen "through the ranks" :

....Hic Romam veniens sub sanctae memoriae Adeodato pontifice, inter clerum Romanae ecclesiae connumeratus est; et quia studiosus erat et capax in officio cantelenae, priori cantorum pro doctrina est traditus. Et acolitus factus, per ordinem

---

[251] Theodore the Lector, *Ecclesiastical History*, *PG* 86/1.193.

[252] THIEL, vol. 1, pp. 685–687. 990–993.

[253] LP I, p. 282, n. 4.

[254] Liberatus the Deacon, *Breviarium in Causae Nestorianorum et Eutychianorum*, cap. 21, *PL* 68.1038–1039.

[255] LP I, pp. 281, 292.

[256] Liberatus, *Breviarium*, cap. 22, *PL* 68.1039.

[257] *Cf.* the letter of Gregory the deacon (28 Dec. 587), in which he confers a donation to the monastery of St. Andrew, known as the *Clivus Cauri*. MGH *Epp.* 2, appendix I.

[258] Gregory I, *Reg.* 5.6, MGH, *Epp.* 1, p. 286.

[259] According to Andrieu, "La Carrière", p. 93, n. 31, based on a reference to him in Gregory I *Reg.* 5.6, MGH *Epp.* 1, p. 287, n. 2.

[260] According to Jaffé-Wattenbach, *Regesta Rom. Pont.*, vol. 1, p. 227, based on Bede, *Historia ecclesiastica gentis anglorum*, Book II.19, ed. Charles Plummer (Oxford: Clarendon Press, 1896), pp. 122–123.

[261] LP I, p. 368.

[262] Liberatus, *Breviarium*, cap. 22, *PL* 68.1039.

[263] Kelly, *Popes*, p. 40.

[264] LP I, p. 285, n. 1.

[265] LP I, p. 363.

[266] LP I, p. 368.

ascendens, a sanctae memoriae Leone pontifice in titulo sanctae Susannae, qui et Duas domos vocatur, presbiter ordinatus est....[267]

Bibliographical information, then, is further evidence of Roman practice of electing and ordaining either deacons or presbyters to the episcopate as reflected in the Dionysian (and subsequently the *Concordia canonum*) modification of Canon XIII of the Council of Sardica, permitting bishops to be drawn from either the presbyterate or the diaconate. This modification was likely made in order to conform to current Roman practice.

b. Ambrose of Milan

An important, though somewhat controversial, example of a lay person and neophyte being ordained directly to the episcopate is Ambrose of Milan (*ca.* 339–397). As governor of Milan, Ambrose was elected bishop while still a catechumen, and consecrated directly to the episcopate after baptism on December 7, 374. His is one of the most celebrated instances of ordination *"per saltum"*.

Yet many commentators assert that between his baptism one Sunday, and his consecration on the next, Ambrose was admitted to all of the minor and major orders, one day at a time. F. Homes Dudden, for example, states:

> On Sunday, the 24th of November, Ambrose was baptized and confirmed; on Monday, the 25 of November, he was made doorkeeper; on Tuesday, the 26th of November, reader; on Wednesday, the 27th of November, exorcist; on Thursday, the 28th of November, acolyte-subdeacon; on Friday, the 29th of November, deacon; on Saturday, the 30th of November, presbyter; and on Sunday, the 1st of December, bishop. Such a passage through the various grades was of course, purely formal; yet it shows that the ideal of gradual promotion was—so far as was possible under the circumstances—respected.[268]

There is, however, no scholarly consensus on the question of whether Ambrose was ordained directly or sequentially to the episcopate.[269]

---

[267] LP I, p. 371.

[268] F. Homes Dudden, *The Life and Times of St. Ambrose*, vol. 1 (Oxford: The Clarendon Press, 1935), pp. 73–74.

[269] There are many examples of historians who claim that Ambrose received all the orders according to the *cursus honorum*. For example, F. Homes Dudden in his life of Ambrose says that he "was apparently made to pass formally through the successive grades of the ministry"; *The Life and Times of St. Ambrose*, p. 68. Dom Gregory Dix in "The ministry of the Early Church, c. A.D. 90–410", *The Apostolic Ministry*, ed. Kenneth E. Kirk (London: Hodder & Stoughton, 1957), p. 284 claims that Ambrose passed through all the

Those who maintain that Ambrose was ordained according to the sequence of the *cursus honorum* cite the account of the event in Book III of the *Vita Sancti Ambrosii* by Ambrose's biographer Paulinus:

> 9. Baptizatus itaque fertur omnia ecclesiastica officia implesse, atque octavo die episcopus ordinatus est summa cum gratia et laetitia cunctum.[270]

A particular reading of this passage has lead scholars such as F. Homes Dudden and others to base their assumption that Ambrose passed sequentially through all the orders. Dudden translates the passage as follows:

> After his baptism he is reported to have fulfilled all the ecclesiastical offices, and on the eighth day he was consecrated bishop.[271]

And yet, an alternative translation, provided by Sr. Mary Simplicia Kaniecka, makes it difficult to support this interpretation:

---

orders. Angelo Paredi in *Saint Ambrose, His Life and Times* (Notre Dame Indiana: University of Note Dame Press, 1964) p. 124 says without comment that Ambrose passed through all the stages of the ecclesiastical hierarchy. In support of his thesis that Cornelius' *cursus* was typical, G. W. Clarke cites Ambrose as evidence; *The Letters of St. Cyprian of Carthage* vol. 3, Ancient Christian Writers 46 (New York: Newman Press, 1986), p. 174. W. H. C. Frend also supports this view in *The Early Church*, p. 179, as well as in *The Rise of Christianity*, p. 618 . Henry Chadwick holds this view as well, *The Early Church*, p. 167. Richard Toporoski reflects the same view in his article "Ambrose, St.," *The Dictionary of the Middle Ages*, vol. I, ed. Joseph R. Strayer (New York: Charles Scribner's Sons, 1982), p. 230.

There are scholars, however, who postulate that Ambrose was ordained directly to the episcopate. E.g., Lafontaine, in *Les Conditions*, supports the view that Ambrose was baptised and ordained a bishop, despite his assertion that *per saltum* means primarily omission of the interstices, and not the intermediary orders, p. 246. Balthasar Fischer, "Hat Ambrosius von Mailand in der Woche zwischen seiner Taufe und seiner Bischofskonsekration andere Weihe empfangen?," *Kyriakon*, vol. 2 [Festschrift Johannes Quasten], eds. P. Granfield and J. A. Jungmann (Muenster: Verlag Aschendorff, 1970), pp. 527–531. Faivre also supports the theory that Ambrose was baptised and ordained a bishop, *Naisssance*, pp. 408–409. The brief entry on Ambrose in *The Oxford Dictionary of the Christian Church*, 2nd ed., (Oxford: Oxford University Press, 1978) pp. 42–43, seems to support the view that Ambrose was simply baptised and ordained. Karl Baus, *et al.*, *The Imperial Church from Constantine to the Early Middle Ages*, The History of the Church, vol. 2, maintain that Ambrose was baptised and then was consecrated to the episcopate. This view is expressed by Louis J. Swift in his article "Ambrose", *Encyclopedia of Early Christianity*, ed. Everett Ferguson (New York: Garland Press Inc., 1991), p. 30.

[270] Michele Pellegrino, ed., *Paolino di Milano, Vita di S. Ambrogio: Introduzione, testo critico et note* (Rome: Editrice Studium, 1961), p. 62; *PL* 14.32.

[271] Dudden, *The Life and Times*, p. 73. *Cf.* "Battizzato, passò, com'è riferito, per tutti i gradi della gerarchia ecclesiastica." Pellegrino, *Vita S. Ambrogio*, p. 63.

> And so being baptized he is said to have fulfilled all the ecclesiastical offices and
> on the eighth day he was consecrated bishop with the greatest favor and joy of
> all.[272]

Whatever "all the ecclesiastical offices" means, according to this interpretation it was through baptism that Ambrose is said to have fulfilled them, not through a series of ordinations.

Furthermore, despite Paulinus' significance as a source for the life of Ambrose, his biography is problematic. Paulinus' purpose is primarily hagiographical rather than historical, and so he is prone to omit important details. As Kaniecka has written in her commentary on Paulinus' *Vita S. Ambrosii*:

> There is one serious charge, however, which we must make against him: that he did
> not use Ambrose's own works as much as he should have for source material. The
> Letters of St. Ambrose especially would have been a rich mine of information for
> him, as those which are extant are, for us, for many details of his hero's life, yet he
> cites them but very seldom.[273]

Ambrose' own account of the event in *Epistle* 59, to the Church at Vercelli, does not suggest anything other than baptism and ordination to the episcopate:

> 65. Quam resistebam ne ordinarer! Postremo cum cogerer, saltem ordinatio prote-
> laretur! Sed non voluit praescriptio, praevaluit impressio. Tamen ordinationem
> meam occidentales episcopi judicio, orientales etiam exemplo probarunt. Et tamen
> neophytus prohibetur ordinari, ne extollatur superbia. Si dilatio ordinationi defuit,
> vis cogentis est; si non deest humilitas competens sacerdotio, ubi causa non haeret,
> vitium non imputatur.[274]

Ambrose says that though pressure prevailed, he fought against being ordained. There is no mention of there being any other ordination than that to the episcopate. He refers to the Eastern bishops having approved of his ordination by their example. It is likely that he is referring to the ordination of Nectarius of Constantinople in 381, who was likewise baptised and immediately ordained a bishop.

---

[272] Sr. Mary Simplicia Kaniecka, ed. and trans., *Vita Sancti Ambrosii a Paulino eius Notario: A Revised Text and Commentary with an Introduction and Translation*, The Catholic University of America Patristic Studies, vol. 16 (Washington: Catholic University of America, 1928), p. 47.

[273] Kaniecka, *Vita Sancti Ambrosii,* p. 11.

[274] *PL* 16.1258.

Ambrose also refers to his own ordination briefly in Book I of *De officiis ministrorum*:

> I.4. Quod ne ipsum quidem mihi accidit. Ego enim raptus de tribunalibus atque administrationis infulis ad sacerdotium, docere vos coepi, quod ipses non didici.[275]

Once again, there is no mention of any other ordination than that to the "priesthood".

Moreover, the fifth-century historians say nothing about Ambrose receiving any orders other than the episcopate. Socrates "Scholasticus" (*ca*.380-450) in Book IV.30 of his *Ecclesiastical History* states that after Ambrose was baptised, he would have been consecrated immediately afterwards had he not objected. Socrates says that once the Emperor Valentinian supported the election, Ambrose was forthwith ordained a bishop.[276] There is no indication of any previous ordination.

In a slightly different version of the incident, the historian Sozomen (early fifth century) in Book VI.24 of his *Ecclesiastical History* also records that Valentinian ordered Ambrose to be ordained a bishop as quickly as possible. Sozomen differs from Socrates in one respect: Sozomen states that Ambrose "was initiated and ordained at the same time."[277]

In a similar version, Theodoret of Cyrrhus (*ca*.393-*ca*.466) in Book IV.6 of his *Ecclesiastical History* affirms that "Ambrose then received the divine gift of holy baptism, and the grace of the archiepiscopal office" at the same time.[278] Once again, there is no suggestion that Ambrose received ordination to any order prior to his episcopal consecration.

Even if one might admit that a particular reading of Paulinus' account is true, that is, that Ambrose did receive seven orders in seven days, the fifth-century historians reflect the prevailing opinion that it was also possible for a lay person to be ordained directly to the episcopate without prior ordination to any of the intervening offices.

Jerome's objection to Ambrose' ordination in *Epistle* 69.9 to Oceanum has already been noted above. Jerome's objection is perhaps equally

---

[275] *PL* 16.27.

[276] *PG* 67.544.

[277] *PG* 67.1356; Charles D. Hartranft, trans., *Nicene and Post-Nicene Fathers*, vol. 2 (New York: Christian Literature Association, 1892), p. 361.

[278] *PG* 82.1132; Blomfield Jackson, trans., *Nicene and Post-Nicene Fathers*, vol. 3 (1892) p. 111.

motivated by his dislike of Ambrose as well as the manner of his ordination as such.

The contemporary evidence, then, cannot support the theory that Ambrose was ordained through a series of offices. There are no concurrent examples of such ordinations; on the contrary, other instances of direct ordination to both the presbyterate and the episcopate abound. The extraordinary feature about Ambrose's election to the episcopate was that he was only a catechumen, not the fact that he had never been ordained to any other order. It would have been equally extraordinary, however, for Ambrose to have been "rushed" through the grades of doorkeeper, lector, exorcist, acolyte-subdeacon, deacon, presbyter, and bishop—all within the space of a week. Lastly, in contrast to the positions advocated by Lafontaine (who does not support the theory that Ambrose received any other ordination than that to the episcopate) and Leclerq,[279] Ambrose's ordination demonstrates that *per saltum* ordination in the fourth century means omission of the minor orders, as well as the diaconate and the presbyterate.

c. Augustine of Hippo

Another significant fourth-century exception to the *cursus honorum* is the career of Augustine of Hippo (354–430). Augustine was ordained to the presbyterate in 391 after his baptism in 387; he was ordained bishop in 395. In *Sermo* 355 (*De vita et moribus clericorum suorum*) preached on December 18, 425, Augustine recounts the event:

> 2. ....Ego, quem Deo propitio videtis episcopum vestrum, juvenis veni ad istam civitatem, ut multi vestrum noverunt. Quaerebam ubi constituerem monasterium, et viverem cum fratribus meis. Spem quippe omnem saeculi reliqueram, et quod esse potui, esse nolui: nec tamen quaesivi esse quod sum. Elegi in domo Dei mei abjectus esse, magis quam habitare in tabernaculis peccatorum. Ab eis qui diligunt saeculum, segregavi me: sed eis qui praesunt populis, non me coaequavi. Nec in convivio Domini mei superiorem locum elegi, sed inferiorem et abjectum: et placuit illi dicere mihi, Ascende sursum.

> Usque adeo autem timebam episcopatum, ut quoniam coeperat esse jam alicujus momenti inter Dei servos fama mea, in quo loco sciebam non esse episcopum, non illo accederem. Cavebam hoc, et agebam quantum poteram, ut in loco humili salvarer, ne in alto periclitarer. Sed, ut dixi, domino servus contradicere non debet. Veni ad istam civitatem propter videndum amicum, quem putabam me lucrari posse Deo, ut nobiscum esset in monasterio; quasi securus, quia locus habebat episcopum. Apprehensus, presbyter factus sum, et per hunc gradum perveni ad

---

[279] Lafontaine, *Les Conditions*, p. 237; Leclerq, "Ordinations irrégulières", col. 2391.

episcopatum. Non attuli aliquid, non veni ad hanc Ecclesiam, nisi cum iis indumentis quibus illo tempore vestiebar....[280]

Augustine recounts how he avoided places that lacked a bishop, such was his fear of being appointed to episcopal office. He narrates how on a visit to a friend at Hippo he was virtually kidnapped and ordained to the presbyterate: "and through this grade I came to the episcopate".

In Book IV of the *Vita Sancti Augustini episcopi*, Augustine's biographer Possidius relates that as he was brought before Bishop Valerius to be ordained a presbyter, Augustine was in tears:

> 2. ....nonullis quidem lacrymas ejus, ut nobis ipse retulit, tunc superbe interpretantibus, et tanquam eum consolantibus ac dicentibus, quia et locus presbyterii, licet ipse majore dignus esset, appropinquaret tamen episcopatui....[281]

People thought that he was disappointed not to have been made a bishop instead, though this appears to have been furthest from Augustine's mind at the time. Augustine was evidently afraid that he would be ordained directly to the episcopate.

There is no indication that Augustine was ever ordained a deacon, or to any other order of ministry. Given the importance of the diaconate in the fourth century, it is unlikely that if he had been ordained deacon, Augustine would have omitted all references to it.

Augustine indicates that he came to the episcopate by way of the presbyterate. Yet his ordination to the presbyterate was not according to the rules of a *cursus* or as a preparatory step towards the episcopate. Rather, it was a way for Valerius to ensure that Augustine would remain in the church of Hippo.[282] Moreover, the interval between ordination to the presbyterate and to the episcopate was only four years; hardly the ten year interval enjoined by Pope Siricius, Augustine's contemporary.

d. Other Western Examples

i.

There are many examples of flexibility with regards to *cursus honorum* and the interstices in other parts of the Western church in this period as

---

[280] *PL* 39.1569.

[281] *PL* 32.37.

[282] *Cf.* Peter Brown, *Augustine of Hippo* (London: Faber and Faber, 1967), p. 139.

well. Again, the list of clerical careers touched upon here is intended to be indicative rather than exhaustive.

In North Africa, Caecilian (d. *ca.* 345) was a deacon when ordained bishop of Carthage at the beginning of the Donatist schism in the early fourth century. He was the archdeacon of his predecessor, Mensurius. As bishop of Carthage (*ca.*311–345), Caecilian was the only Latin African bishop to attend the Council of Nicaea.

Hilary, first bishop of Poitiers (*ca.*315–367) was a lay person, and married, when he was ordained a bishop (*ca.* 353). The needs of a newly created "diocese" required the abilities that were provided by the upper echelons of the laity, such as Hilary, with his superior education and training.

Already noted in this study through his writings, Jerome (*ca.*347–*ca.*420) was perhaps the greatest scholar of the fourth century. After his baptism in *ca.* 366, Jerome was reluctantly ordained to the presbyterate at Antioch, *ca.* 378,[283] on the condition that it not affect his position as a monk. There is no evidence to suggest he was ever ordained a deacon, or to any of the minor orders.

Germain (*ca.* 378–448), bishop of Auxerre, was a lay person at the time of his ordination to the episcopate. Trained as a Roman lawyer and governor of Amorica in Gaul before he was thirty, Germain was virtually seized by the people, tonsured and ordained a bishop in 418.

ii.

The *Historia francorum* of Gregory of Tours contains many instances of both the observance of the *cursus honorum* and its omission. For example, in Book I.44 Gregory discusses Uburcus, who was a lay person when he was consecrated bishop.[284] Book I.46 discusses one Arthemius, who after an illness "became a member of the holy Church," was ordained as a presbyter, and subsequently became the fifth bishop of Clermont-Ferrand.[285]

---

[283] J. D. N. Kelly notes that there is little documentation about Jerome's life between 377–382; *Jerome: His Life, Writings, and Controversies* (Westminster, Maryland: Christain Classics, Inc., 1980), p. 57.

[284] Gregory of Tours, *Historia francorum*, I.44, W. Arndt & Br. Krusch, eds., *Monumenta Germaniae Historica Scriptores Rerum Merovingicarum*, vol. 1 (Hannover: 1884), pp. 28–29.

[285] MGH *SRM*, vol. 1, p. 30.

Book II.41 describes two laymen, Chararich and his son, who were both forcibly ordained directly to the presbyterate and the diaconate respectively. Chararich and his son were ordained on the orders of Clovis who thereupon took possession of their lands and wealth.[286]

In Book IV.6 Gregory recounts the election of Caton as bishop of Clermont-Ferrand in 551. At the death of his predecessor, St. Gall, Caton offered himself as a candidate on the grounds that he had served in all the offices of the church:

> ....Nec me dominus Deus meus patitur hac ordinatione privari, cui tantum famulatum exibui. Nam et ipsos clericati grados canonica sum semper institutione sortitus. Lector decim annis fui, subdiaconatus officium quinque annis ministravi, diaconatui vero quindecim annis mancipatus fui, presbiterii, inquam, honorem viginti annis potior. Quid enim mihi nunc restat, nisi ut episcopatum, quem fidelis servitus promeretur, accipiam?...[287]

Caton explains that he had been promoted through all the ranks of the clergy "according to canonical precept". He was a lector for ten years, subdeacon for five years, a deacon for fifteen years, and a presbyter for 20 years. The sequence of this *cursus* is similar to that prescribed by Siricius, Innocent, and Zosimus. One notes the two classes of minor orders in this *cursus*: lectorate and subdiaconate. The interstices of this *cursus* are not reflected in canonical texts, but the length of time spent in the offices—fifty years—is similar that outlined in the entry for Silverius in the *Liber pontificalis* in the early sixth century. In the end, Caton asks what remains except ordination to the episcopate as a reward for his services. He did, in fact, become the next bishop of Clermont-Ferrand.

Book V.5 describes a lay person, Mundederic, who was tonsured and made archpresbyter.[288] Book V.5 also discusses a layman named Sylvester, who was tonsured, ordained directly to the presbyterate (*tonso capite, presbiter ordinatur*), and later ordained a bishop.[289] Book V.20 relates how two deacons, Salonius and Sagittarius, were both ordained bishops.[290]

---

[286] MGH *SRM*, vol. 1, p. 91.

[287] MGH *SRM*, vol. 1, p. 145.

[288] MGH *SRM*, vol. 1, p. 201.

[289] MGH *SRM*, vol. 1, p. 201.

[290] MGH *SRM*, vol. 1, p. 227.

Book V.36 mentions Maracharius, a layman who was tonsured and conse-crated to the episcopate.[291]

In Book VI Gregory describes the election of a bishop for the see of Le Mans in 581, after the death of its bishop, Domnolus. Prior to his death, Domnolus had directed that he be succeeded by Abbot Theodulf. While Domnolus was still alive, King Lothar, however, chose Badegisil, a lay-man and mayor of the palace instead. Badegisil was tonsured and promot-ed through the grades so that as soon as Domnolus died, he could be ordained a bishop:

> Qui tonsoratus, grados quos clerici sortiuntur ascendens, post quadraginta diebus, migrante sacerdote, successit.[292]

In this instance the sequence of the *cursus honorum* was observed, while the interstices were completely disregarded.

iii.

The *Historia ecclesiastica gentis anglorum* of the Venerable Bede also provides valuable information on clerical careers in the early medieval English Church. Bede offers a useful Anglo-Saxon alternative to the assorted situations described by Gregory of Tours.

Most of the bishops cited by Bede had been presbyter-monks, often ab-bots, at the time of their election and ordination. For instance, Book III.5 indicates that Aidan was an abbot and presbyter when he was ordained a bishop.[293] Book III.21 related that Diuma was a presbyter when consecrat-ed to the episcopate,[294] as were Cedd (Book III.22),[295] Wilfrid (Book III.28),[296] and Chad (Book III.29).[297] In Book V.19 Bede mentions that Wilfrid (634–709) received the clerical tonsure and was ordained a pres-byter; there is no mention of any intervening grades. He was ordained a

---

[291] MGH *SRM*, vol. 1, p. 242.

[292] MGH *SRM*, vol. 1, p. 255.

[293] Bede, *Historia ecclesiastica gentis anglorum*, ed. Charles Plummer (Oxford: Claren-don Press, 1896), p. 135.

[294] Bede, *Historia*, p. 170.

[295] Bede, *Historia*, p. 172.

[296] Bede, *Historia*, p. 194.

[297] Bede, *Historia*, p. 195.

bishop at thirty years of age,[298] in apparent indifference to the standard Western interstices canons.

Bede also records at least two deacons who were ordained bishops. For example, in Book III.20 he mentions a deacon, Thomas, who was made a bishop in East Anglia, 653.[299] Book V.18 mentions a Pecthelm, bishop of Galloway, who was a deacon-monk before he was a bishop.[300]

The *Historia ecclesiastica* of Bede is a primary source for the life and career of Theodore of Taursus, Archbishop of Canterbury (*ca.* 602–690). Book IV.1 relates that after his appointment, Theodore, a Greek monk, was ordained a subdeacon, then bishop:

> ....Qui subdiaconus ordinatus IIII exspectavit menses, donec illi coma cresceret, quo in coronam tondi posset; habuerat enim tonsuram more orientalium sancti apostoli Pauli. Qui ordinatus est a Vitaliano papa anno dominicae incarnationis DCLXVIII, sub die VII, Kalendarum Aprilium, dominica....[301]

Bede explains the four-month interval between the reception of the subdiaconate and episcopal consecration in terms of allowing Theodore's hair to grow out, in conformity with the western tonsure. Curiously, there is no mention of Theodore's having received any orders between the subdiaconate and the episcopate.

Bede concludes his History with a brief biographical note in which he mentions certain details of his own ecclesiastical career:

> Nono decimo autem vitae meae anno diaconatum, tricesimo gradum presbyteratus, utrumque per ministerium reverentissimi episcopi Iohannis, iubente Ceolfrido abbate, suscepi.[302]

Bede relates that he was ordained deacon at age nineteen (six years before the canonical age), and presbyter at the canonical age of thirty.

e. Nectarius of Constantinople

If Ambrose of Milan is cited as the great Western patristic example of ordination *per saltum*, the Eastern counterpart is Nectarius of Constantinople (d. 397). Nectarius was consecrated during the second ecumenical Council

---

[298] Bede, *Historia*, pp. 322–325.

[299] Bede, *Historia*, p. 169.

[300] Bede, *Historia*, p. 320.

[301] Bede, *Historia*, p. 203.

[302] Bede, *Historia*, p. 357.

of Constantinople in 381. The council was fraught with trouble. For example, the president of the council, Melitius of Antioch, died during the proceedings. Further, Gregory of Nazianzus, the bishop of Constantinople, retired in disgrace during the council. According to the early fifth-century *Ecclesiastical History* of Sozomen (Book VII.8), the Emperor Theodosius in an effort to find someone disassociated with the controversy to replace Gregory as bishop of Constantinople, and to replace Melitius as president of the council, appointed Nectarius, a civil servant.[303]

In a slightly different account of the incident, the early fifth-century *Ecclesiastical History* (Book V.8) of Socrates Scholasticus reports:

> Now there was a person named Nectarius, of a senatorial family, mild and gentle in his manners, and admirable in his whole course of life, although at the time he bore the office of prœtor. This man was seized upon by the people, and elected to the episcopate, and was ordained by one hundred and fifty bishops then present.[304]

The accounts of Sozomen and Socrates agree on one important detail: like Ambrose, Nectarius was unbaptised when elected, and was consecrated to the episcopate immediately after baptism.

As bishop of Constantinople, Nectarius presided over the final stages of the Council of Constantinople. It is possible that when Ambrose years after his consecration mentioned that the Eastern bishops supported his election "by their examples" he is referring in retrospect to the consecration of Nectarius. Unlike the ordination of Ambrose, no one has ever doubted that Nectarius was ordained directly to the episcopate after baptism, without receiving any other orders.

f. Other Eastern Examples

Like the Western churches in the fourth century, the East also offers many well-attested instances of deacons being consecrated bishops, and of lay people being ordained presbyters and bishops. The situation in the Eastern churches with respect to the *cursus honorum* was similar to that of the West in the fourth century.

As noted in chapter 2 of this study, after the Council of Nicaea the Alexandrian church amended the custom of electing its bishops from among the presbyterate followed by presbyteral installation. Hence, the Council of Nicaea marked the end of the absolute *cursus* between presbyterate and

---

[303] *PG* 67.1433, 1436.

[304] *PG* 67.577. Hartranft, trans., *Nicene and Post-Nicene Fathers*, vol. 2, p. 121.

episcopate in the Alexandrian church. The fourth century saw a broadening of candidacy for the episcopate. The consecration of Athanasius as bishop of Alexandria in 328 is the first example of the new order. Athanasius (*ca.* 295–373) was ordered lector in 312 and ordained a deacon in 318. He is likely the first bishop of Alexandria to have been ordained from the diaconate directly to the episcopate.

The ecclesiastical career of John Chrysostom (*ca.*347–407) followed the *cursus*: he was made a lector (372), ordained deacon (381) and presbyter (386) before his consecration to the episcopate (398). He does not appear to have been a subdeacon. Yet the careers of many other leading bishops of the Eastern church in the fourth century did not follow this pattern.

The three Cappadocian fathers do not appear to have corresponded to the sequence of the *cursus honorum*. Basil of Caesarea (*ca.*330–379) was ordained to the presbyterate in 364 after living as a monk and a hermit. He was later made a bishop in 370. There is nothing to suggest that he was ever a deacon. His brother, Gregory of Nyssa (*ca.*330–*ca.*395), was a lector at the time of his reluctant consecration to the episcopate in 371. Gregory of Nyssa was a monk as were both Basil and Gregory of Nazianzus.

Gregory of Nazianzus (329–389), a mentor of Jerome, was likewise ordained to the presbyterate without having been ordained a deacon. Yet Gregory is often cited as a fourth-century apologist for the *cursus honorum*. In *Oration* 43.26, Gregory states:

> For I do not praise the disorder and irregularity which sometimes exists among us, even in those who preside over the sanctuary. I do not venture, nor is it just, to accuse them all. I approve the nautical custom, which first gives the oar to the future steersman, and afterwards leads him to the stern, and entrusts him with command, and seats him at the helm, only after a long course of striking the sea and observing the winds. As in the case, again in military affairs: private, captain, general.[305]

Here Gregory clearly commends sequential ordination, making an analogy to both naval and military practice. A prescribed, lengthy series of offices is offered as a corrective to the "disorder and irregularity" which exists in the church, by providing opportunity for probation and preparation.

Gregory states that he does not presume or venture to judge all; one wonders whether he is including himself in this exception, since his own career does not correspond to the prevailing sequence of offices. In

---

[305] *PG* 36.532–533;. C. G. Browne & J.E. Swallows, trans., *Nicene and Post-Nicene Fathers*, vol. 7 (New York: Christian Literatur Association, 1894), p. 404.

Oration 2.5, *Apologeticus de fuga* (*ca.* 362) Gregory offers a defense for having fled into the desert after having been forcibly ordained a presbyter by his father in *ca.*361.[306] Like Augustine of Hippo, Gregory makes no reference to ever having been a deacon. Given the importance of the office of deacon in the fourth century, it is unlikely that if Gregory had been made a deacon, he would have omitted all reference to it.

In addition, in his father's funeral oration, *Oration* 15.12–15, Gregory indicates that his father (also called Gregory and bishop of Nazianzus) was consecrated bishop after his baptism.[307] There is no suggestion that Gregory's father was ordained to any other order than the episcopate.

The history of clerical careers in the patristic and late patristic periods reveals that despite papal and conciliar endorsement and growth in practice, observances of the *cursus honorum*, the interstices, and the ages of clerics, were neither universal nor uniform in the Western and Eastern churches in this period.

9. Summary

From the conversion of Constantine to the death of the Venerable Bede, ordained ministry, like the church itself, underwent remarkable developments. Many of the modifications, particularly in the fourth and fifth centuries, were clearly adoptions from the recently Christianized Roman Empire; others were adaptations to the new situation in which the church found itself. To which category is the emergence of the *cursus honorum* to be assigned: adoption or adaptation?

a. The *Cursus Honorum:* Adoption or Adaptation?

Questions around the emergence of the ecclesiastic *cursus honorum* are not insignificant, despite the lack of attention it receives in histories of the church and holy order,[308] and the relative lack of attention it received from

---

[306] *PG* 35.412.

[307] *PG* 35.1000–1001, 1004.

[308] E.g., J. Gaudemet, "Holy Order in Early Conciliar Legislation (IVth and Vth centuries," *The Sacrament of Holy Orders* (Collegeville: the Liturgical Press, 1962), pp. 183–201. Gaudemet does not mention the *cursus honorum* or the interstices, though he deals

councils and popes in the patristic period in comparison with other issues relating to holy orders, especially celibacy and later simony. As Paul-Henri Lafontaine states in the conclusion of his substantial study *Les Conditions positives de l'Accession aux Ordres dans la première législation ecclésiastique (300–492)*: "Nous pourrions déjà conclure que les deux conditions primordiales de l'accès aux ordres résident dans la chasteté cléricale et l'observation des interstices."[309]

As the wealth, power and prestige of the church grew in the fourth and fifth centuries, bishops gradually came to adopt the signs and the status of the empire. From the pontificates of Damasus and Siricius, bishops of Rome adopt the form and style of the imperial decretal as a means of conveying their decisions. One notes the use of ceremonial honours once proper to imperial officials, such as being preceded by incense or tapers, or the use of the pallium, adopted by Christian bishops.

In what sense can sequential ordination in the patristic period be similarly understood as a conscious (or unconscious, for that matter) borrowing from imperial practice? It has been noted that the *cursus honorum* was a well established practice in the Roman military and civil services. The vocabulary used in the texts surveyed frequently reveals an assimilation of terms from the imperial military and civil services. For instance, in the decretal to Himerius, Siricius uses the expression *ad sacrum militiam*; in the letter of Hesychius, Zosimus speaks of the *coelesti militia*; in the letter to the bishops of Mauritania Caesariensis Leo speaks of *omnes gradus militiae christianae*. Both Zosimus and Celestine use the term *stipendia*, which originally referred to payment given to soldiers. The use of expression such as *ordo, honor, dignitas, meritum*, etc., are all drawn from secular society.[310]

Again, the use of the word *gradus* was correspondingly adopted from civil usage, though the Christian use of the term predates the Constantinian

---

with the gender of clerics, the ages of clerics, examination, the functions of the minor orders. Canon XIII of the council of Sardica is not mentioned by Gaudemet in this article. *Cf.* Kenan Osborne, *Priesthood: A History of the Ordained Ministry in the Roman Catholic Church* (New York: Paulist Press, 1988), mentions the *cursus* in passing in an excursus on the minor orders, pp. 197–199.

[309] Lafontaine, *Les Conditions*, p. 360.

[310] *Cf.* P. M. Gy, "Notes on the Early Terminology of Christian Priesthood," *The Sacrament of Holy Orders* (Collegeville: The Liturgical Press, 1962), pp. 98–115.

era;[311] *gradus* had a clear association with the military and civil *cursus*. The word means "step" and is related to the verb *gradior* meaning "to take steps." And so, the use of the word *gradus* has an implicit sense of movement through the orders of ministry. As David Power has noted:

> It [i.e., the term *gradus*] meant each of the different stages through which public functionaries ascended in the course of their career. This idea of a strict hierarchy of office and of an ascent through the ranks, in order to be suited to the highest office, is what is principally retained in the application of the term to ecclesiastical office.[312]

The term *gradus* appears frequently in papal letters. The first instance of its use in a conciliar text is the Council of Sardica: *ut per singulos gradus (si dignus fuerit) ascendat ad culmen episcopatus.* This canon is one of the rare instances where the word *gradus* appears in a conciliar text. It is absent from the Gallican councils examined, and appears in only two of the Hispanic councils surveyed: Canon XX of Braga I (561), and Canon III of Barcelona II (599). It is also found in the two liturgical texts surveyed of this period: the *Leonensis* and the *Liber ordinum*.

At one level it is easy to surmise that the *cursus honorum* is but one of the many examples of "inculturation" in the fourth century. It has been noted that both Damasus of Rome and Gregory of Nazianzus advocated progression through the grades based on the parallel of the Roman military. The sources examined in this chapter, however, reflect a concern for the integrity of the church's leaders in new and foreboding circumstances. After the conversion of Constantine, the older way of appointing clergy was frequently abused by the unscrupulous, the ambitious, and the unworthy, since ecclesiastical office had become enviable because of its wealth, power, and prestige. As the patristic ecclesiastical histories such as the *Historia francorum* report, unsuitable candidates for the episcopate were often nominated by civil authority; often the unsuited sought office themselves out of greed and ambition. One of the greatest violations the church had to face was simony, the purchasing of ecclesiastical office. Civil appointment, ambition, and simony were often accompanied by direct ordination to the higher offices.

As a result, unsuited and ill-prepared candidates were often made bishops. Sometimes individuals were pagan one day, and Christian bishops the next. Candidates without adequate probation and preparation were often

---

[311] *Cf.* Cyprian, *Epistle* 38.2, CSEL 3.2, p. 580.

[312] Power, *Ministers of Christ*, pp. 63–64.

devoid of the faith and morals they were supposed to teach. Celestine (*Epistle* 4) complained that known criminals were made bishops. In the letter to the bishops of Mauritania Caesariensis (*Epistle* 12), Leo protested that those ignorant of the church's lawful institutions, lacking in all humility, inexperienced and unskilled were likewise made bishops. The Council of Arles, 524, complained of the "unsuitable and disordered prayers of the priest". Gregory the Great commented to Brunhilda, that the "illicit promotion of the few" is becoming the ruin of many, through the lack of respect for the governance of the church.

The texts surveyed frequently speak of the need for *probatio*—the testing of orthodox faith and morals. There were no ecclesiastical selection committees in the patristic church. The requirement for probation was provided by the *cursus honorum* and the interstices, which, when observed, would have tested the holiness and worthiness of clergy for periods of years in the lower offices. This procedure was an attempt to ensure that those unworthy of the "dignity" of the episcopate or the presbyterate would not find themselves in these offices. The texts also speak of progression through the grades in terms of *praeparatio*—training and education; of becoming a disciple before becoming the teacher. After the Peace of the Church, episcopal candidates were needed who were well trained in theology, liturgy, diplomacy, and administration. Bishops who were unprepared for the tasks of episcopal leadership were as undesirable and unsuitable as the candidates who had never been tested. Since there were no seminaries or schools of theology in the early church, the need for preparation was likewise met by the *cursus honorum* with the interstices. By this procedure, the church could ensure that its leaders were well prepared for the demanding tasks of the new situation. As Lafontaine has observed:

> Toutes ces lois sont inspirées par une même idée: l'exigence d'une formation soignée pour les clercs, plus particulièrement pour les clercs majeurs.[313]

In *The Ministers of Christ* Power likewise observes that the positive aspect of the appropriation of Roman terms and practice for the church's ministry is that it accented the need for adequate preparation and moral goodness for promotion to the higher offices.[314]

Clearly, the insistence of both councils and popes that the higher clergy, particularly bishops, undergo a long period of probation and

---

[313] Lafontaine, *Les Conditions*, p. 237.

[314] Power, *Ministers of Christ*, p. 65.

preparation was not motivated by the desire to imitate civil and military institutions, nor was it an uncritical assimilation of imperial practice. Rather,
it was a practical and pastoral adaptation of an imperial practice in order to
combat the problem posed by the ordination of the unworthy and incapable
to ecclesiastical leadership in the newly-christianized Roman Empire and
the Frankish kingdom. The texts themselves bear witness to this concern.
The *cursus honorum* and the interstices, then, were the means the church
used to safeguard the integrity of, rather than to corrupt, its leadership.

b. The Demise of the Interstices

Within a few centuries of the first conciliar and papal legislation prescribing sequential ordination and the interstices, it is clear that the process and
its two-fold purpose, preparation and probation had begun to break down.
This dissolution is associated with the modification and neglect of the
interstices canons.

It has been noted that the observance the *cursus* and the interstices established by Siricius would have taken twenty-nine years to complete for
adult candidates; those who began as boys would be at least forty-five
years old at the time of ordination to the episcopate. According to the intervals established by Zosimus one would have been twenty-nine at the
time of ordination to the diaconate. The *cursus* and interstices prescribed
by Canon I of the Council of Toledo II (527) had a two year interval between receiving the tonsure at age eighteen, and the subdiaconate at twenty, followed by a five year interval prior to being made a deacon at age
twenty-five. The sequence advocated by Silvester in the *Liber pontificalis*,
or followed by Bishop Caton in the *Historia francorum* took over fifty
years to complete. These lengths of time (the *tempora constituta* or the
praefixa tempora) would have provided adequate opportunity for the probation and preparation for candidates for the major orders.

As long as the *cursus honorum* was combined with the observance of
the lengthy interstices, it ensured both probation and preparation. This purpose could not adequately be served once the interstices became modified
and eventually curtailed. In the letter of Innocent to Felix (*Epistle* 7), one
observes the appearance of this phenomenon in the early fifth century. Leo
complains about shortened interstices in the mid-fifth century (*Epistle* 6).
By the pontificate of Gelasius towards the end of the fifth century, it has
become licit to ordain members of the laity through all the clerical grades
from lector to presbyter in a year (*Epistle* 14.2). The letter of Pelagius to

Sapaudus of Arles (*Epistle* 5) reflects the fact that rapid se
tions through the sequence of the *cursus honorum*—in a single ___
become of problem by the mid-sixth century. In these instances where the
two-fold process of the *cursus honorum* was violated, it was the interstices
rather than sequential ordination which was abandoned.

While the conferral of a rapid series of ordinations on a single candidate
stood in marked contrast to papal and conciliar legislation, the practice indicates a shift in the understanding and use of the *cursus honorum*. Such a
rapid series of ordinations, within either a full year or a full day, could
hardly have met the expressed need for preparation and probation envisaged by the early legislators of the clerical *cursus* and the interstices canons.

c. The Effects of the *Cursus Honorum*

The *cursus honorum* affected holy orders in a variety of ways in the patristic period. Generally candidates for the presbyterate and the episcopate
tested and trained in the lower orders in the prescribed times would have
been much better prepared and selected in comparison to those who were
ordained without the requisite time served in a sequence of the lower
orders (though there are many notable exceptions).

Some of the minor offices changed dramatically in function. The lectorate, for example, was changed from an office for those who read at the
liturgy, to an office for the training of boys destined for a clerical career.
Likewise, the exorcistate, among other things, became a training ground
for adult candidates for holy orders.

It is argued that the *cursus honorum* was responsible for the decline of
the diaconate in the patristic period.[315] And yet one notes the numbers of
deacons in this period who were chosen bishops, particularly in the church
of Rome. It has also been noted that at Rome, at least, the diaconate was
not necessarily one of the sequence of grades for either the presbyterate or
the episcopate. It is just as possible that it was neither the clerical *cursus*
nor the presbyterate which threatened the position of the diaconate, but the
minor orders of acolyte and subdeacon, which assumed more and more of

---

[315] E.g., "The decline of the diaconate springs more from the development of the idea of
the *cursus honorum* than from any other single factor." Barnett, *The Diaconate*, p. 106.
Cf. Gregory Dix, "Ministry in the early Church," p. 284.

the deacons' functions.[316] In addition, Duchesne argues that the ministries of subdeacon and acolyte are a development of that of the deacon.[317]

d. Ordination *Per Saltum*

In spite of Canon XIII of the Council of Sardica, and the various papal and conciliar statements enjoining the clerical *cursus*, the *cursus* was neither universal nor uniform. Although the list of *per saltum* ordinations noted is not exhaustive, it sufficiently demonstrates that it was possible for lay people to be ordained directly to the presbyterate and episcopate, for deacons and subdeacons to become bishops, for subdeacons to become presbyters, and in at least one instance, for a subdeacon to become a bishop: the old order had not completely died out. As Lafontaine observes: "Il est donc permis de croire que la fin du IVe siècle constitue un sommet dans cette pratique déplorable."[318] Once again, it is difficult to conclude with Wright that the practice of sequential or cumulative orders became a standard of the church catholic after the mid-third century.[319]

In light of the repeated censures against the ordinations of neophytes and members of the laity to the episcopate, it would appear that the legislation which enjoined the *cursus* and the interstices was often ignored. Clearly, throughout the patristic period the *cursus honorum* with the interstices as enjoined in conciliar and papal legislation was the ideal, rather than the actual practice. As Paul Bradshaw has observed: "Legislation is better evidence for what it seeks to prohibit than for what it seeks to promote."[320]

Some of the more "deplorable" reasons for the perpetuation of *per saltum* ordinations have been noted. There were, however, more positive reasons why the practice continued. After the Decian persecution, the numbers of the clergy were seriously depleted. Likewise the barbarian invasions depleted the numbers of clergy. Due to the scarcity of catholic clergy in some places, such as at Milan at the time of Ambrose's election, it was necessary to chose episcopal candidates from even the

---

[316] As suggested by C. H. Turner, "The Organization of the Church," in *The Cambridge Medieval History*, vol. 1 (Cambridge, The University Press, 1911), p. 152.

[317] Duchesne, *Christian Worship*, p. 345.

[318] Lafontaine, *Les Conditions*, p. 245.

[319] Wright, "Sequential Orders," p. 248.

[320] Bradshaw, *The Search*, pp. 68–70.

catechumenate. As Lafontaine reminds us, in such instances one cannot discount the operation of the Holy Spirit.[321]

e. Variance and the *Cursus Honorum*

In the patristic period there was great flexibility in terms of the structure of the *cursus honorum*. Not all the texts surveyed in this chapter reflect the same sequence of grades, nor the same intervals between them. The sequence of grades of Sardica XIII (lector, deacon, presbyter, bishop) is not evident elsewhere. There are variations between the sequences of grades in the decretals of Siricius, Innocent, and Zosimus, in spite of their proximity to one another in time. The sequence of grades in the *Statuta ecclesiae antiqua* is similar to that of Isidore's *Etymologiae*, which differs from the sequence in Isidore's *De ecclesiasticis officiis*. The flexibility, variations, and inconsistencies in the *cursus honorum* and the interstices point to its slow evolution as an ordination practice.

There is no evidence of questions about the "sacramental validity" of *per saltum* ordinations; perhaps this question is more medieval than patristic. Patristic bishops who had been promoted without the requisite *cursus* were often suspect because they were unprepared and untested; they might have been considered "bad" bishops, but no one doubted that they were nonetheless "true" bishops. The scandal was the fact that such bishops were untested, unprepared, and ill-suited for their office. In short, the primary impetus behind the *cursus honorum* in the patristic period was a pastoral concern, rather than theological, namely the calibre of the clergy.

f. Conclusion

Clearly the *cursus honorum* was neither uniform nor universal in the patristic period. As a prescribed canonical requirement for ordination to the higher offices, the *cursus honorum* emerged shortly after the Peace of the Church to serve the practical and pastoral needs of the patristic church by ensuring the proper selection, probation, and preparation of its ordained leadership.

---

[321] Lafontaine, *Les Conditions*, pp. 263–267.

III

THE *CURSUS HONORUM*
FROM THE EIGHTH CENTURY
TO THE END OF THE TENTH

1. Introduction

This chapter will examine the developments of the *cursus honorum* and the interstices from the beginning of the eighth century to the end of the tenth, a period which witnessed increased stability and uniformity with regards to the *cursus honorum* and the further disintegration of the interstices. Evidence will be considered from conciliar and papal legislation (particularly with regard to the Photian controversy), canonistic collections, liturgical rites, early medieval literature on holy order, and biographical information.

2. The *Cursus Honorum*
in Early Medieval Conciliar Legislation

The first section will examine evidence of the *cursus honorum* in the early medieval councils. The six Carolingian councils which dealt with the clerical *cursus* will be investigated, as well as the Council of Rome (769) and the fourth Council of Constantinople (869). Although chronologically the Frankish councils to be studied are later than the Council of Rome, they will be treated first since the Roman and Constantinopolitan councils will be considered in sequence. The last conciliar legislation to be surveyed is from the Council of Rome (964).

a. Carolingian Councils

The substantial conciliar activity in the Carolingian period dealt with a variety of issues such as doctrine, church property, schools, monasteries, and the clergy.[1] In terms of holy order, canons dealing with the *cursus honorum* are rare; the councils focused largely on issues of clerical celibacy and simony. This section will examine evidence relating to the *cursus* and the interstices from the Councils of Frankfurt (794), Ripense, Freising, and Salzburg (800), Rheims (813), Aachen (816), Soissons (853), and Savonnières (859).

While the Council of Frankfurt (June 794) dealt chiefly with doctrinal matters, it produced some disciplinary canons. Canon XLVIII reiterates a patristic canon, ultimately from the Council of Neocaesarea, which established thirty as the minimum age of presbyters:

> XLVIIII. De presbyteris ante tricesimo aetatis non ordinandis.[2]

Although the canon deals with neither the clerical *cursus* nor the interstices *per se*, it does reveal that five centuries after Canon XI of the Council of Neocaesarea some churches in the West were still trying to establish thirty as the minimum age for presbyters.

The coterminous Councils of Ripense, Freising, and Salzburg (800) dealt with the *cursus honorum* in a single, curious, canon:

> VII. De non ordinandis presbiteris et diaconibus nisi in legitimis temporibus, sicut in decretis Zosimi papae continetur in kap. III. necnon et in decretis Gelasii papae cap. XI.[3]

The canon enjoins the interstices of Zosimus from the letter to Hesychius (*Epistle* 9.3) and also the interstices established by Gelasius (*Epistle* 14.2) which took just a year to fulfil from lector to presbyter. According to Zosimus, one would have been twenty-nine years old at the time of ordination to the presbyterate; older men would spend a five year period in the lectorate/exorcistate, a four year period as an acolyte or subdeacon, and a five year period in the diaconate. Although the intent of Canon VII is unclear,

---

[1] Between 742–859 there are one hundred and nineteen councils recorded in the Monumenta Germaniae Historia, *Concilia aevi Karolini*, vols. 1–3 (Hannover: Hahnsche Buchhandlung, 1979, 1979, 1984).

[2] MGH *Concilia* vol. 2, pt. 1, p. 171.

[3] MGH *Concilia* vol. 2, pt. 1, p. 208. *Cf.* P. Jaffé, *Regista pontificum Romanorum ab condita ecclesia ad annum post Christum natum MCXCVIII*, ed. G. Waatenbach, 2nd ed.(Leipzig: 1885), # 636.

clearly the bishops of the council were encouraging the clerical *cursus* with appropriate interstices.

Canon III of the Council of Rheims (May 813) deals with the *cursus*:

> III. Ut quicumque ad gradus ecclesiasticos condigne ascendere voluerit, unus-
> quisque intellegeret, qualiter secundum possibilitatem intellectus sui in eo gradu,
> ubi constitutus est, Deo militare et se ipsum valeret custodire.[4]

The canon assumes an ascent through the grades. The intent of the canon appears to be the encouragement of those in the lower grades to serve God in the grade in which they find themselves. There appears to be an attempt to give each grade an integrity of its own, rather than simply to use a grade as an inevitable step to the next.

The Council of Aachen, held in 816, is significant for the development of the sequence of grades in the Western church. Canons II–VIII describe the grades of ministry according to the Romano-Gallican sequence (i.e., doorkeeper, lector, exorcist, acolyte, subdeacon, deacon, presbyter, and bishop).[5] Significantly, the compiler(s) of the canons used material from Isidore's DEO, but rearranged Isidore's sequence (doorkeeper, exorcist, psalmist, lector, subdeacon, sacristan, deacon, presbyter, bishop) to con-form to Frankish usage. Material for the acolyte (Canon V), absent in the DEO, is taken from Isidore's Etymologiae. The Council of Aachen did much to strengthen and secure the Romano-Gallican sequence of grades in the Western church.

The Council of Soissons (April 853) dealt with an incident at the mon-astery of Altivillaris. Its newly appointed abbot, Halduinus, had apparently been ordained to the presbyterate without examination. This event caused a mild controversy, as recorded in the minutes of the negotiations at the council. The minutes provide an interesting insight into the developments of holy order and the clerical *cursus*:

> .... Tunc de presbitero quodam et monachorum abbate in Altivillaris monasterio,
> nomine Halduino, qui ab eodem Ebone diaconus visus fuerat ordinatus, et a Lupo
> postea venerabili episcopo Catalaunensi presbyter sine examine fuerat consecratus,
> mota est questio.

> Unde surgens idem Lupus episcopus porrexit volumen, in quo continebatur, quia
> metropolis Remorum ecclesia carebat pastore, iussus est regiis litteris domni Karo-
> li, ut in confectione chrismatis et in aliis necessitatibus videlicet ut suae matri ec-
> clesiae pro sua possibilitate in ecclesiasticis negotiis consulere procuraret. Qua de

---

[4] MGH *Concilia*, vol. 2, pt. 1, p. 254.

[5] MGH *Concilia*, vol. 2, pt. 1, pp. 319–326.

re cum epistola regia, ut ipsum fratrem nomine Halduinum et presbiterum ordinaret et abbatem monachorum in monasterio Altivillaris sacraret, archidiaconus Remensis ecclesiae, cum aliis comministris tam canonicis quam monachis, eundem illi ad ordinandum in gradu diaconii ad presbiterium optulit; quem secundum consuetudinem, quam in offerendo ordinandis ex canonica et monasteriis ipsa metropolis ecclesia habebat, ordinandum suscepit, et ad votum praecipientis principis et offerentium ordinavit. De quo iudicatum est a synodo secundum sacros canones, sicut scriptum est: "Ut qui presbyteri sine examine" per ignorantiam vel per ordinantium dissimulationem "sunt provecti," cum fuerint cogniti, deponantur; "quia quod inreprehensibile est catholica defendit ecclesia." Et ostensum est in eodem scripto secundum canonica formam concilii Sardicensi cap. XVIIII et ex aliis conciliis ac decretis eundem episcopum nihil dampnationis [*sic.*] de illius ordinatione attigisse. Sed qui saltu sine gradu diaconii ad sacerdotium prosilerat, in degradationem debitam resilire deberet.[6]

The circumstances which led to objections to Halduinus as presbyter and abbot are unclear. The grounds given, however, are quite clear: Halduinus had not been examined before his ordination. This circumstance suggests that adequate examination of a candidate was considered a necessity, and probably reflects an actual practice. Bishop Lupus countered this argument by saying that he had received a royal mandate to look after the church; he considered the ordination of Halduinus, the archdeacon of Rheims, to fall within the purview of that mandate. The members of the synod countered with a denunciation of ordaining candidates to the presbyterate without examination, based on Canon IX of the Council of Nicaea (transmitted by the *Dionysiana*).

It is the last sentence of this material from the Council of Soissons which is most interesting, and curiously out of place:

Sed qui saltu sine gradu diaconii ad sacerdotium prosilerat, in degradationem debitam resilire deberet.

"But whoever will have jumped by a leap to the priesthood without the grade of deacon, he is destined to jump back in due degradation." The term *sacerdotium* in this period largely means presbyter rather than bishop.[7] There is no suggestion elsewhere in this text that Halduinus had not been a deacon; the issue was that he had not been examined.

More significantly, however, this text demonstrates that by the mid-ninth century in the Frankish church, the diaconate had become a necessary part of the cursus; any one who has been ordained to the presbyterate

---

[6] MGH *Concilia*, vol. 2, pt. 3, p. 275.

[7] *cf.* Osborne, *Priesthood*, p. 160.

without the diaconate, is degraded, presumably to the previously held office or state. Hence, presbyteral ordination is incomplete without prior diaconal ordination. And yet there must have been some presbyters who had never been deacons, otherwise it would have been unnecessary to make such a statement. Such ordinations are not only illicit, they now appear invalid.

The last Carolingian council to be examined is the Council of Savonnières, 14 June 859. Canon VIII stresses the importance of a lengthy period of training and testing:

> VIII. Ut hi, qui ordinandi sunt, secundum ordinem ecclesiasticum et institutionem sanctorum patrum ordinentur. Videlicet, "ut episcopi iudicio metropolitanorum et eorum episcoporum, qui circumcirca sunt, provehantur ad ecclesiasticam potestatem; hi videlicet, qui plurimo tempore probantur, tam verbo fidei, quam recte conversationis exemplo". Et excerpta Martini: ut "non liceat electionem facere eorum, qui ad sacerdotium provocantur, sed iudicium sit episcoporum, ut ipsi eum, qui ordinandus est, probent, si in sermone et in fide et in" episcopali "vita edoctus est".[8]

The canon states that candidates must be ordained according to the institutes of the fathers. In particular, candidates for the episcopate are to be promoted only if they have undergone a lengthy period of testing in terms of their word of faith and example of their manner of life. The quotation is from Canon XII of the Council of Laodicea (transmitted by the *Dionysiana*), supported by a quotation of Martin of Braga from the Council of Braga. The emphasis in the canon is on the selection and training of bishops after a lengthy period of probation and preparation: the classical reasons behind the *cursus honorum*.

b. The Council of Rome, 769

The purpose of the Council of Rome, held in April, 769, was to restore canonical order to the church of Rome after the usurpation of the papacy by the antipope Constantine (767–768), and to prevent another seizure of the papacy by a lay man. Called by Pope Stephen III, the council legislated that bishops of Rome must be chosen only from among the cardinal presbyters and deacons of the Roman church.

The account of the council begins during the pontificate of Stephen II (752–757), the time when the papacy sought the protection of the Franks

---

[8] MGH *Concilia*, vol. 2, pt. 3, p. 477.

under Pepin against the Lombards. Pepin turned over the Exarchate of Ravenna and all its land to the authority of the pope, thus creating the papal states. Stephen's successor (and brother) Paul I (757–767) consolidated the papal states, but was noted for his severity and reliance on the papal bureaucracy. Towards the end of Paul's pontificate the duke of Nepi plotted to have him murdered and replaced by someone the Roman nobility could influence. The lay nobility were increasingly eager to control the papacy since it had become a temporal power in its own right after the annexation of the Exarchate of Ravenna. The candidate chosen to replace Paul was a layman, Constantine, brother of Toto, duke of Nepi. After Paul I's death (of natural causes) on 28 June 767, Constantine was proclaimed pope by the soldiers of the duke of Nepi. Accordingly, Constantine was rushed through the grades of the *cursus honorum*, perhaps in a matter of days.

There are two accounts of Constantine's consecration to the episcopate. The first comes from the *Liber pontificalis*, which reports that after being made a cleric, Constantine was ordained to the subdiaconate and the diaconate, prior to episcopal ordination—*contra sanctorum canonum instituta consecratus est*.[9] This is the standard account of Constantine's sequence of ordinations to the episcopate.[10]

There is, however, an alternate and little appreciated account of Constantine's ordination from the *acta* of the Council of Rome (769). This account is preserved in an early eleventh-century manuscript of a canon law collection: Wolfenbüttel, Herzog-August-Bibliothek, MS Helmst. 454. The collection had been attributed to Rotger, archbishop of Trier (918–*ca.* 930), by H. Wasserschleben in 1839.[11] Rotger instituted a canonical collection based on patristic and papal sources which he submitted to a

---

[9] LP I, pp. 468–469.

[10] E.g., M. Andrieu, "Les ordres mineurs dans l'ancien rite romain", *Revue des sciences religieuses* 5 (1925) p. 258; "Il y a tout lieu de croire que l'énumeration est ici complète." p. 271; M. Andrieu, "La carrière ecclésiastique," p. 97; Harald Zimmermann, *Papstabsetzungen des Mittelalters* (Köln: Hermann Böhlaus Nachf, 1968), p. 15; Peter Llewellyn, *Rome in the Dark Ages* (London: Faber & Faber, 1970), p. 222; J. N. D. Kelly, *The Oxford Dictionary of Popes* (Oxford: Oxford University Press, 1986), p. 94; Jaffé, p. 283. Eugene Ewig, "The Papacy's Alienation from Byzantium and Rapprochement with the Franks", in *The Church in the Age of Feudalism*, describes Constantine as having "received the various orders *per saltum*," p. 25.

[11] H. Wasserschleben, *Beiträge zur Geschichte der vorgratianischen* (1839), p. 162 ff. Cited by A. Werminghoff, MGH *Concilia* vol. 2, pt. 1, p. 78.

provincial synod at Trier in 927. It is now impossible, however, to associate the Wolfenbüttel manuscript with this collection, or with Rotger at all. As Herwig John has shown, the discovery of the authentic Rotgeran *capitula* makes this ascription impossible.[12] Furthermore, as John indicates, while the provenance of the manuscript remains Trier, it cannot have been written prior to 964, since its latest chronological note is the exile of Pope Benedict V to Hamburg in 964. According to John, although the Wolfenbüttel may be dated as early eleventh-century, it was certainly written after 964.[13]

According to this version after being made a cleric, Constantine received the minor orders of the Gallican *cursus*, and was then consecrated deacon and bishop:

> Concilium Stephani tercii pape habitum temporibus dominorum regnum Caroli at Carlomanni, in quo dampnavit Constantinum neophitum et invasorem sanctae sedis apostolicae, qui a Georio Penestrine civitatis episcopo in palatio Lateranensi contra canonica instituta et sanctorum patrum decreta subito clericus factus est, deinde hostiarius, lector, exorcista, acolitus, subdiaconus et diaconus et mox consecratus in pontificem ab ipso et Eustratio et Citonato episcopis, omnesque, qui ab eodem neophito irregulariter ordinati fuerant.[14]

The text relates how Constantine, against the "canonical institutes and decretals of the holy fathers" was suddenly (*subito*) admitted a cleric, and made doorkeeper, lector, exorcist, acolyte, subdeacon, and finally deacon by George, bishop of Praeneste. George was then joined by the bishops of Eustratius and Citano in the consecration of Constantine as bishop. This account differs from the first most notably in the list of grades received by Constantine prior to his episcopal consecration.

One must be judicious about the degree of authority to be accorded to the account of the Wolfenbüttel manuscript; it was written nearly two centuries after the event, and may reflect tenth-century practice. Yet, if this account is authentic, it reports remarkable things about the *cursus honorum* in Rome in the mid-eighth century. The sequence of grades (doorkeeper,

---

[12] Herwig John (ed.), *Collectio canonum Remedio Curiensi episcopo perperam ascripta, Monumenta Iuris Canonici*, Series B, col. 2 (Vatican: Biblioteca Apostolica Vaticana, 1976), p. 52, n. 99.

[13] ". . . die vielleicht aus dem frühen 11. Jahrhundert stammt, sicher aber nach 964 geschriben wurde, dem Termin der Verbannung Papst Benedikts V. nach Hamburg. . ." John, *Collectio canonum*, p. 52.

[14] MGH *Concilia* vol. 2, pt. 1, p. 78; Wolfenbüttel, Herzog-August-Bibliothek, MS Helmst. 454, fol. 73.

lector, exorcist, acolyte, subdeacon, and deacon) received by Constantine is noteworthy, for it is not the standard *cursus* of other bishops of Rome at this time (another reason for questioning the authenticity of this text). Rather, it is the Romano-Gallican sequence of the *Statuta ecclesiae antiqua*, and the sixth-century material in the *Liber pontificalis* under the entry for Pope Gaius and is similar to the sequence ascribed to Silvester.

The same sequence of the grades is found in the Eighth-Century Gelasian sacramentaries and the tenth-century *Pontificale romano-germanicum*. It can be argued that the Wolfenbüttel account may reflect the *cursus* of the PRG and the sequences of grades received by Leo VIII and John XI-II. Conversely, Roger Reynolds argues that the ordination rites of the Eighth-Century Gelasian Sacramentary were not unknown in Italy at this time, based on the existence of the *Collectio Teatina*, a late-eighth or early-ninth-century canon law collection which contains the Eighth-Century Gelasian ordination rites, including the Romano-Gallican sequence of grades.[15] This discovery may well account for the particular sequence of grades received by Constantine, adding more credence to the Wolfenbüttel manuscript account of Constantine's series of ordinations.[16]

It is noteworthy that neither account includes the presbyterate in the sequence of grades received by Constantine; this omission was common in Rome during this period. And yet, if the Wolfenbüttel account is authentic, it is interesting that in following a sequence of grades which was not typically Roman, the presbyterate was nonetheless omitted in the case of Constantine.

Despite the apparent efforts to obtain a "traditional" election and consecration, the council of 769 held Constantine's consecration to be invalid on the grounds that he was a member of the laity when he was "elected". The account of Constantine's response is recorded:

> Sequenti autem die presentatus est iterum concilio et interrogatus, cur tam nefariae novitati consentiret. At ille [i.e. Constantinum], superbiae spiritu inflatus, ait: Profiteor me nihil novi fecisse, quia Sergius Ravennas archiepiscopus laicus ad honorem electus est et Stephanus Neapolitanus episcopus similiter. Hec eo respondente contra sanctorum patrum instituta, iussus est colaphis caedi et eici

---

[15] Roger Reynolds, "The Ritual of Clerical Ordination of the *Sacramentarium Gelasianum Saec. VIII*: Early Evidence from Southern Italy," *Rituels: Mélanges offerts au Père Gy op*, eds. Paul de Clerck & Eric Palazzo (Paris: Cerf, 1991), pp. 437–445.

[16] Southern Italian manuscripts are extant from this period which contain the Gelasian ordination rites, including the Romano-Gallican sequence of grades.

extra ecclesiam. Tunc allatae sunt inscriptiones eius et gesta decreti in presbiterio et presente concilio conbusta sunt. Deinde constitutum est a sancto concilio sub anathematis interdictione, ut ne quis deinceps ad pontificatum presumeret accedere nisi cardinalis presbiter aut diaconus eiusdem ecclesiae, qui per distinctos gradus ascenderet. De illis vero, qui ab eodem neophito consecrati fuerant, statutum est, ut in eodem gradu permanerent, in quo consistebant, cum eos ipse ad altiorem proveheret; qui autem ex eis digni postea reperirentur, iterum a clero et a populo eligerentur et a domino Stephano papa consecrarentur. De laicis vero, qui ab ipso presbiteri aut diaconi consecrati fuerant, sancitum est, ut ubique voluissent, in religioso habitu solummodo permanerent. sicque factum est, ut omnes episcopi ab eodem Constantino neophito consecrati ad propria remearent et in pristino gradu aliquantulum temporis permanerent et postea, a clero et a plebibus electi, a domino Stephano papa episcopi consecrarentur et omnia ecclesiastica misteria iterarentur preter sacrum baptisma et misticum chrisma....[17]

In his defence, Constantine argues that his election as a lay person was not a novelty. He notes two other known examples of lay men being elected from the laity to the episcopate in Naples and Ravenna. This argument did not convince the members of the synod who forcibly ejected him, and then burned his inscriptions and decrees. Moreover, they declared all the ordinations he performed invalid; those ordinations performed by any bishops he ordained were likewise considered invalid, effectively declaring their own consecrations invalid as well.

The issue of Constantine's election is both canonical and theological. In spite of a careful observance of the sequence of *cursus honorum*, his episcopal consecration was considered sacramentally invalid. Not only were *per saltum* ordinations considered invalid, but *per saltum* elections as well. Constantine was referred to as a "neophyte", despite his seven-fold (or three-fold) appointment to office. The Council of Rome is indicative of a shift from the language of legality to that of validity with respect to election and sequential ordination. This shift moves the discussion from canon law to sacramental theology.

The text makes some noteworthy references to those who were ordained by Constantine and his bishops, and then demoted to their former grades. For example, the council refers to laity who were ordained either presbyters or deacons by the false bishops, who are to retain the religious habit only. Another text directs that the presbyters and deacons ordained by Constantine, be returned to the orders from which they came, specifically "the former subdiaconal order or another":

---

[17] MGH *Concilia*, vol. 2, pt. 1, pp. 78–79

....At vero presbyteri illi vel diaconi, quos in hac sancta Romana ecclesia ordinavit,
in pristino subdiaconatus ordine vel alio, quo fungebantur, officio revertantur....[18]

The text indicates that candidates were ordained to either the presbyterate
or the diaconate, but not necessarily to both. Furthermore, not only did
both presbyters and deacons typically come from the subdiaconate, but
possibly from other grades as well.

The *acta* of the Council of Rome record the solution to prevent the
usurpation of the papacy by a member of the laity from happening again:

...Tunc adlatis sacratissimis canonibus iisque liquido perscrutatis prolata est sententia ab eodem sacerdotale concilio sub anathematis interdictu, nullus umquam
praesumi laicorum neque ex alio ordine, nisi per distinctos gradus ascendens diaconus aut presbiter cardinalis factus fuerit, ad sacrum pontificatus honorem promoveri.[19]

"It was constituted by the holy synod under the interdict of anathema, that
no longer shall any one presume to accede to the pontificate except a cardinal presbyter or deacon, having risen through the distinct grades." The
cursus through the minor ministries to either the diaconate or to the presbyterate is requisite for promotion to the episcopate. Promotion to the pontificate from the laity, or from a minor order, is prohibited. "Promotion" in
this sense probably means "election". This development cannot be regarded as new; it simply gives canonical authority to the traditional Roman
practice of electing either a deacon or a presbyter as bishop.

The events surrounding the accession and demise of Constantine are
important in the development of the *cursus honorum*. They demonstrate
the extent to which the *cursus honorum* had become normative by the mid-
eighth century; even Constantine and his colleagues realised the importance of adhering to the *cursus*. The fact that Constantine, his brother Toto,
and the ordaining bishops, believed that a candidate could be "rushed"
through the grades (either the subdiaconate, diaconate and episcopate, or,
the minor orders and the diaconate and the episcopate) indicates the extent
to which the *cursus honorum* had become dissociated from the interstices.
Such adherence to sequential ordination without the requisite observance
of the interstices can hardly be understood as anything other than as a

---

[18] MGH *Concilia*, vol. 2, pt. 1, p. 86.

[19] MGH *Concilia*, vol. 2, pt. 1, pp. 76–77.

skewed canonical rigidity. Nonetheless, the documents from the council reveal the flexibility in practice, if not in law.[20]

c. The Fourth Council of Constantinople, 869–870

The fourth Council of Constantinople (869–870) belongs to the history of the Photian controversy. The Photian controversy (or schism) is a significant milestone in the deterioration of the relationship between the Eastern and Western Churches in the Middle Ages. In the history of sequential ordination, the canons and ancillary material of the council are of particular importance. The role the debate over the *cursus honorum* and interstices played at the council, however, is often ignored in historical accounts of the controversy. The assortment of texts to be surveyed in this section illustrate the importance of the *cursus honorum* in the conflict between the see of Rome and Photius.

Although the council occurred in Constantinople, it largely reflected Western interests, particularly with regard to the clerical *cursus*. Since the eleventh century, the fourth Council of Constantinople has been regarded as the eighth ecumenical council by the Western church. This opinion has not been maintained by the Eastern church, which seems to have completely ignored the council. Canons from the fourth Council of Constantinople are not found in any of the canonical collections of the Eastern church.[21]

The historical account of the council begins in 858 when Ignatius, the patriarch of Constantinople, was deposed by Emperor Michael III. Ignatius was arrested and exiled on charges of treason. By all accounts a holy man, Ignatius had become involved in the political machinations of Constantinople and quarrelled with Michael's uncle and regent Bardas. Because Ignatius was deposed by the emperor, not by a synod, finding a successor was to be a delicate matter. Ignatius was prepared to resign if his successor would agree to recognise the legitimacy of his patriarchate, uphold his decrees, and maintain communion with him.

Michael and Bardas proposed a compromise candidate in the person of Photius (820–895), a layman and a distinguished scholar, politician, and diplomat, who was head of the imperial chancery at the time. Photius was

---

[20] Of the systematic collections examined in this study, the promulgation of the Council of Rome (769) appears in the *Collectio canon* of Deusdedit.

[21] Norman Tanner, *Decrees of the Ecumenical Councils*, vol.1 (Georgetown: Georgetown University Press, 1990), p. 157.

politically neutral, orthodox, and well-connected: his uncle Tarasius was the patriarch of Constantinople who convened the second Council of Constantinople which ended the iconoclastic controversy. Photius was duly elected by a synod of bishops, and was ordained in late December of 858. By all accounts, he seems to have received the tonsure on 20 December, and then the orders according to the Byzantine *cursus*: lector (*anagnostes*), subdeacon, deacon, and presbyter during the rest of the week. He was consecrated bishop on 25 December in order to preside at the Christmas liturgy at Constantinople as patriarch.[22] As a ninth-century (anti-Photian) account of the event records:

> Nam primo die monachus ex laico, altero lector, tum hypodiaconus, ac diaconus et presbyter: sexto deinde, qui fuit Christi natalis, et ipse sacrum conscedens tribunal, pacem populo, nihil vera pace dignum cogitans, nuntiavit.[23]

While such rapid sequential ordinations through the grades were rare and contrary to the *nomocanone* of the Byzantine Church, the practice was not unknown in Constantinople. For example, in 687 Patriarch Paul III was similarly ordained,[24] as were Patriarchs Tarasius in 784,[25] and Nicephorus

---

[22] Cf. J. Hergenröther, *Photius, Patriarch von Konstantinopel*, vol. 1 (Regensburg: Georg Joseph Manz, 1867), p. 379; Asterios Gerostergios, *St. Photius the Great* (Belmont Mass.: Institute for Byzantine and Modern Greek Studies, 1980), p. 39; Daniel Stiernon, *Constantinople IV*, Histoires des Conciles Oecuménique vol. 5 (Paris: Éditions de l'Orante, 1967), p. 29; Francis Dvornik, *The Photian Schism: History and Legend*, (Cambridge: University Press, 1948), p. 50. However, Despina Stratoudaki White, *Patriarch Photios of Constantinople*, (Brookline, Mass.: Holy Cross Orthodox Press, 1981) p. 23 writes: ".... in five successive days he received all the offices and degrees of the priesthood: lector, subdeacon, and priest [sic.], and was consecrated bishop and enthroned as Patriarch of Constantinople on Christmas Day 858." The entry for "Anagnostes" (i.e. lector) in the *Oxford Dictionary of Byzantium*, vol. 1, ed. Alexander P. Kazhdan (New York: Oxford University Press, 1991), p. 84, claims that the lectorate was the first stage of Photius's career. Hans-Georg Beck in his article "The Byzantine Church in the Age of Photius," *The Church in the Age of Feudalism* simply describes Photius's ordination as "*per saltum*", p. 176.

[23] Niketas-David Paphilagon, *Vita S. Ignatii*, PG 105. 511; not *PG* 105.235, *pace* D. White, *Patriarch Photios of Constantinople*, p. 42, n. 58.

[24] Dvornik, *The Photian Schism*, p. 50.

[25] Ignatius the Deacon, *Vita Tarasii archiepiscopi Constantinopolitani*, PG 98.1391–1393; Dvornik, *The Photian Schism*, p. 50.

in 806.[26] Nonetheless, the method of Photius's ordination to the episcopate was to be a major issue in the ensuing controversy.

Early in 859 a schism in Constantinople occurred when Ignatius refused to abdicate. As a way of settling the growing schism between the patriarchate and the party which regarded Ignatius as the legitimate patriarch, Photius and Michael sought recognition from the other historic patriarchs of the church, including Pope Nicholas I, patriarch of the West. In 860 they sent a delegation to Nicholas with a request for his judgement. Nicholas responded by sending two legates, Bishop Zacharias of Anagni and Bishop Radoald of Porto, to a council at Constantinople in 861. Nicholas directed them to examine the legitimacy of Photius' election. In addition, they were to secure for the Roman church the territories of Illyricum and southern Italy. Zacharias and Radoald recognised Photius, but did not secure the return of the territories.

In 862 Nicholas annulled the decisions of the council of 861, and hence the positions of his own legates. In 863 he excommunicated and deposed Photius, declaring him uncanonically elected and all his ordinations invalid. In return, at a council at Constantinople in 867, Photius deposed and excommunicated Nicholas. Unbeknownst to Photius, however, Nicholas was dead at the time. Thus, a period of schism ensued between Rome and Constantinople.

In 868 Emperor Michael was murdered and succeeded by Basil who immediately deposed Photius and restored Ignatius. Pope Hadrian II (867–872) convened a council in Rome in 869 which anathematised Photius. In the same year, the fourth Council of Constantinople was convened at the initiative of Emperor Basil, who was eager to restore communion with Rome after the period of schism. Three legates from Rome, bishops Donatus and Stephen, and the deacon Marinus (later Pope Marinus I, 882–884), not only attended the council but had intended to presided over it. In fact, Emperor Basil appointed his deputy, Baanes, as president of the council. The council largely confirmed the sentence of the Council of Rome (869) deposing Photius.

Despite Photius' deposition, Ignatius' restoration, and the renewed communion between the churches of Rome and Constantinople, problems continued between the patriarch of Constantinople and the papacy,

---

[26] Paul J. Alexander, *The Patriarch Nicephorus of Constantinople* (Oxford: Clarendon Press, 1958), p. 69; Dvornik, *The Photian Schism*, p. 50.

particularly in regards to the conversion of the Bulgarian people of Illyricum. The council of 869–870 upheld Constantinople's jurisdiction over Illyricum and the Bulgarian people, a policy which Ignatius supported.

In 877 Ignatius died and Photius was restored. At the Council of Constantinople of 879–880, which papal legates also attended, Photius' restoration was ratified and the judgments of the Council of Constantinople IV annulled. Photius was deposed again in 886, and spent the rest of his life in obscurity, and died at the convent of Armeniaki at the end of the ninth century.

The Photian controversy was compounded by other outstanding issues between the sees of Rome and Constantinople: for example, issues around the extent of the Roman primacy, conflicts over the conversion of Bulgaria, theological disputes over the *filioque* clause, and territorial disputes over Illyricum and southern Italy. On all these issues, Patriarch Photius took a contrary position to that of the Roman Church. Nicholas I, then, had many reasons for wanting Photius deposed.

One of the principal denunciations used against Photius by Popes Nicholas I, Hadrian II, and John VIII was the fact that he was a lay person at the time of his election—the same pretext used in the deposition of the antipope Constantine a century earlier in Rome. Hence, the texts from the controversy reflect much of the current opinion about the *cursus honorum*. It is, however, argued that Nicholas was much more interested in Illyricum and southern Italy than in questions over the validity of Photius's orders.[27]

One is confronted with an abundance of material from the Fourth Council of Constantinople from which to choose. The following selections are meant to be an illustrative rather than an exhaustive list.

The letter of Nicholas I to Michael III of 28 September 865,[28] which was read at the fourth session of the council, reveals the papal concerns that the *cursus* and interstices have not been followed in Photius's consecration:

> ....Quod quam sit reprehensione dignum, testes illi qui ei oppositi fuerant manifestant; quia tales, quos in epistola vestra legimus, canonica institutio prohibet.... Ceterum, his etiam sic injuste peractis, ad detestabiliora inconsiderationis suae votum supradictam populi catervam dirigendo, de laicorum habitu qui ei praesset elegit pastorem. O quam praesumptuosa temeritas! ille praeponitur ovili divino qui nescit adhuc dominari spiritui suo: nam qui ignorat disponere vitam suam per gradus

---

[27] A. Gerostergios, *St. Photius the Great*, p. 48.

[28] Identified by Stiernon as 25 September 860. *Constantinople IV*, p. 250.

ecclesiae minime ductus, quomodo corrigere quibit vitam alienam subito electus? Latuisse vos non credimus, quid apostolorum egerit coetus post acceptum donum sancti Spiritus.

Ecce etenim ipsi visione Domini, et locutione illius assidua, ejusdemque resurrectione laetificati, atque gratia spiritalis descensus consolidati, non praesumpserunt de electis septuaginta duobus eligere tam audacter duodecimum, qui Judae praevaricatoris suppleret locum, sed per gradus quosdam (ut ita dicatur) de septuagenario binarioque numero elegerunt duos, Joseph qui vocabatur Justus, et Matthiam. Et sic ex his quem alteri praeponerent interim ignorantes, divinum examen postulavere, electioneque data, qui humanis obtutibus justior videbatur, coram divinitatis conspectu inferior est inventus. Igitur illius congregationis conatus, nihil horum studens exercere, visi sunt a recto itineris tramite declinasse, cum in custodiam dominici gregis non taliter ut decuit studerunt pastorem praeponere. In notitia siquidem saecularium literarum nemo magistri nomine merito censetur, nisi per gradus disciplinarum procedens fuerit doctus.

Verum iste Photius videlicet antea doctor prorupit, quam doctus extiterit: prius magister videri cupiit, quam discipulus audiri. Prius auditor esse debuit, ac institutor: sed hic doctoris e contrario cathedram eligens, docere prius elegit, ac deinde coepit doceri; prius sanctifcare curavit, ac demum sanctificari; prius illuminare voluit, et postmodum illuminari.

Haec itaque catholicus ordo prohibet: et sancta nostra Romana ecclesia talem electionem semper prohibuit per antecessores nostros catholicae fidei doctores. Quorum nos tenorem observantes, instituta ipsorum esse inviolabilia censemus. Sardicense denique concilium, ut de laicis non eligeretur antistes in capite tertiodecimo per omnia prohibuit, ita inquiens: Si forte aut dives, aut scholasticus de foro, aut ex administratore episcopus fuerit postulatus, ut non prius ordinetur, nisi ante lectoris munere, et officio diaconii, aut presbyterii fuerit perfunctus, ut per singulos gradus, si dignus fuerit, ascendat ad culmen episcopatus. Et reliqua.[29]

The letter continues with citations from the letters of Celestine (*Epistle* 5), Leo (*Epistle* 12), and Gelasius (*Epistle* 14.3). This section from the letter reveals Nicholas' concern that Photius had not served in the grades prior to his election as patriarch. The injustice of deposing Ignatius is compounded by the audacity of choosing a pastor from among the laity. Nicholas asks how someone who has been promoted without observing the ecclesiastical degrees can correct the lives of others without knowing how to rule his own life?

Nicholas cites as evidence the election of Matthias from the Acts of the Apostles. Claiming that Matthias had been one of the seventy-two

---

[29] MANSI XVI.59–60; *Epistle* 82, Monumenta Germanica Historica, *Epistolae*, vol. 6, Epistolae Karolini Aevi, vol. 4, (Berlin: Weidmanns, 1925), pp. 434–439; *PL* 119.773–779; Jaffé, # 2682.

disciples, he understands the election of Matthias as conforming to the clerical *cursus*. It is worth noting that the account in the Acts of the Apostles says nothing about Joseph and Matthias ever having been among the Seventy-two, only that they had been among the disciples of Jesus. As noted in Chapter II, there is no evidence in the New Testament of service in one office as a prerequisite for service in another, or that the Twelve had ever been members of the Seventy-two, or of the Seven. By the ninth century the *cursus* had become such an assumed part of catholic order that biblical texts are interpreted according to its usages.

In a style reminiscent of Celestine, Leo, Hormisdas, Gregory, and other papal predecessors, Nicholas emphasises that one must be a disciple before being a teacher. As further evidence against the election of lay people as bishops, Nicholas cites Canon XIII of the Council of Sardica (in the Dionysian form) and the practice of the Roman church, with citations from the letters of Celestine (*Epistle* 5), Leo (*Epistle* 14), and Gelasius (*Epistle* 14.3). Nicholas unequivocally asserts that ".... our holy Roman church has always prohibited elections of such a kind," reflecting a ninth-century opinion that the clerical *cursus* had always been unvarying practice of the Roman church. Once again, the *cursus honorum* has become such an intrinsic and fixed feature of holy order that it is impossible to admit its gradual emergence and development.

Nicholas does not take into account the different sequences of grades leading to the episcopate in Rome itself: sequences which included the diaconate but not the presbyterate, or which included the presbyterate but not the diaconate. Nicholas's own career, for instance, did not include the presbyterate.

In another letter to Emperor Michael, read at the council, Nicholas further elaborates on the necessity of observing the *cursus honorum* and the interstices:

.... Nos quidem de nobilissimo viro Ignatio patriarcha non tantum haec, verum et illud comperimus, quod non solum genere claruit, verum etiam a primaevo suae aetatis per singulos ecclesiasticos gradus ascendens ex monastica vita, omni ecclesiastico coetu consentiente, sicut in apicibus quos sanctissimo Leoni praesuli praedecessori nostro destinaveratis comperimus, episcopatus culmen promeruit.

Photium autem novimus per nullos ecclesiasticos gradus ascendentem, sed tantummodo ex laicali militia episcopum pertinaciter ordinatum. Quamobrem necessario in sententia nostra, qua stetimus, persistimus; et neque venerabilem Ignatium patriarcham in aliquo damnamus, neque Photium modo quolibet suscipimus. Verum quia omnibus accusationibus remotis, quibus strennum virum Ignatium patriarcham ad apostolicam sedem asserebatis notabilem, unum opponentes tantummodo, quod potentia saeculari sedem pervaserit, vestro speciali deposuistis, damnastis, et expulistis arbitrio, et Photium ex laicali agmine vobis improvide in ejus loco subrogastis episcopum, aequanimiter ferre omnino non possumus; maxime cum horum duorum negotium investigari, et nobis renuntiari, non definiri mandaverimus. Quapropter, ut diximus, nullo modo prudentis viri Ignatii patriarchae depositioni, vel Photii subrogationi assensum praebemus, quosque veritas, omni falsitatis suco nudata, in praesentia nostra eluceat. Quia consuetudinem vestram novimus in regia urbe minime apicem archieraticae potestatis aliquem posse habere sine ecclesiasticae plebis consensu, atque imperiali suffragio, et ob id Ignatium patriarcham damnare nolumus, nec debemus.

Praeterea Photii, quem ex militia subito ad tanti culmen regiminis consecrastis, ordinationem ratam haberi decernitis, eo quod Nectarius non solum ex laico habitu, verum etiam ex Pagano, sancto synodo secunda ordinante, meruerit episcopus fieri: qui tamen Nectarius verae religionis catholicus, nullius depositionis catholici conscius, sedis gubernacula, sine scandalo, sine vi, sine omni schismate suscepit: quem Spiritus sancti auxilio, et talento sibi credito, haereticorum perfidiis restitisse, eorumque dogma, quod jam ex longo tempore pullulaverat, et plurimos sui contagione infecerat, destruxisse ipsi recolitis: et idcirco bene et optime sanctae secundae synodo, apostolicae sedis auctoritate fultae, ita de Nectario placuisse testamur.

Sed et beatus nihilo minus fulgidissimus doctor Ambrosius, quem similiter ex militia et catechumeno asseveratis episcopum, cum divinitus per miraculorum signa ab ipsis cunabulis usque ad conscreationis suae tempus fuisset evocatus,et a dissidentibus populis, subito in unam sui concordiam provocatis, compelleretur ad regimen ecclesiasticum suscipiendum, minime seditioni, vel schismati studuit; quin potius eas quas reperit, semetipsum non ultro sed coacte populo offerens, repulitet removit....

.... Pro quo aeque haec sancta Romana ecclesia eos rite suscepit: ideoque hoc ad tempus necessitatis probe suscepit, quia contra canonum privilegum sibi concessum nihil novit temere perpetratum. Vos autem non ita horum illustrium virorum comparationem perpendistis, ubi saepe dictum virum Ignatium patriarcham juste a vobis ordinatum injuste de patriarchatu ejicientes, Photium subito ex laicali militia in episcopali dignitate elevatis:et ob id nihil valere patimur: quia sanctae Romanae ecclesiae nunquam extitit mos improvide vel injuste unum ejicere,et alterum subrogare....[30]

This section of the text begins with Nicholas' commendation of Ignatius, who as a monk ascended through all the grades before "he was promoted to the height of the episcopate". Nicholas goes on to say: "The most inexperienced Photius, on the other hand, ascended through none of the ecclesiastical grades, but was obstinately ordained a bishop from out of the lay

---

[30] MANSI XVI.65–66. *Cf.* The Letter of Nicholas to the archbishops, metropolitans, and bishops of the church of Constantinople, MANSI XVI.101–102.

militia." It is on these grounds that Nicholas states that he cannot accept Photius.

Nicholas repudiates the comparison between Photius's promotion and the examples of Nectarius of Constantinople in 381, and Ambrose of Milan in 374. Nicholas dismisses the comparison with Nectarius on the grounds that Nectarius had not replaced a deposed patriarch (Gregory of Nyssa having resigned). Moreover, Nicholas argues, Nectarius was a catholic, and his election was without scandal. Likewise, Nicholas rejects the comparison between Photius and "the most shining doctor Ambrose," because the latter's election was revealed through miracles. Moreover, Ambrose was reluctant to accept ecclesiastical rule and was forced to accept it by the people.

Despite the charges against Photius' orthodoxy and ambition, Nicholas does not deny the comparison between the nature of the elections of Photius with those of Ambrose and Nectarius. This comparison, however, raises the question of whether Nicholas believed Photius was ordained directly to the episcopate (*per saltum*) or whether he believed Photius was elected from the laity and subsequently rushed through the grades of the *cursus*. The comparison with Nectarius suggests the former. Furthermore, Nicholas states: "*Photium autem novimus per nullos ecclesiasticos gradus ascendentem, sed tantummodo ex laicali militia episcopum pertinaciter ordinatum.*" These and similar inferences in the letter suggest that in Nicholas's mind Photius was ordained, not just elected, *per saltum* from the laity.

A letter of 18 March 862 from Nicholas to Photius himself, also read at the proceedings of the council, adds further confusion to this question. Nicholas writes:

....Nam in hoc quo noster apostolatus vestram prudentiam commonuit, quia ex laicali ordine sine canonica approbatione ad patriarchatus dignitatem subito transcendere contra patrum promulgationes non recusastis, sed temere atque impudenter ad tanti honoris culmen accedere praesumpsistis, assumentes vobis quasi sanctissimo viro Nectario occasionem, quem sancta secunda synodus non ob aliud ad sacerdotalem eligere atque ordinare ex laicali ordine voluit dignitatem, nisi quia magnae necessitatis contritione anxiabatur, eo quod in sancta Constantinopolitana ecclesia nullus clericorum inveniri poterat, qui pessimae haereseos nimbosa caligine non fuerit impeditus....[31]

---

[31] MANSI XVI.69–70.

.... De Tarasii siquidem promotione, qui similiter ex laicali coetu ad patriarchatus extemplo culmen promotus est, quamet vos quasi in auctoritatem vestrae defensionis assumere vultis, si sanctam (quae apud vos tempore sanctissimi viri domini Hadriani papae celebrata est) synodum diligentius scrutati fueritis, atque attentius intenderitis, invenietis quid in ea idem sanctissimus vir consultus decreverit,et quod dum ejus consecrationis reprehenderet actus,et moerorem se pro tam praesumptiva factione nimium sustinere profiteretur. Dicit enim, quod nisi in erigendis imaginibus ferventius contra illarum depositores atque conculcatores ut verus miles Christi resisteres, nequaquam vestrae consecrationi assensum praeberemus, aut in ordine patriarchatus vestram dilectionem susciperemus: quae tantum declaratur inordinate promota, quantum comprobatur contra apostolica decreta enormiter praesumpta.

Beatissimum quoque Ambrosium clarissimamet splendidissimam lucernam ecclesiae, qui ex catechumeno, divino praesagio, ad episcopalem per continuos gradus promotus est dignitatem, cur nobis pro vestro tutamine opponitiset ad vestram illicitam promotionem antefertis? qui non instinctu hominum, sed divina vocatione per miraculorum prodigia electus est....[32]

.... Qui, dum multis ac variis voluisset occultare argumentis,et a tanto honore delitescere, tandem superatus, ad sacerdotalem ab omni populoet clero divinitus est dignitatem electus,et a catechumeno per singulos gradus ecclesiasticos proficiscens, octavo die ab omni catholicorum, divina annuente clementia, consensu est consecratus episcopus. Attendat igitur prudentiae vestrae dilectio,et intimo cordis prospiciat oculo, si debent ea, quae per miraculorum signa fidelibus proveniunt, his aequari, quae proprio tantum libitu ad dignitatis gloriam percipiendam peraguntur:et sic ad auctoritatis vestrae excusationem praefatos assumite viros. Ecce propter necessitatemet inopiam clericorm Nectarius, ecce propter ecclesiastica dogmata,et haereticorum expugnationem, qui venerandas deponere imagines praesumpserunt, Tarasius, ecce per miraculorum signa Ambrosius, ad regendas ecclesias promoti sunt.

De vobis autem, quibus perplures auctoritates conciliorum atque decreta sanctissimorum pontificum resistunt, quid aliud sentiendum, nisi inopinatam a vobis consuetudinem adolevisse credendum? Et secundum sanctorum patrum sententiam, non solum quia ex laicali ordine contra canonicas auctoritates ad regendam Constantinopolitanam ecclesiam subito tranvolastis, sed etiam quia, vivente viro,et incolumi persistente (videlicet religiosissimo Ignatio patriarcha) cathedram illius, scilicet Constantinopolitanam ecclesiam, ut moechus, surripuistis,et invadere praesumpsistis, postponentes illud, quod scriptum est: "Quod tibi non vis fieri, alii ne feceris":et ideo vestrae consecrationi aequitatis libramina tenentes, assensum praebere (quia enormiteret contra sanctorum patrum institutiones peracta est) minime praesumimus.

Quod vero dicitis, neque Sardicense concilium, neque decretalia vos habere sanctorum pontificum, vel recipere, non facile nobis facultas credendi tribuiter: maxime

---

[32] MANSI XVI.70.

cum Sardicense concilium, quod penes vos in vestris regionibus actum est,et omnis
ecclesia recipit: qua ratione convenerat, ut hoc sancta Constantinopolitana ecclesia
abjiceret,et (ut dignum est) non retineret?[33]

Arguing on the basis of the patristic reasons behind sequential ordination—*canonica approbatione*—and drawing on Canon XIII of the Council
of Sardica and the decrees of the earlier popes, Nicholas refuses to recognise Photius as patriarch on the grounds that his consecration was "irregu-
larly accomplished and contrary to the institutes of the holy fathers."
Furthermore, Nicholas noted that Photius's predecessor, Ignatius, was still
alive.

Again, Nicholas refuses to admit the comparison between Photius and
Nectarius because of the circumstance which led to Nectarius' election. He
refuses to compare Photius to Tarasius (d. 806),[34] the eighth-century Patriarch of Constantinople who was elected as a lay person due to the need of
an orthodox patriarch in 784.

Nicholas again refers to Ambrose, though in this instance it is clear that
he believed Ambrose to have been admitted to all the ministries of the
church from the time of his baptism to his consecration as bishop a week
later: "*qui ex catechumeno, divino praesagio, ad episcopalem per continuos gradus promotus est dignitatem,*" and later, "*.... a catechumeno per
singulos gradus ecclesiasticos proficiscens, octavo die ab omni catholicorum, divina annuente clementia, consensu est consecratus episcopus.*"

Nicholas's treatment of Ambrose is notable. It reflects the ninth-century conviction that Ambrose was rushed through the clerical *cursus* in eight
days. This conviction remains in many quarters today.[35] Although it has
been noted that Nicholas seems to have believed that Nectarius was ordained directly from the laity to the episcopate, one wonders why Nicholas
did not ascribe a similar sequence of grades to him as well. As noted in the
previous chapter, the same fifth-century historians ascribe *per saltum* ordinations to both Ambrose and Nectarius.

By including two references in a single letter to Ambrose's consecration does Nicholas suggest that Photius was likewise admitted to all the

---

[33] MANSI XVI.70–71; *Epistle* 86, MGH *Epp.* 3, pp. 448–450. *Cf.* cols. 89–90; the letter
of Nicholas to Photius, MANSI XVI.335, ff.

[34] Tarasius was the uncle, or great-uncle, of Photius.

[35] This is the first instance, apparently, where Ambrose is said to have been ordained
sequentially to all the grades of the clerical *cursus* in one week.

grades? Or is the reference in this letter to Ambrose intended to accentuate further the difference between Photius and Ambrose, specifically, that Photius was ordained *per saltum* and Ambrose was not? At any rate, Nicholas's conviction that Ambrose was ordained through all the grades demonstrates that the *cursus honorum* was such an accepted practice by the ninth century, that well-known fourth- century events were interpreted in its light.

On the other hand it is just as likely that for Nicholas, admission to the grades of lector, subdeacon, deacon, presbyter, and bishop in the space of a week constitutes *per saltum* ordination. This understanding could reflect a Western appreciation of the significance of the interstices in relation to the clerical *cursus*, namely that they are thoroughly interrelated. The letter is further evidence of the extent to which the conciliar and papal texts enjoining the *cursus honorum* were known and cited in the ninth century. In any case, Nicholas attacks this practice, and uses it as the pretext for refusing to recognise Photius.

In a letter to the archbishops, metropolitans, and bishops subject to the see of Constantinople, 13 November 866, Nicholas renewed his attack on the practice of *per saltum* ordination:

.... Nec de clericorum catalogo permittunt ad sacros ordines provehi, qui vitam eorum tanto audacius, quanto diutius ac familiarius sub Christo duce forti militantes, fortius comprimere possent: sed ex seipsis eligunt, qui facta eorum tanto minus praesumant arguere, quanto se paulo ante de eorum coetu favore ipsorum promotos meminerint: quod illis partibus tanto familiarius agitur, ista praesumptio videlicet ut ex laicis subito tondeantur,et in episcopus consecrentur, quanto ex consuetudine hac inolevisse testantur, quam nos econtra tanto studiosius ex ecclesia Dei eradicare volumus, quanto nimium noxae jam esse clericiset omni religiosae plebi supra docuimus, quantoque scimus ex sacris canonibus, quod non minus mala consuetudo, quam perniciosa corruptela vitanda sit;et scimus, quod paulatim crescens jam pestiferae nequitae germine multos invaserit, adeo ut temeritas haec tantum excreverit, ut jam minime clericis egeant, dum contra sacros canones ex seipsis subito tonsuratum quem voluerint eligant,et ad labores clericorum mentis oculos non inflectant.

Ac per hoc sit, ut alienus comedat ipsorum fructus laborum,et stipendia meritorum extraneus hostis insperatus surripiat, ita ut nihil proficiat clericis in castris dominicis militasse, vel gradatim per singulos ecclesiasticos ordines ascendisse, dum alter saltu hos omnes transcendit,et repente principatus eis, qui inter eos nec contra spiritales hostes arma sustulit, nec diversis ecclesiae adversariis pro veritate praelians aliquando restitit. Quantum autem ne de laicis temere quilibet a episcopatum eligatur, sacri canones cum aliis prohibeant, Sardicenses ostendunt, Osio episcopus capite 13 dicente: Et hoc necessarium arbitror....[36]

In this letter, read at the seventh session (*actio* VII) of the council, Nicholas again censures the practice of promoting recently tonsured men to episcopal office. This custom, the pope says, "we wish to eradicate so much more diligently from the church of God". Recalling the letter of Celestine to the bishops of Apulia and Calabria, Nicholas says that the practice of ordaining someone by a leap from the laity to the episcopate is not good for the clergy who have laboured in the Lord's camps, while another by a leap "devours the fruits of the labourers themselves, and an unexpected strange enemy pilfers the tributes of rewards." He then points out that such a practice is contrary to the "sacred canons" and cites Canon XIII of the Council of Sardica in the Dionysian form which permits service in either the diaconate or the presbyterate before the episcopate.

Additionally, insights into the scope of the debate are provided in the *Admonitio ad lectorum de pseudosynodo Photii*. The "pseudo-synod of Photius" refers to the council convened by Photius at Constantinople in 867.

.... Cum vero legati dixissent, nihil in epistolis pontificis contineri, quod a justo alienum esset, respondit aliorum nomine Procopius quidam Caesariensis episcopus, in epistolis contineri, ut nemo ex laico ad episcopalem dignitatem promoveatur; eosque non decere, qui hoc faciunt. Et quia propter Photii electionem decretum hoc videbatur editum, conantur illud multis argumentis infringere. Et primum quidem Sardicensis concilii canonem, qui hoc idem confirmat, non de quocumque laico, sed de forensiet curiali loqui contendunt; cuijusmodi nunquam a Constantinopolitana ecclesia receptum esse.

Deinde si canonum de quovis laico loqueretur, cum contraria esset Constantinopolitanae ecclesiae consuetudo, canonibus asserunt jam esse derogatum: quia nulla ratio clericum potius aut monachum improbum, quam probum laicum deligi sinit. Quare dicunt Sardicensem canonem non prohibere laicum probatae vitae atque examinae virtutis, episcopum deligi; qualis fuit Nectarius a secunda synodo electus, sanctus Ambrosius,et alii.

Addunt praeterea in Romana ecclesia laicos quoque ad pontificalem sedem esse promotos. Sed haec omnia, quae a Photiana pseudosynodo dicta sunt, uno vel ipsius Photii testimonio refelli possunt. Nam in synodo quam habuit adversus Ignatium, canone XVII ut in ipsius Photii Nomocanone habetur, hac statuit: In omnibus boni ecclesiastici curam gerentes, hoc quoque definire necessarium duximus; ut nullus deinceps laicus, vel monachus repente ad episcopalem altitudinem eveheretur: sed in ecclesiasticis gradibus primum examinatus, sic episcopalis dignitatis

---

[36] MANSI XVI.118–119; *Epistle* 91, MGH *Epp.* 3, pp. 531–532; Jaffé, # 2819.

ordinationem susciperet. Etsi enim adhuc quidam ex monachiset laicis exigente necessitate, episcopli honore statim digni facti sunt, quiet virtute excellenti fuere,et suam ecclesiam in altum extulere; id tamen quod raro evenit, ecclesiae legem nequaquam statuentes, decernimus ut deinceps id minime fiat: nisi is qui rite ordinatur, per gradus sacerdotales processerit, in unoquoque ordine tempus praestitum adimplens.

Sardicensis vero concilii non is est sensus, quem illi perperam asserunt: sed si quis, inquit, e foro, hoc est saeculari statu, sive dives ille sit, sive studiis vacans, dignus habeatur episcopatu, hunc minime provehendum esse, nisi priuset lectoriset diaconi,et prebyteri ministerio fungatur per longissimi temporis probationem; quandoquidemet beatissimus apostolus, inquiunt, qui doctor etiam gentium fuit, prohibuisse videtur, ne celeres fiant ordinationes. Cum ergo apostolus omnem excludat absolute neophytum, perspicuum est, Sardicensem quoque canonem de quovis laico pronuntiare. Et si qui etiam ex laicis vel catechumenis facti sunt episcopi, id tamen raro,et vel necessiate urgente, ut Nectarius in secunda synodo: vel divina aliqua inspiratione, ut in sancti Ambrosi electione accidit: id quod Nicholaus in epistola sexta, quae habetur in octava synodo, satis aperte demonstrat. Quod autem raro accidit, (ut ipsemet Photius consitetur) id universalis ecclesiae legem abrogare non poterit. Quare cum idem Photius canonem hac de re in Constantinopolitana ecclesia jam edidisset, falsum est quod Photiani dixere, canonem hunc in Constantinopolitana ecclesia locum non habere.

Quod autem in Romana ecclesia laicus aliquando sit pontifex electus, falsum omnino est. Nullus enim reperitur ante Photii tempora laicus ad summum pontificatum evectus: nam Constantinus schismaticus fuit, ut Anastasius in Stephani papae IV vita fusius narrat. Ergo ab eodem Stephano propter huijusmodi Constantini factum constitutum fuit, ut summus pontifex ex presbyteris aut diaconibus cardinalis eligeretur.[37]

This letter, directed against the proceedings of the council in Constantinople of 867, gives a good indication of the nature of Photius's defense of his promotion. For instance, he must have cited Canon XIII of the Council of Sardica. First, he argued that the church of Constantinople never received the canon. Second, he argued that the intent of Canon XIII was to exclude the untested, including untested monks and clerics. According to Photius's interpretation the canon does not prohibit a lay person of tested life and examined virtue to be ordained to the episcopate. He must have also cited Nectarius, Ambrose, and others as examples. Photius argued that Rome itself knew the practice of ordaining lay people to the pontificate.

The opponents of Photius argue that the *nomocanone*, the collection of canon law of the Eastern church, also prohibits a lay person or monk to be raised suddenly to the episcopacy without a succession of offices, and

---

[37] MANSI XVI.467, 470.

commends examination through the sacerdotal grades in the fixed times—*tempus praestitum.* While it is recognised that there have been instances that have required that certain monks or lay people of recognised excellency be ordained immediately to the episcopate, such instances are rare, and arise out of necessity as in the case of Nectarius, or by divine inspiration as in the case of Ambrose. No such circumstances are evident in the election of Photius.

Photius's opponents contest his interpretation of Canon XIII of Sardica. They urge a more literal interpretation: one must discharge the ministries of lector, deacon, and presbyter, before becoming a bishop. A person is rightly ordained who has passed through the sacerdotal orders according to the prescribed times, the interstices. It is noteworthy that the presbyterate is seen as a regular part of the *cursus.* Because Canon XIII is cited, there is no mention of the subdiaconate.

Photius's assertion that members of the laity had been ordained bishop in Rome is flatly denied. It seems as though Photius must have cited the antipope Constantine as one such example, for his opponents state that Constantine was a schismatic. Moreover, on account of the act of Constantine it is declared that the supreme pontiff must be chosen from among the cardinal presbyters and deacons.

At the tenth session of the Council of Constantinople, twenty-seven canons were enacted. Historically, the most significant legislation of the council is Canon XXI, which acceded to the Roman church's primacy amongst the patriarchates, followed by Constantinople. But for this study, Canon IV is notable:

> Amorem principatus, utpote quamdam malam radicem exortorum in ecclesia scandalorum, radicibus excidentes, eum qui temereet praevaricatorie ac irregulariter, veluti quidam gravis lupus, in Christi ovile insiliit, Photium scilicet, qui mille tumultibuset turbationibus orbem terrae replevit, justo decreto damnamus, promulgantes nunquam fuisse prius aut nunc esse episcopum, nec eos qui in aliquo sacerdotali gradu ab eo consecrati vel promoti sunt manere in eo quod provecti sunt: insuperet eos qui ab illo consuetas orationes ad praepositurae promotionem susceperent, ab hujusmodi patrocinio coercemus....[38]

This canon declares that Photius was never a bishop, and that the ordinations performed by him were similarly invalid.

In terms of the history of the *cursus honorum* and the interstices, the most significant rubric and canon of the council is Canon V:

---

[38] MANSI XVI.162.

V. Quod non oporteat de senatoria dignitate, vel de aliquo laicorum ordine, nuper tonsum eligi vel suscipi patriarcham, nisi secundem definitionem, quae prolata est ab hac sanctaet magna synodo, inveniatur.

Omnem canonicam stabilitatem in ecclesiis semper manere in Christo providere cupientes, renovamuset confirmamus terminoset vocationes, quae olim a sanctis apostoliset beatis patribus nostris editae, legem in ecclesia posuerunt, non oportere antistitem promovere quemquam, qui est vel secundum fidem, vel secundum sacerdotalem sortem neophytus, "ne inflatus, in judicium incidat,et laqueum diaboli", sicut dicit apostolus.

Prioribus ergo canonibus concordantes, definimus; neminem de senatoria dignitate, vel mundana conversatione nuper tonsum super intentione vel expectatione pontificatus, vel patriarchatus honoris, clericum, aut monachum factum, ad huijusmodi scandere gradum; licet per singulos ordines divini sacerdotali plurimum temporis fecisse probetur: neque enim propter religionem vel amorem Dei, aut propter expectationem transeundi viam virtutum, sed ob amorem gloriae, ac principatus tonsus hujusdmodi reperitur: magis autem coercemus hujusmodi, si ab imperatoria dignitate ad hoc compellatur.

Si vero quis per nullam suspicionem praedictae concupiscentiae expectationis, sed propter ipsum bonum humilitatis, quae est circa Christum Jesum, abrenuntians mundo, fiat clericus, aut monachus,et omnem gradum ecclesiasticum transigens, per definita nunc tempora irreprehensibilis inventus extiterit,et probatus, ita ut in gradu lectoris annum compleat, in subdiaconi vero duos, sitque diaconus tribus,et presbyter quattor annis, bene placuit huic sanctaet universali synodo eligi huncet admitti.

Circa hos autem qui religiose morati sunt ordine clericorum,et monachorum, digni judicati sunt pontificatus dignitate pariteret honore; praedictum tempus abbreviamus, nimirum secundum quod episcoporum praelati probaverint qui per tempora fuerint. Si vero praeter hanc definitionem nostram quisquam ad jam fatum supremum honorem provectus extiterit, reprobetur,et ab omni sacerdotali operatione prorsus abjiciatur, utpote qui extra sacros canones sit promotus.[39]

Canon V renews and affirms the decisions of "the holy apostles and blessed fathers" that it is not fitting to ordain neophytes as bishops. In particular, recently tonsured members of the "senatorial dignity or from worldly conversation" who intend on being made patriarch are mentioned specifically. Ambition is ruled out as a motive for episcopal consecration, even in the case of one who has been proven through each of the orders. One must become a cleric or a monk, and be tested through the ecclesiastical grades of lector, subdeacon, deacon, presbyter, before episcopal consecration.

---

[39] MANSI XVI.162–163. *Cf.* col. 402.

The canon also indicates the intervals of time to be spent in the orders: one year as a lector, two as a subdeacon, three as a deacon, and four as a presbyter. In the case of those who have been clerics or monks for a long time, and have been judged worthy of the pontificate, however, the interstices may be shorted. If anyone is made a bishop beyond this decree he is to be rejected and degraded since he would be promoted contrary to the sacred canons. In many ways, the canon appears to be a revision of Canon XIII of the Council of Sardica.

The canon affirms the traditional *cursus* of the Eastern church: lector, subdeacon, deacon, presbyter, bishop. It reflects the sequence of Canon XIII of the Council of Sardica, except for the inclusion of the subdeacon. The minor orders are grouped in two classes: the lectorate and the subdiaconate. Missing from the minor orders are the Western offices of doorkeeper, exorcist, and acolyte; this arrangement was no doubt necessary to be inclusive of the Eastern church which did not know these orders. The *cursus* does not resemble the Roman version of the *Dionysiana*, for the presbyterate is clearly prescribed in the sequence of grades.

The interstices established by the council are noteworthy: there is a minimum ten year interval between the lectorate and the presbyterate, similar to the interstices envisaged by Zosimus and Siricius in the patristic period. The canon permits the interstices, however, to be modified in the case of a monk or cleric of long standing who is chosen bishop. Once again, the *cursus* is seen as essential, while the interstices are dispensable.

At the death of Ignatius on 23 October 877, Photius was restored as patriarch. After the restoration of Photius, in part of a letter to the emperors Basil, Leo, and Alexander (August, 879), Pope John VIII (872–882) admonishes the emperors to observe in the future the canons enjoining the *cursus honorum*:

....Eo tamen tenore ista statuentes, apostolica dumtaxat auctoritatet sanctorum patrum venerabilibus institutis decernimus, ut post hujus patriarchae obitum, nullus de laicis vel curialibus in patriarchatus eligatur vel consecretur honore, nisi de cardinalibus presbyteriset diaconibus Constantinopolitanae sedis, secundum sacros canones spiritu Dei conditos,et totius mundi reverentia consecratos; quia nec praepropere contra canones ecclesiasticos, decretaque majorum cito quilibet lector, cito acolytus, cito diaconus, cito sacerdos vel episcopus fiat: qui in minoribus officiis sic diu perdurent,et vita eorum pariteret obsequium comprobetur, ut per tempora a majoribus instituta, comprobatis prius moribus,et bonae vitae meritis refulgentibus, ad summum sacerdotium postmodum veniat. Quoniam non est subito praeripiendum vel usurpandum, quod vita diu probata meretur accipere. Nam si in quislibet ecclesiae gradibus providenter curandum est, ut in Domini domo nihil sit inordinatum; quanto magis elaborandum est, ut in electione ejus qui supra omnes gradus constituitur, non erretur?....[40]

The letter is further papal indictment of Photius' election. Rather than reiterating Canon V of the council of 869–870, John cites the canon of the Council of Rome of 769, which limits papal candidates to the cardinal presbyters and deacons. While the interstices are not specified, the letter denounces hasty ordinations through the grades—*cito lector, cito acolytus, cito diaconus, cito sacerdos vel episcopus.* John insists that only those tested through each of the ecclesiastical grades be promoted to the "high priesthood". John offers the classical reason for sequential ordination: testing.

The sequence of grades (lector, acolyte, deacon, "priest" or (*vel*) bishop) in the letter is interesting, for it is not that of the council of 869–870; the subdeacon (proper to both East and West) has been replaced by the Western office of acolyte. Like the Dionysian version of Canon XIII of the Council of Sardica, it is not clear whether the presbyter is part of the sequence prior to bishop, for the text specifies "priest or (*vel*) bishop"—*cito sacerdos vel episcopus.* Like Nicholas I and many other papal predecessors, John VIII had been elected bishop of Rome from the diaconate without ordination to the presbyterate.

In 879–880, a synod was held in Constantinople which annulled the condemnations against Photius and abrogated the decisions of the council of 869–870. The council of 879–880 was ignored by the Western church, which, referred to it as the "pseudo-synod of Photius." Moreover, from the second half of the eleventh century the West has regarded Constantinople IV as the eighth ecumenical council.

The council of 879–880 was presided over by Cardinal Peter the presbyter, legate of John VIII, who appears to have been acquiescent towards Photius. Rome needed Byzantine aid to deal with the threat of Islam in southern Italy. Yet the *cursus honorum* was still on the papal agenda, as evidenced in a portion of the letter of John VIII to the Emperors Basil, Leo, and Alexander, read by Cardinal Peter:

..... Etiam ut hoc statuatis, adhortamur vestrum a Deo custodium imperium, ut post obitum sanctissimi Photii, comministriet fratris nostri, nemo e saeculari magistratu ad pontificalem dignitatem eligaturet ordinetur; sed aut ex presbyteris cardinalibus, vel in ecclesia Catholica conscriptis, aut ex ejus diaconis, aut ex aliis sacerdotibus

---

[40] MANSI XVII.138; *Epistle* 207, MGH *Epp.* 7, Karolini Aevi, vol. 5 (1928), pp. 172–173; Jaffé, # 3271.

qui subjecti sunt sedi Constantinopolitanae, juxta divinoset sacros canones: ne quid agatis contra ecclesiasticam disciplinam,et canones Patrum. Procedere autem hunc volumus, probatum per singulos ecclesiae gradus: primo lectorem, deinde aco-lythum, postea diaconum, deinde presbyterum: posthaec episcopum. Ita nimirum ut bonum habeat testimonium de innocentia morumet discendi studio: quoniam dum in inferioribus ordinibus aliquo tempore immoratur, virtus ejus,et in omni alio genere probatis, exploratur. Hoc pacto progredi patriarchas vestros oportet, nec sta-tim unumquemque dignitatem arripere: ut in domo Domini nihil inveniatur incom-positum aut inordinatum. Nam qui supra omnes gradus ascendit, irreprehensibilis in omnibus debet inveniri, ne quando ex hoc ruina nascatur omnis doctrinae eccle-siasticae.

Neque vero quoniam nos ecclesiae vestra paci constituendae providentes ac pros-picientes, Photium religiosissimum fratrem nostrum suscepimus, quemadmodum olim Hadrianus Tarasium avunculum ejus, istud a vobis pro consuetudineet regula reputetur. Nam quae sunt rata bona, non possunt esse multis pro lege. Verum a Domino nostro Jesu Christo visceraet ipsi misericordiae accipientes, vobis in hac parte compassi sumus:et petitioni vestrae tam in de ipso, quam de aliis sacerdoti-bus, qui sunt ex altera ordinatione, omnino concessimus. Quisquis autem posthac ausus fuerit id committere, sine venia erit quae a canoneet a nobis poena condem-natioque irrogabitur....[41]

.....Hoc autem rogamus, etiam, ut fraternitas tua nobiscum decernat, ne posthac e laicis quisquam repente ad summam Pontificatus sedem evehatur, quae tremenda est,et jus apud Deum intercedendi obtinet: sed per graduset ordine ad ministerium progrediens,et convenientem in uniuscujusque gradus ascensu virtutem ostendens, sic demum Pontificalis sedis consecrationem obtineat. Nam qui aliter agit, contra ecclesiasticos nostros canones facit. Et volumus hanc consuetudinem sane im-probandam, quae ab initio in ecclesia vestra inventa est, deinceps abolitam perma-nere. Hoc autem dicimus juxta canonem editum a synodo, temporis Hadriani sanctissimi Papae,et Tarasi felicis recordationis patriarchae Constantinopolitani.

Synodum vero, quae contra tuam reverentiam ibidem est habita, rescidimus, dam-navimus omnino,et abjecimus: tum ob alias causas, tum quod decessor noster bea-tus Papa Hadrianus in ea non subscripsit....[42]

In the letter John VIII confirms Photius as the rightful patriarch, in spite of his unconventional promotion, which continued to be regarded as contrary to ecclesiastical discipline and the canons of the fathers. At the same time, the church of Constantinople is admonished to observe the canons requir-ing the clerical *cursus*. The sequence of grades is that prescribed by John in an earlier letter to Basil, Leo and Alexander: lector, acolyte, deacon,

---

[41] MANSI XVII.403, 406.

[42] MANSI XVII.415.

presbyter, and bishop. Again, the primary purpose of the *cursus* as indicated by John VIII is the testing of morals and virtue.

John concludes his letter with another plea that the *cursus honorum* be observed: "For whoever acts otherwise, does so against our ecclesiastical canons. And we wish this custom, which from the beginning was invented in your church, to be sensibly abandoned and henceforth to remain abolished." In the end, John confirms Photius and rescinds the council of 869–870, on the basis of the recognition by Hadrian II of Patriarch Tarasius in the previous century.

Censure for the abrogation of the *cursus* and the interstices was not limited to Photius in the controversy. A letter from the Council of Constantinople to Pope Hadrian II (867–872) suggests that Hadrian had complained that Byzantine missionaries to Illyricum had ignored the *cursus* and the interstices in ordaining Bulgarian lay people directly to the diaconate:

> .... Intelleximus autemet alia multa a vobis contra patrum decreta fieri, inter quaeet hoc est; nuper quosdam contra statuta patrum priscorum,et synodi oecumenicae proxime celebrata, et laicis repente diaconos creatos, cum sciatis Photii casum inde originem traxisse.[43]

In summary, the issue of the clerical *cursus* played a critical role in the Photian crisis and in the fourth Council of Constantinople. While there were many outstanding issues which contributed to the course of events, it was the *cursus honorum* and the interstices which were used as the pretext for the deposition of Photius. The documents of the council, together with the preliminary and concluding papal letters, reveal something of the nature of the debate. Moreover, the Photian crisis called forth a restatement of the place and purpose of the *cursus honorum*.

Patristic texts, both conciliar and papal, were used and interpreted in different ways; for example, Photius's (probable) interpretation of the meaning of a "tested life" from the Council of Sardica. Patristic instances of *per saltum* ordinations were used as evidence, specifically those Ambrose of Milan and Nectarius of Constantinople, as well as Tarasius in the eighth century. The texts reveal the prevailing ninth-century Western opinion that Ambrose was ordained sequentially through all the grades prior to his episcopal consecration.

Some of the papal documents from the Photian controversy reflect a complete lack of awareness that *per saltum* ordination was not only

---

[43] MANSI XVI.414.

possible in the early church, but was known in Rome itself in the person of Fabian in the early third century. John VIII goes so far as to identify the practice of *per saltum* ordination as an Eastern one. The council and its ancillary material reflect the extent to which the *cursus honorum* had become such an assumed part of the western practice and understanding of holy orders.

The fourth Council of Constantinople also reflects the flexibility and confusion which continues to surround the *cursus* in the ninth century. The texts identify three different sequences of grades: lector, deacon, presbyter and bishop from the Council of Sardica; lector, deacon or presbyter, then bishop from the Dionysian version of Sardica (supported by references to the Council of Rome of 769 which specify bishops be drawn the cardinal presbyters or deacons); lector, subdeacon, deacon, presbyter, and bishop from Canon V of the council, and lector, acolyte, deacon, presbyter, bishop from the letters of John VIII. He is not clear whether the subdeacon or the acolyte is part of the *cursus*. In addition, it remains unclear whether or not the presbyterate was considered to be an indispensable grade in the sequence of grades leading towards the episcopate. The interstices were also variable. For instance, Canon V, which prescribed a ten year interval between ordination as lector and episcopal consecration, permitted the interstices to be shortened.

Despite the degree of flexibility and the contradictions evidenced in the texts from the fourth Council of Constantinople, the *cursus honorum* was discussed and confirmed in the context of a major council, and was declared to be the practice of the church, East and West.

d. The Council of Rome, 964

The Council of Rome of 964 was convened by Pope John XII (955–964) in order to depose and excommunicate his rival for the papacy, Leo VIII (963–965). The corrupt and scandalous pontificate of John XII is chiefly remembered in connection with the coronation of Emperor Otto I in 962, inaugurating the Holy Roman Empire.

In December, 963, Otto convened a synod in Rome which deposed John XII on account of his scandalous life-style. Leo, the chief notary (*protoscriniarius*) of Rome and a lay person, was elected as John's successor on 4 December, contrary to canon law. On 5 December 963, Leo was ordained to all the lower orders and the next day he was consecrated bishop by the bishops of Ostia, Porto, and Albano, again, contrary to canon law.

In January, 964, there were revolts in Rome forcing Leo VIII to leave the city. John XII returned and at a council held in Rome on 26–27 February 964 deposed and excommunicated Leo as a usurper of the Roman see. The first session (*actio prima*) of the council describes Leo's ordination:

> ....Post haec autem interrogavit idem papa sanctum concilium, dicens: Dicite, dilectissimi fratres, si episcopi a nobis ordinati, in nostro patriarchio ordinationem facere potuerunt, an non? Sanctum concilium respondit: Minime. Piissimus ac sanctissimus papa dixit: Quid censetis de Sicone episcopo a nobis dudum consecrato, qui in nostro patriarchio Leonem curialemet neophytum, atque perjurum nostrum, jam ostiarium, lectorem, acolytum, subdiaconum, diaconum, atque subito presbyterum ordinavit, eumque sine aliqua probatione contra cuncta sanctorum patrum statuta in nostra apostolica sede consecrare non formidavit? Sanctum concilium respondit: Deponatur ipse qui ordinavit,et qui ab eo est ordinatus. Piissimus atque sanctissimus papa dixit: Nescitur ubi latet. Sanctum concilium respondit: Requiratur diligenter, si placet, usque ad tertium conventum. Quod si minime repertus fuerit, canonica feriatur sententia. Piissimus ac sanctissimus papa dixit: Placet.[44]

Leo is described as a "neophyte of the imperial court," reminiscent of patristic texts which inhibit such a kind from ordination without the *cursus*. According to the council he was quickly ordained doorkeeper, lector, acolyte, subdeacon, deacon, presbyter, and bishop, "without any testing against all the statutes of the holy fathers."[45] As a result, both Leo and the bishop who ordained him, Bishop Sicone, were deposed.

In Leo's rapid promotion through the grades the interstices were abrogated altogether. For the purpose of this study, it is the sequence of Leo's *cursus* which is most interesting. According to some scholars,[46] Leo was ordained according to the rites of the PRG, recently introduced to Italy by Otto I. Their argument is based on the sequence of grades received by Leo, considered more Frankish than Roman. Unlike Constantine, elected in a similar fashion two centuries earlier, Leo was ordained a presbyter, but not an exorcist. The inclusion of the presbyterate in the *cursus* of Leo might be due to the influence of Frankish practice as reflected in the PRG or possibly OR XXXV. Andrieu, for instance, argues the similarity of Leo's sequence of grades with the Gallican sequence, based chiefly on the mention

---

[44] MANSI XIX.472; *actio tertia* acc. Jaffé, p. 467.

[45] Friedrich Kempf, in his article "The Church and the Western Kingdoms from 900–1046" in *The Church in the Age of Feudalism*, refers to Leo's ordination as a "notorious violation of the law", p. 209.

[46] E.g., Vogel, *Medieval Liturgy*, pp. 235, 244, n. 247.

of the doorkeeper.[47] However, the Romano-Gallican sequence in the PRG includes the orders of psalmist and exorcist, which are missing from Leo's *cursus*.

As noted above, Reynolds has shown that it is equally possible that Leo was ordained according to the rites of the Eighth-Century Gelasian sacramentary which had been known in southern Italy, at least at Chieti, a century prior to the introduction of the PRG into Italy by Otto.[48] Furthermore, while not identical, the sequence of the grades received by Leo is not too dissimilar to that received by Constantine in 767.

A comparison between Leo and Constantine was made in the third session (*actio tertia*) of the council:

> .... Eos vero quos ipse Leo neophytuset invasor sanctae catholicaeet apostolicae Romanae ecclesiae in quolibet ecclesiastico ordine provexit, apostolica atque canonica auctoritateet synodali decreto in pristinum revocamus gradum, quia ordinator eorum nihil sibi habuit, nihil illis dedit. Sicuti olim noster praedecessor piae memoriae Stephanus sententiam tulit de iis qui ordinati fuerant a Constantino quodam neophytoet invasore sanctae sedis apostolicae,et postmodum quosdam eorum sibi placabiles presbyteros aut diaconos consecravit, statuens ut qui ab eo consecrati erant nunquam ad superiorem honorem ascenderent, nec ad pontificatus culmen promoverentur, ne talis impiae novitatis error in ecclesia pullularet....[49]

Like Constantine, Leo was condemned and his ordination and the ordinations performed by him were declared invalid. John XII died soon after the council, and the peculiar efforts to find a successor continued.

The Council of Rome of 964 may be of little general historical importance, but in the history of the *cursus honorum* it is very significant. The council records the account of Leo's election and promotion through the grades. The sequence of grades identified in the text is a puzzle: it follows neither the PRG, nor the native Roman ordination rites, nor precisely the sequence of the Gelasian sacramentaries.

It is noteworthy that Leo received the presbyterate, though it is not clear why, since Roman deacons continued to be ordained to the episcopate in the tenth century. In a parallel eighth-century situation, care was taken that the usurper Constantine follow the traditional *cursus*, and yet he did not receive the presbyterate. Two centuries later the presbyterate was perceived

---

[47] Andrieu, "Les Ordres Mineurs," p. 248.

[48] Reynolds, "The Ritual of Clerical Ordination," pp. 437–445.

[49] MANSI XVIII.474.

as a necessary grade in Rome, at least by Otto and those responsible for the consecration of Leo VIII.

3. Papal Letters and Decretals

The previous section has already surveyed some of the early medieval papal material on the *cursus honorum* and the interstices from the pontificates of the anti-pope Constantine (767–768), Nicholas I (858–867) and John VIII (872–882). These letters are connected with the councils surveyed.

A significant eighth-century papal letter on the related issue of the ages of clerics appears during the pontificate of Zacharias (741–742). In *Epistle* XIII to a bishop Boniface, Zacharias writes:

> ....Regulam catholicae traditionis suscepisti, frater amantissime; sic omnibus praedica, omnesque doce, sicut a sancta Romana, cui Deo auctore deservimus, accepisti Ecclesia. Inquisisti etiam et hoc, si ante tricesimum annum liceat sacerdotem ordinari. Bonum et congruum est, charissime frater, si fieri et inveniri potest, ut provectae aetatis et boni testimonii viri, juxta sacrorum canonum instituta, ordinentur sacerdotes. Si autem minime reperiuntur, et necessitas exposcit, a viginti quinque annis et supra levitae et sacerdotes ordinentur, quemadmodum in lege Domini continentur....[50]

Zacharias commends thirty as the minimum age for ordination to the presbyterate. In the case of necessity, where few presbyters are found, Zacharias permits presbyters, like deacons, to be ordained at the age of twenty-five. It is not specified whether in such an instance a candidate for the presbyterate would be ordained directly from the minor orders, or whether he would have been ordained to deacon and presbyter in the same year. The latter is more likely, permitting an interval of less than a year between the diaconate and the presbyterate. The christological significance of the year thirty for presbyters (and bishops) seems to have been overlooked.[51]

---

[50] *PL* 89.952; MANSI XII.348; Jaffé, # 2292.

[51] Of the systematic collections surveyed in this study, *Epistle* XIII of Zacharias is found in the *Decretum* of Gratian.

4. Early Medieval Canonistic Collections

The early medieval period is significant in the study of Western canon law. As noted, there was substantial conciliar activity from the eighth to the tenth centuries. The period also saw a proliferation of canonistic collections which were important for the transmission of the canons relating to the *cursus honorum*. The canonists in this period arranged many of their collections systematically rather than historically. Thus, the choice of texts dealing with the clerical *cursus* by the compilers was deliberate and intentional.

This section will survey five early medieval canonistic collections: the *Collectio canonum hibernenis* from the early eighth-century Irish church, the *Collectio Dacheriana* from the Carolingian period, the Pseudo-Isidorian collection from the mid-ninth-century Frankish church, the late ninth-century northern Italian *Collectio Anselmo dedicata*, and finally the early tenth-century *Libri duo de synodalibus causis et disciplinis ecclesiasticis* of Regino of Prüm.

a. The *Hibernensis*

The *Collectio canonum hibernensis* [52] may have been compiled in Ireland as early as *ca.* 700. It is a collection of canons and decretals arranged systematically. The "A" recension of the *Hibernensis* contains nearly 1600 canons, 646 of which are drawn from patristic texts.[53] This collection was popular in northern and western France in the late eighth and early ninth centuries; it became one of the more popular collections in Italy from the tenth to the twelfth century. While the collection also includes new material, the author often modified the conciliar and papal texts, reworking, abridging, or expanding some of the original canons.

There are several instances in the *Collectio canonum hibernensis* where reference is made to the *cursus honorum*. Chapter 7 of Book I, titled *De eo qui ordinandus est*, draws on biblical and patristic sources. For instance, the citation from 1 Timothy 3.6 against the ordination of neophytes is

---

[52] H. Wasserschleben, ed., *Die Irische Kanonensammlung (Collectio Hibernensis)* (Leipzig: Scientia Verlag Aalen, 1966).

[53] Reynolds, "Law, Canon," p. 403.

included.[54] A section from Canon I of the *Statuta ecclesiae antiqua*, attributed to the fourth Council of Carthage, is included: *Qui episcopus ordinandus est, ante examinetur, si natura prudens....*[55] With the exception of the text inhibiting neophytes, and the reference to the testing of bishops (*ante examinetur*) there is nothing else in chapter 7 regarding the *cursus*.

Chapter 11, entitled *De aetatibus quibus provehitur quis ad episcopatum* is a reworking of material from Siricius and Zosimus on the *cursus* and the interstices:

> Tribus ordinibus aetas episcopalis eligitur.
>
> a. Primo de virginitate et ecclesiasticis institutis. Sinodus: Puer autem ab infantia ecclesiasticis ministeriis deditus usque ad XX aetatis suae annum lector sive exorcista stet; ostiarius et subdiaconus XXIIII anno, diaconus XXV, presbyter XXX, episcopus vel XL vel XXX [sive LX anno] [*sic*.] sacerdos efficiatur, ut Isidorus ait, quia in ea aetate Christus predicare orsus est. b. Secundo de unius uxoris viro juvene. Sinodus eadem: Qui autem ab accessu adolescentiae usque XXX annum aetatis suae probabiliter vixerit una tantum virgine uxore sumpta contentus, IV annis subdiaconus et V annis diaconus, XL anno presbyter, L episcopus stet. c. Tertio de grandevo laico. Sinodus eadem: Si vero grandis aetatis sit laicus et necesse sit, ut episcopus fiat, bienno sit lector, V subdiaconus, X diaconus, post XII annos presbiter sive episcopus subrogetur.[56]

There are three different sets of interstices in this section, loosely based on both the decretals of Siricius (*Epistle* 1. IX.13; X.14) and of Zosimus (*Epistle* 9.III.5). Wasserschleben identifies the first section ("a") as derivative from both Siricius and Zosimus; it is an extensive reworking and amalgamation of the two. A candidate is to be made a lector or acolyte at twenty years of age, a doorkeeper and subdeacon at twenty-four, a deacon at twenty-five, a presbyter at thirty, and a bishop at either thirty or forty [or fifty]. While the papal texts provide either the intervals between the grades, or the minimal ages for admission to the grades, they have been combined here.

The sequence of the minor orders in *De aetatibus* is peculiar since it does not include the acolyte, similar to the *Liber ordinum*, Isidore's DEO of the Hispanic Church, the DDG or the D7OG, and like the *De gradibus in quibus Christus adfuit* of the *Hibernensis* itself. In fact, where Zosimus refers to the second class of minor ministries as "acolyte *or* subdeacon",

---

[54] Wasserschleben, *Hibernensis*, p. 5.

[55] Wasserschleben, *Hibernensis*, pp. 5–6.

[56] Wasserschleben, *Hibernensis*, p. 8.

the *Hibernensis* reads "doorkeeper *and* subdeacon". As Roger Reynolds comments in *The Ordinals of Christ*, "...the grades of lector, exorcist, doorkeeper, subdeacon, presbyter, bishop, and deacon are the ones most commonly found in Hibernian texts on the ecclesiastical hierarchy."[57]

The second section ("b") is identified by Wasserschleben as deriving from the decretal of Siricius (*Epistle* 1). One becomes a subdeacon at age thirty, for a period of five years, then a deacon for five years. At forty the cleric becomes a presbyter, and at fifty a bishop. In the decretal to Himerius (IX.13) Siricius mentions the lectorate, which is omitted here. He also says that a candidate is to be admitted an acolyte and a subdeacon at age thirty; only the subdeacon is mentioned in the *Hibernensis*. Siricius does not indicate the interval between the subdiaconate and the diaconate; a four year interval is included here. The ten-year interval between the presbyterate and the episcopate is the same in both.

The final section ("c") is again identified as coming from the decretal to Himerius (X.14). This section provides the interstices between the grades, rather than ages. One is a lector for two years, subdeacon for five, a deacon for ten, and a presbyter for twelve before ordination to the episcopate. The two-year interval between the lectorate and the subdiaconate is identical to the decretal to Himerius, though Siricius also includes the exorcistate, which is omitted here. The five-year period in the subdiaconate is the same. The rest of this section does not match the Sirician text at all, which says nothing about being a deacon five years, nor a presbyter for ten.

It is difficult to ascertain the purpose of *De aetatibus quibus provehitur quis ad episcopatum*. The author has obviously taken the time to abridge and expand on texts from both Siricius and Zosimus, but has not harmonised them. This text does not refer to the acolyte, which features in both the papal originals. The doorkeeper appears, but is coupled with the subdeacon; the doorkeeper is mentioned by neither Siricius nor Zosimus.[58]

Book VIII, cap. 1 of the *Hibernensis* includes a short Ordinal of Christ, entitled *De gradibus in quibus Christus adfuit*:

---

[57] Roger Reynolds, *The Ordinals of Christ from their Origins to the Twelfth Century*, Beiträge zur Geschichte und Quellenkunde des Mittelaters, vol. 7 (Berlin: 1978), p. 57.

[58] While this text draws on earlier sources, it became itself a canonical text. Of the systematic collections found in this study, the *De aetatibus quibus provehitur quis ad episcopatum* of the *Hibernensis* appears in the *Collectio canonum in V libris* of the early eleventh century.

Ostiarius fuit, quando aperuit ostia inferni, exorcista, quando ejecit septem demo-
nia de Maria Magdalena, lector, quando aperuit librum Esaiae, subdiaconus, quando fecit vinum de aqua in Cana Galileae, diaconus, quando lavit pedes
discipulorum, sacerdos, quando accepit panem ac fregit et benedixit, episcopus
fuit, quando elevavit manus suas ad coelum et benedixit apostolis.[59]

The enumeration of seven grades reflects the Irish fascination with the
theological significance of numbers.[60] Here the grades appear in the hierarchical sequence of doorkeeper, exorcist, lector, subdeacon, deacon,
"priest", and bishop, rather than the chronological sequence in which
Christ fulfilled them, common to other Irish Ordinals of Christ.[61] The
sequence of the *De gradibus in quibus Christus adfuit* is similar to the
Romano-Gallican sequences of the *cursus*, with two exceptions. First, the
exorcist precedes the lector as in the Hispanic *cursus* where the lector is
superior to the exorcist, which shows the influence of Isidore's DEO.[62]
Second, there is no mention of the acolyte, again, like the DEO.[63]

Chapter 2 of Book VIII, of the *Hibernensis*, entitled *De distantia graduum*, outlines the duties of the various orders:

Episcopum decet judicare et interpretari et consecrare et consummare et ordinare
et baptizare et offerre; sacerdotem autem oportet offerre et benedicere et bene
praeesse, praedicare et baptizare. Levitam i.e. ministrum oportet ministrare ad altare et baptizare et communicare; subdiaconum decet ministrare aquam altari diacono et dehonustare altare. Exorcistam oportet abicere demones et dicere his, qui
communicant, ut requirant aquam ministerii effundere; lectorem oportet legere ei,
qui praedicat et lectiones decantare et benedicere panes et fructus novos, ostiarium
percutere cymbala, aperire ecclesiam et sacrarium et codicem tradat, ex quo praed-
icatur aut legitur.[64]

This text is the earliest form of the later *De officiis VII graduum*. In its Irish
form it is included in the *Collectio canonum in V libris*. The sequence of
grades is similar to that of the preceding *De gradibus in quibus Christus
adfuit*, with the exception of the inversion of the exorcist and the lector

---

[59] Wasserschleben, *Hibernensis*, p. 26.

[60] Roger Reynolds, "'At Sixes and Sevens'—And Eights and Nines: The Sacred Mathematics of Sacred Orders in the Early Middle Ages", *Speculum*, vol. 54.4 (October 1979),
pp. 672–673.

[61] Reynolds, *Ordinals of Christ*, p. 62.

[62] Reynolds, *Ordinals of Christ*, p. 62.

[63] Of the systematic collections of this study, the *De gradibus in quibus Christus adfuit* is
found in the eleventh-century *Collectio canonum in V libris*, with some modifications.

[64] Wasserschleben, *Hibernensis*, p. 26.

according to the Gallican sequence. Once again, there is no mention of the acolyte. The number seven is characteristic of the Irish sequence. Though the office of acolyte was not necessarily part of the Irish church at the beginning of the eighth century, Book IX of the *Hibernensis* deals with both the acolyte and the psalmist. Chapter 1, dealing with the acolyte, merely reproduces the ordination material for the order from the *Statuta ecclesiae antiqua*.[65] Chapter 2, dealing with the psalmist, includes an abridged version of Isidore's treatment of the office in *De ecclesiastic officiis* (II.12, i–ii) as well as the ordination rite from the SEA.[66] It is interesting to note that the compiler of the *Hibernensis* did not use the segment on acolytes from the *Etymologiae*, which was available to him.

b. The *Collectio Dacheriana*

Known as simply the *Collectio Dacheriana* after its seventeenth-century editor, Jean Luc d'Achéry, the *Dacheriana* is a systematically arranged Carolingian canonistic collection. Its compiler is probably Florus of Lyons, though it is sometimes ascribed to Bishop Agobard of Lyons.[67]

The Carolingian renaissance is noted for its attempts at ecclesiastical reform after the chaos of the Merovingian period. The compilation of the *Collectio Dacheriana* belongs to the process of Carolingian ecclesiastical reform. It includes material from two Hispanic collections, the *Collectio hispana gallicana* and the *Collectio hispana systematica*, as well as the *Collectio Dionysio-Hadriana* which was sent to Charlemagne by Pope Hadrian I.

A section of Book III of the *Dacheriana*, entitled the *Collectio antiqua canonum poenitentiarum*, contains many conciliar texts of the patristic period dealing with sequential ordination and related issues. For example, Canon III (V) of the Council of Carthage, establishing twenty-five as the minimum age for deacons is found in cap. 79,[68] and Canon XI of Neocaesarea establishing thirty as the age for presbyters in cap. 101.[69] The

---

[65] Wasserschleben, *Hibernensis*, pp. 26–27.

[66] Wasserschleben, *Hibernensis*, p. 27.

[67] *Cf.* Reynolds, "Law: Canon," p. 404.

[68] J.L.D'Achery, ed., *Spicilegium sive Collectio Veterum Aliquot Scriptorum* I (Paris, 1793) p. 555.

[69] *Dacheriana* I, p. 557.

ordination rites of the *Statuta ecclesiae antiqua* are found in two chapters in Book III: caps. 94 and 102.[70] Canon XIII of the Council of Sardica is included in Book III, cap. 142, according to the version from the *Dionysiana*.[71]

In addition to the conciliar texts, the *Collectio antiqua canonum poenitentiarum* of Book III of the *Dacheriana* also contains four papal texts which deal with the *cursus honorum*. The letter of Innocent to Felix of Nocera, condemning hasty ordinations appears in cap. 17,[72] as well as the intersices texts of Zosimus in cap. 18,[73] and Siricius in cap. 20.[74] The fourth papal text dealing with the *cursus* is the letter of Celestine to the bishops of Vienne and Narbonne, condemning the ordination of lay people to the episcopate, cap. 23.[75]

There are relatively few canons dealing with the *cursus honorum* and the intersices in the *Collectio Dacheriana*. The classic conciliar and papal texts are present, however, and were transmitted by the collection during the Carolingian reform.

c. The Pseudo-Isidorian Decretals

The Pseudo-Isidorian *Decretalium collectio* is one of the largest and most influential of the medieval canonistic collections. The Decretals are the largest of the series of forgeries compiled in the archdiocese of Rheims in the mid-ninth century (*ca.* 847–852).[76] The identity of the compiler of the Pseudo-Isidorian Decretals is unknown, though they are attributed to an author using the pseudonym of Isidore Mercato (or Peccator). Although it was known in the ninth century that they were forgeries, the Pseudo-Isidorian collection became immensely popular and influential.

---

[70] *Dacheriana* I, pp. 556, 557.

[71] *Dacheriana* I, p. 561. The canon is enumerated as XIV in the collection.

[72] *Dacheriana* I, p. 548.

[73] *Dacheriana* I, p. 548.

[74] *Dacheriana* I, p. 549.

[75] *Dacheriana* I, p. 549.

[76] Other scholars, however, argue for a Le Mans provenance for the decretals. E.g., Gerald Ellard, *Ordination Anointings in the Western Church before 1000 AD* (Cambridge, Mass.: The Mediaeval Academy of America, 1933), p. 51; Walter Goffart, *The Le Mans Forgeries*, (Cambridge, MA: Harvard University Press, 1966), pp. 90–94.

The principal intent behind the creation of the collection was political. The canons were to settle questions about the relationship between church and state, between bishops and secular powers, between bishops and metropolitans, and between bishops and chorbishops. The collection did much theoretically to enhance the position of the papacy as the final source of appeal.

The Pseudo-Isidorian Decretals contain about 10,000 fragments of earlier canons.[77] The collection, arranged historically, includes both genuine and false conciliar and papal texts. Because of its tremendous size, it is not surprising that the collection contains a vast array of conciliar and papal texts relating to the *cursus honorum*, the interstices, and related issues. Not only are the classical patristic councils represented, but many of the Gallican and Hispanic councils as well.

Of the patristic conciliar canons, the collection includes Canon II[78] and Canon IX[79] of the Council of Nicaea; Canon XVII of the Council of Ancyra dealing with bishops who are not received in their sees, and who are urged to sit amongst the presbyters whence they came;[80] and Canon XI of Neocaesarea, establishing thirty as the minimum age of presbyters.[81] Canon XIII of the Council of Sardica is found in the Pseudo-Isidorian Decretals.[82] It is worth noting that the version used for this canon is not the *Collectio Dionysiana*, for the text does not allow bishops to have served in either the diaconate or the presbyterate, but rather:

> .... non prius ordinetur, nisi ante lectoris munere, et officio diaconi *et* presbyteri fuerit perfunctis....[83]

---

[77] E. Seckl, "The Pseudo-Isidorian Decretal and Other Forgeries," *The New Schaff- Herzog Religious Encyclopedia*, vol. 9, gen. ed. S. M. Jackson (New York: Funk and Wagnells, 1911), p. 345.

[78] *PL* 130.257.

[79] *PL* 130.258.

[80] *PL* 130.264.

[81] *PL* 130.268.

[82] *PL* 130.276.

[83] *PL* 130.276.

The source of the transmission of this version is most probably the *Collectio hispana*[84] through the forgers of the *Collectio hispana gallica Augustodunensis*.[85]

From the patristic Gallican councils, the Pseudo-Isidorian Decretals include Canon I of the third Council of Arles (524) identifying twenty-five

as the minimum age for deacons and thirty for presbyters.[86] The collection also incorporates material from the SEA, identified as the fourth Council of Carthage; Canon I of the SEA concerning the qualities of candidates for the episcopate is included,[87] as well as the ordination rites.[88]

Canons from various Hispanic councils are incorporated in the decretals. Canons I, II, and III from the Council of Toledo I (397–400) examined above are incorporated.[89] These canons deal with clerical continence, but are important for the *cursus* in that they reflect ascending movement from one grade to another inhibited by sexual incontinence, and descending movement within the minor orders as punishment for such offenses. Canon I of the Council of Toledo II (527) is found in the decretals,[90] dealing with children who are offered into the ministry of the church and establishing twenty as the minimum age for subdeacons, and twenty-five for deacons.

Canon XX from the Council of Braga I (561), directing a lay candidate for the "priesthood" to spend one year as either a lector or a subdeacon for the purpose of training and preparation, is included in the collection;[91] the text has been slightly altered by Pseudo-Isidore. While the original indicates that the episcopal candidate is to become either a lector or a subdeacon, the Pseudo-Isidorian text says:

> Item placuit, ut ex laico ad gradum sacerdotii nemo veniat, nisi prius anno integro in officio lectorum, vel diaconatus disciplinam ecclesiasticam discat....[92]

---

[84] *PL* 84.119

[85] Reynolds, "Law: Canon," p. 405.

[86] *PL* 130.381.

[87] *PL* 130.342–343.

[88] *PL* 130.343–344.

[89] *PL* 130.433–434.

[90] *PL* 130.439.

[91] *PL* 130.570 It is referred to as canon XXXVIII.

[92] *PL* 130.570.

The subdiaconate has been replaced by the diaconate. The source for this modification is perhaps the *Collectio hispana*. Of the canonistic collections surveyed in this study, the Pseudo-Isidorian Decretals is the only collection noted which includes Canon XX of the Council of Braga I.

Many papal patristic texts are found in the Pseudo-Isidorian *Decretalium collectio*. For example, the material dealing with the *cursus honorum* in the decretal of Siricius to Himerius (*Epistle* 9.IX.13; X.14; XIII.7) appears without alteration.[93] The letter of Siricius *Ad diversos episcopos* (*Epistle* 6.III.5) is also included.[94] Likewise, the text from the letter of Innocent to Felix of Nocera (*Epistle* 37.V.6)[95] and the text from the letter of Zosimus to Hesychius (*Epistle* 9.I.1–2; III.5)[96] are found in the decretals, without alteration. The portions dealing with the *cursus honorum* from the letter of Celestine to the bishops of Vienne and Narbonne (*Epistle* 4.4), in which Celestine acknowledges and condemns the practice of ordaining lay people to the episcopate, are included.[97] The letter of Leo to Anastasius of Thessalonica (*Epistle* 14.3), which inhibits neophytes and lay people from being consecrated bishops appears,[98]as well as the letter of Leo to the bishops of Mauretainia Caesariensis (*Epistle* 12.4).[99] The letter of Gelasius to the bishops of Lucania, Bruttii, and Sicily is included, shortening the interstices to one year from doorkeeper to presbyter.[100] Finally, the letter of Hormisdas to the Spanish bishops (*Epistle* 25, I.2) appears in the collection, recalling the necessity of training and preparation and condemns the practice of ordaining one from the laity to the episcopate.[101]

The Pseudo-Isidorian Decretals contain spurious material from the *Liber pontificalis* dealing with the *cursus honorum*. For example, the ascription of the clerical *cursus* to Pope Gaius (282–295) has been

---

[93] Paul Hinschius, ed., *Decretales Pseudo-Isidorianae* (Leipzig: Bernhard Tauchnitz, 1863), p. 522.

[94] Hinschius, *Decretales*, pp. 524–525.

[95] Hinschius, *Decretales*, p. 533.

[96] Hinschius, *Decretales*, p. 553.

[97] Hinschius, *Decretales*, p. 560.

[98] Hinschius, *Decretales*, p. 619.

[99] Hinschius, *Decretales*, p. 622.

[100] Hinschius, *Decretales*, p. 650–651.

[101] Hinschius, *Decretales*, p. 690.

included.[102] The ascription of the interstices to Pope Silvester (314–335) is likewise incorporated, though with some modification;[103] the *LP* indicates that one was a lector for thirty years, and an exorcists for thirty days.[104] The Pseudo-Isidorian version, however, states that the time in the lectorate and the exorcistate will be according to the time constituted by the bishop. The Pseudo-Isidorian version also mentions the doorkeeper, which is not found in the *LP*.

The Pseudo-Isidorian *Decretalium collectio* has gathered most of the patristic texts surveyed in chapter III of this study, with few modifications. Given the influence of the collection, it was a significant vehicle for the transmission of the canonical texts dealing with the *cursus honorum* and the interstices in the Middle Ages.

d. The *Collectio Anselmo dedicata*

The *Collectio Anselmo dedicata* is a systematically arranged collection of northern Italian provenance, compiled in the late ninth century, *ca.* 885.[105] It is so named because of its dedication to a bishop Anselm, probably Anselm II of Milan (882–896). The collection was popular in the Frankish church as well as in Italy.

The *Anselmo dedicata*, which embodies much of the Pseudo-Isidorian material, includes many patristic texts dealing with the *cursus honorum* and the interstices.[106] Of the patristic conciliar texts found in the collection are Canon XI of Neocaesarea (II.19),[107] Canon XVII of the Council of Ancyra (II.44),[108] Canon II of Nicaea (V.2),[109] and Canon XIII of the Council

---

[102] *Epistola Gai.* Cap. VI.7, Hinschius, *Decretales*, p. 218; *Cf.* LP I, p. 161.

[103] *Ex synodalibus gestius Silvestri*, Cap. VI, Hinschius, *Decretales*, p. 450.

[104] LP I, pp. 171–172.

[105] Reynolds, "Law: Canon," p. 406.

[106] In the edition of Jean-Claude Besse, *Collectio Anselmo dedicata: Étude et Texte, Histoire des Textes du Droit de l'Église au Moyen-Age*, (Paris: Librairies Techniques, 1960), only the incipits of the canons are included, making textual comparisons impossible.

[107] Besse, *Anselmo dedicata*, p. 9.

[108] Besse, *Anselmo dedicata*, p. 10.

[109] Besse, *Anselmo dedicata*, p. 31.

of Sardica (II.40).[110] Of the Gallican material dealing with the *cursus*, only Canon XVII of the Council of Agde is included in Book II.20.[111] Of the Hispanic councils, Canon I of the Council of Toledo II (V.1),[112] and Canon XX of the Council of Toledo IV (IV.20)[113] are found in the collection.

The *Collectio Anselmo dedicata* incorporates many patristic papal decretals on the *cursus honorum* and the interstices. For example, the decretal of Siricius to Himerius (*Epistle* 1. IX–X, XIII) is found in Book V.7–8;[114] later in Book VI.11, cap. XIII from the same letter appears, dealing with monks and the *cursus*.[115] The decretal of Zosimus to Hesychius of Salone (*Epistle* 9, I.1, III.5) is likewise found in two books of the collection; cap. I.1 appears in Book VI.12,[116] and cap. III.5 in Book IV.14.[117]

Two letters from the pontificate of Celestine are included: the letter to the bishops of Vienne and Narbonne (*Epistle* 4.4) (II..6)[118] and the letter to the bishops of Apulia and Calabria (Epistle 5.2) (II.41).[119] The letter of Pope Leo to Anastasius of Thessalonica (*Epistle* 14.3) is found twice in the collection: in Book I.106[120] and in Book II.42.[121] The letter of Gelasius to the bishops of Lucania, Bruttii, and Sicily is included ((VI.19).[122]

Letters surveyed in this study from the pontificate of Gregory the Great appear in the *Collectio Anselmo dedicata*. For example, the letter of Gregory to Brunhilda (*Reg.* IX.213) is found in Book II.237.[123] The letter to Syagrius, Etherius, and Desiderius (*Reg.*IX.218) is found in Book

---

[110] Besse, *Anselmo dedicata*, p. 10.

[111] Besse, *Anselmo dedicata*, p. 9.

[112] Besse, *Anselmo dedicata*, p. 31. The incipit of the canon in Besse's edition, however, does not correspond with the text of Toledo II.

[113] Besse, *Anselmo dedicata*, p. 25.

[114] Besse, *Anselmo dedicata*, p. 31.

[115] Besse, *Anselmo dedicata*, p. 37.

[116] Besse, *Anselmo dedicata*, p. 37.

[117] Besse, *Anselmo dedicata*, p. 25.

[118] Besse, *Anselmo dedicata*, p. 9.

[119] Besse, *Anselmo dedicata*, p. 10.

[120] Besse, *Anselmo dedicata*, p. 7.

[121] Besse, *Anselmo dedicata*, p. 10.

[122] Besse, *Anselmo dedicata*, p. 37.

[123] Besse, *Anselmo dedicata*, p. 14.

II.239).[124] The letter to Theodoric and Theodobert (*Reg*.IX.215) appears in two places: Book IIIa.203[125] and much later in Book XIIa.2.[126]

The *Collectio Anselmo dedicata* contains many of the classic patristic papal and conciliar texts on the *cursus honorum* and the interstices. It demonstrates how widely these canons were known and disseminated in at least one late ninth-century canonistic collection.

e. Regino of Prüm

The last canonistic collection to be surveyed in this chapter is the *Libri duo de synodalibus causis et disciplinis ecclesiasticis* of Regino of Prüm (840–915), compiled *ca.* 906 at Trier. Regino relied on the *Dacheriana*, the Pseudo-Isidorian corpus and other sources.[127] What is astonishing about Regino's collection is the dearth of texts relating to the *cursus honorum* and the interstices, though the related issues of probation and the ages of clerics are cited.

Of the patristic texts surveyed in the previous chapter, only three canons appear in Book I of the *Libri duo*. In specific, cap. 421 of the *Libri duo* is Canon XI of the Council of Neocaesarea, which established thirty as the minimum age of presbyters.[128] Likewise Canon IV of the third Council of Carthage establishing twenty-five as the age of deacons is included in cap. 422.[129] Lastly, Canon I of the SEA, on the examination and probation of a bishop (which makes no reference to the *cursus per se*) is included in cap. 455.[130]

The absence of any other texts relating to the *cursus* and the interstices in the *Libri duo* is noteworthy. Given the many canons relating to the clergy and issues surrounding their ordinations such as continence, and the relation between clerics and their feudal masters, Regino is clearly interested

---

[124] Besse, *Anselmo dedicata*, p. 14.

[125] Besse, *Anselmo dedicata*, p. 22.

[126] Besse, *Anselmo dedicata*, p. 65.

[127] Reynolds, "Law: Canon," p. 407.

[128] F. G. A. Wasserschleben, ed., *Regionis Abbatis Prumiensis: Libri duo de synodalibus causis et disciplinis ecclesiasticis* (Leipzig: Englemann, 1840), p. 191.

[129] Wasserschleben, *Regionis...Libri duo*, p. 191.

[130] Wasserschleben, *Regionis...Libri duo*, p. 204.

in the state of the clergy. Either the *cursus honorum* was an issue he did not need to deal with, or was not prepared to handle.

5. Ordination Liturgies

The ordination liturgies of the eighth, ninth, and tenth centuries are critical in the study of the *cursus honorum*. From the eighth century, evidence of the *cursus* will be examined from the *Ordines Romani*, specifically OR XXXIV, the *Missale francorum*, and the Gelasian Sacramentaries. From the ninth century, the Gregorian Sacramentary will be examined, and from the tenth-century OR XXXV and the *Pontificale romano-germanicum*.

a. The Eighth Century

i.

The first ordination rite from the eighth century to be examined is OR XXXIV.[131] This text is dated mid-eighth century, making it the oldest extant description of Roman ordination practice since the *Apostolic Tradition*. The *Ordines romani*, while Roman in origin, were copied in Gaul or Germany. OR XXXIV is largely a series of rubrical directions, but also contains some prayers. In the rite of episcopal ordination it reproduces fully the presentation and examination of the candidate. With the exception of the blessing of the acolyte, however, no ordination prayers are provided.

OR XXXIV describes the rites of ordination, in an ascending sequence, for the orders of acolyte, subdeacon, deacon, presbyter, and bishop; there are no rites for the doorkeeper, lector, or exorcist. Vogel contends that the doorkeeper and exorcists are omitted because these orders had fallen into desuetude at this time, though he notes the lectorate was still in use.[132] In his introduction to OR XXXIV, Andrieu argues the same point though he too notes that the text is equally silent about the lectorate, which had always been maintained in Rome.[133] Bradshaw, on the other hand, suggests

---

[131] Michel Andrieu, ed., *Les Ordines Romani du haut Moyen Age*, vol. 3, (Louvain: Spicilegium Sacrum Lovaniense, 1951), pp. 603–613.

[132] Vogel, *Medieval Liturgy*, p. 174.

[133] Andrieu, *Les Ordines Romani*, vol 3, pp. 543–544.

that only the acolyte and the subdeacon are included because they are the only minor orders which served at the altar.[134]

It is possible to query the position of Vogel and Andrieu on the grounds that the anti-pope Constantine in the middle of the eighth century was ordained doorkeeper, lector, exorcist, acolyte, subdeacon, and deacon, at least according to the Wolfenbüttel account.[135] This query depends on the authenticity of the Wolfenbüttel version over against the more generally accepted account from the *Liber pontificalis* which, like OR XXXIV, omits any reference to the doorkeeper, exorcist, and lector. Yet, many eighth-century Hispanic and Frankish texts (e.g., *Epistula ad Leudefredum*, *De ordinibus VII graduum*, the *Missale francorum*) include references to these orders. Moreover, as Reynolds has shown, there is evidence that the Eighth-Century Gelasian sacramentaries, with the Romano-Gallican sequence of grades, were known in southern Italy in the eighth century.

There is an apparent assumption in OR XXXIV that candidates will proceed sequentially through the grades. For instance, in OR XXXIV.3, after the ordination of the acolyte the text says: *Et si ad subdiaconatus officium voluerit eum provocare....;*[136] after the ordination of the subdeacon in OR XXXIV.6, the text reads: *Et si ad diaconatus ordinem voluerit eum provocare....;*[137] and after the deacon is ordained OR XXXIV.11 directs:

> Si vero voluerit eum consecrare presbyterum, tenens eum archidiaconus ducit foras rugas altaris, exuit eum dalmatica et sic eum induit planetam et ducit iterum ad episcopum.[138]

The *eum* in each of these sentences refers to the person who was just ordained to the preceding order. It ought not to be understood that the orders were received one after the other within the course of the same liturgy. This procedure would have been impossible between the grades of subdeacon and deacon; subdeacons were ordained before communion while deacons were ordained after the gradual. However, between the

---

[134] Paul Bradshaw, *Ordination Rites of the Ancient Churches of East and West* (New York: Pueblo Publishing Co., 1990), p. 101.

[135] The *Liber pontificalis* notes only the tonsure, subdiaconate, and diaconate as part of Constantine's *cursus*. Missing from this sequence is the grade of acolyte, which is present in OR XXXIV and the lector, which Vogel notes was still in use, and the presbyterate.

[136] Andrieu *Les Ordines Romani*, vol. 3, p. 604.

[137] Andrieu, *Les Ordines Romani*, vol. 3, p. 604.

[138] Andrieu, *Les Ordines Romani*, vol. 3, p. 606.

grades of deacon and presbyter the text would seem to make ordination to two orders at the same liturgy plausible. Andrieu comments:

> Je serais donc incliné à croire que l'expression «*Si vero voluerit eum consecrare presbiterum*» marque une alternative et je l'entendrais ainsi: *Mais, si c'est un prêtre qu'il veut ordonner*....[139]

Andrieu says he knows of no Roman historical document which exhibits an instance of a person receiving the diaconate and the presbyterate on the same day, with the exception of Leo VIII in 964.[140] This position marks a dramatic shift for Andrieu, who had earlier maintained the position that according to the rites of OR XXXIV, subdeacons were ordained deacons, some of whom were immediately ordained presbyters without ever having exercised the diaconal ministry; i.e., candidates were ordained both deacons and presbyters at the same liturgy.[141] This view is also expressed by Louis Duchesne in the chapter on ordination in *Origines du Culte Chrétien*:

> Cet *ordo* suppose, comme aussi les deux autres documents de même nature, que les diacres et les prêtres étaient ordonnés en même temps, les sous-diacres destinés à la prêtrise recevant d'abord la bénédiction du diaconat, puis, aussitôt après, celle de la prêtrise.[142]

An interesting perspective on this question is found in the *Liber pontificalis*. Some, though not all, of the entries for eighth-century popes list the numbers of ordinations performed by the bishops of Rome. For example, the entry for John VI (701–705) says:

> Hic fecit ordinationem presbiterorum et diaconorum I, id est presbiteros VIIII, diaconos II.[143]

Similarly, Constantius (708–715) performed one ordination in which he ordained ten presbyters and two deacons.[144] Gregory II (715–731) ordained thirty-five presbyters and four deacons.[145] Gregory III (731–741)

---

[139] Andrieu, *Les Ordines Romani*, vol. 3, p. 561.

[140] Andrieu, *Les Ordines Romani*, vol. 3, p. 562; p. 562, n. 1.

[141] Andrieu, "La carrière ecclésiastique," p. 99.

[142] Louis Duchesne, *Origines du Culte Chrétien*. 2nd ed. (Paris: A. Fontemoing, 1898), p. 342.

[143] LP I, p. 383.

[144] LP I, p. 393.

[145] LP I, p. 410.

ordained twenty-four presbyters and three deacons.[146] Zacharias (741–752) ordained thirty presbyters and five deacons.[147] Stephen II (752–757) is said to have ordained two presbyters and two deacons on one occasion: *"Qui fecit ordinationem I per mens. mart., presbiteros II, diaconos II."*[148] While there is nothing to suggest that the two presbyters and two deacons were the same people, this is as close as the LP comes to supporting the theory that a person could receive two orders at the same liturgy. Paul I (757–767) ordained twelve presbyters and two deacons.[149] The antipope Constantine ordained eight presbyters and four deacons.[150] Stephen III (768–772) ordained five presbyters and four deacons.[151] At the end of the eighth century Hadrian (772–795) ordained twenty-four presbyters and seven deacons.

While such a regular abrogation of the interstices canons seems unlikely given the abhorrence for rapid sequential ordination in the period, one might admit the possibility that all presbyters listed in these entries from the *Liber pontificalis* passed through the diaconate immediately prior to their presbyteral ordinations, as Andrieu suggested in "La carrière ecclésiastique des papes" (1947). One might further suggest that since such presbyters never exercised any diaconal ministry, their ordinations to the diaconate were simply ignored by the authors of the LP. These two hypothesis, however, remain unsubstantiated on the basis of the text of the LP itself. On the basis on the numbers of ordinations performed by the popes in the eighth century, it seems equally (if not more) likely that not all the presbyters ordained by the eighth-century bishops of Rome were ever ordained to the diaconate; that in fact many, if not most, of the eighth-century Roman presbyters were ordained directly to that office from the subdiaconate. This alternate view is supported by Cyril Vogel. Commenting on OR XXXIV, Vogel writes: "Clerics do not have to pass through each stage of the *cursus* in order to reach the higher rank."[152] While the biographical information of the *Liber pontificalis* seems to confirm this assertion, it

---

[146] LP I, p. 421.

[147] LP I, p. 435.

[148] LP I, p. 456.

[149] LP I, p. 465.

[150] LP I, p. 469.

[151] LP I, p. 480.

[152] Vogel, *Medieval Liturgy*, p. 174.

remains possible that the text of OR XXXIV assumes that candidates will ordinarily pass sequentially from one order to the next.

The one unequivocal exception to this assumption in OR XXXIV is the rite of episcopal ordination, which presumes that the candidate will be *either* a deacon *or* a presbyter. In OR XXXIV.22, the pope asks those who are presenting the candidate:

> Quo honore fungitur? Resp. Diaconus, presbyter aut quod fuerit.
>
> Interrogantur: Quantos annos habet in diaconato aut presbiterato? Resp. quantos et quomodo.[153]

The pope ask the same question of the candidate in the examination (OR XXXIV.27).[154] Later, when the pope invites the assembly to pray for the one to be consecrated bishop he refers to him by name as a deacon or presbyter (OR XXXIV.38).[155] Furthermore, the rite itself is identical for both diaconal or presbyteral candidates to the episcopate.

The practice of ordaining bishops from among either the deacons or presbyters of Rome is attested in the biographies of the popes in the *Liber pontificalis* and in canonistic texts such as the Dionysian version of Canon XIII of the Council of Sardica. The rite for the ordination of a bishop in OR XXXIV, however, is the first liturgical evidence corroborating the long-standing practice of ordaining both deacons and presbyters to the episcopate in the church of Rome.

ii.

The second eighth-century liturgical text to be examined is the *Missale francorum* (Cod. Vat. Reg. Lat. 257), from the early eighth century.[156] Despite its title, the *Missale francorum* is not a pure Gallican rite; in fact, there are no purely Gallican liturgical texts extant. Gallican usages remain in composite rites such as the *Missale francorum* which combine both Roman and Gallican texts. Hence, Bradshaw refers to it as the "more-or-less Gallican book known as the *Missale Francorum*."[157]

---

[153] Andrieu, *Les Ordines Romani*, vol. 3, p. 608.

[154] Andrieu, *Les Ordines Romani*, vol. 3, p. 610.

[155] Andrieu, *Les Ordines Romani*, vol. 3, p. 612.

[156] Leo Cunibert Mohlberg, ed., *Missale francorum* (Rome: Herder, 1957), pp. 3–19.

[157] Bradshaw, *Ordination Rites*, p. 14.

Two sequences of grades appear in the *Missale francorum*. The first, included with the SEA, introduces the ordination material. Here the grades appear in the ascending sequence of doorkeeper, acolyte, exorcist, deacon, presbyter, and bishop;[158] missing from the sequence of the SEA is (the psalmist and) the lector and the subdeacon. In the *Missale francorum* the acolyte appears between the doorkeeper and the exorcist, whereas in the SEA he is hierarchically superior to the exorcist. Finally, the grades appear in the SEA in a descending sequence, rather than in the ascending sequence as reproduced in the *Missale francorum*.

The second sequence is the arrangement of the ordination rites, which appear in the following ascending sequence: doorkeeper, acolyte, lector, exorcist, subdeacon, deacon, presbyter, and bishop. The lector and subdeacon appear in this sequence. Again, the acolyte does not appear in the usual Romano-Gallican place between the exorcist and the subdeacon, but is found after the doorkeeper. The placing of the acolyte after the doorkeeper is similar to the sequence of grades in Isidore's *De ecclesiasticis officiis* and the pseudo-Isidorian *Epistula ad Leudefredum*. Since both these texts invert the positions of the lector and acolyte, however, the similarity ends here.

Within the ordination liturgies of the *Missale francorum* there is no explicit evidence of movement between the clerical grades. For instance, unlike the Leonine Sacramentary and the *Liber ordinum*, there is no petition in the blessing of the deacon, *In ordinatione diaconi*, that he might ascend to the "higher grade". Rather, in the *Missale francorum* the bishop prays that the new deacon may be worthy of the rank given by the apostle to Stephen and the seven:

> ....et indulgentia purior eorum gradu, quos apostoli tui in septinario numero beato Stephano duce ac praevio sancto spiritu auctore elegerunt, dignus existat....[159]

A significant feature of the *Missale francorum* is the inclusion of a ceremonial anointing of the hands of a new presbyter. The *Missale francorum* is the first witness of this practice. Two formulae are provided:

> Consecratio manus. Consecrentur manus istae et sanctificentur per istam unctionem et nostram benedictionem, ut quaecumque benedixerint benedicta sint, et quaecumque sanctificaverint sanctificentur: per dominum.

---

[158] Mohlberg, *Missale francorum*, p. 3

[159] Mohlberg, *Missale francorum*, p. 7.

Item alia. Unguantur manus istae de oleo sanctificato et crismate sanctificationis: sicut uncxit Samuhel David in regem et prophetam, ita unguantur er consummentur in nomene dei patris et filii et spiritus sancti, facientes imaginem sanctae crucis salvatoris domini nostri Iesu Christi, qui nos a morte redemit ad regna caelorum perducit...[160]

The first prayer asks that the new presbyter's hands be consecrated and hallowed by unction and episcopal blessing, so that whatsoever they bless might be blessed, and whatsoever they sanctify might be sanctified. There are liturgical, "priestly" implications associated with this prayer.

The second prayer asks that the hands of the new presbyter be anointed with holy oil and the chrism of holiness, so that as Samuel anointed David to be king and prophet, so too the newly ordained may be anointed and perfected. The implications here are less liturgical and "priestly", and directed more towards governance and leadership.[161]

It is notable that there is no corresponding anointing of a new bishop's hands in the *Missale francorum*. While this does not demonstrate a liturgical expectation of sequential movement from the presbyterate to the episcopate, it does beg the question. It is hard to imagine that a presbyter "received" something in ordination that a bishop did not, unless, however, bishops were all drawn from the presbyterate.

The Frankish practice of ordination anointing stemming from the *Missale francorum* will become increasingly significant in the discussion of sequential ordination from the presbyterate to the episcopate, as reflected in the ordination rites.

iii.

A third eighth-century liturgical book is the so-called "Old" Gelasian sacramentary (Cod. Vat. Lat. 316; Paris, B.N. 7193, 41/56).[162] This sacramentary, a composite rite, is a Gallican recension of a Roman sacramentary.

---

[160] Mohlberg, *Missale francorum*, p. 10.

[161] As Gerald Ellard notes, the Samuel-David motif appears in the Bobbio Missal (MS. B.N. lat 13246, f. 117) in a prayer for the anointing of the dying. *Ordination Anointings*, p. 21.

[162] Leo Cunibert Mohlberg, ed., *Liber sacramentorum Romanae Aeclesiae ordinis anni circuli* (Cod. Vat. Lat. 316; Paris, B.N. 7193, 41/56) (Rome: Herder, 1981), pp. 115–122; Chavasse, Antoine, ed., *Le Sacramentaire Gélasien Vaticanus Reginensis 316* (Tournai: Desclée, 1958); H. A. Wilson, ed., *The Gelasian Sacramentary* (Oxford: 1894), pp. 22–29, 144–152.

Thus, it is less Gallican than the *Missale francorum*. It was copied at Chelles (near Paris), *ca.* 750, though its Roman ancestor could have been composed *ca.* 628–715,[163] hence it cannot be attributed to the pontificate of Pope Gelasius. While the model for the book is likely seventh-century, the Chelles manuscript belongs to the eighth.

Some of the most distinctive Gallican features of the Old Gelasian sacramentary are found in the ordination material, particularly the minor orders. The ordination rites (*Ordo de sacris ordinibus benedicendis*) begin with the interstices text from the letter of Zosimus to Hesychius (*Epistle* 9, III.5), accurately rendered.[164] The introduction is followed by the ordination canons of the *Statuta ecclesiae antiqua* with the rites appearing in the original descending sequence of bishop, presbyter, deacon, subdeacon, acolyte, exorcist, lector, doorkeeper, and psalmist.[165] The ordination rites themselves are treated in the same, though ascending, sequence. The rites for the minor orders from psalmist to subdeacon are Gallican. There are no rites for either the deacon or presbyter in the Gallican ordination rites.[166] Rather, propers for the anniversary of the ordinations of a deacon and presbyter are provided (*In natale consecracionis diaconi*; *In natale consecracionis praesbiteri qualiter sibi missam debeat celebrare*).[167] The inclusion of anniversary propers is noteworthy for this study. The fact that there is a liturgical expectation that deacons will celebrate the anniversaries of their ordination signifies that some deacons, like most presbyters, would have remained in that office for many years. It also demonstrates that normally there must have been an interval of at least one year before ordination to the presbyterate. As noted, the ordination rites in the Gelasian sacramentary are introduced by the interstices text of the letter of Zosimus to Hesychius, which indicates an interval of five years.

---

[163] On the provenance and date of the "Old" Gelasian sacramentary see Vogel, *Medieval Liturgy*, pp. 67–69; Deshusses, "Les sacramentaires," p. 28.

[164] Mohlberg, *Liber sacramentorum*, pp. 115–116.

[165] Mohlberg, *Liber sacramentorum*, pp. 116–117.

[166] Ordination prayers for the presbyter and deacon appear earlier in the Roman section of the sacramentary. Mohlberg, *Liber sacramentorum*, pp. 24–28; Wilson, *Gelasian*, pp. 22–29.

[167] Mohlberg, *Liber sacramentorum*, pp. 119–120.

iv.

A new class of sacramentaries emerged in the eighth century in the Frankish church known as the Frankish Gelasian or Eighth-Century Gelasian sacramentaries. These sacramentaries are likewise Romano-Frankish composite rites containing materials from the "Old" Gelasian sacramentary (Vat. Lat. 316), the Gregorian Sacramentary, and Gallican elements. The archetype was probably compiled late in the reign of Pepin III (751–768) by Benedictine monks, *ca.* 760–770.[168]

The earliest and best example of the archetype of the Eighth-Century Gelasian is the Sacramentary of Gellone.[169] The ordination rites in the Gellone[170] treat the orders in the usual Romano-Gallican sequence: doorkeeper, lector, exorcist, acolyte, subdeacon, deacon, presbyter, and bishop. The rites for presbyter, deacon, and subdeacon appear under a new heading, a sign of the shifting significance of the subdiaconate. Other Eighth-Century Gelasian sacramentaries follow the same pattern. The Phillipp's Sacramentary of Autun (*ca.* 800) introduces the rites with interstices text from the letter of Zosimus,[171] as does the Sacramentary of Angoulême.[172]

No rubrical directions specify movement between the orders. The consecration of the deacon contains the petition that the new deacon might merit to rise from the inferior to the greater grade.[173] The presbyteral ordination rites in the Eighth-Century Gelasian sacramentaries include the anointing of the hands, from the *Missale francorum*. The formula for the anointing is the first form from the *Missale francorum*: *Consecrentur manus isti quesumus domine....*[174] The episcopal ordination rites also contain an anointing of the hands, from the second form in

---

[168] On the date of the archetype of the Frankish Gelasian, see Vogel, *Medieval Liturgy*, pp. 75–76.

[169] Vogel, *Medieval Liturgy*, p. 76.

[170] A. Dumas, ed., *Liber Sacramentorum Gellonensis* CCSL 159 (Turnhout: Brepols, 1981), pp. 381–395.

[171] O. Heiming, ed., *Liber sacramentorum Augustodinensis* CCSL 159b (Turnhout: Brepols, 1984), p. 181.

[172] P. Saint-Roch, ed., *Liber Sacramentorum Engolismensis* CCSL 159c (Turnhout: Brepols, 1987), p. 313.

[173] Dumas, *Gellonensis*, p. 387.

[174] Dumas, *Gellonensis*, p. 391

the *Missale francorum*: *Unguantur manus iste de oleo*....[175] The two prayers request different things; the first for priestly and liturgical grace, the second for the grace of leadership and governance. It is significant, though not surprising, that the prayers have been thus assigned to the presbyterate and the episcopate respectively. Again, there is no explicit suggestion that bishops would already have had a previous anointing as presbyters. It is difficult, however, to imagine that presbyters were given a particular grace necessary to the presbyterate and the episcopate, while the bishop was given only a grace in anointing for the tasks of leadership and oversight, that is, unless bishops had already received the first anointing as presbyters.

The Eighth-Century Gelasian sacramentaries were not limited to the Frankish church. Again, as noted above, the ordination rites of the Gelasian sacramentary are found in a late eighth-early ninth-century canon law collection, the *Collectio Teatina* (Vatican, BAV Reg. lat. 1997) from Chieti in southern Italy.[176] These ordination rites are virtually identical to other eighth-century manuscripts of the Gelasian sacramentary, such as the Gellone, Phillipp's, or the Angoulême sacramentaries of the Frankish church. Reynolds notes:

> But the appearance of the ite in the Chieti manuscript is dramatic evidence that this Frankish ordination rite was known in southern Italy well over a century before the supposed advent of the PRG.[177]

The ordination material of the *Collectio Teatina* contains ordination liturgies for the doorkeeper, lector, exorcist, acolyte, subdeacon, deacon, and presbyter.

b. The Ninth Century

i.

The end of the eighth century saw the introduction of the Gregorian-type sacramentary into the Frankish church.[178] The Gregorian prototype was probably redacted in Rome during the pontificate of Honorius I (625–

---

[175] Dumas, *Gellonensis*, p. 395.

[176] Reynolds, "The Ritual of Clerical Ordination," pp. 437–445.

[177] Reynolds, "The Ritual of Clerical Ordination," p. 441.

[178] Jean Deshusses, ed., *Le Sacramentaire Grégorien*, vol. 1, *Spicilegium Friburgense* 16 (Fribourg: Éditions Universitaires Fribourg Suisse, 1971); Hans Lietzmann, ed., *Das Sacramentarium Gregorianum: Nach dem Aachener Urexemplar* (Münster: Aschendorffsche Verlagbuchhandlung, 1921); H. A. Wilson, ed., *The Gregorian Sacramentary under Charles the Great*, (London: Henry Bradshaw Society, 1915).

638).[179] An example of a Gregorian sacramentary is the *Hadrianum*. Following the "romanizing" programme of Pepin, Charlemagne requested of Pope Hadrian a copy of a "pure" Roman liturgical text free of Gallican interpolations. The book sent by Hadrian, known as the *Hadrianum*, appeared in Charlemagne's court in the last decade of the eighth century.[180] Throughout the ninth century, however, editions of the *Hadrianum* increasingly came to incorporate many features of the Gallican rites which had been fused to the Gelasian sacramentaries a century earlier.

The *Hadrianum* includes rites for the ordination of bishops, presbyters, and deacons. The rite for the ordination of a deacon contains the petition that he might ascend to the higher order.[181] Another type of Gregorian, the revised *Hadrianum* and Supplement, attributed to Benedict of Aniane (d. 821), contains rites for the minor orders as well, in the Romano-Gallican sequence, according to the ritual of the SEA. The Supplement to the *Hadrianum* is a ninth-century example of the gallicanization of Roman liturgical books. The sources for the Supplement are the *Missale francorum*, the Old Gelasian sacramentary, and the Eighth-Century Gelasian sacramentaries. The inclusion of the Gallican rites of ordination and sequence of grades in the Gregorian sacramentary eventually altered the rites and sequences of grades in Rome itself.

ii.

An example of the *Hadrianum* and Supplement is the ninth-century Sacramentary of the Abbey of Marmoutiers,[182] in northern France.[183] Known as the Raganaldus Sacramentary after Raganaldus, abbot of Marmoutiers, Tours, it is one of the oldest exemplars of the *Hadrianum*.

A particularly noteworthy feature of the Raganaldus Sacramentary is a portrait of the seven ecclesiastical grades.[184] The upper panel portrays the

---

[179] Vogel, *Medieval Liturgy*, p. 79.

[180] Vogel, *Medieval Liturgy*, p. 81.

[181] Deshusses, *Grégorien*, vol. 1, p. 98.

[182] Autun Bibl. mun. MS Lat. 19.

[183] Roger E. Reynolds, "The Portrait of the Ecclesiastical Officers in the *Raganaldus Sacramentary* and its Liturgico-Canonical Significance," *Speculum*, vol. 46.3 (July 1971), pp. 432–442.

[184] Folio 1v.

bishop, presbyter, and deacon; the lower panel portrays the doorkeeper, lector, exorcist, acolyte, and subdeacon. In the lower panel, the subdeacon appears in the middle of the other grades, raised above them, reflecting the shifting position of the subdeacon above the minor orders. The subdiaconate still appears as part of the minor grades, but has a preeminent place among them. With regards to the arrangement of the minor ministers, Reynolds notes: "The other officers are placed so that one reads from left to right the sequence which *per ordinem* a cleric had to pass." That is, the sequence of the SEA.[185]

c. The Tenth Century

i.

The first tenth-century ordination rite to be examined is OR XXXV.[186] The text is largely based on OR XXXIV but contains many more Frankish elements making it a Romano-Gallican rite. Andrieu notes that the manuscript used for his OR XXXV, the Ordinal of Besançon (London: British Museum, Cod. *Addit.* 15222), was copied in the diocese of Besançon, *ca.* 1000.[187] He notes that its archetype must have been redacted in Rome during the first quarter of the tenth century. Vogel likewise attests that it was compiled in Rome *ca.* 925 at the latest, and *ca.* 900 at the earliest since the compilers of the PRG used it.[188]

Like its predecessor OR XXXIV, OR XXXV contains the rubrical directions for the rites of ordination. It also includes liturgical texts such as the ordination prayers, and in episcopal ordination, the texts for the presentation and examination of the candidate. In addition to the rites for acolyte, subdeacon, deacon, presbyter, and bishop, OR XXXV contains a rite for the ordination of lectors, absent from OR XXXIV. The subdiaconate is treated as one of the minor orders; the text refers to the "*subdiaconum vero vel ceteros gradus inferiores....*"[189]

---

[185] Reynolds, "Portrait of Ecclesiastical Officers," p. 436.

[186] M. Andrieu, *Les Ordines Romani du haut moyen age* vol. 4 (Louvain: Spicilegium Sacrum Lovaniense, 1956), pp. 33–46.

[187] Andrieu, *Les Ordines Romani*, vol. 4, p. 3.

[188] Vogel, *Medieval Liturgy*, p. 176.

[189] Andrieu, *Les Ordines Romani*, vol. 4, p. 36.

There are a number of points of interest in OR XXXV for the study of the *cursus honorum* and the interstices. For instance, after the ordination of the acolyte the text says:

> Et si ad presens voluerit eum ad subdiaconatus ordinem promoveri, tollitur ab eo sacculus....[190]

The same is found in OR XXXIV. The addition of the words *"ad presens"* to the text, however, gives the impression that such a promotion would have taken place at that time, implying that the offices of acolyte and sub-deacon could have been conferred at the same liturgy.

A similar impression is given between the reception of the diaconate and the presbyterate. After the ordination of the deacon, the text reads:

> Nam, si statim eum voluerit consecrare presbiterum, tenens eum archdiaconus et ducit foras rugas altaris in presbiterio, exuensque dalmatica induit eum planeta et deportat eum iterum ad pontificem et dat illi benedictionem consecrationis solus per se.[191]

The interpolation of the word *statim*, in addition to the rubric directing the new deacon to replace the dalmatic with a chasuble and to appear again (*iterum*) before the pontiff, naturally lead one to assume that the diaconate and the presbyterate could conferred on the same candidate at the same liturgy. This question was also raised in connection with OR XXXIV.

Here, Andrieu surmises that the addition of the word *statim* underlines the fact that those who receive the orders of deacon and presbyter are the same individuals. Yet he adds cautiously: "Et cependant je ne suis pas sans quelque doubte."[192] Such an abrogation of the interstices in a liturgical text is difficult to reconcile with the (albeit often abused) concurrent canonical tradition. If Andrieu's surmise is correct, the text of OR XXXV continues to underline the normative character of the *cursus* between deacon and presbyter. Yet this view must be qualified against the careers of many popes at this time who were either never deacons or never presbyters.

From the *Liber pontificalis* it appears that in the ninth and tenth centuries, as the eighth, more presbyters than deacons continue to be ordained in the Roman church. Such presbyters likely were never deacons. The details of the ordinations performed by popes decline after the eighth-century entries in the LP. The following details are available from the ninth

---

[190] Andrieu, *Les Ordines Romani*, vol. 4, p. 35.

[191] Andrieu, *Les Ordines Romani*, vol. 4, p. 38.

[192] Andrieu, *Les Ordines Romani*, vol. 3, p. 561.

century: Leo III (795–816) ordained thirty presbyters and twelve deacons.[193] Sergius II (844–847) ordained eight presbyters and three deacons.[194] Leo IV (847–855) ordained nineteen presbyters and eight deacons.[195] Benedict III (855–858) ordained six presbyters and one deacon.[196] Nicholas I (858–867) ordained seven presbyters and four deacons.[197] The only tenth-century papal biography is for John XII (955–964), who is reported to have ordained seven presbyters and two deacons.[198]

Throughout the ninth century, and most likely throughout the tenth (if John XII's pontificate can be taken as an example in this respect), more presbyters were ordained than deacons in Rome, probably meaning that not all presbyters had ever passed through the diaconate. This assertion, as noted above, is corroborated by the careers of some of the popes in this period.

The presbyteral ordination rite in OR XXXV contains an anointing of the hands, according to the formula: *Consecrentur et sanctificentur manus iste per istam unctionem....*[199] This ceremony in OR XXXV is clearly a Gallican interpolation.

Like OR XXXIV, OR XXXV assumes that candidates for the episcopate will be either deacons or presbyters. At the presentation, the pope asks:

> Interrogantur: Quo honore fungitur? Respondent: Diaconi, presbiteri, aut quod fuerit.

> Interrogantur: Quantos annos habet in diaconatu aut presbiterato? Resp.: quantos et quomodo.[200]

The same questions are asked of the candidate at the examination.[201]

---

[193] LP II, p. 34.

[194] LP II, p. 101.

[195] LP II, p. 134.

[196] LP II, p. 148.

[197] LP II, p. 167.

[198] LP II, p. 246.

[199] Andrieu, *Les Ordines Romani*, vol. 4, pp. 39–40.

[200] Andrieu, *Les Ordines Romani*, vol. 4, p. 41.

[201] Andrieu, *Les Ordines Romani*, vol. 4, p. 42.

In OR XXXV there is one major distinction in the way that deacons and presbyters are consecrated bishops: the rite enjoins the Gallican practice of anointing the hands of the new bishop:

> Hac expleta, consecrat ei manus si nondum habuit consecratas, ordine quo supra prefiximus.[202]

Although the formula is not provided, it must have been the same one used in the ordination of a presbyter—*ordine quo supra prefiximus*—conferring the priestly and liturgical graces. If a presbyter is ordained to the episcopate, his hands are not anointed; such an anointing would have taken place at his ordination to the presbyterate. By comparison, if the episcopal candidate is a deacon, then his hands are anointed for the first and only time.

In "La carrière ecclésiastique des papes", Andrieu asserted that the anointing rubric applies only to deacons; there is no mention of presbyters who had not been anointed.[203] Andrieu later speculated, however, that this direction could equally apply to presbyters ordained under a rite such as OR XXXIV who like deacons, would never had had their hands anointed.[204] Commenting on this text, Gerald Ellard wonders:

> How shall one interpret that unique prescription: 'consecrat ei manus si nondum habuit consecratas'? Was the legal-minded Roman of the view that at least *one* anointing of the hands was necessary as a sort of prerequisite for the fullness of Orders? Or is it not rather written with the knowledge that bishops would be consecrated according to this book, whose hands at priestly ordination had not known any anointing? Which ever way it is understood, the rubric itself is eloquent testimony that the rite was new at Rome.[205]

It is beyond the scope of this study to consider whether presbyters ordained under an older rite would have received an anointing when consecrated bishop under this rite. Given the fact, however, that deacons are still envisaged as candidates for episcopal consecration in OR XXXV, it seems reasonable that they are to be considered the primary object of this rubric. Moreover, a liturgical grace is not asked for presbyters which is not equally asked for bishops.

The fact that deacons are eligible for ordination directly to the episcopate in the Romano-Gallican OR XXXV stands in marked contrast to the

---

[202] Andrieu, *Les Ordines Romani*, vol. 4, p. 45.

[203] Andrieu, "La carrière ecclésiastique," p. 103.

[204] Andrieu, *Les Ordines Romani*, vol. 4, p. 20.

[205] Ellard, *Ordination Anointings*, pp. 76–77.

insistence on sequential ordination to the presbyterate for diaconal candidates for the episcopate in the Frankish Church, as evidenced in the concurrent *Epistle* 29 of Hincmar to Adventius of Metz. In OR XXXV, direct ordination to the episcopate is likely an instance of Roman conservatism.

ii.

The second tenth-century example of an ordination liturgy is from the *Pontificale romano-germanicum* of the tenth century.[206] The PRG is an amalgamation of materials from the *ordines* and the sacramentaries compiled *ca.* 950–962 in the city of Mainz.[207] Although Germanic in origin, it is the successor to the composite Romano-Gallican sacramentaries. These composite rites received their permanent shape in the PRG, which rapidly became the first universal pontifical of the Western church.

The ordination rites of the PRG were originally introduced by the *De ordinibus VII graduum,* with its ascending sequence of doorkeeper, lector, exorcist, subdeacon, deacon, presbyter, and bishop, with no mention of the acolyte.[208] The ordination liturgies for the minor orders appear in the sequence of psalmist, doorkeeper, lector, exorcist, and acolyte. The rites for subdeacon, deacon, and presbyter appear separately, indicating the shifting place of the subdiaconate as it becomes regarded as a major order.

There is little in the rites themselves which indicates progression through the grades, such as the *"Si vero voluerit eum consecrare...."* of the *Ordines.* The only internal evidence is from the Roman consecration prayer of the deacon, which prays that he might merit the higher grade:

.... in Christo firmi et stabiles perseverent dignisque successibus de inferiori gradu per gratiam tuam capere potiora mereantur.[209]

A more significant sign of sequential ordination from the diaconate to the presbyterate is found in an easily overlooked rubric in the vesting of the new presbyter:

Hic reflectat orarium super humerum eorum dextrum, dicens ad eos per singulos: Accipe iugum domini...[210]

---

[206] Cyrille Vogel, *Le Pontifical Romano-Germanique du Dixième Siècle* vol. 1 (Vatican: Biblioteca Apostolica Vaticana, 1963), pp. 12–36, 198–227.

[207] On the date and provenance of the PRG, see Vogel, *Medieval Liturgy,* pp. 232–235.

[208] PRG, pp. 12–13.

[209] PRG, p. 26

[210] PRG, p. 34.

The rubric directs the stole of the newly ordained to "be changed, over their right shoulder." The giving of a stole is not new; the direction that it be adjusted, however, is. The clear implication is that these presbyters were already wearing stoles over their *left* shoulders, that is, deacon-wise. This innovation in the rite establishes that in the PRG the assumption is that all candidates for the presbyterate are deacons.

The new presbyter's hands are anointed according to the usual formula: *Consecrare et sanctificare digneris, domine, manus istas per istam unctionem....*[211] The episcopal ordination rite, which appears elsewhere in the pontifical, includes the Frankish formula for bishops: *Unguantur manus istae de oleo sanctificato....*[212] There is an additional anointing of the new bishop's thumb:

> Completa benedictione, confirmet pollicem consecrati cum chrismate, dicens:

> Deus et pater domini nostri Iesu Christi, qui te ad pontificatus sublimari voluit dignitatem, ipse te chrismate et misticae delibationis liquore perfundat, et spiritualis benedictionis ubertate fecundet, ut quicquid benedixeris benedicatur, quicquid santificaveris [*sic.*] sanctificetur, et consecratae manus istius vel pollicis impositio cunctus proficiat ad salutem.[213]

This formula recovers a sense of the liturgical and priestly nature of episcopal office.

iii.

A third tenth-century example is the pontifical roll made for Landolf of Benevento.[214] Compiled in the second half of the tenth century (*ca.* 975) the Landolf Pontifical is a supplemented Gregorian sacramentary. It contains a *rotulus consecrationis*, a roll from which the rite was used.

The *rotulus* contains twelve scenes depicting the rites of clerical ordination. The sequence of the minor orders is the same as that of the Raganaldus Sacramentary, which shows some dependence on both the Eighth-Century Gelasian and Gregorian sacramentaries, although there is no mention of the psalmist. The scenes explicitly depict doorkeepers becoming lectors, subdeacons becoming deacons, and deacons becoming presbyters,

---

[211] PRG, p. 35.

[212] PRG, pp. 219–220.

[213] PRG, p. 220.

[214] Rome, Biblioteca Casanatense 724. See Roger E. Reynolds, "Image and Text: The Liturgy of Clerical Ordination in Early Medieval Art," *Gesta*, vol. 22.1 (1983), pp. 31–35.

evidence that sequential ordination through the clerical *cursus* will follow the hierarchical sequence of the grades. In particular, the roll indicates an assumed sequence from subdeacon, to deacon, to presbyter in the late tenth century.

6. Early Medieval Literature on Holy Orders

A considerable body of literature on holy orders emerged in the Carolingian period. This section will survey a small portion of this material as related to the *cursus honorum*. From the eighth century the *Epistula ad Leudefredum*, the *De officiis VII gradum*, and a short tract by Pseudo-Bede from the *Collectaneum* will be examined. From the ninth century this section will examine the *Disputatio puerorum* of Alcuin, the *Liber officialis* of Amalarius of Metz, the *Formulae antiquae promotionum episcopalium* of Hincmar of Rheims, and the *De clericorum institutione* of Rabanus Maurus. Lastly, from the tenth century the *Liber de divinis officiis* of Pseudo-Alcuin and the *Canones Aelfrici ad Wulfinum episcopum* by Aelfric the Grammerian will be examined.

a. The Eighth Century

i.

An important early medieval Hispanic tract on the duties of clerics is the *Epistula beati Ysidori iunioris episcopi Spalensis eclesiae ad Leudefredum aepiscopum Cordobensis aeclesie directa*.[215] It later was used as an introduction to the offices of the church in numerous medieval canonical, theological, and liturgical texts, such as the *Sententiae* of Peter Lombard and the canonistic collections of Burchard of Worms and Ivo of hartres. In spite of its Isidorian ascription and the similarities it shares with genuine Isidorian texts such as the *Etymologiae* and the DEO, there is no conclusive evidence that establishes Isidore of Seville as the author of the

---

[215] Text: Roger Reynolds, ed., "The 'Isidorian' *Epistula ad Leudefredum*", *Mediaeval Studies*, 41 (1979), pp. 260–262; *PL* 83.893–898.

Epistula ad Leudefredum (EL). Moreover, it is much later than Isidore, originating in the eighth, or perhaps the seventh century.[216]

The EL is a tract on the duties of the various orders of the church. There is no discussion on the question of sequential movement from one order to another. The arrangement of the grades indicates the sequence of the *cursus*. In the EL the orders are presented in the following sequence: doorkeeper, acolyte, exorcist, psalmist, lector, subdeacon, deacon, presbyter, and bishop. Moreover, the offices associated with the bishop are discussed: archdeacon, secretary (*primicerius*), treasurer (*thesaurius*), and steward (*economus*). The duties of the abbot (*pater monasterii*) are also described. A second sequence of the minor grades appears under the duties of the secretary, who is charged to direct them. The second sequence (acolyte, exorcist, psalmist, and lector) is the same as the first, though it omits the doorkeeper and the subdeacon.[217]

The sequence of the grades in the EL reflects the Hispanic *cursus*, particularly the position of the lector above the exorcist. And yet the acolyte, which appears in neither the *Liber ordinum* nor the DEO, is found here between the doorkeeper and the exorcist. The position of the acolyte itself is curious, as it neither appears in its position in sequences of grades of the SEA, the *Liber pontificalis* (Gaius and Silvester), nor of the other texts which contain the Gallican arrangement.[218]

ii.

A second eighth-century text to be examined is the *De officiis VII graduum*. The *De officiis VII graduum* (DO7G) is a series of brief sentences describing the functions of each of the ecclesiastical orders. Like the EL,

---

[216] Reynolds, "The 'Isidorian' *Epistula ad Leudefredum*," p. 282. On the discussion of the authorship, date, and provenance of the text, see pp. 269–282.

[217] Reynolds cites this example as evidence of the descending Gallican sequence of acolyte, exorcist, psalmist, and lector, "The 'Isidorian' *Epistula ad Leudefredum*," p. 275. It is not clear why this is identified as a descending Gallican sequence; it appears to be a repetition of the ascending Hispanic sequence earlier in the text, in which the acolyte seems to be hierarchically inferior to the exorcist, psalmist, and lector. Moreover, the psalmist appears as he does in both Hispanic and Gallican sequences, that is, below the lector.

[218] Of the canonistic collections surveyed in this study, the EL is partially reproduced in the pre-Gregorian Reform collection of Burchard; the EL appears in the *Liber de vita christiana* of Bonizo, Ivo's *Panormia* and *Decretum*.

the DO7G became widely dissimulated (and modified) in medieval texts dealing with holy orders. From the mid-tenth-century Anglo-Saxon Egbert Pontifical onwards, the sentences of the DO7G are used in the introductions to the various ordination rites, such as the PRG.[219]

Like the EL, the DO7G is often ascribed to Isidore of Seville; such is the ascription in the tenth-century PRG. It is impossible to ascertain the exact provenance and date of the DO7G. The nucleus may have been in existence as early as the fifth century; it was possibly in existence by the time of the *Collectio hibernensis* (*ca.* 700), because an earlier form of the DO7G appears in Book VIII.2 of the collection in the *De distantia graduum*.[220] On the other hand, the DDG may be the earliest form of the DO7G.

Although the DO7G does not describe movement within the grades, its sequence of grades is significant. The orders appear in the ascending sequence of: doorkeeper, lector, exorcist, subdeacon, deacon, presbyter, and bishop. (The DO7G is another eighth-century example of the early medieval fascination for the number seven.) The sequence is much like that of the SEA. The sequence of grades is identical to that of the *De distantia graduum* of the *Hibernensis*, the original form of the DO7G. The lector and exorcist are in their Gallican, not Hispanic, places in the *cursus*. There is no mention of the psalmist or the acolyte.

The sequence of the grades is neither Hispano-Celtic nor Gallican, though it has features of both. Reynolds postulates that the provenance of the DO7G might be a location where Celtic and Gallican influences meet, such as continental areas visited by Irish missionaries. He notes that the British Isles also might be the location, where there were both Gallican and Celtic influences at work.[221] The DO7G, like the EL, is further evidence that the sequence of the grades in the *cursus honorum* was far from uniform in the early eighth century.

iii.

A third eighth-century text on orders is the *Collectaneum*, placed amongst the *opera dubia* of the Venerable Bede.[222] The chapter entitled *De septem*

---

[219] PRG, pp. 12–13.

[220] For a discussion on the date, provenance, and possible models for the DO7G, see Roger E. Reynolds, "The *De officiis VII graduum*: Its Origins and early Medieval Development," *Mediaeval Studies*, vol. 34 (1972), pp. 117–128.

[221] Reynolds, "The *De officiis VII graduum*," p. 128.

[222] *PL* 94.553–555.

ordinibus outlines the origins and duties of clerics. Much of it is based on Isidore. The orders are treated in the ascending sequence of doorkeeper, lector, exorcist, acolyte, subdeacon, deacon, and presbyter. Bishops are included under the entry on presbyters. The *Collectaneum* possibly reflects the Romano-Gallican sequence of grades in the Anglo-Saxon church.

b. The Ninth Century

i.

An important ninth-century Carolingian tract on holy orders is found in the *Disputatio puerorum per interogationes et responsiones* attributed to Alcuin of York (*ca.* 735–804). In chapter IX, entitled *De gradibus totius ecclesiae dignitatis*, in a catechetical form, Alcuin discusses the duties of the orders, and the etymologies of the names of the orders.[223]

The sequence in which the grades appear in *De gradibus totius ecclesiae* is noteworthy. Alcuin lists the grades in the ascending sequence of doorkeeper, psalmist, lector, exorcist, acolyte, subdeacon, deacon, and presbyter. Except for the omission of the bishop, the sequence of grades is identical to the first sequence of Isidore's *Etymologiae*. The description of the presbyter is from Isidore. Except for the inversion of the psalmist and the doorkeeper, the sequence is similar to the SEA.

ii.

The second ninth-century text is the *Liber officialis* of Amalarius of Metz (*ca.* 780–*ca.* 850). A pupil of Alcuin, Amalarius was the premier liturgical scholar of the Carolingian renaissance. Amalarius drew on a variety of sources such as the SEA, Isidore, the Ordinals of Christ, and the *Ordines*.

In Book II, caps. 4–13 of the *Liber officialis* Amalarius describes the duties of the ecclesiastical orders, the rites of ordination, and the theological significance of orders.[224] He treats the orders in the following ascending sequence: doorkeeper, lector, exorcist, acolyte, subdeacon, deacon, presbyter, and bishop (*de pontifice*). This sequence is similar to that of Alcuin's *Disputatio puerorum* with the exception that the bishop is included and the psalmist is excluded. It is also similar to the SEA, again with the

---

[223] *PL* 101.1131–1134. Migne places the treatise among the *opera dubia* of Alcuin.

[224] J. Hanssens, ed., *Liber officialis, Amalarii episcopi Opera liturgica omnia* vol. 2, Studi e Testi, vol. 139 (Vatican: Bibliotheca Apostolica Vaticana, 1984), pp. 209–236.

exception of the psalmist. It is identical to the Roman sequence of grades of Cornelius and the *Liber pontificalis*. One of Amalarius's goals in the *Liber officialis* was to fuse Roman and Gallican usages.

Amalarius not only assumes movement from one grade to another, but finds a rationale for it. In Book II, cap. 6.6, he concludes the chapter which introduces the discussion of the grades by saying:

> De istis sat est ad demonstrandum unumquemque sacerdotem habere in se subdita ministeria, sed propter multitudinem hominum non posse omnia illum adimplere, ac ideo adiectos esse sibi socios, qui minora adimpleant. Nunc ordo poscit, quantum Dominus dederit, ut de singulis ordinibus dicamus specialiter.[225]

As the "priest" has within himself the lower ministries but cannot fulfil them himself, other ministers do so. This introduction leads to the description of the different ministries.

In Book II, cap. 12.14, Amalarius speaks of the movement between the diaconate and the "priesthood" in the discussion on deacons, *De diaconis*:

> Si enim qui voluerit dicere, quid necesse est toties inponere manus super captita eorum qui consecrantur? Imponuntur enim super diaconum, imponuntur postea super presbyterum. Quare hoc? nisi quia per consecrationem de opere ad opus transit, sicut de ministerio diaconi transit ad immolationem sacerdotalem....[226]

Amalarius asks why the deacon receives the imposition of hands when later a presbyter does as well? The answer appears to lie in the fact that the work of the deacon "passes over" into the priestly sacrifice.

Amalarius also reflects sequential ordination from the presbyterate to the episcopate. In cap. 14 on bishops, *De pontifice*, Amalarius writes:

> Secundum auctoritatem patrum, scilicet Paulum apostolum, et Ambrosium archiepiscopum, et Hieronimum presbyterum, consecratio ad immolandum facta est episcopi in ordinatione presbyteri, sed quod additur ex canonica auctoritate, ut plures assint episcopi, dicendum est cur addatur.[227]

It is by their ordination to the presbyterate that bishops have received the power to offer the eucharistic sacrifice. This assertion is perhaps related to the formulae for anointing of the hands of presbyters and bishops in the Frankish ordination rites. It is the presbyteral formula, rather than the episcopal, that asks for liturgical and priestly graces associated with the eucharistic offering.

---

[225] Hanssens, *Liber officialis*, p. 215.

[226] Hanssens, *Liber officialis*, pp. 225–226.

[227] Hanssens, *Liber officialis*, p. 233.

The *Liber officialis* is one of the best known liturgical expositions of "presbyterianism" prior to the eleventh century.[228] In the section on presbyters Amalarius argues for the original equation of bishops and presbyters. Here he insinuates that to be a bishop (which entails celebrating the eucharist) one must be first a presbyter.

iii.

A third ninth-century example comes from the works of Rabanus Maurus (776 or 784–856), one of the greatest theologians of the Carolingian renaissance. Rabanus, like Amalarius a pupil of Alcuin, was abbot of Fulda and archbishop of Mainz. The ecclesiastical orders are dealt with in Book I, caps. 1–13 of Rabanus's *De clericorum institutione.*[229] Using sources such as the DEO and the *Etymologiae* of Isidore, Bede, and the SEA, Rabanus describes the origins and the duties of the different orders; he describes the ordination rites for the minor orders.

Rabanus introduces the description of the orders with the following ascending sequence: doorkeeper, psalmist or (*sive*) lector, exorcist, acolyte, subdeacon, deacon, presbyter, and bishop. His descriptions of the orders follow the same sequence, but in a descending order. This particular sequence is similar to Alcuin's with the exception of the inclusion of the bishop, and the alternative between psalmist and lector, which are treated under one heading in chapter XI: *De lectoribus.* Otherwise, the sequence of grades is that of the Romano-Gallican *cursus.* In the chapter on bishops, Rabanus describes a three-fold episcopate: patriarchs, metropolitans, and bishops. He also deals with the *chorepiscopus*, of which he seems to approve. It is interesting to note how Rabanus reorders Isidore's material from the *Etymologiae* to conform to the Gallican sequence of grades.

In Book I, cap. 13, entitled *Quos oportet ad sacrum ordinem accedere, et quo ordine*, Rabanus discusses the *cursus honorum* itself and the interstices based on the decretal of Zosimus to Hesychius:

> Canones et decreta Zozymi papae decernunt ut clericus qui ad sacrum ordinem accedit, inter lectores sive exorcistas quinque annos exsolvat, exinde acolythus vel subdiaconus quattor annis fiat. Ad benedictionem quoque diaconatus non minoris aetatis quam viginti quinque annorum accedat, in quo ordine quinque annis

---

228 Reynolds, "Patristic 'Presbyterianism' in the Early Medieval Theology of Sacred Orders," *Mediaeval Studies*, vol. 45 (1983), p. 324.

229 *PL* 107.297–306; A. Knoepfler, ed., *Rabani Mauri De clericorum institutioni libri tres* (Munich: 1899), pp. 98–102.

expletis, si inculpabiliter ministraverit, ad presbyteratus honorem promoveri poterit, non tamen ante triginta annos aetatis, licet valde dignus sit, quia et Dominus noster non ante tricesimum annum praedicare exorsus est. De quo gradu si eum auctior ad bonos mores vita perduxerit, summum pontificatum accipere poterit, hac tamen lege servata, ut neque bigamus, poenitens, nec neophytus ad hos gradus possit admitti.[230]

Here he has edited and paraphrased Zosimus' decretal. For instance, Zosimus says nothing about ages of clerics, only the interstices. Moreover, he says nothing about the length of time spent in the presbyterate. Like Canon XI of the *Collectio hibernensis*, Rabanus has added what Zosimus has not included. The sentence dealing with the age of the presbyter ultimately looks to Canon XI of the Council of Neocaesarea. It is noteworthy that in the sentence dealing with the deacon, Rabanus says that boys (*minoris aetatis*) are not to be ordained deacons and he reiterates twenty-five as the minimum age for ordination to the diaconate. Is he trying to correct a situation where much younger men were being admitted to the diaconate?

iv.

Two final ninth-century examples are found in two letters of Hincmar (*ca.* 806–882), archbishop of Rheims, regarding the promotion of bishops. In one, *Epistle* 39, Hincmar writes to the church in Beauvais concerning the election of a new bishop after the death of bishop Hodon:

Quia defuncto dilecto, vel venerabili, confratre ac sacerdote nostro, patare videlicet ac pastore vestro Odone, electione canonica a domino nostro rege vobis solita benignitate concessa, necesse erit ut de eligendo atque constituendo vobis pastore, vel doctore atque rectore, secundum ecclesiasticas regulas, votis nostris in unum Domino mediante convenientibus....[231]

.... De cujus videlicet a nobis consecrandi episcopi electione, pro imposito nobis ministerio, et cura totius provinciae secundum mysticae Nicaenae synodi canones delegata, fraternitati vestrae auctoritatem divinitus promulgatum intimare satagimus....Deinde, ut de ecclesia vestra, sive sit in civitate, sive in monasteriis, his disciplinis institutum, et ita apostolicae formae convenientem, de diaconibus vel presbyteris eligatis vobis, auctoreet fautore Domino, consecrandum episcopum, sicut cum de eligendo atque constituendo episcopo ageret, Tito et Timotheo Paulus depingit apostolus. Et si, quod absit, de civitatis ac parrociae vestrae clericis, ordinandus episcopis nullus dignus, vel idoneus summo sacerdotio, quod evenire non credimus, poterit inveniri: tunc alterum de altera dioceseos nostrae ecclesia, unde nobis secundum Africanum concilium, sine cujusquam contradictione, ordinandi

---

[230] *PL* 107.306.

[231] *PL* 126.258.

quemquam canonice electum et petitum est attributa licentia, eligere, procurate; qui merito vitae et scientiae doctrina vobis praeeese valeat, et prodesse: quique sacris canonibus praecipue capitulo Carthaginensis concilii: Qualis debeat ordinari epis-copus, non debeat obviare, et a decretis Patrum, Siricii videlicet, Innocentii, Co-elestini, Leonis, Gelasii, atque Gregorii, quantum patitur humana fragilitas, et poteritis conspicere, non valeat quoquomodo discrepare....[232]

.... Ante omnia autem cavete in electione pontificis malum simoniacae haereseos, ne pro data aliquo, vel promissione illicita, neque pro gratia cujuscunque vel famil-iaritate aut propinquitate alicujus, quempiam attentetis eligere. Non eum, cui nulla natalium, nulla morum dignitas suffragetur: vel qui originali, aut alicui conditioni obligatus detineatur. Neminem ex laicis neophytum, id est noviter attonsum, et sine disciplina, vel non per tempora constituta ad eclesiasticos gradus provectum. Quod ideo specialiter designamus quia cum canones dicant, "Nullus ex laicis ordinetur", demonstrant quod non de omnibus sit laicis constitutum....[233]

In the election, conceded to the clergy and people by the king, the church in Beauvais is directed by Hincmar to elect its bishop "according to the ecclesiastical rules". Further, they are to choose a deacon or a pres-byter from either the clergy or the monks to become their new bishop, just as the apostle Paul directed Titus and Timothy. If they cannot find worthy and suitable candidates in Beauvais, they may look to other dioceses, ac-cording to the "African council." Hincmar instructs them to choose a can-didate according to the Council of Carthage, and according to the decretals of Siricius, Innocent, Celestine, Gelasius, and Gregory. They are warned to beware of the evil heresy of simony in the election of a bishop. No one recently tonsured is to be elected, nor any one who has "not advanced through the established times to the ecclesiastical grades". Again, no one from the laity is to be ordained.

Hincmar calls the church of Beauvais to observe the ecclesiastical dis-cipline of the *cursus honorum* and the interstices in the selection of the next bishop. Either deacons or presbyters are eligible. The chapter from the Carthaginian council no doubt refers to Canon I of the *Statuta ecclesiae antiqua* which outlines the qualities sought in a bishop. Hincmar refers to the decretals of the popes already surveyed; missing from the list is Zosi-mus.

Lastly, in his attack against simony, Hincmar prohibits laity from being elected for the episcopate, or those who have not *per tempora constituta*

---

[232] *PL* 126.259.

[233] *PL* 126.259–260; *Formulae antiquae promotionem episcopalium* IV, MANSI XVII. appendix cols. 411–412.

ad ecclesiasticos gradus provectum. In this restatement of the classic *cursus honorum* and interstices, Hincmar seeks to ensure that no lay person will be elected as bishop of Beauvais as a gift, or because of friendship, nepotism, or nobility.

Yet in an earlier letter, *Epistle* 29 to Adventius of Metz, again concerning episcopal elections, Hincmar advocates sequential movement from the diaconate to the presbyterate:

> Sicut jussistis, mitto vobis consecrationem episcopi, et exemplar decreti, quod in ampla pergamena debet scribi, ut confirmationes cleri et legatorum singulorum monasteriorum, et primorum presbyterorum parochiae ac plebis, ibi valeant scribi: et si isdem electus in diaconii gradu adhuc est, canonico tempore debet presbyter ordinari....[234]

While Hincmar admits that bishops may be chosen from among the deacons, he states unequivocally that a bishop-elect who is a deacon must first be ordained to the presbyterate, according to the canonical interval— *canonico tempore debet presbyter ordinari.*

The Frankish church seems to have insisted on sequential ordination from the diaconate to the presbyterate, or rather, from the presbyterate to the episcopate, much earlier than the Roman church. Commenting on the letter to Adventius, Andrieu writes:

> A Rome, il faudra attendre le XIe s. pour trouver des exemples concrets de diacres élus à l'épiscopat qui, avant le sacre, aient jugé nécessaire de se faire conférer la prêtrise. Aux VIIIe et IXe s., on pouvait encore passer directement du diaconat à l'épiscopat.[235]

While the ninth-century Frankish church elected both deacon and presbyters to the episcopate, according to Hincmar, exclusively presbyters were ordained to the episcopate.

c. The Tenth Century

i.

In comparison with the ninth century, the tenth century is not noted for an abundance of original theological tracts and commentaries on holy orders. The first tenth-century tract on orders to be surveyed is from the *Liber de*

---

[234] *PL* 126.186.

[235] M. Andrieu, "Le Sacre Épiscopal d'après Hincmar de Reims," *Revue d'histoire ecclésiastique*, vol. 48(1953), p. 27.

divinis officiis of Pseudo-Alcuin,[236] considered the most important tenth-century text on orders, although it was not especially popular in the medieval period.[237] Cap. 34, entitled *De dignitate ecclesiasticis ordinis*, deals with the biblical origins of the grades. It treats the orders in the standard Romano-Gallican sequence: doorkeeper, lector, exorcist, acolyte, subdeacon, deacon, presbyter, and bishop.

A slightly different ascending sequence is found in cap. 36, *De gradibus ecclesiasticis*, which deals with the duties of clerics. While Pseudo-Alcuin's *De gradibus ecclesiasticis* is based in part on the *Etymologiae* of Isidore and on the tracts of Amalarius and Rabanus Maurus, it reflects some innovation on the part of the compiler.[238] For example, the particular sequence here is rare, since it places the acolyte between the lector and the exorcist. There is no intimation of movement between the grades in cap. 36—it is assumed. *De gradibus ecclesiasticis* contains a noteworthy sentence in the section dealing with the exorcist:

> ....Istud ministerium, ut canones dicunt, nemo debet usurpare, nisi qui idem officium habent, aut diaconus, aut subdiaconos, aut exorcista.[239]

"No one is to usurp this ministry, unless they already have it, that is, either the deacon, subdeacon, or the exorcist himself." The implication here is that in process of ascending through the grades, one retains the ministries given in the lower orders.

ii.

A second tenth-century exemplar is a short Anglo-Saxon tract on holy orders attributed to Aelfric the Grammarian (*ca.* 955–1020), the *De septem*

---

[236] *PL* 101.1231–1236.

[237] Roger Reynolds, "Marginalia on a Tenth-century Tract on the Ecclesiastical Officers," *Law, Church, and Society: Essays in Honor of Stephen Kuttner*, eds. K. Pennington and R. Somerville (University of Pennsylvania Press: 1977), p. 116.

[238] Reynolds, "Marginalia", pp. 116–117. Reynolds notes that the anomalies between the two sequences of grades in the *Liber de divinis officiis* was noted by medieval copyists who would rearrange the sequence of grades in XXXVI to correspond to the Romano-gallican sequence of XXXIV. E.g. the eleventh century *Exposition Rabbani de celebratione misse et de ordinibus* (Vatican, MS Reg. lat. 234); the twelfth century Brescia Pontifical (Bologna, Biblioteca Universitaria, MS lat. 794).

[239] *PL* 101.1234.

gradibus aecclesiasticis, contained in the *Canones Aelfrici ad Wulfinum episcopum.*[240]

In canons X–XVII, Aelfric deals with the clerical grades in the following ascending sequence: doorkeeper, lector, exorcist, acolyte, subdeacon, deacon, and presbyter.[241] The bishop is dealt with, in a "presbyterian" way,[242] under the canon on presbyters. Except for the omission of the psalmist, this particular sequence is evidence of the place of the Romano-Gallican *cursus* in the Anglo-Saxon church of the tenth century. This is noteworthy in itself, for the *Canones Aelfrici* predates the arrival of the PRG at the Conquest in the English Church. Canon VI dealing with the deacon includes a verse from the *De distantia graduum* of the *Hibernensis.*[243] Thus, although Aelfric is plainly aware of the Irish sequence, he uses the Romano-Gallican.

7. Biographical Material

In addition to the conciliar and papal statements, canonistic collections, ordination rites, and the literature on holy orders, biographical information from the eighth, ninth, and tenth centuries is an indispensable source of information on the development of the *cursus honorum*. The details of the careers of bishops, specifically the sequence of the orders they received (or did not receive), indicate a more flexible exercise of the *cursus* than implied in the canonical and liturgical texts. Biographical information will be surveyed from the Roman church and, to a lesser extent, the Frankish church.

a. The Roman Church

Again, thanks to the work of M. Andrieu, the clerical careers of the bishops of Rome in the early medieval period are made easily accessible.[244]

---

[240] Bernhard Fehr, ed., *Die Hirtenbriefe Aelfrics in altenglisher und lateinischer Fassung*, Bibliothek der angelsächsischen Prosa, vol. 9 (Hamburg: 1914; reproduced with a supplement by Peter Clemoes, Darmstadt: 1966), pp. 256–258; MANSI XVIII.699–670.

[241] Fehr, *Die Hirtenbriefe Aelfrics*, p. 256.

[242] Reynolds, "Patristic 'Presbyterianism'," pp. 328–329.

[243] Reynolds, "*De officiis VII graduum*," p. 133.

[244] Andrieu, "La carrière ecclésiastique," pp. 90–119; *cf.* Andrieu, "Les ordres mineurs," pp. 232–274.

i.

As noted in the previous chapter, during the Byzantine period (the sixth to the mid- ighth centuries) the bishops of Rome were regularly chosen from among the seven deacons of the Roman church, primarily the archdeacon. According to the *Liber pontificalis*, throughout the eighth century deacons continued to be elected as bishops of Rome. The following eighth-century popes were ordained from the diaconate: Gregory II (715–731),[245] Zacharias (741–752),[246] Stephen II (752–757),[247] Paul I (757–767),[248] and Hadrian I (772–795).[249] By all accounts the antipope Constantine was also in deacon's orders when consecrated bishop in 767.[250]

The eighth century also included presbyters who were elected bishops in Rome. For example, the LP records that Gregory III (731–41),[251] Stephen III (768–772)[252] and Leo III (795–816)[253] were all presbyters when elected bishops of Rome.

In the ninth century there was a tendency to elect bishops of Rome from among the presbyters. For example, Paschal I (817–824),[254] Eugene II (824–827),[255] Gregory IV (827–844),[256] Sergius II (844–849),[257] Leo IV (847–855),[258] Benedict III (855–858), [259] Hadrian II (867–872),[260]

---

[245] LP I, p. 396.

[246] LP I, p. 423, n. 13.

[247] LP I, p. 440. This Stephen is not to be confused with the Stephen who succeeded Zacharias in 752, but only lived four days, LP I, p. 440.

[248] LP I, p. 463.

[249] LP I, p. 486.

[250] LP I, pp. 468–469.

[251] LP I, p. 415.

[252] LP I, p. 468.

[253] LP II, p. 1.

[254] LP II, p. 52.

[255] LP II, p. 69.

[256] LP II, p. 73.

[257] LP II, p. 86.

[258] LP II, p. 106.

[259] LP II, p. 140

[260] LP II, p. 173.

Stephen V (885–891),[261] and Romanus (897)[262] were presbyters or arch-presbyters. The *Liber pontificalis* also reflects the fact that deacons contin-ued to be elected bishops of Rome in the ninth century, albeit with less frequency. In particular, Stephen IV (816–817),[263] Valentine (827),[264] and Nicholas I (858–867)[265] were all deacons or archdeacons. As noted above, the Frankish church at this time, as reflected by Hincmar, continued to elect deacons as bishops, but required presbyteral ordination prior to epis-copal ordination.

The tenth century saw a similar tendency to elect bishops of Rome from among the presbyters, as reflected in the catalogue of popes by archbishop Sigeric of Canterbury, included by Duchesne in the introduction to his edi-tion of the *Liber pontificalis*.[266] For example, Christopher (903–904),[267] Leo VI (928),[268] Stephen VIII (928–931),[269] John XI (931–935),[270] Leo VII (936–939),[271] and John XV (985–996)[272] were presbyters. As ob-served above, the presbyterate was the last order received by Leo VIII in the rapid series of ordinations prior to episcopal ordination in 963.

Nevertheless, in the tenth century deacons continued to be chosen bishops of Rome, albeit rarely. In particular, Benedict V (964–966),[273] Benedict VI (973–974),[274] and the antipope Boniface VIII (974, 984–

---

[261] LP II, p. 191.

[262] LP II, p. 230.

[263] LP II, p. 49.

[264] LP II, p. 71.

[265] LP II, p. 212.

[266] LP II, p. xv.

[267] LP II, p. xiv.

[268] LP II, p. xv.

[269] LP II, p. xv.

[270] LP II, p. xv.

[271] LP II, p. xv.

[272] LP II, p. xv.

[273] LP II, p. xv.

[274] LP II, p. 255. Identified by Andrieu as Benedict IV, "La carrière ecclésiastique des papes," p. p. 109, Benedict VI is sometimes identified as a cardinal presbyter before election as bishop of Rome, e.g., J. D. N. Kelly, *The Oxford Dictionary of Popes* (New York: Oxford University Press, 1986), p. 130. The LP, however, identifies him as a dea-con, as does Sigeric of Canterbury: "Item Benedictus sancti Theodori sedit annos I et dimidium, dies XII." LP II, p. xv.

985)[275] were deacons. Benedict VI and Boniface VIII are the last deacons noted by Andrieu who were elected directly to the episcopate. Andrieu adds: "Mais nous ignorons s'ils demeurent diacres jusqu'à leur sacré."[276]

A new phenomena emerged in the late ninth and early tenth centuries: the translation of bishops from other dioceses to the see of Rome. The translation of clergy, including bishops, was condemned by Canon XV of the Council of Nicaea.[277] The first bishop to be translated to Rome, without incident, was Marinus (882–884), bishop of Caere (Cereveteri).[278] The most notable instance of such a translation is that of Formosus (891–896), who became bishop of Rome after a stormy career as bishop of Porto.[279] His translation was not held against him until nine months after his death. Formosus's successor, Stephen VI (896–897), in the infamous "Synod of the Corpse," condemned Formosus and degraded him from office on the grounds that he had violated Canon XV of Nicaea regarding the translation of bishops. Ironically, Stephen VI had been bishop of Anagni prior to his election to the see of Rome.[280]

In the tenth century John X (914–928),[281] John XIII (965–972),[282] John XIV (983–984),[283] the antipope John XVI (997–998),[284] and Silvester II (999–1003)[285] were all bishops of other dioceses before becoming bishop of Rome.

---

[275] LP II, pp. 255, 257, n. 1.

[276] Andrieu, "La carrière ecclésiastique des papes," p. 109.

[277] Tanner, *Decrees*, vol. 1, p. 13.

[278] LP II, p. 224, n. 1.

[279] LP II, p. 227.

[280] LP II, p. 229.

[281] LP II, p. 240.

[282] LP II, p. 252.

[283] LP II, p. 259.

[284] LP II, p. 261.

[285] LP II, p. 263.

ii.

Some of the entries in the LP provide details about the careers of the eighth- and ninth-century popes, prior to elections from either the diaconate or the presbyterate.[286]

The LP reports that Sergius I (687–701) was an acolyte, then "rose through the ranks", and was a presbyter before election as bishop.[287] Gregory II (715–731) was a subdeacon, deacon, then bishop.[288] Stephen II (752–757) was ordained through the ecclesiastical grades to the diaconate before election to the episcopate.[289] According to the LP, Constantine (767) was rapidly ordained subdeacon, deacon, then bishop;[290] according to the Wolfenbüttel account he was made doorkeeper, lector, acolyte, subdeacon, deacon, and finally bishop.[291] Hadrian I (772–795) was a subdeacon, deacon, then bishop.[292] Leo III (795–816) was a subdeacon, presbyter, then bishop.[293] Stephen IV (816–817) was a subdeacon, deacon, then bishop.[294] Paschal I (817–824) was likewise a subdeacon, presbyter, then bishop.[295] Valentine (827) "rose through the ranks," was a subdeacon, (arch)deacon, then bishop.[296] Gregory IV (827–844) was a subdeacon, presbyter, then bishop.[297] Sergius II (844–847) was an acolyte, subdeacon, (arch)presbyter, then bishop.[298] Leo IV (847–855) was a subdeacon, presbyter, then bishop,[299] as was Benedict III (855–858).[300] Nicholas I (858–

---

[286] *Cf.* the chart of papal careers in Andrieu, "La carrière ecclésiastique," p. 97.

[287] LP I, p. 371

[288] LP I, p. 396.

[289] LP I, p. 440.

[290] LP I, pp. 468–469.

[291] Wolfenbüttel, Herzog-August-Bibliothek, MS Helmst. 454, fol. 73; MGH *Concilia,* vol. 2, pt. 1, p. 78.

[292] LP I, p. 486.

[293] LP II, p. 1.

[294] LP II, p. 49.

[295] LP II, p. 52.

[296] LP II, p. 71.

[297] LP II, p. 73.

[298] LP II, p. 86.

[299] LP II, p. 106.

[300] LP II, p. 140.

867) was a subdeacon, deacon, then bishop.[301] Hadrian II (867–872)[302] and Stephen V (885–891) [303] were both subdeacons, presbyters, and subsequently bishops.

iii.

The two parallel entries for a tenth-century bishop of Rome in the LP, John XIII, are evidence of the growing importance of the Romano-Gallican *cursus* in Rome. John XIII, the successor of Benedict V, was bishop of Narni according to one account, or the bishop of Ravenna according to the other. One account in the LP describes John XIII's ecclesiastical career as follows:

> Mortuo vero domno Leone, omnes Romani.... elegerunt sibi domnum Iohannem, reverentissimum et pium episcopum sanctae Narniensis ecclesiae, bene doctum et honorifice eruditum de divinis et canonicis libris. Nam a cunabulis ad clericatus ordinem in Lateranensi palatio est ductus, et hostiarius, psalmista, lector, exorcista, acolitus, subdiaconus, diaconus, in eadem Romana ecclesia per distinctos ordines est ordinatus, et ita, Deo volente, legitime et canonice est pontifex consecratus.[304]

The parallel account of John's *cursus* omits the grade of psalmist.[305] The purpose of these entries in the LP was to act as a foil to the career of Leo VIII, who received all the grades in forty-eight hours. It is noteworthy that Leo was ordained deacon *and* presbyter, while John received only the diaconate.

John's *cursus honorum* follows more or less the Romano-Gallican sequence of grades; this is the first mention of the office of psalmist in the LP.[306] Yet the Romano-Gallican sequence is not precisely followed in the sequence of grades received by Leo VIII (doorkeeper, lector, acolyte, subdeacon, deacon, presbyter, bishop) nor by John XIII (doorkeeper, [psalmist] lector, exorcist, acolyte, subdeacon, deacon, bishop). The sequence of grades is identical to the sequences described by Alcuin in the *Disputatio*

---

[301] LP II, p. 151.

[302] LP II, p. 173.

[303] LP II, p. 191.

[304] LP II, p. 247.

[305] LP II, p. 247.

[306] Andrieu, "Les ordres mineurs," p. 249.

puerorum[307] and by Rabanus Maurus in *De clericorum institutione*[308] (doorkeeper, psalmist, lector, exorcist, acolyte, subdeacon, deacon, [presbyter] bishop). Yet John received the grades from doorkeeper to deacon while he was in Rome.

Presumably John received the various orders in Rome during the pontificate of John XII, under whom he served as librarian. Since there is no evidence of a Romano-Gallican rite (which would have contained the doorkeeper, psalmist, lector, and exorcist) in Rome at this time, the question is asked again: according to what rite was John XIII admitted to the various clerical grades?

As noted above, it is possible that the ordination rites of the PRG, brought to Italy by Otto, were used in the ordinations of Leo VIII. It is more probable, as suggested by Reynolds, that John XIII, like Leo VIII, was not ordained according to the PRG, but according to the rites of a Gelasian Sacramentary of the Eighth-Century contained in the late eighth-early ninth-century *Collectio Teatina*,[309] or the related tenth-century Landolf Pontifical. This is only a probability. As Reynolds points out, there have been no examples found in Rome of the Chieti texts.[310]

iv.

A number of observations arise from the details about the clerical careers of the bishops of Rome recorded in the LP and the catalogue of Sigeric. First, only two minor orders are mentioned: the acolyte and subdeacon, though the office of acolyte is mentioned only twice. There is only one apparent instance, that of Sergius II, where a pope has received sequentially the offices of acolyte and subdeacon. Despite the canonical legislation of the fourth and fifth centuries, and even the fourth Council of Carthage, the minor orders would, on the evidence of the LP, appear dispensable.

Second, the office of subdeacon appears to lead to both the two major orders of deacon and presbyter. In "La carrière ecclésiastique des papes", Andrieu notes that in the primitive church, subdeacons were ordained directly to the presbyterate without any intervening ordination, but that soon became insufficient. He asserts that subdeacons destined to the

---

[307] *PL* 101.1131–1134.

[308] *PL* 107.296–306.

[309] Reynolds, "The Ritual of Clerical Ordination," pp. 441–442.

[310] Reynolds, "The Ritual of Clerical Ordination," p. 444.

presbyterate would have been ordained deacons and presbyters at the same liturgy, and hence would never have exercised their diaconal ministry. This, he explains, is why the *Liber pontificalis* says nothing about the diaconate in the cases of popes elevated to the presbyterate from the subdiaconate.[311] Duchesne, as noted, is of the same opinion. With respect to the evidence from the *Liber pontificalis* he states:

> The custom of conferring simultaneously the diaconate and the priesthood explains why the pontifical biographers of the ninth century, in describing the *cursus honorum* of the Popes chosen from among the cardinal priests, never make mention of the diaconate, but pass always from the subdiaconate to the priesthood.[312]

As noted above, however, later in the introduction to OR XXXIV in *Les Ordines Romani du haut moyen age*, Andrieu adopted a quite different position in which he claims to know of no instance where the offices were conferred on the same day, despite the inferences to the contrary in both OR XXXIV and OR XXXV.[313] The lists of ordinations performed by popes from the eighth to the tenth century would support this view. Furthermore, sequential ordination to the diaconate and to the presbyterate on the same day would have been in violation of the interstices canons.

In addition, one recalls that the Council of Rome in 769, after it declared Constantine's ordinations invalid, directed those who were ordained deacon or presbyter by him "to return to the subdiaconal grade":

> ....At vero presbyteri illi vel diaconi, quos in hac sancta Romana ecclesia ordinavit, in pristono subdiaconatus ordine vel alio, quo fungebantur, officio revertantur....[314]

This direction intimates that subdeacons were ordained by Constantine to either the diaconate or to the presbyterate, but not both. It is likely, then, that the diaconate was a dispensable grade as well in the clerical *cursus* of the Roman church in the eighth and ninth centuries.

Third, deacons and presbyters were both eligible for consecration to the episcopate in the eighth, ninth, and tenth centuries; on this point there is little doubt.[315] Canon law (the Dionysian version of Canon XIII of the

---

[311] Andrieu, "La carrière ecclésiastique," p. 99.

[312] Duchesne, *Christian Worship*, p. 355–365, n. 2.

[313] Andrieu, *Les Ordines Romani*, vol. 3, p. 561.

[314] MGH *Concilia*, vol. 2, pt. 1, p. 86.

[315] "Prêtres et diacres étaient également éligibles au souverain pontificat et le rituel de l'ordination papale était identique pour les uns et pours les autres. Un diacre ordonné pape passait donc directement du diaconat àl'épiscopat, sans avoir jamais reçu la prêtrise. Sur ce point, il ne saurait y avoir le moindre doute." Andrieu, "La Carrière Ecclésiastique des Papes," p. 99.

Council of Sardica transmitted through the various canonistic collections) and the liturgies corroborate the fact that deacons as well as presbyters could be, and were, ordained bishops. Thus, the presbyterate was also a dispensable grade in the *cursus* towards the episcopate.

b. The Frankish Church

The election of deacons to the episcopate was not isolated to the Roman church in the early medieval period. It has been noted, from the letters of Hincmar, that both deacons and presbyters were eligible for election to the episcopate in the Frankish church. It would appear, however, that diaconal bishops-elect were required to be ordained to the presbyterate. There are examples of deacons being elected as bishops well into the late ninth century. For instance, two letters of Pope John VIII (872–882) written in 879 to Carloman, commending a deacon, Gospertus (Conspertus), as bishop of Vercelli.[316] There is also a letter from John VIII to Theodosius, bishop-elect of "Nonensis", also of 879. The letter is addressed to "the venerable deacon Theodosius": *Teodosio [sic.] venerabili diacono, et electo sanctae ecclesia Nonensis*.[317]

There are at least two well-known instances of deacons exercising great influence, yet remaining in deacon's orders for the rest of their lives. Alcuin (*ca.* 735–804), Abbot of St. Martin's in Tours and advisor to Charlemagne was one of the greatest scholars of the Carolingian renaissance, yet remained a deacon. A native of York, it is difficult to know by which rite he was ordained deacon. If it was a rite with roots in the Roman church, the bishop would have prayed that he might "persevere strong and stable in Christ, and be found worthy to advance from the inferior grade to take up higher things." Alcuin's life demonstrates that he was certainly worthy, yet he did not advance to "higher things." Albeit only one example, Alcuin's career demonstrates that the diaconate had not unequivocally become a mere "stepping-stone" to the presbyterate. Although a deacon, Alcuin was Abbot of St. Martin's Abbey in Tours. This situation must have been exceptional. By comparison, it has been noted that the Council of Soissons (853) dealt with the appointment of a deacon, Halduinus, as Abbot of the monastery of Altivillaris. Yet in this instance, Halduinus was

---

[316] *Epistle* 171, MANSI XVII.116; *PL* 126.83; Jaffé, # 3243. *Epistle* 187, MANSI XVII.127; *PL* 126.840; Jaffé, # 3257.

[317] *Epistle* 183, MANSI XVII.124; *PL* 126.838; Jaffé, # 3255.

ordained a presbyter (albeit without proper examination) in order to become abbot of the monastery.

The second example is that of Florus of Lyons (*ca.* 790–*ca.* 860). Canonist, liturgical scholar, and theologian, Florus was a canon of the cathedral of Lyons. While he was one of the great theological leaders of his day, he remained a deacon.[318]

8. Summary

The early medieval period is notable in the history of the *cursus honorum*. While the eighth and ninth centuries reveal much diversity and flexibility, by the tenth century, there is evidence of a growing consensus and uniformity, particularly in the number and sequence of the grades received in the *cursus honorum*. While the period reflects continued diversity in the practice of sequential ordination, there is growing consistency.

a. The Sequence of the *Cursus Honorum*

The eighth and ninth centuries reflect an assortment of sequences of ecclesiastical grades, in particular, the minor orders. These variations are generally associated with different liturgical traditions: Frankish, Hispanic-Irish, and Roman. Yet even within these traditions one observes some diversity. For instance, within the Frankish church one notes the slightly different sequences of grades in the *Missale francorum* (doorkeeper, acolyte, lector, exorcist, subdeacon, deacon, presbyter, bishop), the Gelasian sacramentaries (psalmist, doorkeeper, lector, exorcist, acolyte, subdeacon, deacon, presbyter, bishop), and Pseudo-Bede (doorkeeper, lector, exorcist, acolyte, subdeacon, deacon, presbyter, bishop). The *Missale francorum* places the acolyte beneath the lector instead of beneath the subdeacon. The Gelasian is the only one to include the psalmist.

The Hispanic-Irish sequence of grades has its own peculiarities. The sequence of the Ordinal of Christ contained in the *Collectio canonum hibernensis* (doorkeeper, exorcist, lector, subdeacon, deacon, "priest") is

---

[318] The medieval necrologies would also be an area of fruitful study, as they contain much information on the careers of medieval clerics. They reveal many deacons, subdeacons, and those in the other minor orders who remained in their respective orders until death.

different from that of the *De distantia graduum* (doorkeeper, lector, exorcist, subdeacon, deacon, presbyter, bishop) which is also found in the *Hibernensis*. The former reflects the more usual Hispanic-Irish arrangement which places the lector above the exorcist, while the latter reflects the typically Gallican sequence where the lector is beneath the exorcist.

The place of the exorcist and the lector in the Hispanic sequence is reflected in the "Isidorian" *Epistula ad Leudefredum* (doorkeeper, acolyte, exorcist, psalmist, lector, subdeacon, deacon, presbyter, bishop), yet the acolyte and psalmist are included in this list, which are distinctive of the Gallican *cursus*. The *De distantia graduum* of the *Hibernensis* and the "Isidorian" *De ordinibus VII graduum* (doorkeeper, lector, exorcist, subdeacon, deacon, presbyter, bishop) reflect the Hispanic sequence, since they omit the acolyte, but place the lector and exorcist in the Gallican position.

The eighth-century Roman OR XXXIV contains rites for the acolyte, subdeacon, deacon, presbyter, and bishop. There are no rites for the minor orders below the acolyte, including the lectorate which was always maintained in Rome. Scholars assume that this omission reflects the reality that the other minor ministries had fallen into desuetude in Rome; the biographies in the *Liber pontificalis* confirm this view.

One of the most significant events in the history of the *cursus* in the ninth century was the fourth Council of Constantinople (869–870) which put the clerical *cursus* and the interstices on the agenda of an ecumenical council (at least according to Western reckoning). The nature of Photius's election and consecration gave rise to a debate on the place of the *cursus* and the interstices. The debate at the council reveals the extent to which the *cursus honorum* had become entrenched in Western understandings of holy orders. Biblical texts such as the appointment of Matthias, and historical events such as the election of Ambrose, were understood in light of the contemporary ecclesiastical *cursus*. Canon V of the council prescribed both the *cursus* and an interval of ten years between the lectorate and the episcopate. The sequence deacon, presbyter, and bishop is specified in the canon. Though the Western church continued to regard this as an ecumenical council and its enactments valid (despite the fact that the council and its decisions were abrogated ten years later), the papacy does not appear to have followed Canon V in the ninth and (perhaps) tenth centuries, since deacons, including Nicholas I and Hadrian II, continued to be elected and consecrated bishops in Rome.

The sequence of grades prescribed by Canon V of the fourth Council of Constantinople is the standard *cursus* of the Eastern church: lector, subdeacon, deacon, presbyter, bishop. Yet in a letter to the emperors Basil, Leo, and Alexander, Pope John VIII describes the clerical *cursus* as lector, acolyte, deacon, presbyter, and bishop. The Roman church does not appear to have observed either sequence.

The ninth-century Western texts surveyed reflect a somewhat more stable picture in relation to the arrangement of the minor orders in comparison with the preceding century. The inclusion of the Gallican sequence of grades in the Supplement to the *Hadrianum* (doorkeeper, lector, exorcist, acolyte, subdeacon, deacon, presbyter, and bishop) would have far reaching consequences for the stability of the clerical *cursus*. Some ninth-century texts, such as the *De clericorum institutionem* of Rabanus Maurus, reorder texts such as the *Etymologiae* of Isidore, to correspond with the dominant sequence of the Gallican *cursus honorum*. Both Alcuin and Rabanus Maurus rehearse the same sequence (doorkeeper, psalmist, lector, exorcist, subdeacon, deacon, presbyter, bishop) which is not the traditional Gallican *cursus* since the doorkeeper and psalmist are inverted. The sequence of Amalarius is the same, except that he omits the psalmist altogether.

Apparently there was some difficulty in knowing where to place the psalmist. Some ninth-century writers, such as Rabanus Maurus, combine it with the lectorate, while others, such as Amalarius and Benedict of Aniane in the supplement to the *Hadrianum*, omitted it.

It was during the tenth century that the sequence of the minor orders seems to have received its final shape in the Western church. While OR XXXV contains rites for only the lector, acolyte, subdeacon, deacon, presbyter, and bishop, the PRG contains the standard Romano-Gallican sequence: psalmist, doorkeeper, lector, exorcist, acolyte, subdeacon, deacon, presbyter, bishop. This sequence, with roots in the Roman church of the third century as witnessed by Cornelius, as well as the fifth-century Gallican church of the *Statuta ecclesiae antiqua*, came to dominate and replace all others with the emergence and extension of the PRG across the Western church, and eventually beyond the Frankish empire into the Anglo-Saxon and Hispanic churches.

The hierarchical ordering of the major orders of bishop, presbyter, and deacon had been stable since at least the second century. The actual series or sequences of major orders clerics might receive, however, remained flexible in the eighth, ninth, and tenth centuries. For example, deacons throughout this period were ordained bishops in Rome, without prior ordination to the presbyterate. This practice appears to have ended in the Frankish church by the time of Hincmar's *Epistle* 29, though deacons continued to be elected bishops.

It is not clear whether there was the same degree of flexibility between the diaconate and the presbyterate. There are many indications, especially in the *Liber pontificalis,* that one could be ordained a presbyter directly from the subdiaconate, though as noted, there are differing opinions on this question. The liturgical rites, OR XXXIV and especially OR XXXV and the PRG, strongly imply that those to be ordained as presbyter were deacons. This position finds support in the fact that the Council of Soissons (853) identified ordination to the diaconate as a prerequisite for ordination to the presbyterate:

> Sed qui saltu sine gradu diaconii ad sacerdotium prosilieret, in degradationem debitam resilire.[319]

b. The *Cursus* in Canon Law and Theology

While the exact sequence of the *cursus honorum* was still transitional in the early medieval period, the overall significance of sequential ordination was increased, both canonically and theologically.

The Council of Rome, 769, legislated the place of the *cursus* in respect to episcopal elections, turning what had been a long-standing Roman tradition into law. The patristic *cursus* and interstices texts appear in all but one (the *Libri duo de synodalibus causis et disciplinis ecclesiasticis* of Regino of Prüm) of the canonistic collections surveyed in this chapter. The decretals of popes and conciliar decisions were well known in the period, and were appealed to frequently. Failure to observe the interstices, for example, in the instance of a rapid series of ordinations by a papal aspirant, would lead to deposition.

The *cursus honorum* in the eighth, ninth, and tenth centuries acquired a theological significance unknown in the patristic church. In the primitive church, as well as during the patristic period, the ordination of lay people directly to the presbyterate and to the episcopate, without ever having received any of the lower ministries, was not an unusual occurrence.

---

[319] MGH *Concilia*, vol. 2, pt. 3, p. 275.

Patristic instances of ordination *per saltum* were just that: a leap over the intervening offices. In the early medieval period, the ordination of neophytes, i.e., members of the laity, to the episcopate invariably entailed the reception of the grades of the clerical *cursus* in rapid succession. For example, Constantine (767) and Leo VIII (963) in the Roman church, and Photius in the East (857) have been observed in this respect. Although a *pro forma* reception of the lower orders in these instances entailed no possibility of probation and preparation, they were conferred nonetheless.

Though admittedly the practice of "rushing someone through the grades" in a matter of days had its roots in the late patristic period, generally it would have seemed quite odd from the fourth to the sixth centuries;[320] a lay person would more likely have been ordained directly to the presbyterate or the episcopate. The regular insistence on the reception of the lower grades for lay people elected to the episcopate in the medieval period indicates a new perception of the *cursus honorum*. Once the canonical prescriptions of the interstices were ignored and the pastoral rationale for sequential ordination (i.e., preparation and probation) was overlooked, another rationale for sequential ordination had to be sought.

Patristic bishops of Rome might decry the ordination of the laity to the episcopate; Siricius called it heretical;[321] Leo the Great referred to it as "contrary to the precepts of divine law;"[322] Gregory the Great called it "that detestable evil."[323] There is no evidence, however, from the patristic period that such bishops were not regarded as real bishops, however unsuited for office they might have been. This view had changed by the eighth century: Constantine, Photius, and Leo VIII were all declared invalid bishops by the respective councils which dealt with them, because they were elected from out of the lay state. The series of ordinations they received through the *cursus* were held to be uncanonical and invalid because the interstices had not been observed. Hence, a valid episcopal ordination was one that was preceded by the observation of the *cursus honorum* with the observation of the corresponding interstices between the grades. Once the vocabulary around the *cursus honorum* has moved from

---

[320] *Pace* the scholars who believe that Ambrose was so ordained.

[321] *Epistle* 6.III.5, *PL* 13.1166.

[322] *Epistle* 12.2, *PL* 54.647.

[323] *Reg.* 9.215, MGH *Epp.* vol. 2, p. 202.

legality to validity, the discussion has shifted from canon law to sacramental theology.

The letter of Hincmar of Rheims to Adventius of Metz indicates that by the late-ninth century presbyteral ordination had become a prerequisite for episcopal consecration, at least within the Frankish church. In one sense this trend simply conforms to the patristic texts dealing with the *cursus honorum*. On the other hand, the absolute requirement of presbyteral ordination prior to episcopal consecration was not the universal practice of the Western church until the late eleventh century.

The ninth-century Frankish church also reflects a rationale for sequential ordination from the presbyterate to the episcopate. For example, Amalarius indicates the opinion in the *Liber officialis* that the bishop receives the power to offer the eucharistic sacrifice in ordination to the presbyterate; thus, one must be first a presbyter in order to be a bishop. This view belongs to a "presbyterian" view of the relationship between the presbyterate and the episcopate.

There is growing indication in the early medieval period that the diaconate was indispensable for ordination to the presbyterate. One notes evidence from the liturgical rites, especially OR XXXIV and OR XXXV, as well as the statement from the Council of Soissons that presbyters must have been deacons. Regardless, it seems likely that throughout this period there were many omissions of the diaconate between the subdiaconate and the presbyterate, particularly in the Roman church. The anomalies with respect to the place of the diaconate cause one to question whether or not it was universally dispensable in the clerical *cursus*.

c. Conclusion

From the eighth to the tenth century the *cursus honorum* became more uniform and stable, and increasingly consequential in the church's practice and theology of holy orders; it was no longer simply a matter of the preparation and probation of clergy. Yet one notes much flexibility in this period, particularly regarding the minor orders in the eighth and ninth centuries, and the major orders well into the tenth. The period from the eighth to the tenth century, then, is one of continuing development and transition in the history of the *cursus honorum*; it had by no means achieved its final form.

IV

THE *CURSUS HONORUM*

IN THE ELEVENTH AND TWELFTH CENTURIES

1. Introduction

With the wide distribution of the PRG in the tenth century, the hierarchical sequence of the minor orders was fixed; hence, the sequence of the *cursus honorum* had reached its final shape in the Western church. The exact sequence of grades actually conferred, however, was not ultimately settled until the eleventh century, especially in relationship to the major orders. While the presbyterate was hierarchically superior to the diaconate in the sequence of grades, it was not universally conferred in the sequence of the *cursus*. Throughout the eighth and ninth centuries deacons continued to be elected and ordained as bishops of Rome; most likely the last such bishops to be ordained as deacons were Benedict VI and Boniface VIII in the tenth century. The Frankish church required candidates for episcopal ordination to be presbyters from at least the time of Hincmar in the late ninth century. By the eleventh century the presbyterate had become a requisite part of the *cursus honorum* in Rome, and hence throughout the Western church. In addition, the indispensable place of the subdiaconate within the sequence of the clerical *cursus* was settled in the same century.

The eleventh century was a period of economic and social change in the West; it was also a period of upheaval and reform for the medieval church. Many factors called for reform: clerical standards and morality were low, clerical celibacy, especially among the rural clergy, had fallen into virtual desuetude, and simony and lay investiture were serious problems. Though often associated with the pontificate of Gregory VII in the second half of the eleventh century, reforms were initiated as early as the tenth century in the monastic reforms associated with Cluny. Eleventh-century reforms

were initiated north of the Alps by lay rulers such as the emperors Henry
II and III, and the German popes nominated by the latter (Clement II,
1046–1047; Damasus II, 1048; Leo IX, 1049–1054; Victor II, 1055–
1057). Major papal reforming impetus is associated with the pontificate of
Leo IX (1049–1054) and those he gathered to Rome, principally Cardinal
Humbert, Bruno of Silva Candida, and Hildebrand, who later became Gregory VII. The concerns of the reformers were manifold: papal primacy,
clerical celibacy, simony, relations to temporal power (especially lay investiture), and monastic life. In the midst of these major reforms the *cursus
honorum* received its final shape.

This chapter will examine the development of the *cursus honorum* and
the related issues of the interstices and the ages of clerics in the eleventh
and twelfth centuries. Evidence will be gathered from conciliar legislation
and papal decrees, the eleventh and twelfth-century canonistic collections,
liturgical rites, other writings on holy order, and from biographical information available in these centuries.

2. The *Cursus Honorum* in Conciliar Legislation

The period of the eleventh and twelfth centuries was one of the most prolific in terms of conciliar activity.[1] Issues around the *cursus honorum*, the
interstices, and the ages of clerics were of minor significance in comparison with other issues dealt with by councils and popes. In this section eight
eleventh-century councils which dealt with the *cursus* and related issues
will be examined. None of the twelfth-century councils examined touched
upon the *cursus honorum* or the interstices, though one of the twelfth-century councils legislated on the ages of clerics.

The Synod of Ravenna (1014) is remembered chiefly for its legislation
on the ages of clerics, and the reforms initiated against simony and other
abuses. The synod was held under both Pope Benedict VIII (1012–1024)
and the recently crowned emperor Henry II (1002–1024), an active supporter of the Cluniac reforms. Canon II of the council declared:

---

[1]   E.g. in the MANSI collection there are 349 councils from the eleventh century and 309
councils from the twelfth century. MANSI IX, XX, XXI, XXII.

The *Cursus Honorum* in the 11th and 12th Centuries

> De etatibus [*sic.*] quibus clerici consecrandi sunt. Heinrici regis.
>
> Si quis episcopus ante XXX. annum presbiterum consecraverit, vel diaconum ante XXV. annum, anathema sit, et ordinatus deiciatur usque ad prefinitam etatem, nisi summa compellat necessitas. Quod si inevitabilis causa advenerit, permittamus presbiterum consecrari in legitima aetate diaconorum. Subdiaconus ante XII. annum nullatenus fiat.[2]

The canon confirms the ages of thirty and twenty-five for presbyters and deacons respectively. In exceptional circumstances, however, presbyters may be ordained at the same age as deacons, that is, twenty-five. The age for subdeacons is twelve, making a twelve-year interstice between reception of the subdiaconate and the diaconate. This interstice is the longest noted thus far. Moreover, it implies that the minor orders below the subdiaconate would be received prior to twelve years of age, that is, by boys.[3]

The Council of Toulouse (1056) legislated on the ages of clerics, and on the observation of the interstices. Canon II states:

> Item placuit confirmare, sicut scriptum est, ut episcopus, vel abbas, presbyter, ante triginta annos, diaconos vero ante viginti quinque non ordinetur: nisi aut studio sanctitatis aut sapientiae ornati, providentia episcopi simul et cleri promoveantur. Et eadem ordinatio ne fiat, nisi temporibus secundum canones statutis: aliter quidem irrita fiat ordinatio.[4]

While confirming thirty as the minimum ages for bishops, abbots, and presbyters, and twenty-five as the age for deacons, the canon permits bishops, with the consent of the clergy, to abrogate these age requirements if candidates are "adorned with wisdom" and show "zeal of holiness".

The canon adds that such ordinations must follow the times established by the canons. To neglect the interstices makes an ordination not just illicit, but invalid: *aliter quidem irrita fiat ordinatio*. This canon is evidence that the clerical *cursus* and the observance of the interstices have accrued not just canonical significance, but theological and sacramental significance as well. It is also evidence of the degree of latitude and flexibility allowed by bishops in ordaining candidates, at least to the diaconate and the presbyterate.

---

[2] L. Weiland, ed., *Monumenta Germaniae Historica, Constitutiones et Acta Publica Imperatorum et Regum*, vol. 1 (Hannover: Impensis Bibliopolii Hahniani, 1893), p. 62. The Ravannese origin is now contested.

[3] Of the systematic collections examined in this study, Canon II of the Synod of Ravenna in found in the *Collectio in V libris*.

[4] MANSI XIX.847.

The Council of Compostello, also held in 1056, likewise legislated on the ages of clerics. Canon II from the council states:

Abjungimus ut per omnes dioceses tales eligantur Abbates, qui mysterii S. Trinitatis rationem fideliter faciant, et in divinis Scripturis, et sacris Canonibus sint eruditi. Hi autem Abbates per proprias Ecclesias canonicas faciant scholam, et disciplinam componant, ut tales deferant ad Episcopos clericos ordinandos. Subdiaconos annos XVIII habeat, diaconos 25. presbyter 30. et ipsi qui totum Psalterium, cantica et hymnos, salisparsionem, baptisterium, insufflationem, et commendationem, et horas, et ipsum cantare de festis unius justi, unius confessoris, unius virginis, de virginibus, de defunctis, et omnia responsoria perfecte sciant. Et nullus praesumat Simoniacus esse quaerens sibi ipsam ordinationem....[5]

The objective of the canon is primarily the education of clerics and the prevention of simony. It is interesting to note the ages of clerics specified in the canon: eighteen for subdeacons, twenty-five for deacons, and thirty for presbyters. Though the minimum age of eighteen for subdeacons is older than that prescribed by the Synod of Ravenna (twelve years), it nonetheless implies a lengthy interstice between the subdiaconate and the diaconate: seven years. Moreover, the implication is that all the minor orders below the subdiaconate would have been received before a candidate reached eighteen years of age.

The Council of Rome of 1059 legislated against rapid promotion through the ecclesiastical grades. Canon XIII from the council states:

Ut nullus laicus ad quemlibet gradum ecclesiasticum repente promoveatur: nisi, post mutatum habitum saecularem, diuturna conversatione inter cleros fuerit comprobatus. Vos ergo haec et alia sanctorum patrum statuta fideliter et Christiana reverentia observate, si vultis de sanctae Romanae ecclesiae, et apostolicae sedis, pace et communione atque benedictione gaudere.[6]

The canon forbids members of the laity to be promoted suddenly to any ecclesiastical grade. Promotion to the grades is restricted to those who have "changed the worldly habit", and "who will have been approved after a long manner of living among the clergy".

That such a restatement of the ancient tradition of the church was necessary in the mid-eleventh century is made clear in cap. V of the decretal of Nicholas II (1058-1061) to the council:

De ordinatis infra annos grave nobis periculum imminet, quia prius se de victoria jactant, quam bellare viderint aut sciant; idest prius officia sacrae castitati conscia

[5] MANSI XIX.856.
[6] MANSI XIX.899.

per cupiditatem arripiunt, quam jacula incentiva naturae experiri possunt. Idcirco sacri canones sanxerunt, ut subdiaconis non ordinetur ante annos 14. nec diaconus ante annos 25. nec presbyter ante 30.[7]

Apparently candidates were being ordained below the established ages. If this was an actual problem, there is every reason to suppose that laity were also being ordained to ecclesiastical office without the requisite testing in the ranks of the clergy.

The canon is also noteworthy in the minimum ages it prescribes for clerics. Deacons and presbyters retain the traditional ages of twenty-five and thirty respectively. Nicholas decrees that the minimum age for subdeacons is fourteen years; this age for subdeacons is four years below that prescribed by the Council of Compostello, and two years above that prescribed by the Synod of Ravenna. The interstice between the subdiaconate and the diaconate according to Nicholas would have been eleven years.[8]

The Council of Rouen (1072) dealt with the question of clerics who had been ordained deacons without having first received the minor orders. Canon X of the council states:

Quod depositione digni sunt, qui furtim aut indebite ad sacros ordines provebuntur.

Item clerici, qui non electi, nec vocati, aut nesciente episcopo, sacris ordinibus se intromittunt: aliquibus vero episcopus, ut diaconibus, manum imponit: alii caeteros ordines non habentes, diacones aut presbyteri consecrantur: hi digni sunt depositione.[9]

The canon directs that those who have been ordained deacons and presbyters secretly or unduly, and who never received the orders below the diaconate, are "worthy of deposition". The minor orders are clearly necessary for promotion to the diaconate and beyond. That such a canon would need to be promulgated at all would suggest that at Rouen there were individuals who were being ordained *per saltum* to the diaconate, contrary to the canons and practice of the church.

Further abuses in Rouen are evident in a subsequent council held there in 1074. Canon IV of that council states:

---

[7] MANSI XIX.915.

[8] Of the systematic collections surveyed in this study, cap. V of the decretal of Nicholas II in the Council of Rome is found in Ivo's *Panormia*.

[9] MANSI XX.37.

> Ne ordines ab acolyto usque ad sacerdotium una die vel uno tempore tribuantur, sacra canonum auctoritate prohibemus.[10]

The canon forbids the grades from the acolytate to the presbyterate to be conferred on a single day, or at one liturgy (*uno tempore*). The intent of the canon seems to be directed at the practice of conferring the successive offices of acolyte, subdeacon, deacon, and presbyter on a particular cleric in one day or at one liturgy, as opposed to conferring the different grades on different clerics in a day. Once again, the appearance of such a canon implies that rapid ordinations were an actual abuse. While Canon X of the council of 1072 demonstrates that the *cursus* was illicitly dispensed with, Canon IV of the council of 1074 demonstrates the extent to which the *cursus* was observed, while the interstices were completely ignored. Both practices were condemned.

Canon VI from the Council of Rouen of 1074 legislated on the minimum ages of clerics, and by implication, the interstices between the grades:

> Ut ordines juxta SS. Patrum statuta dentur. Scilicet ut nullus ordinetur subdiaconus ante XX. annos, diaconus ante XXV. annos, presbyter ante XXX. nisi summa necessitate. Sed tamen presbyter nullus ordinetur ante XXV. annos.[11]

The canon states that the minimum age for the subdiaconate is twenty, considerably older than the minimum age prescribed by Nicholas II at the Council of Rome in 1059. The age for deacons remains at twenty-five. The ages for presbyters is thirty; presbyters may be ordained at an earlier age for reason of great necessity. They may not, however, be ordained below the age of twenty-five. While the canon raises the age of subdeacons, it significantly permits the lowering of the age of presbyters. This reduction of the age of presbyters is the first noted in this study since *Epistle* 13 of the eighth-century Pope Zacharias to Boniface.[12]

The Council of Melfi (near Bari in southern Italy; 1089/90) also dealt with the ages of clerics. Canon IV of the council states:

> Igitur ut haec, annuente domino valeant conservari, sanctorum patrum decretis obsecundantes, et eorum praecepta apostolico moderamine temperantes, constituimus ut nemo ante annos quindecim, aut quatuordecim, subdiaconos ordinetur, nemo

---

[10] MANSI XX.399.

[11] MANSI XX.400.

[12] *PL* 89.952.

ante annos viginti quinque vel viginti quatuor diaconus fiat, nemo ante trigesimum in presbyterum consecretur.[13]

The minimum ages for subdeacons are fifteen or fourteen; for deacons twenty-five or twenty-four. The age for presbyters is thirty.

The Council of Benevento (1091) insisted that candidates for the episcopate be deacons and presbyters. Canon I states:

> Nullus deinceps in episcopum eligatur, nisi qui in sacris ordinibus religiose vivens inventus est. Sacros autem ordines dicimus diaconatum ac presbyteratum. Hos siquidem solos primitiva legitur ecclesia habuisse: super his solum praeceptum habemus apostoli. Subdiaconos vero, quiaet ipsi altaribus administrant, opportunitate exigente concedimus, sed rarissime, si tamen spectatae sint religioniset scientiae. Quodet ipsum sine Romani pontificis, vel metropolitani licentia non fiat.[14]

The canon directs that no one is to be elected a bishop except those who have been living religiously in holy orders, which are said to be the diaconate and (*ac*) the presbyterate. The canon permits subdeacons on rare occasion to be elected, if they are religious and of tested knowledge, but only with the permission of the pope or the metropolitan. Such subdeacons, it is assumed, would be ordained deacons and presbyters.

This canon is noteworthy in that it understands that the orders preceding election and consecration to the episcopate are "the diaconate *and* the presbyterate" rather than "the diaconate *or* the presbyterate". This modification is evidence of the place the presbyterate had won as an indispensable grade in the *cursus* towards the episcopate in the eleventh century. In light of papal affirmations on the place of the subdiaconate as an holy order, especially from Alexander II and Urban II, it is odd that only the diaconate and the presbyterate are said to be the *sacros ordines*.[15]

An interesting contrast to Canon I of the Council of Benevento is Canon V of the Council of Clermont-Ferrand (1095) which succinctly asserts:

> Ut nullus laicus, clericus, vel tantum subdiaconus in episcopum eligatur.[16]

In this instance lay persons, clerks and subdeacons are specifically inhibited from being elected bishops, likely reflecting an abuse in which they were.

---

[13] MANSI XX.723.

[14] MANSI XX.738–739; *cf.* letter to Ubran II, Jaffé, p. 667.

[15] Of the systematic collections found in this study, Canon I of the Council of Benevento appears in the *Decreta* of Ivo and Gratian.

[16] MANSI XX.817.

A final example from the period is Canon XII of the Council of Dalmatia (1199), which also legislated on the age of presbyters:

Ut nullus ante trigesimum annum ad sacerdotium promoveatur.

Similiter prohibemus, ut nullus ordinetur in sacerdotem, nisi trigesimum expleverit annum.[17]

At the end of the twelfth century thirty continues to be upheld as the minimum age for ordination to the presbyterate.

Conciliar legislation in this period attempted to rectify a number of aberrations. While many of the abuses revolve around simony, the councils proscribe against a variety of deviations from the *cursus honorum*. In particular, the canonical ages seemed to have been ignored. The minor orders, even the subdiaconate, seem to have been ignored. The interstices seem to have been abrogated to the point of being completely neglected (e.g. acolyte to presbyter in a day). Members of the laity, those in minor orders and the subdiaconate continue to be elected to the episcopate. As well as remedying a situation of laxity, the councils reflect a certain development. The conciliar texts continue to reflect the traditional ages for deacons and presbyters, though the age of the presbyterate may be reduced to twenty-five, though thirty continues to be upheld as the ideal. The minimum ages of subdeacons varies considerably. From the councils of Ravenna, Rome, and Melfi, it appears that in Italy the subdiaconate is conferred on young adolescents. From the Councils of Compostello and Rouen, it would appear that the church north of the Alps continued to confer the subdiaconate on young men between eighteen and twenty years of age. While the councils, specifically the Councils of Rome and Rouen, reflect a situation in which the minor grades of the *cursus* were omitted, they insist that the grades of the clerical *cursus* correspond to the hierarchical sequence of the grades; there are to be no omissions of the grades in the *cursus honorum*.

3. Papal Letters and Decretals

The writings of the bishops of Rome throughout this period, especially Alexander II and Urban II in the eleventh century, continue to reflect and legislate on the *cursus honorum* and the related issues. The letter of

---

[17] MANSI XXII.704.

Nicholas II to the Council of Rome (1059) regarding the minimum a subdeacons, deacons, and presbyters, was dealt with in the previous section. The pontificate of Alexander II (1061–73) is important in the history of holy orders, especially in clarifying the status of the subdiaconate as a major order which enjoined clerics to celibacy. Of particular significance for the place of the subdiaconate in the sequence of grades is *Epistle* 32, to Rumoldus, bishop of Constance (1063):

> De eo qui subdiaconatus ordine post posito, diaconuset presbyter est ordinatus.
>
> Solicitudo dilectionis tuae studuit consulere, utrum portior istarum litterarum, diaconatuset presbyteratus officium sit idoneus peragere, necne: cum ad id praepropero cursu, videlicet sine subdiaconatus ordine, negligentia potius quam superbia, cognoscatur adscendisse. Unde nos consulendo caritati tuae mandavimus, ut ab officio sacerdotali eum prohibeas, donec proximo quatuor temporum jejunio subdiaconatus ministerium sibi rite imponas,et sic deinceps ad majora officia eum redire concedas.[18]

Alexander writes to Rumoldus concerning deacons and presbyters who through negligence had never been ordained to the subdiaconate. Alexander directs that "priests" in such a predicament (and presumably deacons) be inhibited from the exercise of their office until the next embertide, when they are to be ordained to the subdiaconate; they do not lose the orders of deacon and presbyter.

This letter indicates a number of things. First, there were deacons and presbyters in the church of Constance who had not been ordained to the subdiaconate. One recalls Canon X of the Council of Rouen which similarly dealt with clerics who had not received the subdiaconate. Second, the letter demonstrates the extent to which the subdiaconate in the eleventh century was held by the reformers to be indispensable in the sequence of the *cursus honorum*; both the "priesthood" and the diaconate are thought to be deficient without subdiaconal ordination. The obligation to celibacy is related to the growing understanding of the subdiaconate as a major order. Third, the use of terminology is significant; Alexander speaks of a "hasty career"—*praepropero cursu*. The letter of Alexander to Rumoldus marks the first instance in this study where the terminology of *cursus honorum* is actually used in a papal (or any other) text.[19]

---

[18] MANSI XIX.963; *PL* 146.1349; Jaffé, # 4510.

[19] Of the systematic collections surveyed in this study, the letter of Alexander to Rumoldus is found in the *Decreta* of both Ivo and Gratian.

A second text from the pontificate of Alexander II, *De quodam sacerdote male ordinato*,[20] also deals with the issue of deacons and presbyters who have not received the subdiaconate:

> De quodam Sacerdote male ordinato.
>
> Quidam in clericalibus officiis educatus subdiaconatus gradum suscipere neglexit,et diaconatus, ac presbyteratus honorem, non quidem ambitiose, sed negligenter conscendit. In quo praeceptum canonicum non nos invenisse meminimus; consilium autem ex praerogativa authoritatis apostolicae damus. Ab utriusque itaque idest sacerdotalis,et leviticae, quos inordinate suscepit, officio suspendatur; donec congruo tempore intersit ejus, qui ad subdiaconum benedicendum honorem,et cum eis subdiaconatus suscipiat benedictionem. Prius tamen discutiendum si ejus vita digna officio habeatur;et sic, si vitae canones non obviaverit, in priore ordinatione diaconus,et presbyter teneatur.[21]

Alexander again writes about clerics who through neglect, not ambition, have been ordained to the diaconate and the presbyterate without having first received the subdiaconate. Such clerics are suspended from the exercise of both the diaconate and the presbyterate until such time as they have received subdiaconal ordination.

Once again, Alexander effectively declares the subdiaconate to be an indispensable grade in the *cursus honorum*. A presbyter who has not received the subdiaconate is considered to have been "erroneously ordained" (*male ordinato*) and suspended from office until the missing order has been received.

The text assumes that a presbyter has also received the diaconate. Alexander speaks of the cleric's preceding ordination as deacon and presbyter (*in priore ordinatione diaconus,et presbyter*).

Long before the eleventh century, the subdiaconate had been a regularly conferred grade in the clerical *cursus*. It was noted in earlier chapters of this study that most bishops of Rome had been subdeacons prior to ordination to either the diaconate or to the presbyterate. Nevertheless, there must have been instances in the eleventh century when the subdiaconate was neglected in the clerical *cursus*. Alexander suspends such clerics from the exercise of their ministry until they have been ordained subdeacons thus defining the indispensable nature of the subdiaconate.

---

[20] Ex M.S *Codex Pistoriensis*

[21] MANSI XIX.984; *Cf.* Jaffé, # 4584, letter of Alexander II to Archbishop Gervais of Rheims, 1065.

It is not clear whether Alexander's suspension of clerics without the subdiaconate was intended in some way as a deterrent to those who would neglect the subdiaconate, or whether omission of this grade rendered one's diaconate and presbyterate "invalid". It is worth noting that Alexander did not insist that such deacons and presbyters be re-ordained to these offices. At any rate, from either a canonical or theological point of view, the diaconate and the presbyterate are held to be incomplete without prior ordination to the subdiaconate in accordance with the *cursus honorum*. As Reynolds has summarised:

> For Alexander the subdiaconate was not simply another step to the higher orders which could be sidestepped at will, but an order which had to be episcopally confirmed and which demanded a life worthy of the higher orders.[22]

An interesting letter written during the pontificate of Urban II (1088–1099) describes the continued practice of *per saltum* ordination, in this instance to the presbyterate. In *Epistle* 263 to Bernard, archbishop of Toledo, Urban writes:

> Litterarum praesentium lator ad nos veniens ab exorcista usque ad sacerdotium nullum ordinem se accepisse confessus est. Quod audientes plurimum mirati sumus. Et quia ejus persona nobis ignota sine litteris et sine ullis indiciis nostro se praesentavit conspectui, eum strenuitati tuae remisimus, praecipientes ut causam ejus diligenter inquiras; et si quod refert verum esse constiterit, a sacerdotio male et inorindate accepto, indicta quam dignam duxeris poenitentia, per annum cessare jubebis. Anno vero transacto, si ejus viteat conversatio talis visa fuerit et alia non impediunt ut honore digna sit tanto, omnes ordines quos non accepit cum ipso pariter presbyteratu, siquidem presbyteratum gratis assumpserit, illi restituas.[23]

Apparently a cleric confessed to having been made an exorcist and subsequently ordained to the presbyterate without having received any of the intervening orders. Urban directs that the cleric spend a year in penance and probation before receiving all the intervening grades which he had not received, as well as the presbyterate itself—*cum ipso pariter presbyteratu*.

The letter is significant in a number of respects. First, it reflects that the practice of direct ordination (*per saltum*) still continued. Second, it shows that such a practice was considered invalid; the cleric had been ordained *a sacerdotio male et inordinate*. Without the intervening grades, the cleric's

---

[22] Roger Reynolds, "Sacred Orders in the Early Middle Ages: Shifts in the Theology of the Lower and Higher Ecclesiastical Orders from Late Patristic Antiquity through the Early Middles Ages, as Reflected in the Ordinals of Christ and Related Literature," diss., Harvard University, 1966, p. 256.

[23] *PL* 151.525; MANSI XX.701; Jaffé, # 5734.

first ordination to the presbyterate was considered invalid and had to be repeated after the candidate received all the other grades. Urban's instructions to Bernard are much more severe than those of Alexander to
Rumoldus. Alexander merely inhibited presbyters and deacons who had
not received the subdiaconate until they had received the grade; they were
not ordained again.

4. Canonistic Collections Prior to the Gregorian Reform

It is maintained that the period from the tenth to the mid-eleventh century
was one of decline in the history of canon law.[24] Yet a number of canonistic collections pre-date the Gregorian reforms of the mid-eleventh century.
Associated with the reforms initiated in the early eleventh century are a
number of canonistic collections that dealt with many areas of church life,
including the clerical grades. This section will examine the treatment of
the *cursus honorum* and related issues in two collections from the period:
the transalpine *Decretum* of Burchard of Worms, and the Italian *Collectio
canonum in V libris*.

a. Burchard of Worms

One of the most important early eleventh-century collections is the *Decretorum Libri XX* of Burchard, bishop of Worms (1000–1025). The *Decretum* was complied between 1008–1012 by Burchard, in collaboration with
Bruncicho, *praepositus* of the cathedral at Worms, Walter, bishop of Spey-
er, and Olbert, later abbot of Gembloux.[25] The *Decretum* sets out the principles which were to guide imperial reform; it was widely used by the early
eleventh-century reformers, and continued to be copied long into the thirteenth century. The *Decretum* contains 1,785 capitula, arranged systematically, on a variety of ecclesiastical topics, including holy order. Three
canonistic collections already surveyed in this study were among the
sources used by Burchard in the compilation of the *Decretum*: the *Libri
duo de synodalibus causis et disciplinis eccesiasticis* of Regino of Prüm,

---

[24] *Cf.* Charles Munier, "False Decretals to Gratian: Canon Law, History of", *New Catholic
Encyclopedia*, vol. 3 (New York: McGraw-Hill Book Company, 1967), p. 39.

[25] Reynolds, "Law, Canon," p. 407.

the *Anselmo dedicata*, and the *Collectio hibernensis*. Burchard is noted for altering his sources and rearranging material to correspond to contemporary needs.[26] There are only thirteen capitula in the *Decretum* which touch upon the clerical *cursus*, the interstices, and the ages of clerics; these caps. are found in Books I–III.

In Book I, *De primato ecclesiae*, Burchard deals with the qualities sought for in candidates for the episcopate. For example, cap. V reproduces a section of the letter of Leo to Anastasius of Thessalonica (*Epistle* 14.3) forbidding the ordination of members of the laity, bigamists, and widowers to the episcopate.[27] Cap. VIII is the lengthy first canon of the SEA (known here as the Council of Carthage), concerning the qualities sought in a bishop.[28] Cap. IX, from Canon XII of the Council of Arles directs that only those who have been tested for a long time be elected bishops.[29] Cap. XVI, from canons I and II from the Council of Arles, 524 (*not* Canon VII as purported in the text), directs that members of the laity not be ordained to the episcopate or to the presbyterate until either they have reached thirty years of age, or within a year of their conversion (or manner of living):

> Episcopatus vero vel presbyterii honorem nullus laicus ante anni conversationem, vel ante triginta annos accipiat.[30]

Here Burchard has slightly altered the original text of Canon I:

> ..... episcopatus vero vel presbyterii honore nullus laicus ante praemissa conversatione vel ante triginta aetatis annos accipiat.[31]

Cap. XVII of *De primato ecclesiae* repeats Canon XIII of the Council of Sardica, according to the version of the *Dionysiana*.[32] Cap. XVIII is the letter of Celestine to the bishops of Vienne and Narbonne (*Epistle* 4.4) against the ordination to the episcopate of those who have not served in the minor offices.[33] Cap. XXXVI reproduces Canon XVII of the Council of

---

[26] Reynolds, "Law, Canon," p. 408.

[27] *PL* 140.551.

[28] *PL* 140.551.

[29] *PL* 140.552.

[30] *PL* 140.553.

[31] de Clerq, *Concilia Galliae*, p. 43.

[32] *PL* 140.554.

[33] *PL* 140.554.

Ancyra, which directs that bishops who are not received in their sees may sit with the presbyters.[34]

Book II of the *Decretum, De sacris ordinibus*, deals with the remaining orders below the episcopate. Cap. III, from the letter of Pope Zephrynus to the Egyptian church, insists that presbyters and "levites" be ordained at fitting times, tested and learned.[35] Chapters IX–XIII of Book II deal with the ages of clerics. Cap. IX, is from Canon XVII (*not* Canon VII as purported in the text) of the Council of Agde, 506, confirming thirty as the minimum age for presbyters and bishops.[36] Cap. X from the decretal of Fabian to the East likewise assigns thirty as the minimum age for presbyters.[37] Canon XI, from the third Council of Carthage, 397, confirms twenty-five as the age for deacons.[38] Canon XII from Canon XX of the fourth Council of Toledo, 633, also identifies twenty-five as the age for deacons and thirty as the age for presbyters.[39] Cap. XIII of Book II reproduces Canon IX of the Council of Nicaea, dealing with those who have been admitted presbyters without examination.

Book III, cap. L, *De ordinibus sacris*, is based on the pseudo-Isidorian *Epistula ad Leudefredum*. While it does not describe movement within the sequence of grades, its inclusion by Burchard in the *Decretum* is significant because of the sequence in which the grades arise. In the EL (in its earlier form) the grades appear in the hierarchical sequence of doorkeeper, acolyte, exorcist, psalmist, lector, subdeacon, deacon, presbyter, and bishop. In the *Decretum* the grades appear in the sequence of psalmist, doorkeeper, lector, exorcist, acolyte, subdeacon, deacon, presbyter, and bishop, the standard *cursus* of the Western church since the tenth century.[40]

While *Decretorum libri XX* includes many sources from the patristic period already examined in chapter III of this study, other well-known texts are conspicuously absent. For example, Burchard has omitted the material from the pontificates of Siricius, Zosimus, and Gelasius. Burchard's principal concerns regarding the *cursus honorum* appear to be the quality

---

[34] *PL* 140.560.

[35] *PL* 140.625–626.

[36] *PL* 140.627.

[37] *PL* 140.627.

[38] *PL* 140.627.

[39] *PL* 140.627.

[40] *PL* 140.681–682.

of candidates for the episcopate, an insistence on testing and learning, and the exclusion of lay people (among others) from being elected bishops.

b. *Collectio canonum in V libris*

Another important early eleventh-century collection is the Italian *Collectio canonum in V libris*. The collection contains 1,288 capitula arranged systematically on a variety of topics, including holy orders. Of the canonistic collections surveyed, the *Collectio hibernensis*, the Pseudo-Isidorian Decretals, the *Dacheriana*, and the *Concordia Cresconii*, were all sources for the *Collectio canonum in V libris*.

Book I of the collection contains a number of capitula dealing with the *cursus honorum* and related issues. It begins with Isidore's treatment of the grades from the *Etymologiae*, including the two sequences in which Isidore treats them.[41]

Book I, cap. II is a reworking of the *De septem gradibus quos Christus adimplevit* from the *Collectio hibernensis*.[42] Not only is the text reworked, but the sequence of grades as well. In the *Hibernensis* the grades follow the hierarchical sequence; its recension in the *Collectio canonum in V libris* treats the grades according to the chronological sequence of the life of Christ (lector, exorcist, subdeacon, deacon, presbyter, doorkeeper, bishop). Cap. III is the *De distantia graduum* of the *Hibernensis*, the sequence of grades faithfully replicated.[43]

Two letters of Gregory the Great which condemn the ordination of the untrained, the untested, and members of the laity to the episcopate are included. Cap. XXXVII contains portions of the letter of Gregory to Syagrius (*Reg.*9.218);[44] Cap. XXXVIII contains portions of one of Gregory's letters to Brunhilda (*Reg.* 8.4). A letter of Gregory to Columbus (*Reg.* 3.47) prohibiting the ordination of boys (*pueri*) is included in cap. LXXVI.[45]

---

[41] M. Fornasari, ed., *Collectio canonum in V libris*, CCCM 6 (Turnhout: Brepols, 1970), p. 21.

[42] Fornasari, *V libris*, p. 24.

[43] Fornasari, *V libris*, pp. 24–25.

[44] Fornasari, *V libris*, p. 38. The introduction to cap. XXXVII identifies this text as a letter of Gregory to Brunhilda (*Reg.* 9.213); Fornasari's note concurs. This is, however, clearly Gregory's letter to Syagrius, Etherius, Vergilius, and Desiderius (*Reg.* 9.218); *cf.* MGH, *Epp.* 2.207–208, 209–210.

[45] Fornasari, *V libris*, p. 64.

Cap. XLI reproduces the letter of Jerome to Theophilus (*Epistle* 82, 8.2) advocating twenty-five years as the minimum age for "levites" and thirty for "priests".[46] Canon I of the *Statuta ecclesiae antiqua*, describing the qualities sought in a bishop, is included in cap. XLIII.[47] Cap. LXXXVI includes a pseudo-Silvestrian letter promoting the *cursus honorum* through each of the grades (lector, exorcist, acolyte, subdeacon, deacon, and presbyter) at the appropriate (though undefined) ages.[48]

Cap. LXXXVII, entitled *De aetatibus et meritis quibus provehi debent ad episcopatum*, is based on the *Tribus ordinibus aetas episcopalis eligitur* of the *Hibernensis*.[49] The original is reproduced with two notable exceptions. The second section of *Tribus ordinibus aetas episcopalis eligitur* in the *Hibernensis* (I.11) indicates that a cleric is to be ordained a subdeacon at thirty years of age for an interstice of four years, after which he may be ordained a deacon for a five year period. At forty years of age, one is ordained a presbyter, and at age fifty a bishop.[50] The corresponding text in Book I, cap. LXXXVII.3 of the *Collection canonum in V libris* says:

> Qui enim ab accessu adolescentiae usque ad trigesimum aetatis annum probabiliter vixerit, una tantum virgine uxore contentus, vigesimo anno subdiaconus, trigesimo diaconus, trigesimo quinto presbyter aut episcopus fiat.[51]

Those who have been tested, and content with one wife until age thirty, may be ordered subdeacon at age twenty, deacon at thirty, and presbyter and bishop at age thirty-five. The third section of *Tribus ordinibus* in the *Hibernensis*, witness to another set of interstices, is accurately reproduced in cap. LXXXVIII of the *Collectio canonum in V libris*.[52]

Cap. LXXXIX, from the *Lex Romana* can. compta, VII, identifies thirty as the minimum age for presbyters, twenty-five for deacons, fourteen for subdeacons, and nine years for lectors.[53] Cap. XC is from the "Henrician" Canon II, traditionally attributed to the Synod of Ravenna (1014),

46 Fornasari, *V libris*, pp. 39–40.
47 Fornasari, *V libris*, pp. 40–41.
48 Fornasari, *V libris*, pp. 67–68.
49 Fornasari, *V libris*, p. 68.
50 Wasserschleben, *Hibernensis*, p. 8.
51 Fornasari, *V libris*, p. 68.
52 Fornasari, *V libris*, p. 69.
53 Fornasari, *V libris*, p. 69.

specifying thirty as the minimum ages for presbyters and twenty-five as the minimum age for deacons, and twelve years for subdeacons.[54]

Cap. XCI, *De conversatione ecclesiastica, qui ab infantia se Deo voverit*, is a considerable reworking of the letter of Siricius to Himerius of Tarragona (*Epistle* 1.IX.13).[55] Whereas Siricius mentions only lectors (or exorcists in the case of adults) acolytes, subdeacons, deacons, and presbyters, cap. XCI refers to lectors, doorkeepers, exorcists, acolytes, subdeacons, deacons, presbyters, and bishops.

Cap. XCII faithfully reproduces the letter of Innocent to Felix of Nocera (*Epistle* 37, V.6) condemning hasty ordinations.[56] Cap. XCIII is a portion of the letter of Leo the Great to the bishops of Mauretania Caesariensis (*Epistle* 12.2) condemning the ordination of the untested and unprepared.[57] Whereas Leo seems to have directed his attack at those who are ordained bishops without examination, in the *Collectio canonum* it seems to apply to any of the other grades as well.

Cap. XCIV, from the pseudo-Silvestrian letter to the Council of Nicaea, deals with the ages of clerics.[58] Subdeacons are not to be ordained below twenty-four years, deacons below twenty-five years, and presbyters and bishops below thirty years. Cap. XCVI.1 is from the letter of Zosimus to Hesychius (*Epistle* 9,III.5), faithfully replicated.[59] Cap. XCVI.2 is from the letter of Siricius to Himerius (*Epistle* 1, X.14) dealing with the ordination of older men.[60]

Although identified in the text as the decretal of Siricius, cap. XCVII is from the letter of Gelasius to the bishops throughout Lucia, Bruttii, and Sicily (*Epistle* 14.2), concerning the shortening of the interstices whereby a tested member of the laity would receive the grades of the *cursus honorum* within the space of twelve months.[61] Cap. XCIX.1 is Canon XIII from the Council of Sardica, in the version of the *Dionysiana*.[62] Cap.

---

[54] Fornasari, *V libris*, pp. 69–70.

[55] Fornasari, *V libris*, p. 70.

[56] Fornasari, *V libris*, pp. 70–71.

[57] Fornasari, *V libris*, p. 71.

[58] Fornasari, *V libris*, pp. 71–72.

[59] Fornasari, *V libris*, pp. 72–73.

[60] Fornasari, *V libris*, p. 73.

[61] Fornasari, *V libris*, pp. 73–74.

[62] Fornasari, *V libris*, pp. 74–75.

XCIX.2 is from the letter of Celestine to the bishops of Vienne and Narbonne (*Epistle* IV.4) in which the pope complains that certain bishops have reached the episcopate without having served in any of the lower offices.[63] Cap. XCIX.3 is from the Canon IV of the third Council of Carthage, directing that deacons not be ordained below twenty-five years of age.[64] Cap. C is from Canon IX of the Council of Neocaesarea, designating thirty as the minimum age for presbyters.[65]

The compiler of the *Collectio canonum in V libris* has gathered and presented systematically various texts dealing with the *cursus honorum*, the interstices, ages of clerics, and *per saltum* ordination. The major patristic texts are all present. While some have been altered, most appear in their original forms. The fact that twenty-two capitula dealing with the ecclesiastical *cursus* appear more-or-less together is significant; it is indicative of how important this area had become in the reforms of the early eleventh century. Moreover, since most of the patristic texts are (more-or-less) accurately reproduced, it demonstrates that the early eleventh-century reformers were well aware of the historic reasons behind the *cursus*, that is, probation and preparation.

5. Canonistic Collections from the Mid-Eleventh Century

The reform movement of the eleventh century, under way by the middle of the century, is associated with the reform of the papacy and the strong assertions of papal primacy. The movement is especially identified with the pontificates of Leo IX (1049–1054), Nicholas II (1058–1061), and Gregory VII (1073–1085). Associated with the reforms was increased attention to canon law, resulting in the compilation of a great number of canonistic collections. It is during this period that the study of canon law as a science began.

This section will investigate the most prominent canonistic collections of the Gregorian Reform: the *Diversorum patrum sententiae*, the *Collectio canonum* of Anselm of Lucca, and the *Collectio canonum* of Deusdedit.

---

[63] Fornasari, *V libris*, p. 75.

[64] Fornasari, *V libris*, p. 75.

[65] Fornasari, *V libris*, pp. 75-76.

This section will examine collections of the post-Gregorian period: the *Liber de vita christiana* of Bonizo of Sutri, Ivo of Chartres *Panormia* and *Decretum*. Lastly, the mid-twelfth-century *Concordantia discordantium canonum* of Gratian will be examined.

a. The *Diversorum patrum sententiae*

One of the earliest collections from this period is the Italian *Diversorum patrum sententiae*, or the *Collection in Seventy-Four Titles* (74T). The collection contains 315 capitula arranged systematically under seventy-four titles. Although the date and authorship of the 74T are disputed, it must have been compiled sometime before 1067 since it was known during the pontificate of Gregory VII.[66] One of the primary sources for the 74T was the Pseudo-Isidorian Decretals.[67]

Tituli 15-19 of the 74T deal with clerical ordination; most of the materials dealing with the *cursus* and related issues is found under *titulus* 15, "On prelates who are untrained, unworthy, simoniacal, or neophyte." The first section in *titulus* 15, 15.111, is from the letter of Innocent to Aurelius of Carthage, in which the pope censures the practice of ordaining bishops who have never served in any of the subordinate offices.[68] Caps. 112 and 114 are from the letter of Celestine to the bishops of Apulia and Calabria (*Epistle* 5.1-2) condemning the ordination of members of the laity to the episcopate.[69] Cap. 118 is from the letter of Leo to Anastasius of Thessalonica (*Epistle* 14.3) which condemns the elections of laymen, neophytes, and those twice married to the episcopate.[70] A portion from the letter of Leo to the bishops of Mauritania Caesariensis (*Epistle* 12.4) appears in cap. 122, condemning the ordination to the episcopate of those who "do not want to rise up from the ranks, but desire to start at the top".[71] *Titulus*

---

[66] Reynolds, "Law: Canon," p. 409; John Gilchrist, trans., *The Collection in Seventy- Four Titles: A Canon Law Manual of the Gregorian Reform* (Toronto: Pontifical Institute of Mediaeval Studies, 1980), p. 2.

[67] Gilchrist, *Seventy-four,* p. 15. Gilchrist says that it is doubtful whether the author of the 74T used any other original source, apart from the false decretal of Pseudo-Isidore; he estimates that out of the 315 *capitula,* 252 were from the Pseudo-Isidorian collection.

[68] John Gilchrist, ed., *Diversorum patrum sententiae sive Collectio in LXXIV titulos* [74T], Monumenta Iuris Canonici, Series B, Corpus Collectionum I (Vatican: Biblioteca Apostolica Vaticana, 1973) p. 74.

[69] Gilchrist, 74T, pp. 75, 76.

[70] Gilchrist, 74T, pp. 77–79.

[71] Gilchrist, 74T, p. 79.

15.124, from the letter of Hormisdas to the Hispanic bishops (*Epistle* 25.1) insisting on the importance of probation and preparation in the election of bishops, and condemning the election of members of the laity and penitents to the episcopate.[72]

The 74T contains a number of the letters of Gregory the Great, indicating the importance of Gregory to the eleventh-century reformers. Six chapters from *titulus* 15 are from the pontificate of Gregory I. Cap. 125 is from a letter of Gregory to Brunhilda (*Reg.* 9.213) in which Gregory complains that ambitious Frankish laymen are suddenly promoted from the laity and censures the practice.[73] Cap. 126 is from a letter to Theodoric and Theodobert (*Reg.* 9.215) in which Gregory censures both the practices of simony and the ordination of vain, ambitious members of the laity to the episcopate; Gregory suggests that if Theodoric and Theodobert neglect to amend these practices they will share in the guilt.[74] Capitula 127–131 are from Gregory's letter to Syagrius of Autun (Reg. 9.218); capitula 129–131 deal with ordinations of members of the laity and neophytes to the episcopate.[75]

Cap. 137, ascribed to St. Augustine, is actually based on the letter of Leo to the bishops of Mauritania Caesariensis (*Epistle* 12.2) concerning the hasty imposition of hands without respecting the ages of candidates, the appropriateness of time, obedience, and preparation. There is an interpolation in cap. 137 from the letter of Jerome to Oceanum (*Epistle* 69.9— "Yesterday a catechumen, today a bishop...") from the Pseudo-Isidorian Decretals.[76]

Titulus 16, entitled "To whom Sacred Orders are to be Given, and to whom denied" includes only two capitula on the *cursus honorum* and the related issues. Cap. 138, from the Pseudo-Isidorian Decretals, is from a pseudo-Silvestrian synodal decree commending the clerical *cursus* with corresponding interstices. The ultimate source is the entry for Silvester is the *Liber pontificalis* which ascribes the interstices to him.[77] A cleric is to pass through the offices of doorkeeper, lector, and exorcist at a time specified by the bishop. A cleric is then an acolyte for five years, a subdeacon

---

[72] Gilchrist, 74T, pp. 80–81.

[73] Gilchrist, 74T, pp. 81–82.

[74] Gilchrist, 74T, pp. 82–84.

[75] Gilchrist, 74T, pp. 87–89.

[76] Gilchrist, 74T, p. 93.

[77] LP I, p. 161.

for five years, a deacon for five years, a custodian of martyrs for five years, and a presbyter for three years before becoming a bishop.[78]

Like the Pseudo-Isidorian Decretals, and the *Collectio canonum* of Anselm of Lucca, the 74T is one of the few canonistic collections to use the letter of Siricius *Ad diversos episcopos* (*Epistle* 6, III.5), which is found here under *titulus* 16, cap. 141.[79] In the letter, Siricius complains that members of the laity and neophytes have been ordained as deacons and presbyters, and that laity are chosen bishops. Siricius concludes: "What I caution is that it go on no further."

The 74T contains the requisite texts reflecting the concern that only the probated and prepared be promoted through the grades. What is curious about the collection is that the papal texts which one might expect to be used are missing. For instance, the archetypal papal patristic texts on the *cursus* from the pontificates of Siricius (*Epistle* 1) and Zosimus (*Epistle* 9) are absent. The compiler of the 74T must have been aware of them; they are included in the Pseudo-Isidorian Decretals and a section from Siricius' letter to Himerius not dealing with the *cursus honorum* (*Epistle* 1.14) appears elsewhere in the 74T: *titulus* 15, cap. 140.[80]

b. Anselm of Lucca

One of the canonistic collections influenced by the 74T was the *Collectio canonum* of Anselm II of Lucca, *ca.* 1083.[81] In addition to the papal sources found in the 74T, Anselm also used conciliar material. The *Collectio canonum* is a systematic collection. The material on bishops and their appointments, including the *cursus honorum* and related issues, is found in Book VI of the collection.

Book VI, cap. 15 is a portion from the letter of Leo to Anastasius of Thessalonica (*Epistle* 14.3), excluding neophytes and members of the laity from being elected bishops.[82] Cap. 19, from the letter of Hormisdas to the Hispanic bishops (*Epistle* 25.I.2) condemns the ordinations of members of

---

[78] Gilchrist, 74T, p. 94.

[79] Gilchrist, 74T, p. 95.

[80] Gilchrist, 74T, p. 95.

[81] Not to be confused with Anselm I of Lucca, who became Pope Alexander II in 1061.

[82] Fridericus Thaner, ed., *Anselmi episcopi Lucensis Collectio Canonum una cum Collectione minore iussu instituti Savigniani* (Oeniponte: Librariae Academicae Wagneriane, 1906), pp. 273–274.

the laity to the episcopate, and commends a long probation for candidates.[83] Cap. 20 is a letter of Pope Hadrian to the fourth Council of Constantinople, 869–870, condemning the election of the laity to the episcopate.[84]

Cap. 24 reproduces the letter of Zosimus to Hesychius of Salone (*Epistle* 9.I.1–2, III.5).[85] There are some subtle differences between Anselm's version and the original. Zosimus wrote that those dedicated to the ecclesiastic ministry from infancy are to remain among the lectors until they have reached twenty years of age; Anselm omits this.[86] Zosimus makes provision for both child and adult candidates to the clerical grades; Anselm omits the reference to adults. The rest of the interstices are accurately reproduced.

Cap. 25, from the letter of Gregory I to Syagrius *et al.* (*Reg.* 9.218), condemns the ordinations of neophytes, and commends promotion through the ecclesiastical grades.[87] Cap. 26, from the same letter, again condemns the election and consecration of recently tonsured lay men to the episcopate, and endorses the clerical *cursus*.[88]

Cap. 28 is from a letter of Innocent to Aurelius of Carthage (*Epistle* 17, from the *Collectio hispana*), in which the pope complains that those who have never served in any grade are made bishops.[89] Cap. 29 is from a letter of Leo I to the bishops of Mauritania Caesariensis (*Epistle* 12.2), with the interpolation from the letter of Jerome to Oceanum (*Epistle* 69.9) found in the 74T and the Pseudo-Isidorian Decretals.[90]

The letter of Celestine to the bishops of Vienne and Narbonne (*Epistle* 4.4) in which bigamists and laity are barred from the episcopate appears in cap. 61.[91] A canon from Gregory VII to the Council of Rome (1080)

---

[83] Thaner, *Collectio canonum*, pp. 275–276.

[84] Thaner, *Collectio canonum*, pp. 276–277.

[85] Thaner, *Collectio canonum*, pp. 279–280.

[86] Thaner, *Collectio canonum*, p. 280.

[87] Thaner, *Collectio canonum*, p. 281.

[88] Thaner, *Collectio canonum*, pp. 281–282.

[89] Thaner, *Collectio canonum*, p. 282.

[90] Thaner, *Collectio canonum*, p. 283.

[91] Thaner, *Collectio canonum*, p. 298.

excluding members of the laity from becoming bishops and abbots appears in cap. 62.[92]

Anselm includes material from the pontificate of Gregory the Great. Cap. 67 contains a letter of Gregory I to Brunhilda (*Reg.* 9.213) in which the pope not only complains that ambitious lay men are ordained to the episcopate, but that the episcopate is being bought; disregard for the *cursus* and the interstices is compounded with simony.[93] Cap. 68 is a portion of the letter of Gregory to Theodoric and Theodobert (*Reg.* 9.215) in which Gregory again denounces the ordination of lay people to the episcopate.[94] Cap. 71, again from the letter of Gregory to Syagrius *et al.* (*Reg.* 9.218), condemns the ordination of the married and the laity to the episcopate.[95] Cap. 73 is a segment of the letter of Gregory to Victor (*Reg.* 12.9), condemning the heretical practices of simony and the ordination of neophytes.[96]

In Book VII of the *Collectio canonum*, Anselm includes many texts dealing with the *cursus* and the clerical grades below the episcopate. Cap. 27, from the Council of Rome (769), is from the account of the pontificate of Stephen III in the *Liber pontificalis*. The antipope Constantine is denounced and it is stated that bishops of Rome are to be chosen from among the deacons and presbyters "who have ascended through each of the grades".[97]

Cap. 28, from the letter of Celestine to the bishops throughout Apulia and Calabria (*Epistle* 5.2), prohibits members of the laity from ascending to the major orders.[98] Cap. 29, from the letter of Innocent to Felix of Nocera (*Epistle* 37.V.6), directs that clerics be ordained at the proper times (*tempora constituta*) and inhibits hasty ordinations through the grades.[99]

Cap. 34 is from the letter of Siricius *Ad diversos episcopos* (*Epistle* 6, III.5), in which Siricius complains that neophytes and members of the laity are being ordained deacons and presbyters, a practice which is identified

---

[92] Thaner, *Collectio canonum*, p. 298.

[93] Thaner, *Collectio canonum*, p. 300.

[94] Thaner, *Collectio canonum*, pp. 301–302.

[95] Thaner, *Collectio canonum*, p. 304.

[96] Thaner, *Collectio canonum*, p. 305.

[97] Thaner, *Collectio canonum*, p. 375.

[98] Thaner, *Collectio canonum*, p. 375.

[99] Thaner, *Collectio canonum*, p. 376.

with heretics.[100] Cap. 39 is from a portion of a letter of Gregory I to Columbus (*Reg.* 3.47), in which the pope directs that boys (*pueri*) not be admitted to holy orders.[101] Cap. 40 is from the pseudo-synod of (pseudo-) Silvester, outlining the clerical *cursus* and interstices. The text is the same as the corresponding one in the 74T (*titulus* 16.138) with the exception that in the 74T, one remains a presbyter for three years, while Anselm has altered the text to say four years.[102]

Cap. 41 contains the letter of Zosimus to Hesychius (*Epistle* 9.III.5), outlining the *cursus* and interstices for boys dedicated to the clerical career;[103] the letter to Hesychius appeared earlier in Book VI, cap. 24 of the *Collectio*. Cap. 42 reproduces Canon I of the Council of Toledo II, 527, likewise dealing with the clerical careers of those dedicated from infancy.[104]

Caps. 46–52 reproduce the ordination rubrics from the *Statuta ecclesiae antiqua* for the orders of psalmist, doorkeeper, lector, exorcist, acolyte, subdeacon, and deacon.[105]

Cap. 78 is from the letter of Jerome to Evangelus the presbyter (*Epistle* 146.1–2) on the hierarchical superiority of presbyters over deacons.[106] Cap. 81, Canon XI from the Council of Neocaesarea, directs that none shall be ordained a presbyter under thirty years of age.[107] Cap. 85 is from the letter of Gelasius to Victor (*Fragmentum* 10) in which the pope permits presbyters to be raised from among the acolytes or subdeacons in the situation where deacons are avoiding promotion to the presbyterate.[108]

The *Collectio canonum* of Anselm of Lucca was a major vehicle for the transmission of the patristic texts dealing with the *cursus honorum* and the interstices. The major papal texts are represented, as well as later texts from the pontificate of Stephen III and Hadrian II. Like other eleventh-

---

[100] Thaner, *Collectio canonum*, pp. 376–378.

[101] Thaner, *Collectio canonum*, p. 379.

[102] Thaner, *Collectio canonum*, p. 379–380.

[103] Thaner, *Collectio canonum*, p. 380.

[104] Thaner, *Collectio canonum*, pp. 380–381.

[105] Thaner, *Collectio canonum*, pp.384–385.

[106] Thaner, *Collectio canonum*, pp. 396–397.

[107] Thaner, *Collectio canonum*, p. 398.

[108] Thaner, *Collectio canonum*, pp. 399–400.

century collections, the *Collectio canonum* reflects the importance of Gregory the Great to the Gregorian reformers.

One of the concerns of the *Collectio canonum* of Anselm of Lucca was simony. Often simony was associated with abuses relating to the *cursus honorum*. A way of attacking the practice of simony, therefore, was to insist on sequential ordination through the grades, according to the times prescribed by the interstices canons. There are some curious omissions from Anselm's collection. In particular, one notes the absence of Canon XIII of the Council of Sardica, and the letter of Siricius to Himerius. Nonetheless, the collection is a witness to the cognizance of the eleventh-century Italian reformers about the ancient and early medieval texts on the *cursus honorum*.

c. Deusdedit

Another major Italian collection is the *Collectio canonum* of Cardinal Deusdedit, which appeared *ca.* 1087, making it concurrent with the collection of Anselm of Lucca. The *Collectio canonum* of Deusdedit is likewise a systematic collection, divided into four books. Book II contains most of the material relating to the *cursus* and related issues. Like Anselm, Deusdedit relied on the 74T, and other sources. Nevertheless, he included considerably less material on the *cursus honorum* than either Anselm or the compiler of the 74T.

Book II, cap. XXVIII is based upon Canon XI of the Council of Neocaesarea, establishing thirty as the minimum age for presbyters.[109] Cap. LIV is a portion of the letter of Gelasius to Victor (*Frag.* 10) in which the pope permits those in the minor orders to be made presbyters rather than deacons who avoid the office.[110] Cap. XCV recounts the establishment of the clerical *cursus* by pope Gaius, ultimately from the *Liber pontificalis*.[111] Cap. CXL is from the letter of Jerome to Evangelus the presbyter (*Epistle* 146.1–2).[112]

---

[109] Victor Wolf von Glanvell, ed., *Die Kanonessammlung des Kardinals Deusdedit*, vol. 1 (Paderborn: Druck und Verlag von Ferdinand Schöningh, 1905), p. 201. While thirty is established as the age for presbyters, the text says: "*Nam dominus deus noster XX [recte: XXX] anno etatis sue baptizatus est et sic cepit docere.*"

[110] Glanvell, *Die Kanonessammlung*, p. 211.

[111] Glanvell, *Die Kanonessammlung*, p. 226.

[112] Glanvell, *Die Kanonessammlung*, pp. 259–260.

Capitula CLXI–CLXIII are from the Council of Rome (769) under the pontificate of Stephen III; caps. CLXI–CLXII deal with the clerical *cursus*. Cap. CLXI, from the third session of the synod, decrees that bishops of Rome must be elected from among the deacons and cardinal presbyters.[113] Cap. CLXII, also from the third session, excludes members of the laity from being elected bishop of Rome.[114] The texts selected by Deusdedit for his *Collectio canonum* sufficiently reflect the clerical *cursus*. Nonetheless, the paucity of material on the *cursus honorum* is curious when compared to the *Diversorum patrum sententiae* and the collection of Anselm of Lucca.

d. Bonizo of Sutri

Although written during the pontificate of Urban II (1088–1099), a third example of an Italian collection of the Gregorian reform is the *Liber de vita christiana* of Bonizo of Sutri. The *Liber de vita christiana* is a systematic collection, dealing with a broad spectrum of topics from baptism to penance.

Book II, cap. 14, contains a portion from the letter of Celestine to the bishops of Vienne and Narbonne (*Epistle* 4.4) in which Celestine complains that members of the laity are promoted to the episcopate without having first served in any of the lower ecclesiastical offices. Celestine commends the minor orders for training and preparation.[115] Book V, cap. 71, is based on the pseudo-Isidorian *Epistula ad Leudefredum*. Unlike the sequence of grades in the EL (doorkeeper, acolyte, exorcist, psalmist, lector, subdeacon, deacon, presbyter, bishop), Bonizo's arrangement matches the sequence of grades of the PRG and Burchard's version of the EL (psalmist, doorkeeper, lector, exorcist, acolyte, subdeacon, deacon, presbyter, bishop).[116]

The ordination rubrics of the SEA are reproduced in Book V, caps. 72–76, for the orders from doorkeeper to subdeacon.[117]

---

[113] Glanvell, *Die Kanonessammlung*, p. 268.

[114] Glanvell, *Die Kanonessammlung*, p. 268.

[115] Ernst Perels, ed., *Bonizo: Liber de vita christiana* (Berlin: Weidmannsche Buchhandlung, 1930), p. 41.

[116] Perels, *Liber de vita*, pp. 210–202.

[117] Perels, *Liber de vita*, pp. 202–203.

As in the *Collectio canonum* of Deusdedit, one is struck by the paucity of material on the clerical *cursus* and related issues. This dearth is partly explained by the fact that Bonizo compiled his collection principally to deal with much broader issues of the Christian life.

e. Ivo of Chartres

Two of the most important transalpine collections of the period just after the Gregorian reform are the *Panormia* and the *Decretum* of Ivo (*ca.* 1040–1115), bishop of Chartres, the most learned canonist prior to Gratian.

i.

The shorter, and more popular, of Ivo's canonistic collections is the *Panormia*, a systematic collection in eight books. The material dealing with the *cursus honorum* and related issues is found in Book III of the collection.

Book III, cap. 5, from Canon I of the Council of Benevento (1091) under Urban II, decrees that no one is to be elected a bishop except those already in holy orders, that is, the diaconate and the presbyterate, or with papal permission, the subdiaconate.[118]

Capitula 27–32 deal with the ages of clerics. Cap. 27, ascribed to Canon XVI (though including Canon XVII) of the Council of Agde (506) establishes thirty as the minimum age for presbyters and bishops.[119] Cap. 29, ascribed to a decretal of Fabian to the East at the Council of Neocaesarea, confirms thirty as the minimum age for presbyters.[120] Cap. 30, from the third Council of Carthage (397), confirms twenty-five as the minimum age for deacons, virgins, and lectors.[121] Cap. 31, from Canon XIX of the Council of Toledo V (though actually Canon XX of Toledo IV, 633) established twenty-five as the minimum age for deacons. Although Toledo IV also confirmed thirty as the age for presbyters, cap. XXXI omits the presbyteral reference.[122] Cap. 32 from Canon VI of the decree of Nicholas II to the

---

[118] *PL* 161.1130.

[119] *PL* 161.1135.

[120] *PL* 161.1135.

[121] *PL* 161.1135–1136.

[122] *PL* 161.1136.

Synod of Rome (1059) confirms fourteen as the minimum age for subdeacons, twenty-five for deacons, and thirty for presbyters.[123]

Capitula 33–40 are the ordination rubrics from the *Statuta ecclesiae antiqua*, in a descending sequence from presbyter to psalmist.[124] Cap. 41 is from the *Epistula ad Leudefredum*, with the grades appearing in the original sequence.[125]

Apart from these references, the *Panormia* does not demonstrate much concern for the *cursus honorum* and the interstices. There is, however, considerable interest shown in the patristic texts dealing with the ages of clerics. The *Panormia* makes use of Gallican, Hispanic, and patristic councils, as well as contemporary material such as the Council of Benevento (1091).

ii.

The much larger of Ivo's canonistic collections is the *Decretum*. The *Decretum* is a systematic collection, consisting of 3,760 canons in seventeen books. The concerns of Ivo in the *Decretum* are not only canonical but theological as well. Parts V and VI contain the material on the *cursus*; part V deals with bishops and part VI deals with the orders below the episcopate.

Part V, cap. 59, from the letter of Leo to Anastasius (*Epistle* 14.3; falsely identified in the text as *Epistle* 82.3) excludes neophytes, members of the laity, and bigamists from the episcopate.[126] Cap. 63, based on Canon IX of the Council of Orleans (549), directs that only those tested for a long period of time shall be promoted to the episcopate;[127] Canon IX actually specifies a one year interval from the time of election to ordination as a bishop, for those elected from the laity.[128] Cap. 70, attributed to Canon I of the Council of Arles III, directs that no one be ordained a bishop below thirty years and within the year of his conversion.[129]

---

[123] *PL* 161.1136–1137.

[124] *PL* 161.1137–1138.

[125] *PL* 161.1137–1139.

[126] *PL* 161.346–347.

[127] *PL* 161.348.

[128] de Clercq, *Concilia Galliae*, p. 151.

[129] *PL* 161.349–350. This canon is more likely based on canon IX of the Council of Orleans, 549.

Cap. 71 is Canon XIII of the Council of Sardica, according to the *Dionysiana*.[130] Cap. 72, from the letter of Celestine to the bishops of Vienne and Narbonne (*Epistle* 4.4) as well as Canon I from the Council of Benevento, 1091, insists that bishops be chosen from among those who are deacons and presbyters, that is, not from among the laity.[131] Cap. 102, from a portion of the letter of Zosimus to Hesychius (*Epistle* 9.I.1—not the usually cited section from the letter) insists on ordinations at the proper times of the year, according to the precepts of the Fathers.[132]

Part VI, entitled *De clericis*, includes texts relating to the *cursus* with respect to the grades below the episcopate. Caps. 5–11 are an abridgement and rearrangement of the *De ecclesiasticis officiis* of Isidore of Seville. The original sequence of grades of the DEO (doorkeeper, exorcist, psalmist, acolyte, lector, subdeacon, sacristan, deacon, presbyter, bishop) has been rearranged according to the Romano-Gallican sequence of doorkeeper, lector, exorcist, acolyte, subdeacon, deacon, and presbyter.[133]

Caps. 12–19 are the ordination rubrics from the *Statuta ecclesiae antiqua* for the grades from presbyter to psalmist, in a descending sequence.[134] Cap. 20 is from the *Epistula ad Leudefredum*, the grades appearing in the original sequence.[135]

Cap. 29, from canons XVI and XVII of the Council of Agde, confirms the minimum age for deacons as twenty-five and thirty for presbyters and bishops.[136] Cap. 30, from a decree of Fabian to the East, confirms thirty as the minimum age for presbyters.[137] Cap. 31, Canon IV of the Council of Carthage III, confirms twenty-five as the age for deacons.[138] Cap. 32, from Canon XX of the Council of Toledo IV, 633, again assigns the minimum age for deacons at twenty-five; the sentence setting thirty as the age for

---

[130] *PL* 161.350.
[131] *PL* 161.350.
[132] *PL* 161.358.
[133] *PL* 161.443–447.
[134] *PL* 161.447–448.
[135] *PL* 161.448–450.
[136] *PL* 161.451–452.
[137] *PL* 161.452.
[138] *PL* 161.452.

presbyters in Canon XX is omitted.[139] Cap. 33, Canon IX of the Council of Nicaea, insists on an examination for candidates for the presbyterate.[140]

Capitula 91–92 are from the letter of Siricius to Himerius (*Epistle* I.IX.13–X.14), accurately reproduced.[141] Cap. 106 is from the letter of Gelasius to Victor (*Frag.* 10) in which Gelasius permits the ordination of acolytes and subdeacons to the presbyterate where deacons evaded promotion.[142]

Cap. 409 is from the letter of Alexander II to Rumoldus (*Epistle* 32), insisting that deacons and presbyters who have not received the subdiaconate be suspended until they have been ordained to that office.[143]

While Ivo includes more texts regarding the *cursus* in the *Decretum* than in the *Panormia*, they are clearly not of as great interest to him as they were to Anselm of Lucca or the compiler of the 74T. Ivo again seems more interested in the ages of clerics than in texts reflecting movement from one grade to another, which is perhaps indicative of the abuses he was attempting to suppress.

f. Gratian

Although referred to as the "father of canon" law, little is known about the life of Gratian. He might have been a Camaldolese monk from central Italy; he died no later than 1159. Compiled by Gratian, *ca.* 1140, the *Concordantia discordantium canonum*, known also as the *Decretum Gratiani* or simply the *Decretum*, came to form the first part of the *Corpus Iuris Canonici* of the Roman Church. The compilation of the *Decretum Gratiani* is regarded as the inauguration of the classical period in the history of Western canon law.[144] Gratian's collection is the most important classical text of canon law. Though never an official text, the *Decretum* became the consummate authoritative repository of canon law in the Western church; it is the first scientific treatment of canon law and became the standard manual in the courts and the universities.

---

[139] *PL* 161.452.

[140] *PL* 161.452.

[141] *PL* 161.466.

[142] *PL* 161.470–471.

[143] *PL* 161.533.

[144] *Cf.* Munier, "False Decretals to Gratian," p. 40.

The *Decretum Gratiani* is a systematic collection, containing nearly 4,000 patristic texts, conciliar statements, and papal decrees, on all aspects of the church's life. Given the sheer size of the *Decretum Gratiani* it is not surprising that it contains all the major patristic and medieval texts relating to the *cursus honorum*, the interstices, and the ages of clerics.

The method utilized in the *Decretum* is different from the earlier collections of medieval canon law. Gratian used the dialectical method of Peter Abelard, that is, asking a question or stating a supposition, then playing various texts against one another in order to arrive at a balanced conclusion.

In Part I, *dist.* XLVIII, the discussion begins with an excerpt based on the letter of Jerome to Oceanum requiring that one who is a catechumen one day, not be a bishop the next, that one who is at the theatre one day, be not seated in the church the next, *et cetera*.[145] In support, Canon I cites Canon II of the Council of Nicaea inhibiting the ordination of neophytes;[146] Canon II also cites a portion of the letter of Gregory I to Syagrius*et al.* (*Reg.* 9.218), again condemning the ordination of neophytes (which here means members of the laity) to the episcopate.[147]

In *distinctio* LII, Gratian asserts that sequential progression through the grades is imperative; there can be no omission of any grade in the *cursus* towards the major orders. *Dist.* LII deals with the question of those who have risen to the major orders, but have neglected any grade (*Qui vero pretermissis aliquibus gradibus*); they are to abstain from their ministries until they have received what was neglected. Gratian introduces the section:

> Qui vero pretermissis aliquibus gradibus non superbia, sed negligentia ad maiores conscenderit, tamdiu a maioribus abstineat, quousque congruo tempore pretermissos accipiat.[148]

In support, *dist.* LII, Canon I cites the letter of Alexander II to Rumoldus directing that presbyters and deacons who have neglected the subdiaconate be suspended from office until they have received it.[149]

---

[145] Aemilius Friedberg, ed., *Decretum Magistri Gratiani* (Liepzig: Bernhard Tauchnitz, 1879), col. 174.

[146] Friedberg, *Decretum*, col. 174.

[147] Friedberg, *Decretum*, col. 174.

[148] Friedberg, *Decretum*, col. 205.

[149] Friedberg, *Decretum*, cols. 205–206.

Dist. LIX deals with preparation and probation for those aspiring to the episcopate:

> Item qui ecclesiasticis disciplinis inbuti, et temporum approbatione discussi non sunt, ad summum sacerdotium non aspirent.[150]

In support of this position, Canon I cites a portion of the letter of Zosimus to Hesychius (*Epistle* 9.I.1) prescribing a long time of probation and preparation.[151] Canon II, from the same letter of Zosimus (*Epistle* 9.I.2), speaks of testing through each of the grades.[152] Canon III is from the letter of Gregory I to Syagrius *et al.* (*Reg.* 9.218) in which Gregory castigates the practice of ordaining a lay person to the episcopate and commends the *cursus* through the various ecclesiastical grades.[153] Canon IV, from the letter of Celestine to the bishops of Vienne and Narbonne (*Epistle* 4.4), notes that ordination to the episcopate without any of the lower offices is contrary to the decrees of the fathers, and commends the lower offices for strengthening and preparation.[154]

In *dist.* LX Gratian asks who may be promoted to sacred order, and who may not.[155] In reply, Canon IV repeats Canon I of the Council of Benevento (1091), which limits candidacy for episcopal election to those in holy order, i.e., the diaconate and the presbyterate, or with papal or metropolitical permission, the subdiaconate.[156] Gratian concludes:

> Alterum vero, ut in episcopum vel archiepiscopum nisi in sacris ordinibus constitutus non eligatur, propter dignitatem ordinis statutum est.[157]

In part I of *Distinctio* LXI Gratian again argues that members of the laity not be ordained to the episcopate, but proceed through each of the grades:

> Item laici non sunt in episcopum elegendi, sed per singulos ordines prius sunt probati.[158]

---

[150] Friedberg, *Decretum*, col. 224.

[151] Friedberg, *Decretum*, col. 225.

[152] Friedberg, *Decretum*, col. 225.

[153] Friedberg, *Decretum*, cols.225–226.

[154] Friedberg, *Decretum*, col. 226.

[155] Friedberg, *Decretum*, col. 226.

[156] Friedberg, *Decretum*, col. 227.

[157] Friedberg, *Decretum*, col. 227.

[158] Friedberg, *Decretum*, col. 227.

In support of this assertion, a variety of patristic papal texts are marshalled. For example, *dist.* LXI, Canon I is based on a portion of the letter of Gregory I to Brunhilda (*Reg.* 9.213), in which Gregory condemns the sudden ordination of lay men to the episcopate.[159] Canons II and III, from portions of the letter of Hormisdas to the Hispanic bishops (*Epistle* 25.I.2), cautions against the ordination of members of the laity to the episcopate and commends a long period of probation and preparation.[160] Canon IV, from a portion of the letter of Innocent to Aurelius of Carthage (*Epistle* 12), likens the teacher who has never been taught to the bishop who has never served in any other grade.[161] Canon V, from the letter of Leo to the bishops of Mauritania Caesariensis (*Epistle* 12.1–5), commends the *cursus* and the interstices in terms of probation and preparation.[162] Canon VII, from the letter of Celestine to the bishops of Apulia and Calabria (*Epistle* 5.2), condemns the ordination of members of the laity to the episcopate; such ordinations arise out of immoderate ambition and ignorance of the nature of church office.[163] Gratian concludes: *His omnibus auctoritatis laici prohibentur in episcopum eligi.*[164]

On the other hand, in part II of *Distinctio* LXI, Gratian cites three instances in which members of the laity have been elected bishops: Nicholas, Severus, and Ambrose:

> § 1. Econtra B. Nicolaus ex laico est electus in episcopum, B. Severus ex lanificio assumptus est in archiepiscopum, B. Ambrosius, cum nondum esset baptizatus, in archiepiscopum est electus. § 2. Sed sciendum est, quod ecclesiasticae prohibitiones proprias habent causas, quibus cessantibus cessant et ipsae. Ut enim laicus in episcopum non eligeretur, hec causa fuit, quia vita laicalis ecclesiasticis per ordinem non erudita nescit exempla religionis de se prestare aliis, que in se ipsa experimento non didicit. Cum ergo quilibet laicus merito suae perfectionis clericalem vitam transscendit, exemplo B. Nicholai et Severi et Ambrosii eius electio potest rata haberi.[165]

Gratian acknowledges the examples of a bishop Nicholas, an archbishop Severus, and Ambrose of Milan, who were elected to the episcopate from

---

[159] Friedberg, *Decretum*, col. 227.

[160] Friedberg, *Decretum*, cols. 227–228.

[161] Friedberg, *Decretum*, col. 228.

[162] Friedberg, *Decretum*, cols. 229–229.

[163] Friedberg, *Decretum*, cols. 229–230.

[164] Friedberg, *Decretum*, col. 230.

[165] Friedberg, *Decretum*, col. 230.

the laity. Gratian posits that the reason such elections are prohibited is the fact that a lay person who has not been instructed through the ecclesiastical grades cannot by experience demonstrate an example of reverence. When, therefore, a lay person by merit of his perfection ascends to the clerical life, his election may be approved by the example of Nicholas, Severus, and Ambrose. (Interestingly, Gratian does not discuss whether Ambrose or the others were ordained sequentially through the orders or not after their election.)

In reply, in Canon X, Gratian cites the first section of Canon XIII of the Council of Sardica, in the Dionysian form, that no one be put forward and ordained as a bishop, except those who have served as lectors, deacons, or presbyters.[166]

In *dist.* LXXVII Gratian again takes up questions about the *cursus honorum*, the interstices, and the ages of clerics. Gratian ends the preamble to the section:

> Ex monachis autem vel laicis nullus nisi per gradus ecclesiae ad summum sacerdotium debet pervenire.[167]

"No monk or lay person is to be a bishop except one who has passed through each of the grades." In support, Canon I cites the pseudo-Gaian decretal establishing the *cursus* from the Pseudo-Isidorian Decretals (although it is ascribed to Gelasius).[168] Canon II is based on the letter of Zosimus to Hesychius (*Epistle* 9.III.5), with some alterations, based on the version of the letter in the *Collectio canonum* of Anselm of Lucca.[169] Like Anselm, Gratian has omitted the distinction Zosimus made between child and adult candidates for the ecclesiastical grades:

> In singulis gradibus hec tempora sunt observanda, si ab infantia ecclesiasticis ministeriis nomen dederit, ut inter lectores et exorcistas quinquennio teneatur, exinde acolitus vel subdiaconus quatuordecim annis fiat, et sic ad benedictionem diaconatus, si meretur, accedat, in quo ordine quinque annis, si inculpate gesserit, adherere debebit. Exinde suffragantibus stipendiis, per tot gradus datis propriae fidei documentis, sacerdotium poterit promereri, de quo loco, si eum exactior vita ad bonos mores perduxerit, summum pontificatum sperare debebit. § 1. Defensores etiam ecclesiae, qui ex laicis fiunt, supradicta observatione teneantur, si meruerint in ordine esse clericatus.[170]

---

[166] Friedberg, *Decretum*, cols. 230–231.

[167] Friedberg, *Decretum*, col. 272.

[168] Friedberg, *Decretum*, col. 272.

[169] Thaner, *Collectio canonum*, p. 280.

[170] Friedberg, *Decretum*, col. 272.

Although Zosimus directs that children remain among the lectors until twenty years of age, Gratian (with Anselm) has altered the text to say that children dedicated to the clerical grades are lectors or exorcists for a five year period; afterwards they may be acolytes or subdeacons at fourteen years, deacons for five years, and so on. It is an adult who remains a lector or an exorcist for fifteen years. The alteration in Gratian's *Decretum*, transmitted by Anselm, serves to update the Zosiman text to the eleventh and twelfth centuries, particularly the age of the subdeacon.

Dist. LXXVII, Canon III is from the letter of Siricius to Himerius (*Epistle* 1.IX.13, X.14), the sequence of grades and the interstices faithfully reproduced.[171] Canon IV, from a "Sixth Synod," confirms that subdeacons are not to be ordained below twenty years of age.[172] Canon V, from Canon IV the Council of Carthage III, confirms twenty-five as the minimum age for deacons.[173] Canon VI, from canons XVI and XVII of the Council of Agde, confirms the age of deacons at twenty-five, and thirty for presbyters and bishops.[174] Canon VII, from Canon XX of the Council of Toledo IV, confirms twenty-five as the minimum age for deacons; thirty for presbyters.[175] Canons VIII and IX, from a portion of the letter of Gelasius to the bishops throughout Lucania, Bruttii, and Sicily (*Epistle* 14.2) permit the interstices to be reduced, while the sequence of the *cursus* must be observed.[176]

In *dist.* LXXVIII Gratian discusses the age (*etate*) of presbyters. Canon I, from Canon XI of the Council of Neocaesarea (attributed to Boniface) verifies thirty as the minimum age.[177] Canon II, from the *Cleros apud Iulian. Antec. constit. CXV. c. 19.*, confirming thirty as the minimum age for presbyters, twenty-five for deacons and subdeacons, eighteen for lectors, and forty for deaconesses.[178] Canon III, from the letter of Leo I to the bishops of Mauritania Caesariensis (*Epistle* 12.2) deals with the meaning of the expression "to impose hands suddenly" (from 1 Tim 5.22) and

---

[171] Friedberg, *Decretum*, cols. 272–273.

[172] Friedberg, *Decretum*, col. 273.

[173] Friedberg, *Decretum*, col. 273.

[174] Friedberg, *Decretum*, cols. 273–274.

[175] Friedberg, *Decretum*, col. 274.

[176] Friedberg, *Decretum*, cols.274–275.

[177] Friedberg, *Decretum*, col. 275.

[178] Friedberg, *Decretum*, col. 275.

concludes that it means to ordain someone before probation.[179] Canon IV, from Canon XI of the Council of Neocaesarea, confirms thirty as the minimum age for presbyters, because that was the age when Christ was baptized and began his ministry.[180] Canon V, however, from the letter of Pope Zacharias to Boniface (*Epistle* XIII) allows for presbyters to be ordained at age twenty-five in the case of necessity.[181]

The *Decretum Gratiani* assumes the practice of sequential ordination, according to the sequence of the *cursus honorum* fixed in the eleventh century. For Gratian, all the grades must be received; this is clear from *dist.* LII, and it is amplified throughout. It is not surprising given the volume of texts employed by Gratian, that the *Decretum* should contain so many texts on the clerical *cursus*. While Gratian clearly reflects the position finally achieved in the eleventh century on the immutability of the *cursus*, Gratian's collection also records the historic reasons behind the *cursus* and the interstices: selection, probation, preparation.

6. Ordination Liturgies

Like the ordination liturgies of the earlier periods, the rites of the eleventh and twelfth centuries reflect contemporary practice with regard to the *cursus honorum*. This section will survey two ordination liturgies: a textual variant of OR XXXV from the early eleventh century, and the *Pontificale romanum* of the twelfth century.

a. OR XXXV "B"

The manuscript used for Andrieu's OR XXXV of the tenth century[182] assumes that candidates for the episcopate will be either deacons *or* presbyters. The only possible exception in the rites of ordination to the episcopate for deacons and presbyters would be the anointing of the hands in the case of a deacon, who would offer the eucharistic liturgy for the first time in his capacity as a bishop.[183]

---

[179] Friedberg, *Decretum*, col. 275.

[180] Friedberg, *Decretum*, cols. 275–276.

[181] Friedberg, *Decretum*, col. 276.

[182] London: British Museum, Cod. Addit. 15222

[183] Andrieu, *Les Ordines Romani*, vol. 4, p. 45.

The manuscript Andrieu uses for his OR XXXV "B", the Alexandrinus 173,[184] is a small pontifical containing the rite for the consecration of a bishop. It was transcribed near Rome, a little after the year 1000,[185] though it was probably assembled *ca.* 975–1000.[186] The rite of episcopal ordination in the Alexandrinus is based on *Ordines* XXXIV and XXXV, and the PRG.

Unlike the tenth-century OR XXXV, the Alexandrinus assumes that a candidate for the episcopate will invariably be a presbyter. For instance, at the presentation of the candidate, the following questions are asked:

Interr.: Quo honore fungitur?

Resp. : P[res]b[ite]ratus.

Interr.: Quot annos habet in p[res]b[iter]atu?

Resp. : Decem.[187]

The same questions and answers are repeated in the examination of the candidate.[188] Thus, the candidate for the episcopate can only be a cleric who has been a presbyter for at least ten years. OR XXXV "B" is the first liturgical evidence noted in this study where a presbyter is unequivocally identified as the regular candidate for episcopal consecration. The exclusive ordination of presbyters to the episcopate corresponds to the practice in Rome from the eleventh century onwards, and in the Frankish church from the second half of the ninth century onwards. The ten-year interstice between the presbyterate and the episcopate, however, is reflected in neither the canonical texts nor the biographical information.

b. *Pontificale romanum saeculi XII*

The so-called *Pontificale romanum saeculi XII* (PR12) describes a family of rites rather than one single rite. As noted in the previous chapter, the PRG spread quickly throughout northern Europe in the tenth century and was introduced to Rome sometime late in the century, though there was no single version of the PRG in Rome. The twelfth-century liturgists, possibly from Monte Cassino, attempted to simplify and update the PRG, based on

---

[184] Rome, Biblioteca Alessandrina, Cod. lat. 173.

[185] Andrieu, *Les Ordines Romani*, vol. 4, p. 79.

[186] Vogel, *Medieval Liturgy*, p. 177.

[187] Andrieu, *Les Ordines Romani*, vol. 4, p. 99.

[188] Andrieu, *Les Ordines Romani*, vol. 4, p. 100.

its principal antecedent, the *Mainz Pontifical*. The variety of manuscripts which survive from the twelfth century are known by the generic title of *Pontificale romanum saeculi XII*, and are distinguished from one another depending on their degree of proximity to the PRG.

As noted earlier, the compilers of the PR12 sought to simplify and update the rites. This feature is certainly evident with respect to the *cursus honorum* in the ordination rites. For example, under section IX of the PR12, *Ordo qualiter in romana ecclesia diaconi et presbiteri eligendi sunt*, the Lyons manuscript[189] describes the presentation of the candidate for the diaconate as follows:

> Postquam introitum dixerint et caetera usque ad *Alleluia* sive tractum, veniat archidiaconus et vocet eum qui ordinandus est in diaconum, indutum quidem sicut subdiaconus debet indui in missa, sine tunica, et offerat eum pontifici ita dicendo:[190]

The four manuscripts[191] of the PR12 used in Andrieu's edition agree that the archdeacon presents the candidate to the pope with the words:

> Postulat mater ecclesia catholica ut hunc praesentem subdiaconum ad onus diaconii ordinetis.[192]

The text unequivocally asserts that only a subdeacon will be ordained to the diaconate; the Lyons manuscript directs the candidate to appear vested as a subdeacon (*indutum quidem sicut subdiaconus debet indui in missa*).[193]

After the presentation and before the litany in the rite for the ordination of a deacon, the Lyons manuscript adds:

> 6. Et tunc aliqui de circumstantibus attestentur eum esse dignum et iustum gratia Dei. Hoc peracto, si forte aliquis fuerit ibi ordinandus in sacerdotem, et ipsum quoque indutum more diaconi absque dalmatica vocet archidiaconus et offerat pontifici ita dicendo:
>
> Postulat mater ecclesia catholica ut hunc diaconem ad onus presbiterii ordinetis.[194]

---

[189] Lyons, Bibliothèque municipale, Cod. 570.

[190] M. Andrieu, *Le Pontifical Romain du XIIe Siècle, Le Pontifical Romain au Moyen-Age*, vol. 1, Studi e Testi, vol. 86 (Vatican: Biblioteca Apostolica Vaticana, 1938), p. 130.

[191] Lyons 570; London, British Museum, Add. 17005; Rome, Vatican Library, Barber. lat. 631; Rome, Vatican Library, Ottob. lat. 270.

[192] PR12, p. 130.

[193] PR12, p. 130.

[194] PR12, p. 131.

The clear expectation here is that the deacon will be ordained to the pres-byterate. The rubric and formula anticipate a liturgy in which both orders will be conferred. Again, sequential ordination between the diaconate and the presbyterate is accented by rubric, vesture, and formula.

The *cursus* between diaconate and presbyterate is further highlighted in the rite for the ordination of a presbyter. Three of the manuscripts [195] introduce the *Ordinatio presbiteri* as follows:

> Post lectionem autem et tractum atque letaniam, parato electo qui presbiter ordi-nandus est, diaconi more, orario tantum, et praesentantibus eum....[196]

The candidate for the presbyterate is a deacon and is vested as such. The corresponding text in the Lyons manuscript states:

> Consummatis omnibus quae supra diximus, de electione eius qui in presbiterum est ordinandus, et completa diaconi benedictione, si forte eodem die diaconus ordina-tus est (ordinatur enim aliquando presbiter ita quod eodem die non ordinatur diaconus, et e converso), tunc ille qui consecrandus est in presbiterum a duobus di-aconis deduci debet et dextera laevaque teneri usque ad presbiteros....[197]

Once again, there is the liturgical expectation of sequential ordination from the diaconate to the presbyterate. The rubric indicates, however, that one would not receive the two orders at the same liturgy.

The vesting of the new presbyter in the PR12, like the PRG, assumes that the candidate had been a deacon. The rubric for the giving of the stole states:

> Hic reflectat orarium super humerum dextrum, dicens ad eum: Accipe iugum do-mini....[198]

Like the corresponding text in the PRG, the rubric directs the stole to be changed over the right shoulder, meaning that previously it had been over the left shoulder only, that is, "deacon-wise."

Section X is the order for the calling, examination, and consecration of a bishop: *Incipit ordo ad vocandum et examinandum seu consecrandum electum in episcopum iuxta morem romanae ecclesiae.* The Lyons manu-script describes the entrance of the candidate for episcopal consecration:

---

[195] London, British Museum, Add. 17005; Rome, Vatican Library, Barber. lat. 631; Rome, Vatican Library, Ottob. lat. 270.

[196] PR12, p. 134.

[197] PR12, p. 134.

[198] PR12, p. 136.

> Sabbati die circa vesperam, sedente domno apostolico in atrio iuxta ecclesiam, ven-
> it archipresbiter illius ecclesiae, cuius electus consecrandus est, indutus alba et ca-
> sula, sicut deberet missam cantare, quem iunior diaconus cardinalis deducere debet
> et tenere per manuum dextram et subdiaconus per manuum sinistram. Et aliqui de
> clericis eiusdem electi, cum superpelliciis vel cappis, ipsum archipresbiterum
> modeste et decenter prosequantur....[199]

While the *indutus alba et casula* might refer to the archpresbyter, it seems equally likely that it refers to the candidate, who is accompanied by a deacon on the right hand and a subdeacon on the left. If this interpretation is accurate, it marks another instance of a liturgical expectation that the episcopal candidate is a presbyter, vested to sing the Mass.

Similar to OR XXXV "B", in the presentation of the candidate, the following questions and answers are given:

> Interrogatio: Quo honore fungitur?
> Resp. : Presbiteratu.
> Interrogatio: Quot annos habuit in presbiteratu?
> Resp. : Decem.[200]

The Lyons manuscript adds: *Si plures vel pauciores in presbiteratu annos habeat, certum tempus respondit.*[201] Clearly episcopal candidates are presbyters. Normally there will be an interstice of ten years, though from the Lyons manuscript it is evident that there is flexibility in terms of the interval spent in the presbyterate.

After the epistle, during the singing of the gradual, the PR12 directs the candidate to appear in pontifical vesture. Three of the manuscripts[202] direct the candidate to be vested in dalmatic, chasuble, and episcopal sandals; in addition the Lyons manuscript directs the candidate to wear a tunicle.[203] The implication here is that a bishop has received the (subdiaconate,) diaconate and presbyterate.

The rubric for the anointing of the new bishop's hands in the PR12 suggests sequential ordination from the presbyterate to the episcopate. The Frankish *Unguantur manus istae de oleo....* formula has been removed from the rite. Whereas the rubric in the PRG read: *Completa benedictione,*

---

[199] PR12, p. 138.

[200] PR12, p. 139.

[201] PR12, p. 139.

[202] London, British Museum, Add. 17005; Rome, Vatican Library, Barber. lat. 631; Rome, Vatican Library, Ottob. lat. 270.

[203] PR12, p. 145.

confirmat pollicem consecrati cum christmate, dicens...,[204] the corresponding texts in the PR12 directs:

> Completa benedictione, confirmat manum et pollicem consecrat cum crismate, dicens: Deus et pater domini Iesu Christi....[205]

While the text of the PRG speaks of "confirming" the thumb after the consecration of the hand, the PR12 speaks of "confirming" the hand, and consecrating the thumb. As Andrieu comments on this modification:

> Le choix des termes est intentionnel....Quant aux mains, le mot «confirmer» indique qu'il ne s'agit que de ratifier, de corroborer une consécration antérieure, celle qui avait eu lieu au cours de l'ordination presbytérale du nouveau prélat. Consacrées en cette circonstance, les mains de l'ordinand n'ont pas à l'être une seconde fois. C'est pourquoi on supprime la formule du Romano-germanique *Unguantur manus istae...* Cependent cette consécration déjà ancienne sera revivifée, «confirmée», en même temps que le pouce sera consacré.[206]

By the eleventh and twelfth centuries, the practice of ordaining clerics sequentially through the grades is reflected in the rites of ordination. These same features are evidenced in the subsequent (so-called) Pontifical of the Roman Curia of the XIIIth Century,[207] and even more so in the Pontifical of William Durandus.[208]

7. Medieval Literature on Holy Orders

Theologians of the eleventh and twelfth centuries, like the canonists, addressed a variety of issues, including holy orders. While the *cursus honorum* and the interstices were relatively low on the theologians' lists of priorities, theological tracts of the period nonetheless reflect something of the place sequential ordination played in the medieval theology of orders.

---

[204] PRG, p. 220.

[205] PR12, p. 149.

[206] Andrieu, "La Carrière Ecclésiastique," p. 105.

[207] M. Andrieu, *Le Pontifical de la curie Romaine au XIIIe Siècle, Le Pontifical Romain au Moyen-Age*, vol. 2, Studi e Testi, vol. 87 (Vatican: Biblioteca Apostolica Vaticana, 1940), pp. 337–353.

[208] M. Andrieu, *Le Pontifical de Guillaume Durand, Le Pontifical Romain au Moyen-Age*, vol. 3, Studi e Testi, vol. 88 (Vatican: Biblioteca Apostolica Vaticana, 1940), pp. 358–377.

This section will examine the *Acta synodi Atrebatensis* of Gerard of Cambrai and the *De excellentia sacrorum ordinum et de vita ordinandorum in synodo habitus* of Ivo of Chartres from the eleventh century. From the twelfth century, the treatment of order in the *De sacramentis of Hugh of St. Victor and the Sententiae* of Peter Lombard will be examined.

a. Gerard of Cambrai

The northern French bishop, Gerard Florens of Cambrai (*ca.* 1012–1051) is an example of an early eleventh-century, pre-Gregorian, theologian. Chapter VI of Gerard's "Acts of the Synod of Arras (*Acta synodi Atrebatensis*), entitled *De sacris ordinibus*, is a brief tract on holy orders.[209] Gerard discusses each of the orders in terms of origin, function, and the rite of ordination. Gerard draws largely from the *Etymologiae* of Isidore, the Ordinals of Christ, and the *Statuta ecclesiae antiqua.*

While Gerard deals with each of the orders sequentially, there is nothing in the text of *De sacris ordinibus* which deals with, or reflects, sequential movement from one grade to another. It is possible that such movement is simply assumed by Gerard.

Towards the end of the tract Gerard cites a variety of texts from the pastoral epistles on the imposition of hands and the bishop's office. The last two biblical texts specified are from the first letter to Timothy in which the pseudo-Pauline author instructs Timothy not to impose hands suddenly (1 Tim 5.22) and warns against making a neophyte a bishop (1 Tim. 3.6):

....Jam vero, quod saeculares viri nequaquam ad ministerium Ecclesiae assumantur, eadem apostolica auctoritas docet et dicit: «Manus nemini cito imposueris.» Et iterum: «Non neophytum, ne in superbia elatus» putet se non tam ministerium humilitatis quam administrationem saecularis potestatis adeptum, et in condemnationem superbiae sicut diabolus per jactantiam dejiciatur. Non enim valebit saecularis homo sacerdotii magisterium implere, cujus nec officium tenuit, nec disciplinam cognovit, sed neque docere potest quod non didicit.[210]

Gerard writes that it is inappropriate to confer on "a man of the world, who has held no office and does not know the discipline, the teaching office (*magisterium*) of the priesthood." Following Siricius, Celestine, Leo, Hormisdas, and Gregory, he adds that such a person cannot teach what he has not learned.

---

[209] *PL* 142.1291–1294.

[210] *PL* 142.1294.

It is possible that the abuse Gerard condemns here is simony, whereby worldly men—*saeculares viri*—who have held no office and are ignorant of ecclesiastical discipline, are being promoted through the *cursus* to the episcopate. This abuse is likely associated with the proliferation of simony. While not dealing explicitly with the *cursus honorum*, Gerard elucidates the classical reasons behind it, that is, preparation and probation.

Gerard is often cited as an early eleventh-century example of the revival of "patristic presbyterianism."[211] In the "Acts of the Synod of Arras" Gerard reflects the diminished view of the episcopate in identifying the diaconate and the presbyterate (i.e., levites and priests) as the original grades of the church.[212]

b. Ivo of Chartres

Ivo, bishop of Chartres (*ca.* 1040–1115) was one of the most important theologian-canonists of the eleventh century. Two of Ivo's canonistic collections, the *Panormia* and the *Decretum*, have already been noted. This section will examine a short tract by Ivo on holy orders, the *De excellentia sacrorum ordinum, et de vita ordinandorum, in synodo habitus*, designated in the standard editions simply as *Sermo II*.[213] On the significance of *Sermo II*, Reynolds comments:

> As a tract on orders, *Sermo II* ranks, with Isidore's tracts and several works of the ninth century, as a major landmark in the theological exposition of the sacrament of orders.[214]

Sermo II would be used in the *De sacramentis Christianae fidei* of Hugh of St. Victor and in the *Sententiae* of Peter Lombard.

Like the *De sacris ordinibus* of Gerard of Cambrai, *Sermo II* discusses the functions of each of the clerical grades, their origins, and their rites of ordination. He draws on sources such as the *De ecclesiasticis officiis* of Isidore of Seville, the Ordinals of Christ, and the *Statuta ecclesiae antiqua*. Unlike Gerard, Ivo in *Sermo II* does portray sequential movement through the grades. In the introduction to the seven orders in *Sermo II* Ivo writes:

---

[211] E.g., Reynolds, "Patristic 'Presbyterianism'," p. 329.

[212] *PL* 142.1291.

[213] After the Hittorp-Fronteau edition of the text, *PL* 162.513–519.

[214] Roger Reynolds, "Ivonian Opuscula on the Ecclesiastical Officers," *Mélanges Gerard Fransen, Studia Gratiana*, vol. 20 (1976), p. 312.

....Si ergo ad ambulandum in via Dei, sicut praetaxatum est, affecti estis, et clerici vocari digni estis, et ad majora militiae clericalis officia promoveri. Haec officia septem gradibus sunt distincta, quia sancta Ecclesia septiformis gratiae est munere decorata. Haec officia in propria persona Dominus noster ostendit, et Ecclesiae suae exhibenda reliquit: ut forma quae praecesserat in capite repraesentaretur in corpore.[215]

"Whoever is worthy to be called to the clergy," Ivo states, "is promoted to the clerical militia; there are seven grades because the church is adorned by sevenfold graces."

References to sequential ordination can be found in the sentences introducing the various grades in *Sermo II*. In introducing the doorkeeper, Ivo states: *In his septem officiis primus gradus est ostiariorum*....[216] The section on the lector begins: *Inde promovetur ad officium lectorum*....;[217] the exorcist with the words: *Tertio loco sequitur ordo exorcistam*....;[218] the acolyte with the words: *Quarto loco accedunt acolyti*....;[219] and the subdeacon with the words: *Quinto loco ordinantur subdiaconi*....[220] The terms of movement Ivo uses (*promoveatur, sequitur, accedunt,* and *ordinantur*) clearly indicate sequential movement from one order to the next.

Ivo introduces his treatment of the diaconate by stating:

Diaconorum ordo est in sexto loco, non sine aliquo senarii mysterio, quo, propter sui perfectionem, significatur operum perfectio....[221]

Following Augustine, Ivo speaks of the order of deacons in the sixth place, but not without the "some mysteries" of the "sixness" (*senarii*). This could be taken to mean that the office of deacon requires the lower orders. The diaconate is the only grade in *Sermo II* for which Ivo provides any indication of age. Deacons must be twenty and older: "*a viginti autem annis et supra....*", based on the ages of Levites in the Old Testament.[222] Ivo

---

[215] *PL* 162.514.
[216] *PL* 162.514.
[217] *PL* 162.514.
[218] *PL* 162.515.
[219] *PL* 162.515.
[220] *PL* 162.515.
[221] *PL* 162.516.
[222] *PL* 162.516.

discusses the importance of testing candidates for the diaconate, based on biblical texts from the first letter to Timothy.[223]

In the section on the seventh order, the "priesthood", Ivo discusses the distinctions between presbyters and bishops, but includes no reference to sequential movement between the two grades.

While Ivo does not specifically reflect upon, nor advocate the *cursus honorum* in *Sermo II*, sequential movement from one order to the next (at least from doorkeeper to deacon) is explicit. This witness in *Sermo II* is noteworthy, when compared to Gerard of Cambrai's *Acta synodi Atrebatensis* a generation earlier. Although the two texts are similar in content and in the sources used, Gerard makes no reference to the *cursus* while Ivo explicitly recognises it.

c. Hugh of St. Victor

The first twelfth-century commentator on holy orders to be examined is Hugh of St. Victor. Little is known about Hugh (d. 1142), though his works dealt with a variety of topics from grammar and geometry, to theology and biblical commentaries. This section will consider his treatment of the clerical grades and the *cursus honorum* in the *De sacramentis Christianae fidei*. The *De sacramentis* relies heavily on Ivo's *Sermo II*.

In Book II, part III of *De sacramentis*, entitled *De ecclesiasticis ordinibus*, Hugh contemplates the clerical grades. He discusses the biblical origins of the grades, their functions, and the rites of ordination. Interspersed are sections from the Ordinal of Christ material from Ivo. Hugh's sources here also include the *Statuta ecclesiae antiqua*, Isidore's *De ecclesiasticis ordinibus*, particularly the material on the diaconate.

Hugh includes various references to the *cursus honorum*. In Book II, part III, cap. V, *De septem gradibus sacris*, he writes:

Primum igitur signaculum clerici corona est, quo in partem ministerii sacri consignatur. Sequuntur deinde septem graduum promotiones, in quibus per spiritualem potestatem altius semper ad sacra tranctanda [*sic.*] conscendit, primus gradus est ostiariorum; secundus lectorum; tertius exorcistarum; quartus acolytharum, quintus subdiaconorum; sextus diaconorum; septimus sacerdotum. Hic gradus dispares in eodem ordine habet dignitates. Nam post sacerdotes altiores sunt principes sacerdotum, id est, episcopi....[224]

---

[223] *PL* 162.517.

[224] *PL* 176.423.

Hugh speaks of the "seven promotions in the grades" in which, through spiritual power, one rises to the sacred *tranctanda*. Hugh also links the sevenfold orders to the sevenfold graces distributed to the church, which Jesus fulfilled in his life.[225]

Hugh does not introduce his discussion on the orders with language suggesting sequential movement as did Ivo, though like Ivo he does say in cap. XI, *De diaconis* that the diaconate is not complete without the other mysteries:

> Diaconorum ordo sexto sequitur loco, non sine aliquo senarii mysterio, in quo propter perfectionem sui significatur operum perfectio.[226]

Hugh likewise assigns twenty as the minium age for deacons in this section.[227] In *De diaconis* Hugh cites biblical texts from the First Letter to Timothy insisting that candidates for the diaconate be tested, that they serve without crime.[228] This section shows clear dependence on *Sermo II*.

In cap. XIII, *De episcopis*, Hugh refers to sequential ordination prior to the episcopate:

> Sacri canones definiunt nullum in episcopum eligendum, nisi qui prius in sacris ordinibus religiose fuerit conversatum. Sacros autem ordines diaconatus et presbyteratus tantum appellandos censent; quia hos solos primitiva legitur Ecclesia habuisse, et de his solis praeceptum habemus apostoli. Subdiaconos tamen quia et ipsi sacris altaribus administrant, opportunitate exigente in episcopos eligi concedunt. Sed rarissime et ipsum non sine Romani pontificis sive metropolitani licentia; si tamen spectatae sit religionis, et probabilis scientiae....[229]

As defined in the sacred canons, in particular Canon I of the Council of Benevento (1091) only those who are presbyters and deacons, and in exceptional circumstances, subdeacons, may be elected to the episcopate. Interestingly, Hugh identifies the diaconate and the presbyterate because they are the only orders found in the primitive church and in the ordinances of Paul. A reason for citing this canon is to demonstrate that the episcopate cannot be considered an order independent of the presbyterate.[230] Cap.

---

[225] *PL* 176.423.

[226] *PL* 176.426.

[227] *PL* 176.426.

[228] *PL* 176.427.

[229] *PL* 176.430.

[230] Reynolds, "Patristic 'Presbyterianism'," p. 339.

XIII is another instance of the eleventh-century revival of patristic 'presbyterian' theories.

In cap. XXI, *Quae aetate ordinandi sunt qui ordinantur*, Hugh addresses the minimum ages of clerics:

> De aetate vero ordinandrum [*sic.*] talem nobis definitio sacrae Scripturae discretionem reliquit. Ut subdiaconus quidem non ordinetur ante quartuordecim annos; nec diaconus ante viginti quinque, nec presbyter ante triginta, quatentus deinceps si dignus inventus fuerit in episcopum eligi possit.[231]

Reflecting the decretal of Pope Nicholas II to the Council of Rome in 1059, the minimum age for subdeacons is fourteen. Hugh confirms the traditional ages of twenty-five and thirty for deacons and presbyters respectively; one recalls that in cap. XI, *De diaconis*, Hugh set the minimum age for deacons at twenty. Hugh does not identify an age limit for bishops, though it could not have been less than thirty, the age set for presbyters.

Cap. XXI commends an eleven year interstice between the subdiaconate and the diaconate, a five year interstice between the diaconate and the presbyterate, and no specified interstice between the presbyterate and the episcopate. A possible reason for explaining why no interval is prescribed between the presbyterate and the episcopate is the fact that when deacons were elected bishops in the eleventh century, they were regularly ordained presbyter first, sometimes weeks or days prior to episcopal ordination. Since the interval between presbyteral and episcopal ordinations was frequently a matter of days, it was easier for Hugh to remain silent on the minimum age of bishops and the interval between the presbyterate and the episcopate.

While Hugh of St. Victor neither prescribes nor reflects any new developments in terms of the clerical *cursus* in *De sacramentis*, he does reflect sequential movement through the grades.

d. Peter Lombard

One of the greatest of the twelfth-century theologians was Peter Lombard (*ca.* 1100–1160), the "Master of the Sentences", and bishop of Paris. His most important work is the *Sententiarum libri quattuor*, written *ca.* 1155–1158. Peter Lombard discusses holy orders in Book IV, *dist.* 24, of the *Sententiae*.

---

[231] *PL* 176.432.

ter Lombard describes the orders, their functions and origins, and
ᴜ. rites of ordination. His treatment of the clerical grades was greatly dependent on sources such as the *Statuta ecclesiae antiqua*, Isidore's *De ecclesiasticis ordinibus* and the *Etymologiae*, the pseudo-Isidorian *Epistula
ad Leudefredum*, various patristic sources, Ivo's *Sermo II*, Hugh of St. Victor's *De sacramentis*, and Gratian's *Decretum*.

In cap. 2 of *dist.* 24, Peter Lombard asks: *Quare septem sunt?* In the response he states:

> Septem autem sunt propter septiformem gratiam Spiritus Sancti: cuius qui non sunt
> participes, ad gradus ecclesiasticos indigne accendunt; illi vero in quorum menti-
> bus diffusa est septiformis gratia Spiritus Sancti, cum ad ecclesiasticos ordines ac-
> cedunt, in ipsa spiritualis gradus promotione ampliorem gratiam percipere
> creduntur.[232]

Like the theologians before him, Peter Lombard configures the sevenfold ministry to the sevenfold gifts of the Spirit. For Peter Lombard, however, promotion though the grades is seen as receiving an increase of
spiritual grace. One can conclude that an omission of any of the grades
would imply an incompleteness for the fulfilling of one's particular office.

Peter Lombard's descriptions of the grades do not reflect specific
movement from one grade to another. His introduction to the diaconate,
dist. 24.10, is an abbreviation of that used by Hugh and Ivo:

> Diaconorum ordo sextum tenet locum, propter senarii perfectionem.[233]

He has omitted the expression *"non sine aliquo senarii mysterio, in quo
propter perfectionem sui significatur operum perfectio"* found in both Ivo
and Hugh of St. Victor. Like Ivo and Hugh of St. Victor, Peter Lombard
cites biblical texts from 1 Timothy requiring the probation of deacons.[234]

In *dist.* 25, cap. 7, Peter Lombard discusses the ages of clerics. He cites
Nicholas I (858–867):

> Sacri, inquit, canones sanxerunt ut subdiaconus non ordinetur ante quatuordecim
> annos, nec diaconus ante viginti quinque, nec presbyter ante triginta. Deinde, si
> dignus fuerit, ad episcopatum eligi potest. Quod nos etiam pari modo servare iube-
> mus.[235]

---

[232] Peter Lombard, *Libri IV sententiarum*, ed. PP Collegii S. Bonaventurae, *Magistri Petri
Lombardi Parisiensis episcopi Sententiae in IV libris distinctae*, vol. 2 (Grottaferrata:
1981), p. 394.

[233] Peter Lombard *Libri IV*, p. 401.

[234] Peter Lombard, *Libri IV*, p. 402.

[235] Peter Lombard, *Libri IV*, p. 415.

This cap. is similar to the corresponding text in the *De sacramentis* of Hugh of St. Victor (Book II, part III, cap. XXI),[236] though Peter Lombard ascribes it to Nicholas I.[237] The canon is surely based on the decretal of Nicholas II (1058–1061) to the Council of Rome (1059) though as noted above in Hugh's treatment of the same decretal, Nicholas II does not discuss the episcopate.

None of the four theologians surveyed explicitly prescribes or advocates the *cursus honorum*; in a sense, for them sequential movement from one grade to the next was past the point of needing comment. Ivo's *Sermo II* is the text which is the most explicit about actual movement from one grade of the *cursus* to the next.

A significant step, however, in this period, is the theological reflection upon the sevenfold gifts of the Spirit and the sevenfold clerical *cursus*. Already evident in the writings of Ivo and Hugh of St. Victor, the association between the sevenfold gifts and the seven grades culminates in the *Sententiae* of Peter Lombard who links promotion through the seven clerical grades to the reception or increase of the sevenfold gifts of the Spirit: the more grades, the more gifts of the Spirit. This equation makes sequential movement from one grade to the next even more of a theological imperative.

It is interesting to note that Gerard of Cambrai in the first half of the eleventh century alludes to the classic reasons behind the *cursus honorum*, namely preparation and probation. These reasons, however, are not reflected in the later writers; Ivo, Hugh, and Peter Lombard (all citing 1 Timothy 3.10) do insist, though, that deacons must be tested. With the latter, however, the accent has shift from pastoral and canonical motives for the *cursus honorum* to a more theological justification by associating the ascent through the clerical grades with the seven-fold gifts of the Holy Spirit.

---

[236] *PL* 176.432.

[237] The editor of the *Sententiae*, however, says that this passage is not found among the writings of Nicholas I: *Non invenitur inter decreta vel alia scripta Nicolai I, Libri IV*, p. 415, n. 3.

8. Biographical Material

Biographical information about the careers of bishops in the eleventh and twelfth centuries corresponds with the conciliar, papal, canonistic, and liturgical evidence of the *cursus honorum* from the period. The liturgical and canonical documents of the eleventh and twelfth centuries presuppose that candidates for episcopal ordination would invariably be presbyters. This presupposition did not mean that deacons (and others) ceased to be elected bishops. Once elected, however, they were required to be ordained to the presbyterate prior to episcopal consecration, in accordance with the (now) uniform practice of the *cursus honorum*.

This section will examine information about the clerical careers of bishops first from Rome, and secondly from Italy, France, and England.

a. The Roman Church

Once again, one is indebted to M. Andrieu's article, "La carrière ecclésiastique des papes et les documents liturgiques du moyen âge". As noted in the previous chapter, the last deacons to be elected and ordained directly to the episcopate in Rome were Benedict V (964–966), Benedict VI (973–974), and the antipope Boniface VIII (974, 984–985). In the tenth and eleventh centuries bishops of Rome tended to be elected from among the presbyters or the bishops of other sees. Yet in the last quarter of the eleventh century there was a recovery of the practice of electing deacons. In the late eleventh and twelfth centuries several deacons were elected bishop of Rome; these, however, were all ordained presbyters prior to episcopal consecration.

The first deacon elected as bishop of Rome to receive presbyteral ordination prior to episcopal ordination was Gregory VII in 1073. As Bonizo of Sutri has recorded the event:

> Nam in ieiunio pentecostes sacerdos ordinatur, et in natale apostolorum ad altare eorundem a cardinalibus secundum antiquum morem episcopus consecratur.[238]

As a deacon, Hildebrand was archdeacon of Rome when he was elected pope on April 22, 1073. Bonizo says that he was ordained a presbyter—

---

[238] Bonizo of Sutri, *Liber ad amicum* VII, in P. Jaffé, *Monumenta Gregoriana*, Bibliotheca Rerum Germanicarum 2 (Berlin: Weidmann's, 1865), p. 657.

sacerdos—on the Pentecost ember days (May 22) and ordained a bishop on June (29 or) 30.[239]

The election and subsequent ordinations to the presbyterate and episcopate of Gregory VII mark the *terminus ad quem* for the study of the *cursus honorum* in the Western church. This event marks the acceptance by the church of Rome, and ultimately the Western church, of the complete sequence of the *cursus honorum* from doorkeeper to bishop. As Andrieu has commented on the incident:

> Quand le diacre Hildebrand, élu au souverain pontificat depuis le 22 avril, se fit ordonner prêtre, le 22 mai 1073, aux Quatre-Temps de la Pentecôte, il ne se doutait vraisemblablement pas qu'il renouait avec l'ancienne discipline officielle du Siège apostolique par l'intermédiaire de la liturgie franque.[240]

One must add that an interval of thirty-nine days between the reception of the presbyterate and ordination to the episcopate, however, was hardly part of the "ancienne discipline officielle" of the see of Rome.

Twelfth-century bishops of Rome were similarly elected from the diaconate. Gelasius II (1118–1119) had been a cardinal deacon and chancellor for nearly thirty years when elected pope in 1118. The *Liber pontificalis* relates:

> ....Omnibus igitur undique congregatis, conferabatur ab illis quando certis temporibus papa et promoveri pariter et consecrari deberet. Et quidem diaconus, non presbyter erat.[241]

> .... existente clero ac populo infinito, sancto dictante Spiritu et effectus est presbiter et in papam Gelasium infra k[al]. martii consecratus.[242]

He was ordained to the presbyterate on March 9, and was consecrated to the episcopate on the following day.[243]

Innocent II (1130–1143) was a cardinal deacon when he was (clandestinely) elected pope. As recorded in the *Annales de Margan* he was first ordained a presbyter:

> Hoc anno 16. Kalendas martii defunctus est Papa Honorius apud sanctum Gregorium et in crastino, id est 15. Kal. eiusdem, electus est Gregorius diaconus cardinalis sancti Angeli in Apostolatum, qui et Innocentius nominatus est, et sexta die, scilicet

---

[239] Jaffé I, p. 599.

[240] Andrieu, "Le sacre épiscopal," p. 29.

[241] LP II, p. 314; *cf.* p. 320, n. 24.

[242] LP II, p. 315; *cf.* p. 320, n. 31.

[243] Jaffé I, p. 775.

sequenti sabbata post proximum, ordinatur in presbyterum, in die Cathedrae sancti Petri, et in crastino consecratus est in summum Pontificem apud sanctam Mariam novam. Eo die et Petrus Leonis consecratus est in Apostolicatam apud sanctum Petrum.[244]

Innocent's rival for the papacy, Cardinal Peter (Anacletus II) was already a presbyter; the two were consecrated bishops on the same day.

Celestine III (1191–1198) was eighty-five years old and a cardinal deacon when elected pope; he too was first ordained a presbyter. The event is recorded in Ansbertus's *Historia de expeditione Friderici imperatoris*:

Ipse etiam dominus Papa, prius diaconus et circa mediam quadragesimam recenter electus, sabbato quo dicitur *Sitientes* sacerdos est factus et in die paschae, hoc est XVIII kal. *maii*. Papa est consecratus, qui statim proxima die ipsum regem et reginam augustali dignitate excellenter sublimavit.[245]

Innocent III (1198–1216), perhaps the greatest of the medieval popes, was cardinal deacon of St. Sergius and St. Bacchus when he was elected pope on January 8, 1198. The *Gesta Innocenti papae*, cap. VII, records:

Celebrata est ejus electio sexto Idus Januarii, anno Incarnationis Dominicae millesimo centesimo nonagesimo septimo. Et, quia tunc diaconus erat, dilata est ejus ordinatio in presbyterum usque ad Sabbatum Quatuor Temporum, Nonas Kalendas Martii; et sequenti Dominica, in qua tunc occurrit festum Cathedrae sancti Petri, fuit apud Sanctum Petrum in episcopum consecratus, et in ejusdem apostoli cathedra constitutus, non sine manifesto signo et omnibus admirando....[246]

He was ordained a presbyter on February 21, and a bishop on the next day.

b. Italy, France, England

The instances of deacons being elected bishops, with a presbyteral ordination immediately prior to episcopal consecration, were not limited to the Roman church. For instance, the *Annales Ordinis S. Benedicti* (Book I part LX, cap. XXXIII) record that in 1053 a deacon named Peter was elected bishop of the diocese of Anicium (Puy-en-Velay):

His auditis, electum apud se sisti jubet pontifex, ab ipso consecrandum: quem, quia tantum diaconus erat, Humbertus Silvae—candidae episcopus primo presbyterum

---

[244] qtd. in J.M. Watterich, *Pontificum Romanorum vitae*, vol. 2 (Aalen: Scientia Verlag, 1966), p. 190; Jaffé I, pp. 841–842.

[245] qtd. in Watterich, *Pontificum*, vol. 2, pp. 708–709; Jaffé II, p. 578.

[246] *PL* 214.xx.

ordinavit, eumdemque alia die pontifex apud Arminium cum Heinrico Ravennatis
ecclesiae electo episcopum consecravit.[247]

The bishop of this see was traditionally ordained by the pope. On March
13, 1053, Peter was ordained a presbyter by Cardinal Humbert. The following day he was ordained a bishop by Leo IX.

Similar circumstances are observed in the election of Alfanus as archbishop of Salerno in 1058. The *Chronica Casinense* (Book I, part II, cap.
96) records:

....ipse Romam reversus Alfanum olim Desiderii socium, Salternitae tunc sedis
electum secum duxit, eumque in jejuniis Martii primo presbyterum, dehinc sequenti dominica archiepiscopum consecrans, cum honore Salernum remisit.[248]

Evidently Alfanus was a deacon when elected bishop. He was ordained a
presbyter by Stephen IX during the March ember days, and ordained bishop by the pope on the following Sunday, that is, March 8, 1058.

The *Chronicon Hugonis* (Book I, cap. II) describes the *cursus* of Hugh,
named bishop-elect of Die in 1073:

....Non multo post ipse qui commendabatur advenit, et quia solam clericatus ton-
suram habebat—detestabatur enim Symoniacorum ordinationes—, in mense De-
cembrio per manum ejus usque ad presbiteratus gradum promotus est, cum hoc
aliqui calumpniarentur Romanorum, et promerent morem sanctae Romanae ecclesiae, neminem licet electum antistitem a papa ordinandum nisi in eadem deserviret
aecclesia. Quod tamen in ipso domnus autentica potestate sua fecit; complacuerat
enim sibi in illo anima ejus. In quadragesima vero, sabbato in presbiterum, et sequenti Dominica ad missas in episcopum consecratus est....[249]

Evidently at the time of his election Hugh was a member of the laity; he
had only received the tonsure. In December of 1073, Gregory VII ordained
Hugh sequentially through the grades of the *cursus* "*usque ad presbiteratus gradum*", that is, from doorkeeper to deacon, inclusive. In 1074, on the
Saturday before Lent (*Quadragesima*) Gregory VII ordained Hugh to the
presbyterate and consecrated him bishop on the following day. Again,
presbyteral ordination is closely linked with consecration to the episcopate.

---

[247] J. Mabillon, *Annales Ordinis S. Benedicti*, vol. IV (Lucae: Typis Leonardo Venturini,
1739), p. 495; *cf.* appendix, cap. LXX, pp. 680–681.

[248] *PL* 173.704.

[249] *PL* 154.276.

The *Gesta Virdunensium episcoporum et abbatum* of Laurence of Liège (cap. 15) records that in 1106, Richard of Verdun was chosen archbishop of Rheims:

> Ante illos dies Remorum archiepiscopus Manasses vita decesserat, et illa ecclesia Richardum Virdunensem archidiaconum in pastorem sibi elegerat; .... Proinde Paschalis papa per litteras et legatum suum praedictum Albanensem episcopum eidem archidiacono mandavit, ut ab ipso Albanorum praesule in diaconum ordinaretur—erat enim adhuc subdiaconus—et sic consecraretur Remorum archiepiscopus....[250]

Although he exercised the office of archdeacon of Verdun at the time of his election, Richard of Verdun was in subdeacon's orders. Hence, Pascal II ordered the bishop of Albano to ordain him to the diaconate. The text indicates that the bishop of Albano was then directed to consecrate him to the episcopate. There is no mention of an intervening ordination to the presbyterate; given the theological climate, one can assume, however, that such an ordination did occur, probably on the day before Richard was ordained to the episcopate. The text is more concerned with the fact that Richard was a subdeacon when he was appointed archbishop-elect of Rheims. One recalls Canon V of the Council of Clermont-Ferrand (1095) and Canon I of the Council of Benevento (1091) which discouraged such elections.

A much celebrated instance of a deacon being elected to the episcopate is the election of Thomas Becket (*ca* 1118–1170) as archbishop of Canterbury in 1162. Becket had been ordained a deacon and appointed archdeacon of Canterbury in 1154. As historian David Knowles has observed, little is known about the early career of Thomas Becket prior to his appointment as archdeacon of Canterbury.[251] One of his biographers, Herbert of Bosham sketches Becket's appointment to the diaconate and the office of archdeacon in the *Vita S. Thomae* (Book II.6):

> Et ita inspiratus a Deo pontifex Theobaldus Thomam, quem prius secundum formam canonam ad alios inferios ordines, postea in levitam, simul etiam et ecclesiae suae archilevitam....[252]

According to canonical form, Becket had been admitted to the minor orders, and then deacon and archdeacon.

---

[250] *PL* 204.940.

[251] David Knowles, *Thomas Becket* (London: Adam & Charles Black, 1970), p. 27.

[252] Herbert of Bosham, *Vita Sancti Thomae, archiepiscopi et martyris*, ed. J. C. Robertson, *Rerum Britannicarum Medii Aevi Scriptores* (Rolls Series) 67.3 (London: KrausReprints Ltd., 1965), p. 168.

In 1155 Henry II appointed Becket chancellor of England. In 1162 Henry nominated him to the see of Canterbury. Herbert of Bosham's *Vitae S. Thomae* (Book III.4) describes Becket's ordinations to the presbyterate and the episcopate:

> ....Igitur in sacramentali illo tempore, in illis tam mirae quam mirificae unctionis diebus, in hebdomada Pentecostes, in hebdomadae sabbato, temporis et ordinis, ut mox claruit, consonantibus sacramentis, archilevita ecclesiae electus in sacerdotem ordinatur, in crastino Dominicae diei in antistem consecrandus....[253]

Herbert describes how the archdeacon was ordained a presbyter on the Saturday after Pentecost, and bishop on Trinity Sunday, that is, June 2 and 3, 1162.

The relatively few pieces of biographical information referred to from the Roman church, as well as sees in Italy, France, and England, amply corroborate the evidence from the conciliar, canonistic, and liturgical sources that by the eleventh century there is an unequivocal sequence between the presbyterate and the episcopate, in terms of ordination. There is, however, no corresponding *cursus* in terms of election to the episcopate; deacons, subdeacons, and even untonsured laity continue to be elected to episcopal office. They must receive all the grades of the *cursus honorum*, including the presbyterate. The liturgical rites assume a ten-year interstice between the presbyterate and the episcopate; in reality it was often shorter, on occasion no more than twenty-four hours.

9. Summary

While the exact hierarchical sequence of the minor orders in the West was consummated by the tenth-century PRG, the sequence of the major orders a cleric might receive varied until the eleventh century. In the Frankish church the presbyterate was required for ordination to the episcopate by at least the late ninth century, while at Rome deacons were admitted to the episcopate without having been ordained presbyters well into the tenth century. The presbyteral ordination of Hildebrand prior to episcopal ordination in 1073 is the definitive sign that the Frankish sequence had become universal in the medieval church. Hence, the eleventh and twelfth

---

[253] Herbert of Bosham, *Vita S. Thomae*, p. 188.

centuries mark the final stage in the development of the *cursus honorum* in the Western church.

a. The Gregorian Reforms

The primary objectives of the eleventh-century reformers were the abuses of simony and lay investiture, though these were not the only ones. The reformers paid particular attention to standards and morality of the clergy. For instances, Reynolds has observed:

> Conciliar and papal strictures against the sexual liaisons of the clergy are almost as numerous as those against simony and lay investiture.[254]

One of the abuses which must have confronted the reformers of the eleventh century was a certain laxity with respect to the *cursus honorum*. It would appear that in certain places reception of the minor orders, in particular the subdiaconate, had fallen into desuetude. Councils and popes legislated against the omission of grades within the *cursus*, particularly the subdiaconate; for example, Canon X of the Council of Rouen (1072), and *Epistle* 32 of Alexander II. Legislation from the pontificate of Alexander II (1061–73) confirmed the indispensable place of the subdiaconate within the *cursus*; without it deacons and presbyters were inhibited from the exercise of their offices.

    Conciliar legislation prohibiting members of the laity from being elected to the episcopate, such as Canon XIII of the Council of Rome (1059), Canon I of the Council of Benevento (1091), Canon V of the Council of Clermont-Ferrand (1095), was no doubt directed against the abuse of simony. The same rationale probably accounts for the large number of patristic texts in the canonistic collections, culminating in Gratian's *Decretum*, against the election of members of the laity to the episcopate. Insistence on sequential ordination with a proper observance of the interstices (and the canonical ages), therefore, was part of the arsenal used against the practice of simony. The purchasing of a high ecclesiastical office by the unscrupulous and ambitious would have been rendered senseless by the canonical observance of a long period of probation and preparation in the lower offices.

---

[254] Reynolds, "Sacred Orders," p. 252.

b. The Presbyterate

Gregory VII was not the first bishop of Rome to have received all the grades; that claim can be made by Roman bishops at least as early as Cornelius in the third century. What is significant about Gregory's election is that he was ordained a presbyter in order to be ordained a bishop. Again, this is not the first instance of the practice; Hincmar witnesses to it in the late ninth century. Gregory's ordination marks the first instance of the practice in Rome. Other Roman bishops elected from the diaconate in the eleventh and twelfth centuries followed the same pattern. Roman conservatism had given way to the prevailing norm.

The absolute position of the presbyterate in the sequence of the *cursus honorum* is witnessed in the ordination rites. OR XXXV "B" assumes that candidates for the episcopate are invariably in presbyters' orders. The PR12 reflects sequential ordination from the subdiaconate to the diaconate to the presbyterate; it clearly reflects the liturgical expectation that all candidates for the episcopate are presbyters.

It is interesting to contemplate the extent to which the ordination rites themselves contributed to the insistence that only presbyters may be ordained bishops. Such an insistence is not evident in *Ordines* XXXIV or XXXV; one must therefore turn to the Frankish liturgies, particularly the custom of anointing the hands of the newly ordained. As queried in chapter III of this study, in relation to the *Missale francorum* where only the presbyter's hands are anointed, one wonders why a particular grace would be given to the presbyterate which was necessary to the episcopate as well, unless all bishops had been ordained as presbyters. This question is further accented in the Eighth-Century Gelasian sacramentaries which retain the priestly anointing for the presbyters, but delegate the Samuel-David anointing for governance to the bishop. Again, as noted in chapter III, Amalarius of Metz remarks that the sacerdotal ministry of the bishop is conferred in the presbyteral anointing. The PRG of the tenth century retains the two-fold anointing, whereas the PR12 "confirms" the consecrating of the hands, and proceeds to consecrate the thumb of the new bishop; this direction assumes a previous, presbyteral, anointing of the hands.

To what extent the Frankish insistence on sequential ordination from the presbyterate to the episcopate, and the Frankish anointing ceremonies played in the Roman adoption of both practices is a fascinating question. Certainly Andrieu makes the connection in reference to the consecration of Hildebrand.

> Quand le diacre Hildebrand...se fit ordonner prêtre...il ne se doutait vraisemblable-
> ment pas qu'il renouait avec l'ancienne discipline officielle du Siège apostolique
> *par l'intermédiaire de la liturgie franque.*[255]

In addition, the eleventh century is noted for a resurgence of the patristic 'presbyterian' theories of episcopacy.[256] Commentators argued that bishops and presbyters were originally one office; they pointed out the equality of bishops and presbyters at the eucharist; the term *sacerdotium* came to be equated primarily with the presbyterate, and only derivatively with the episcopate. Given the current theology of orders, it is not surprising that throughout the eleventh and twelfth centuries deacons elected to the episcopate were routinely ordained first to the presbyterate.

While OR XXXV "B" and the PR12 reflect a ten year interval between the reception of the presbyterate and the episcopate, often the interval between the two ordinations was a matter of weeks or days. When bishops-elect were deacons, consecration seems to have been a bi-partite affair: ordination to the presbyterate on one day and episcopal ordination on the next. This practice reflects the sacramental conflation of the two orders.

c. The Interstices

While sequential ordination through all the grades of the clerical *cursus* became an invariable practice in the eleventh and twelfth centuries, the period continues to reflect a considerable degree of flexibility with respect to the interstices and the ages of clerics. There appears to have been a fair bit of abuse of the interstices, again no doubt associated with simony. For example, Canon X of the Council of Rouen censures the practice of conferring all the grades from acolyte to "priest" in a day.

There was a notable variety in the ages of subdeacon. The minimum ages of subdeacons in Italy, for instance, were considerably lower than in the transalpine church. Italian councils, such as Ravenna (1014), Rome (1059), and Melfi (1089/90) prescribe that subdeacons should be ordained at fourteen (or even twelve) years of age. In the transalpine church, however, as witnessed in the Councils of Compostella (1056) and Rouen (1074) the minimum age for subdeacons was eighteen or twenty. These differences in minimum ages of subdeacons would affect the interstice

---

[255] Andrieu, "Le sacre épiscopal," p. 29.

[256] Reynolds, "Patristic 'Presbyterianism'," pp. 328, ff.

between the subdiaconate and the diaconate. The minimum age for deacons remains constant at twenty-five.

The traditional age for presbyters, thirty years, is commended, though there are provisions for the ordination of presbyters at age twenty-five, for example, Canon VI of the Council of Rouen (1074). This provision would affect the interstice between the diaconate and the presbyterate.

Given that both OR XXXV "B" and the PR12 assume a ten-year interval between the presbyterate and the episcopate, it may be inferred that normally the minimum age for bishops was between thirty-five and forty.

d. Conclusion

The eleventh-century clerical *cursus* can be summarized as follows: typically a cleric would pass sequentially through the offices of (psalmist) doorkeeper, lector, exorcist, and acolyte from childhood to the ages of either twelve or fourteen (in Italy), or eighteen or twenty (north of the Alps). A cleric would be ordained to the subdiaconate between the ages of twelve (or fourteen) and eighteen (or twenty). The cleric would then be ordained to the diaconate at age twenty-five, and to the presbyterate between twenty-five and thirty years of age. Normally, a cleric would be a presbyter for ten years before ordination to the episcopate.

Notwithstanding a certain flexibility in terms of the ages of clerics and the interstices between the grades, the *cursus honorum* in the eleventh century received the shape it would retain in the West until the sixteenth century for the churches of the Reformation, and until the 1972 apostolic letter of Paul VI, *Ministeria quaedem*, which abolished medieval sequence of the minor orders in the Roman Catholic Church. The universal practice of sequential ordination through each of the *major* orders achieved in the eleventh-century Western church remains unchanged, though not unchallenged, to this day.

V

CONCLUSION:

THE *CURSUS HONORUM* PAST AND FUTURE

1. Introduction

The final chapter will summarize the development of the practice of sequential ordination outlined in the four historical periods: the pre-Nicene, the patristic and the early medieval periods, culminating in the final shape of the *cursus honorum* in the eleventh and twelfth centuries. Subsequent developments will be sketched in the late medieval period and in the Reformation and Counter-Reformation. Lastly, this chapter will touch on recent changes and challenges to the *cursus honorum* in the Anglican Communion and in the Roman Catholic Church.

The intent of the summary is two-fold: firstly, to recapitulate the historical material presented in the preceding chapters in order to highlight the stages of the development of the *cursus honorum* and the causes of its emergence and evolution. Secondly, the summary will apply the insights from the history of the origins and evolution of the *cursus honorum* to questions about the parameters of its adaptation for the contemporary church, particularly in the wake of the movement for the restoration of the diaconate as a permanent office.

2. Summary of the Development of Sequential Ordination

a. The Pre-Nicene Period

There is no evidence in the New Testament of movement from one ministry to another, prescribed or otherwise. Neither, however, is there evidence of the various ministries associated with the later *cursus honorum* except in their most embryonic form. Likewise, there is no evidence of sequential appointment to office in post-apostolic writings such as the *Didache* and I Clement, the early second-century Ignatian epistles, and the mid-second-century *Apologies* of Justin Martyr.

The second century reveals a variety of patterns in the relationships between the episcopate, the presbyterate and the diaconate which might suggest various series or sequences of ministries. Ignatius of Antioch, for example, offers no evidence for—or against—the custom of sequential ordination. Yet if it was practised at all in the churches he knew, the most likely sequence would have been from the diaconate to the episcopate, since the Ignatian epistles reflect such an affinity between these two ministries. In the Ignatian churches it is unlikely that presbyters would have become bishops, or that deacons would have become presbyters. By comparison, presbyters may have succeeded bishops regularly in office in Gaul in the mid-second century (and in Alexandria until the early-fourth century). One might expect to find the same pattern in the second-century Roman Church, given its collegial presbyteral foundation. Yet in the late second century there are signs that deacons also became bishops in Rome.

The third century provides conclusive evidence of sequential ordination. Although the ordination liturgies of the *Apostolic Tradition* reflect no expectation of sequential appointment, other contemporary evidence confirms its existence. For example, the letters of Cyprian show that the practice was known in North Africa as well as in Rome by the mid-third century. Cyprian's *Epistle* 38 indicates the deliberate use of one office as preparatory to another. *Epistle* 55 reveals that at least one bishop, Cornelius of Rome, was appointed to *all* the ecclesiastical offices. Although neither universal nor prescribed, mid-third-century evidence indicates that sequential ordination was a feature in at least some parts of the pre-Nicene church.

The pre-Nicene period reflects instances of deacons becoming bishops, members of the laity becoming bishops, members of the laity becoming presbyters, and of presbyters becoming bishops. The sequence which is bypassed in this inventory—for which there is very little evidence—is from the diaconate to the presbyterate. Since it is this sequence which has raised contemporary questions regarding the *cursus honorum*, it is significant that there is so little evidence of sequential movement between these two ministries in the first three centuries.

In sum, evidence from the pre-Nicene period reveals the practices of both direct and sequential (or serial) ordination. In the pre-Nicene church the diaconate, presbyterate, and episcopate tended to be primarily life-long vocations to which people were ordained directly. And yet in many instances both deacons and presbyters did become bishops, and thus received a series or sequence of offices. While sequential ordination was neither a sacramental priority nor a canonical necessity, it did without doubt, occur regularly in the pre-Nicene church. Yet sequential appointment in this period was too variable and inconsistent to be seen as a parallel to the concurrent imperial *cursus honorum*.

b. The Patristic Period

The first extant canonical requirement of sequential ordination is Canon XIII of the Council of Sardica (343). Subsequently, councils and bishops repeatedly called for sequential ordination with specific intervals of time—the interstices—between ordination to one office and promotion to the next. The fourth century marked a period of unprecedented growth for the church. After the conversion of Constantine, local churches were no longer the small, closely-knit communities they had once been, in which vocations to ecclesiastical leadership were easily discernible, but had become large communities in which leadership had become highly desirable and sought after. Not only had the presbyterate and the episcopate accrued privilege, power, and financial opportunity, but the duties of bishops from the fourth century required a knowledge of theology, liturgy, canon law, administration, and diplomacy. From the numerous condemnations of the ordinations of the unworthy and untrained found in conciliar legislation, papal decretals, canonistic collections, and in the patristic ecclesiastical histories, it is clear that the new situation of the fourth century necessitated an effective means to train and test the church's leaders. Sequential ordination—the *cursus honorum*—was the method that evolved by which the church could best select, prepare, and prove candidates for the higher offices. The insistence of conciliar and papal legislators that the clergy, particularly bishops, undergo a long period of probation and preparation appears not to have been motivated by a desire to imitate imperial military and civil institutions. Rather, the ecclesiastical *cursus honorum* emerged as a practical and pastoral solution to the problem of appointing the unworthy and incapable to the higher offices, precipitated by the new situation of the fourth century.

From the fourth century the practice of sequential ordination appears to have been the preferred and canonical way of training and selecting members of the clergy. Even so, one cannot conclude that sequential ordination became a standard practice of the patristic church. The *cursus honorum* in the fourth and fifth centuries was still in the early stages of a long process of evolution. Although enjoined by conciliar and papal legislation, and transmitted through the patristic canonistic collections, the practice of sequential ordination was neither uniform nor universal. Thus, candidates continued to be selected for the episcopate from a variety of states of life—neophytes, the laity, the minor orders, the diaconate—in a fashion similar to the pre-Nicene period. By way of illustration, many bishops of Rome were drawn from the diaconate; the Roman recensions of Canon XIII of the Council of Sardica enshrine this practice. In Milan, Ambrose was ordained directly to the episcopate as a neophyte; in Constantinople Nectarius was similarly ordained to the episcopate. In North Africa, Augustine was ordained directly to the presbyterate as a lay person, as was Gregory Nazianzus in Cappadocia. The *Historia francorum* of Gregory of Tours indicates that there was little uniformity with respect to sequential ordination in the Frankish church. Thus, in light of the repeated censures against the ordination of neophytes and lay people in the patristic period, it is clear that the older practice of direct ordination persisted. The exhortations for sequential ordination were either ignored on spurious grounds such as ambition or simony, or dispensed with on pastoral grounds, such as the shortage of clergy or the need to assert orthodox leadership.

Sequential ordination in the patristic period served a pastoral rather than theological function. For all that popes and councils may have decried the practice of ordaining neophytes and lay people directly to the episcopate, they nonetheless regarded such bishops as real bishops, albeit often of poor calibre: hence the scandal of *per saltum* ordinations. Bishops who had been promoted without the requisite *cursus* were often suspect because they were ill prepared, unsuited, and ineffective, and yet such bishops were true bishops. In short, there is no evidence that the "sacramental validity" of *per saltum* ordination was doubted in the patristic period.

As long as the *cursus honorum* was observed with the canonical interstices it appears to have been an effective means of preparation and probation. While there was a variety of prescribed interstices in the patristic period, it would have taken many years to rise from the minor orders to the diaconate, the presbyterate and finally to the episcopate. For example, the series of grades in the entry for Silvester in the *Liber pontificalis* or the sequence followed by Bishop Caton in the *Historia francorum* would have taken over fifty years to complete.

Within the patristic period itself one notes the preliminary dissolution of this two-fold process in the abbreviation and eventual disregard of the interstices. The letters of Innocent and Leo, for instance, indicate this process was under way by the fifth century in some parts of the church. Again, in the late-fifth century Gelasius permitted the grades from lector to presbyter to be conferred on an individual within the space of twelve months. Furthermore, in the sixth century Pelagius suggests that in a least one instance a series of orders was conferred in a single day. The interstices— the *tempora constituta*—enabled the *cursus honorum* to function as an effective means of training and testing. A rapid reception of orders, whether within the space of a day or a year, could in no way serve as a period of preparation and probation. Once dissociated from the interstices, the strict observance of the *cursus honorum* would degenerate into a sort of lopsided canonical rigidity. The practice of sequential ordination without the observance of the interstices altered the very intent of the *cursus honorum*. While the interstices continued to be mandated by popes, councils and canonists, the custom of conferring orders when neither their exercise nor their use as a means of preparation for the reception of a succeeding grade was intended, suggests that ordination through a series or sequences of grades was understood to be for some purpose other than canonical observance. One can anticipate the advent of an implicit sacramental understanding of sequential ordination.

c. Eighth, Ninth, and Tenth Centuries

The medieval period, particularly the tenth century, witnessed to a growing consensus on the number and sequence of the grades received in the ecclesiastical *cursus honorum* in the Western church. In the eight and ninth centuries there was a variety of sequences of minor orders associated with the different Western liturgical traditions: Frankish, Hispanic-Irish, and Roman. These variations were harmonised in the tenth century through the appearance and dissemination of the *Pontificale romano-germanicum* throughout the Western church with its particular sequence of grades. Interestingly, the so-called Romano-Gallican sequence of the PRG— psalmist, doorkeeper, lector, exorcist, acolyte, subdeacon, deacon, presbyter, and bishop—is similar to the sequence of ministers mentioned in the third century by Cornelius of Rome in the letter of Fabius of Antioch, and is identical to the sequence of grades found in the fifth-century Gallican *Statuta ecclesiae antiqua*.

Conversely, a degree of flexibility persists with regards to the number and sequence of the major orders to be received in this period. For example, through the eighth, ninth, and tenth centuries, deacons continue to be elected and consecrated directly to the episcopate in Rome without prior presbyteral ordination. In contrast, this practice seems to have ended in the Frankish church by the time of Hincmar's *Epistle* 29 to Adventius of Metz in the late ninth century. Although deacons continued to be elected to the episcopate in the Frankish Church, they were ordained presbyters prior to episcopal consecration. Admittedly, the insistence that bishops first be presbyters conforms to the Sardican Canon XIII listing the presbyterate as a grade leading to the episcopate. At the same time, it marks a shift away from the inherited Western pattern in which the presbyterate could be omitted. The basis for the Frankish insistence on presbyteral ordination seems to have arisen out of theological and liturgical considerations rather than canonical. Thus, Amalarius writes in the *Liber officialis* that the bishop receives the power to offer the eucharistic sacrifice at his ordination to the presbyterate. Amalarius's assertion is based on the Frankish liturgical practice of anointing the hands of the newly ordained presbyter. And so in this instance, liturgical usage ultimately gives rise to a theological and sacramental priority. In Rome the practice of ordaining deacons to the episcopate, enshrined in the Dionysian form of Canon XIII of the Council of Sardica, continued until the tenth century.

It is not clear whether the same degree of flexibility existed in the Western church with regard to sequential ordination from the diaconate to the presbyterate. While the liturgical rites suggest that normally presbyters would have been deacons, the biographical and historical evidence, especially from the *Liber pontificalis*, suggests that there were many presbyters who had never been deacons.

The early medieval period saw abuses of sequential ordination and the interstices as well as strong conciliar reassertions of their place in ordination practice. Thus, the incident of the anti-pope Constantine, rushed through the minor orders to the diaconate and subsequently ordained to the episcopate in 767, was censured by the Council of Rome (769). The council legislated the long-standing convention of the Roman church that only deacons or presbyters were to be eligible for election and consecration to the episcopate. The election of Photius to the see of Constantinople in 858 inadvertently became important in the history of sequential ordination. Although Popes Hadrian and Nicholas were more interested in the assertion of papal primacy and Roman expansion in southern Italy and Bulgaria than they were in the mode of Photius' election, it was the fact that Photius had been a lay person at the time of his election, counter to the decree of the Council of Rome (769), that became the pretext for his deposition by Nicholas I in 863 and by the Council of Constantinople in 869. Still, the Photian crisis placed the *cursus honorum* on the agenda of the Fourth Council of Constantinople, an ecumenical council by Western reckoning. Canon V stated that candidates for the episcopate must first have been clerics or monks, and tested through the grades of lector, subdeacon, deacon, and presbyter, with a ten year interstice between reception of the lectorate and episcopal ordination. And yet Canon V was promulgated in the midst of considerable diversity with respect to the sequence of the *cursus*. Nicholas I, for instance, had never been a presbyter. The sequence of Canon V was not that of the ninth-century Western church, nor that commended by Pope John VIII—lector, acolyte, deacon, "priest" and bishop—to the Byzantine emperors Basil, Leo and Alexander (879).

It is noteworthy that when medieval bishops chose to violate the canons concerning the *cursus honorum* it was the interstices rather than the sequence of grades which were abandoned. By comparison, in the patristic church the ordination of members of the laity directly to the presbyterate or the episcopate without any intervening ordinations was not an unusual occurrence. While there are some indications of rapid ordinations as early as the early-sixth century, by the medieval period the ordinations of "neophytes" (i.e. members of the laity) to the episcopate invariably entailed a rapid series of ordinations through all the grades of the *cursus*. Though the conferral of the minor and major orders in such cases—in total disregard for the interstices canons—could in no way provide testing and training, they were conferred nonetheless. Something other than training and testing had become operative in the minds of those who could so easily detach sequential ordination from the interstices. On the one hand, this can be attributed to a rigorous, albeit lopsided, legalism. On the other hand, there seems to be a developing sacramental perception associated with sequential ordination.

Constantine, Photius, and Leo were declared to have been invalidly ordained because they were elected from the laity not the clergy. The series of ordinations they received were held to be invalid because the interstices had not been observed. Hence, in the early medieval period a sacramentally valid episcopal ordination was one which complied with the canonical *cursus honorum* and the interstices. Yet inconsistencies abounded. The councils which dealt with Constantine, Photius, and Leo were more interested in political considerations (such as usurpation of episcopal and papal power) than in questions of valid ordinations. These incongruities are apparent in the fact John VIII rescinded the deposition against Photius in 879, for apparently political considerations, and recognised him as a true bishop in contradiction to the statements of his deposition in 863 and in 869 as well as Canons IV and V of Constantinople IV a decade earlier. Nonetheless, once the language around sequential ordination had shifted from legality to validity, the discussion has shifted from canon law to sacramental theology.

In the early medieval period, then, the practice of sequential ordination became more uniform and stable, and more significant in the theology and practice of ordination. Nonetheless, the period continues to reflect a certain flexibility, notably with respect to the sequence of the minor orders in the eighth and ninth centuries, and the places of the diaconate and the presbyterate in the *cursus* throughout all three centuries. Hence, this relatively late period is one of continuing development and transition in the history of the *cursus honorum*.

d. The Eleventh and Twelfth Centuries

The wide distribution of the *Pontificale romano-germanicum* from the mid-tenth century settled the hierarchical sequence of the minor orders in the Western church. Yet the exact sequence of major orders was not settled until the eleventh century with the universal insistence on sequential ordination from the presbyterate to the episcopate. The presbyteral ordination of the deacon Hildebrand in 1073 prior to his episcopal consecration as Pope Gregory VII is the decisive indication that the Frankish sequence and practice has become universal in the Western church.

The eleventh-century reform movements insisted on sequential ordination through all the grades in what must have been a situation of considerable laxity. For instance, it appears that in some places reception of the minor orders, especially the subdiaconate, had fallen into desuetude. Hence, both councils and popes insisted that no grade be received without the reception of the lower. Thus, legislation from the pontificate of Alexander II (1061–1073) directed that without reception of the subdiaconate, presbyters and deacons were inhibited from the exercise of their offices until they had received it. Eleventh-century canonical legislation demanding sequential ordination with an adequate observance of the interstices was part of the effort to stem the abuse of simony. Accordingly, the purchase of the higher ecclesiastical offices would have been rendered pointless by the insistence on long periods of canonical probation and preparation through the grades.

The eleventh century is noted for the resurgence of what Roger Reynolds has termed "patristic presbyterian" theories of episcopacy. Commentators on orders argued that at the eucharist there is a basic equality between bishops and presbyters. Moreover, they argued, it is the presbyter who is primarily the *sacerdos*; episcopal office is only derivatively sacerdotal. It is possible that the final acceptance of the Frankish pattern by the Roman church was related to the Frankish practice of anointing the hands of the newly ordained presbyter in order to preside at the eucharist. At any rate, sequential ordination from the presbyterate to the episcopate had become a theological as well as a canonical principle.

In sum, the sequence of both the minor and major orders became fixed in the eleventh century, though considerable flexibility remained with regards to the ages of clerics and the interstices. Nevertheless, this period marks the final shape of the *cursus honorum* in the Western church until the sixteenth-century Reformation, and in Roman Catholic Church, the 1972 Pontifical of Paul VI.

3. The Aftermath

The eleventh and twelfth centuries effectively mark the *terminus ad quem* of this study of the origins and evolution of the *cursus honorum*. Yet a brief examination of the aftermath is important in order to bridge the history of the practice to the present-day questions about sequential ordination raised in the Introduction of this study. This section will treat the theological interpretations which sequential ordination received from the scholastic theologians of the thirteenth century, in particular, Thomas Aquinas and Richard Fishacre. Subsequent revisions to the *cursus honorum* from the sixteenth century to the present by both the Reformation and Counter-Reformation traditions will be surveyed.

a. The Later Medieval Period

Although the later medieval period saw no new developments in the practice of the *cursus honorum*, scholastic theologians commented on sequential ordination, especially the sequence from presbyter to bishop. For
example, in the Supplement to the *Summa Theologica* (*ca.* 1272), Question
35, article 5, Thomas Aquinas (*ca.* 1225–1274) asks "whether the character of one order necessarily presupposes the character of another order:"

> Respondeo dicendum quod non est de necessitate superiorum ordinum quod aliquis
> minores ordines prius habeat: quia potestates sunt distinctae; et una, quantum est
> de sui ratione, non requirit aliam in eodem subiecto. Et ideo etiam in primitiva Ec-
> clesia aliqui ordinabantur in presbyteros qui prius inferiores ordines non suscep-
> erant: et tamen poterant omnia quae inferiores ordines possunt; quia inferior potestas
> comprehenditur in superiori virtute, sicut sensus in intellectu et ducatus in regno.
> Sed postea per constitutionem Ecclesiae determinatum est quod ad maiores ordines
> se non ingerat qui prius in minoribus officiis se non humiliavit. Et inde est quod qui
> ordinantur per saltum, secundum canones, non reordinantur, sed id quod omissum
> fuerat de praecedentibus ordinibus eis confertur.[1]

Aquinas answers that it is not necessary for the major orders to receive the
minor, since their respective powers are distinct. Noting that in the early
church there were some who were ordained priests without having
received the lower orders, he adds: "it was decided by the legislation of the
church" that candidates for the higher orders must first have humbled
themselves in the lower. And so those who are ordained without the lower
orders are not re-ordained, but receive what was lacking through subsequent ordination to the lower orders. Thus, according to Aquinas one could
validly, though illicitly, be ordained a presbyter without having first been
ordained a deacon.

Aquinas also teaches, however, that there is a theological imperative regarding sequential ordination from the presbyterate to the episcopate. For
Aquinas there are only three sacred orders: the "priesthood", the diaconate,
and the subdiaconate.[2] In Question 40 of the Supplement, Aquinas asks
whether the episcopate is an order:

---

[1] Thomas Aquinas, *Summa Theologiae*, Pars IIIa et Supplementum, De Rubeis, Billuart,
    and P. Faucher, eds. (Rome: Marietti, 1953), p. 758.

[2] "Et sic sunt tantum tres ordines sacri: scilicet sacerdos; et diaconus, qui habet actum
    circa corpus Christi et sanguinem consecratum; et subdiaconus, qui habet actum circa
    vasa consecrata." Suppl. Q. 37, art. 3. p. 766

(Sed contra:) Est quod unus ordo non dependet a praecedenti, quantum ad necessitatem sacramenti. Sed episcopalis potestas dependet a sacerdotali: quia nullus potest recipere episcopalem potestatem nisi prius habeat sacerdotalem. Ergo episcopatus non est ordo.[3]

Aquinas restates the conviction that one order does not depend on a preceding order in terms of validity. With regard to the episcopate, however, he states that "episcopal power depends on the priestly power since no one can be a bishop who has not received priestly power."

For Aquinas and the scholastic theologians, the sacrament of order is related to the eucharist.[4] The presbyterate is the summit of the orders since it is directed to the consecration of the eucharist.[5] Since the episcopate is not directed to the eucharist, they argued, it is not an order. Consequently, episcopal consecration depends on ordination to the presbyterate; without prior ordination as a presbyter a bishop would have jurisdiction, but not order.

The same teaching is held by other scholastic theologians.[6] For example, the less well-known Oxford theologian of the thirteenth century, Richard Fishacre, also recognizes that while one may be validly ordained to the presbyterate without prior ordination to the diaconate, one must be ordained a presbyter prior to episcopal ordination. In the *Commentarium in libros sententiarum* (*ca.* 1241–1245) Fishacre writes:

In consecratione confertur episcopo nec novus ordo, sed novum officium et nova potestas. Si aliquis quippe ordinaretur in sacerdotem, omisso gradu diaconatus, tamen vere sacerdos esset. Sed omisso sacerdotio si quis consecraretur in episcopum, episcopus non esset. Et si hoc verum est, tunc non se habet episcopatus ad sacerdotium ut se habent ordines ad invicem.[7]

Once again, without prior ordination as a presbyter, i.e. a "priest" (*sacerdos*), a bishop is not a bishop. A new order is not conferred in episcopal consecration, but a new office with new power.

---

[3] Suppl. Q. 40, art. 5. p. 780.

[4] "Et ideo aliter dicendum quod ordinis sacramentum ad sacramentum Eucharistiae ordinatur, quod est *sacramentum sacramentorum*...." Suppl. Q. 37, art. 2. p. 765.

[5] Suppl. Q. 37, art. 5.

[6] See Augustine McDevitt, "The Episcopate as an Order and Sacrament on the Eve of the High Scholastic Period," *Franciscan Studies* 20 (1960), pp. 96–127.

[7] Richard Fishacre, *Commentarium*, qtd. in McDevitt, "The Episcopate as an Order," p. 124, n. 95.

Aquinas and Fishacre attest to the degree to which, by the thirteenth century, it had become theologically—as well as canonically and liturgically—impossible for one to be consecrated bishop without having first been ordained a presbyter. This is hardly a new development. Canonists had long insisted on ordination through all the grades, and the liturgical rites from the late tenth-century OR XXXV "B" and the *Pontificale romanum saeculi XII* manifest this sequence. "Patristic presbyterian" theories of the relationship between the episcopate and the presbyterate were current from the eleventh century. The scholastic theologians have advanced the discussion by explicitly associating the prevailing theology of "priesthood" with the standard canonical and liturgical practice of sequential ordination.

On the other hand, it is noteworthy that for the scholastic theologians sequential ordination from the lower orders to the presbyterate remains largely a canonical requirement. While the exercise of an order depends on the reception of the lower orders, one may be validly ordained directly to the presbyterate without passing through the minor orders, the subdiaconate and the diaconate.

b. The Reformation

i.

The sixteenth century was a period of considerable modification and revision for the *cursus honorum* in the Western church. In the Lutheran, Zwinglian, Calvinist and Anabaptist traditions the practice of sequential ordination was lost with the discontinuation of the major and minor orders associated with it.[8]

One of the major Reformation traditions, with which the Council of Trent was to take particular issue regarding the minor orders, was Calvinism.[9] The French reformer and theologian John Calvin (1509–1564) wrote about ordered ministry in Book IV of the *Institutes of the Christian Religion* (first published in 1536, revised in 1543, with the final version

---

[8] Although there are notable exceptions, such as Lutheran churches in Finland and Sweden, and the Reformed tradition in Hungary.

[9] K. Osborne notes that the focus of the second chapter of the twenty-third session of the Council of Trent (1563), was aimed at John Calvin's teaching on the minor orders and sequential ordination. *Priesthood*, p. 255.

appearing in 1559). In common with other reformers, Calvin takes issue with both the theology and structure inherited from the medieval church. His starting point for the ordering of the church's ministry is Scripture, in particular Ephesians 4.11: "The gifts he gave were that some would be apostles, some prophets, some evangelists, some pastors and teachers. . ." Apostles, prophets and evangelists, for Calvin, were extraordinary ministers, associated with the apostolic period. The permanent ministers of scriptural warrant for Calvin were the pastors and teachers, who formed one ministerial order. To the ordained ministries of pastor and teacher were added elders and deacons, lay people who in Calvin's system take part in governance, charitable work, and assist the pastors.[10] While this four-fold structure became characteristic of Calvinism, credit for its conception lies with reformer Martin Bucer (1491–1551).[11] This particular ministerial order became one of the most influential of the Reformation.[12]

Since pastors and teachers form one ministerial order, and since elders and deacons are temporary lay positions, there is no *cursus honorum* in Calvin's system. Yet Calvin appears quite insightful in his historical appraisal of the reasons behind the clerical *cursus*, although he rejects the major and minor orders associated with it. In Book IV.4.9 of the *Institutes* Calvin deals specifically with the minor orders, which he sees as essentially a means of preparation and probation for ecclesiastical office, rather than offices in their own right:

> En ceste manière ils estoyent promeus de degrez en degrez, afin qu'on les approuvast en chacun exercice, devant que les faire Sousdiacres. Mon propos tend là, qu'on cognoisse que ces choses ont esté préparations et rudimens ou apprentissage, plustot que certains offices, comme i'ay dit cy dessus.[13]

Calvin is surprisingly generous in his treatment of the *cursus honorum* and the minor orders. This positive approach is linked to his profound

---

[10] In the first edition of the *Institutes* (1536) Calvin speaks only of pastors and teachers. The fourfold ministry first appears in the *Ecclesiastical Ordinances* (1541), and is reflected in the *Institutes* from 1543. François Wendel, *Calvin: Sources et évolution de sa pensée religieuse* (1950; Genève: Labor et Fides, 1985), p. 50.

[11] Wendel, *Calvin*, p. 50.

[12] Harry G. Goodykoontz, *The Minister in the Reformed Tradition* (Richmond, VA: John Knox Press, 1963), p. 53.

[13] Jean Calvin, *Institution de la Religion Chrestienne: Edition critique avec introduction, notes et variances*, Livre Quatrième, ed. Jean-Daniel Benoit (Paris: Librairie Philosophe J. Vrin, 1961), p. 81.

concern for the election of well-prepared and tested ministers, which he understands the *cursus honorum* to have met in the past. In Book IV.4.10 of the *Institutes* Calvin writes:

> . . . [c]ar nul n'estoit fait Sousdiacre, qu'il n'eust esté esprouvé par longue espace de temps avec telle sévérité comme nous avons dit. Après qu'on l'avoit encore derechef esprouvé en ce degré-là, on le constituoit Diacre; auquel office s'il se portoit fidèlement, il parvenoit au degré de Prestrise. Ainsi nul n'estoit promeu qu'il n'eust esté auparavant longuement examiné, mesme à la veue du peuple.[14]

Given the Reformation insistence on *sola scriptura*, Calvin could do little but reject the minor orders and the subdiaconate (which are not found in the New Testament) and reinterpret the diaconate, presbyterate and episcopate according to his theological perspective and agenda. Hence, Calvin rejected the orders associated with the *cursus honorum* in both theory and practice. Nevertheless, his historical assessment of their function is consistent with both patristic and medieval understandings of the motives for sequential ordination though the grades, i.e. preparation and probation.

ii.

A Reformation tradition which did, in part, retain sequential ordination, was the Church of England. Like Calvinism, the reformed Church of England rejected minor orders as unscriptural. In the fifth book *Of the Laws of Ecclesiastical Polity* (1597), the premier theologian of Elizabethan Anglicanism, Richard Hooker (*ca.* 1554–1600) acknowledges the minor orders, and identifies their purpose as preparation:

> Catechistes, Exorcistes, Readers, Singers, and the rest of like sort, if the nature onlie of theire laboures and paines be considered, maie in that respect seeme clergie men, even as the fathers for that cause terme them usuallie clerkes, as also in regard of the ende whereunto they were trained up which was to be ordered up when yeares and experience should make them able.[15]

Unlike Calvinism, Anglicanism judged the ordered ministries of bishops, presbyters and deacons to be of scriptural warrant. The *Bishops' Book* (1537), a document of the early English Reformation, states that in the New Testament "there is no mention made of any degrees or distinctions

---

[14] Calvin, *Institutions*, pp. 82–83.

[15] Richard Hooker, *Of the Laws of Ecclesiastical Polity*, Bk V.78.10, ed. W. Speed Hill (Cambridge, MA: Harvard University Press, 1977), p. 446.

in orders but only of deacons or ministers, and of priests or bishops".[16] In similar fashion, Richard Hooker, lists the same orders in the *Laws*:

> ...divers learned and skillfull men have so taken it as if those places did intend to teach what orders of ecclesiasticall persons there ought to be in the Church of Christ, which thing wee are not to learne from thence but out of other partes of holie scripture, whereby it clearly appeareth that Churches Apostolique did knowe but three degrees in the power of ecclesiasticall order, at first Apostles, Presbyters, and Deacons, afterwardes in stead of Apostles Bishopes concerning whose order wee are to speake in the seaventh booke.[17]

In preserving the three-fold ministry, the Church of England also maintained the traditional practice of sequential ordination. And yet by abolishing the minor orders, particularly the subdiaconate which for centuries had been held to be indispensable, the English Reformers effectively demonstrated their conviction that the clerical *cursus* had somewhat broader "parameters of adaptation."

From the sixteenth century, Anglicanism has insisted on sequential ordination through the orders of deacon, presbyter and bishop. From the first Anglican ordination rites of 1550 (the "Ordinal", attached to the 1549 *Book of Common Prayer*) to the present, the liturgical texts have clearly reflected the *cursus* between the orders of deacon and presbyter. For example, the final prayer in the ordination rite for deacons contains the petition:

> [that they] ...may so well behave themselves in this inferior office, that they may be found worthy to be called unto the higher ministries in thy Church; through the same...[18]

Furthermore, a rubric at the end of the rite for the ordering of deacons prescribes sequential movement between the diaconate and the presbyterate:

> And here it must be declared unto the Deacon, that he must continue in that office of a Deacon [*sic.*] the space of a whole year (except for reasonable causes it shall otherwise seem good unto the Bishop) to the intent he may be perfect, and well

---

[16] Charles Lloyd, ed., *Formularies of Faith put forth by authority during the reign of Henry VIII* (1825), pp. 104–105, qtd. in Paul Bradshaw, *The Anglican Ordinal* (London: SPCK, 1971), p. 8.

[17] Hooker, *Laws*, Book V.78.9, p. 446.

[18] *The First Prayer Book of King Edward VI 1549*, Everyman's Library, No. 448 (London: Dent, 1952), p. 302; The Church of England in the Dominion of Canada, *The Book of Common Prayer* (Cambridge: The University Press, 1918), p. 622; Protestant Episcopal Church in the United States of America, *The Book of Common Prayer (1928)*, (New York: The Church Pension Fund, 1945), p. 534.

expert in the things pertaining to the Ecclesiastical Administration. If he has been found faithful and diligent, and has satisfied the Bishop that he is sufficiently experienced in the things belonging to the Ministry, he may be admitted by his Diocesan to the Order of Priesthood at the Ember Seasons, or on any Sunday or Holy Day.[19]

The Prayer Book ordination rites amply describe the two principle function of sequential ordination from deacon to presbyter, i.e. preparation and probation.

The *Constitutions and Canons Ecclesiastical* of 1604 are the foundational body of Anglican canon law, synthesizing the medieval canonical tradition and the principles of the English Reformation. With respect to sequential movement from the diaconate and the presbyterate, they parallel the directions and tenor of the Prayer Book Ordinal. Canon 32, entitled *"None to be made Deacon and Minister both in one day"*, states:

> The office of deacon being a step or degree to the ministry, according to the judgement of the ancient fathers, and the practice of the Primitive Church; we do ordain and appoint, that hereafter no bishop shall make any person, of what qualities or gifts soever, a deacon and a minister both together upon one day; but that the order in that behalf prescribed book of making and consecrating bishops, priests, and deacons, be strictly observed. Not that always every deacon shall be kept from the ministry for a whole year, when the bishop shall find good cause to the contrary; but that there being now four times appointed in every year for the ordination of deacons and ministers, there may ever be some trial of their behaviour in the office of deacon, before they be admitted to the order of priesthood.[20]

While the intent of this canon is to prohibit a candidate from being ordained a deacon and a presbyter on the same day—a probable abuse—it clearly describes a traditional Anglican understanding of the order of deacon. In this classical Anglican statement the diaconate is described as a "step or degree to the Ministry" (i.e., the presbyterate) for the purpose of

---

[19] Anglican Church of Canada, *Book of Common Prayer* (Cambridge: The University Press, 1962) [hereafter: Canada 1962], p. 644. *Cf. The First Prayer Book of King Edward VI 1549*, p. 302. Another presumable interstice between reception of the diaconate and the presbyterate was three years. The 1550 ordinal states the minimum ages of deacons and priests as twenty-one and twenty-four respectively, and thirty for bishops. *The First Prayer Book of King Edward VI 1549*, p. 292. *Cf.* By the time of the 1662 *Book of Common Prayer* the ages had risen to twenty-three and twenty-four.

[20] Canon 32, *Constitutions and Canons Ecclesiastical*, 1604, qtd. in John Henry Blunt, *The Book of Church Law* (London: Rivington's, 1872), p. 378; G. R. Evans and J. Robert Wright, eds., *The Anglican Tradition: A Handbook of Sources* (London: SPCK, 1991), p. 192.

preparation and probation. The canon cites as support the judgements of the ancient fathers and the practice of the primitive church.

The current canonical revisions of the Church of England with respect to the *cursus honorum* reflect much of Canon 32 of the *Constitutions and Canons Ecclesiastical* of 1604. The current corresponding canons, promulgated on February 26, 1987, state:

> 3.7. No person shall be ordained both deacon and priest upon one and the same day, unless he have a faculty from the Archbishop of Canterbury.

> 3.8. A deacon shall not be ordained to the priesthood for at least one year, unless the Bishop shall find good cause for the contrary, so that trial may be made of his behaviour in the office of deacon before he is admitted to the order of priesthood.[21]

Again, the purpose of the diaconate appears to be probation. What distinguishes this canonical revision from its 1604 counterpart is the fact that while the original canon expressly inhibits the reception of the two orders on a single day, the revised canon makes it a canonical possibility, if the candidate has "a faculty from the Archbishop of Canterbury." In such a case it would be difficult to ascertain the purpose of such an ordination to the diaconate since it could be neither a genuine period of preparation nor a sufficient trial of behaviour. While the expressed intent of sequential movement between the diaconate and the presbyterate may be ignored, the *cursus honorum* is nevertheless upheld.

An Anglican movement for the reform of the diaconate has resulted in a discussion on the place of sequential ordination. Calls for the restoration of the diaconate as a permanent order in the Anglican Communion began in the nineteenth century. By the mid-twentieth century, the Lambeth Conference of bishops began to give special attention to the restoration of the diaconate. The 1958 Lambeth Conference, in its report the "Order of Deacon", submitted that the time had come when Anglicans must either conclude that there is no place for the order of deacon, or else begin to restore the office of deacon in the worship and witness of the church.[22] The bishops strongly endorsed the latter position. Consequently, Resolution 88 of the 1958 Conference states:

> The Conference recommends that each province of the Anglican Communion shall consider whether the office of deacon shall be restored to its place as a distinctive

---

[21] *The Canons of the Church of England*, 4th ed., 5th supp. (London: Church House Publishing, 1986, October 1991), p. 59.

[22] "The Order of Deacon", *The Lambeth Conference, 1958* (London: SPCK, 1958), Sec. 2, p. 106.

order in the Church, instead of being regarded as a probationary period for the priesthood.[23]

The 1968 Lambeth Conference also dealt with the restoration of the diaconate. In Resolution 32 the bishops recommended that the diaconate be open to men and women, to full time church workers, in addition to candidates for the presbyterate. The same resolution also directed that the ordination rites of the Anglican Communion be revised to take into account the new role of the diaconate, to remove references to the diaconate as an "inferior office", and to emphasize the continuing element of *diakonia* in the ministries of presbyters and bishops.[24]

Resolution 32 of the 1968 Lambeth Conference was dealt with by the Anglican Consultative Council meeting in Trinidad in April of 1976. In Resolution 10 a) in the Section on Ministry, the council cautiously recommended:

> ... that the use of the Diaconate as a period of preparation for the priesthood be retained: and that every church should review its practice to ensure that this period is one of continued training and further testing of vocation; but that it is not to be regarded as necessarily leading to the priesthood.[25]

One of the strongest statements from the Lambeth Conference on the restored diaconate appears in the section reports of the 1988 Conference. A section of the report on "Ministry and Mission", entitled "The Distinctive Diaconate", stressed that:

> We need to rediscover the diaconate as an order complementing the order of priesthood rather than as a merely transitional order which it is at present. We should ensure that such a diaconate does not threaten the ministry of the laity but seeks to equip and further it. Such a diaconate, furthermore, would serve to renew the *diakonia* of the whole Church; laity, deacons, priests, and bishops....
>
> Similarly the long-standing tradition that the diaconate is an "inferior" order (cf. the old ordinals) through which you pass on the way to the priesthood is also an obstacle to the emergence of a distinctive diaconate.[26]

---

[23] Roger Coleman, ed., *Resolutions of the Twelve Lambeth Conferences: 1867–1988* (Toronto: Anglican Book Centre, 1992), p. 140.

[24] Coleman, *Resolutions*, pp. 162–163.

[25] *Anglican Consultative Council—3: Trinidad, 23 March–2 April 1976* (Coventry: Coventry Printers, 1976), p. 44.

[26] Secs. 121, 122, "Ministry and Mission", *The Lambeth Conference, 1988* (London: Church House Publishing, 1988), p. 56.

The report is clearly critical of the *cursus honorum* and cites it as an obstacle to the emergence of a distinctive diaconate; for all that, it does not explicitly offer an alternative.

While no adaptation of the traditional sequence has been ventured, an apparent lack of consensus on the place of the *cursus honorum* amongst the various national liturgical commissions is manifest in the newer ordination rites appearing throughout the Anglican Communion. Some contemporary Anglican ordinals, reflecting the directives of the 1968 Lambeth Conference, have removed all references to the diaconate as an "inferior order" and any allusion to sequential ordination.[27] Other provincial churches of the Anglican Communion have redrafted their newer ordination rites in order to reveal sequential ordination more sharply.[28]

The movement for the restoration of the diaconate as a permanent office has lead to questions about the place of the *cursus honorum* in

---

[27] E.g., *An Australian Prayer Book*, The Standing Committee of the General Synod of the Church of England in Australia (Sydney: Anglican Information Office Press, 1978), pp. 604–621; *The Book of Common Prayer*, The Episcopal Church of the United States of America, (New York: The Church Hymnal Corporation, 1979); the English *Alternative Service Book* (1980), and the Canadian *Book of Alternative Services* (1985). The rubrics of the American *Book of Common Prayer* direct that candidates for all three orders are not to wear stoles "or any other vesture distinctive of ecclesiastical rank or order" (pp. 511, 524, 536). Vesture appropriate to the diaconate, presbyterate, or episcopate is to be worn only after the prayer of consecration to an order. The intent of this rubric is to ensure that at an ordination, it will not be visually apparent that those being ordained presbyters are deacons, and that those being ordained bishops are presbyters.

[28] E.g., The Church of the Province of Southern Africa, *An Anglican Prayer Book* (Cape Town: Collins, 1989). In the charge to the candidates for the presbyterate the bishop says: "My brothers... When you were made deacon, you accepted the call to be servant [*sic*.] of God and of his people. Remember that you never cease to be a deacon, and be ready to offer service wherever God calls." (p. 587). The Ordinal of *A New Zealand Prayer Book* (Auckland: Collins, 1989), considered to be one of the more *avant-garde* of the newer rites, expressly acknowledges sequential ordination. At the presentation of a presbyter, the presenter says: "We give thanks for *N*.'s ministry as a deacon. We believe that *s/he* will serve Christ well as a priest" (p. 901). The 1995 revision of Australian ordinal departs from the 1978 rite by acknowledging liturgically the practice of sequential ordination. At the presentation of those to be ordained presbyter, the archdeacon says: "N, bishop in the Church of God, we present to you *these deacons/*NN to be ordained priest." The bishop further on says to the people: "Dear friends in Christ, you know the importance of this office. We have been assured that *these deacons are* suited to this ministry. . ." The Anglican Church of Australia, *A Prayer Book for Australia* (Alexandria, NSW: Broughton Books, 1995), p. 792.

ordination practice. In recent years Anglican challenges to the practice of sequential ordination have been raised by proponents (largely North American) for the restoration of the diaconate. Making the case that as long as candidates for the presbyterate must first be ordained deacons the diaconate will never be more than a stepping-stone, they argue for direct ordination to the priesthood for those called to that order without an intervening ordination to the diaconate. The positions of James Barnett and J. Robert Wright outlined earlier in the Introduction to this study indicate something of the scope of this debate. At present, the inherited process of sequential ordination appears stable in the churches of the Anglican Communion. The example of the English Reformation, however, ought to remind Anglicans that the clerical *cursus* is far from immutable.

c. The Roman Catholic Church

In the face of the sixteenth-century Protestant Reformation and the need for internal reform, the Council of Trent sought to confirm and defend what was traditional in catholic teaching and structure. The twenty-third session of the Council of Trent dealt with questions around the sacrament of order, and promulgated the final decree on 15 July 1563. This session is remembered particularly for its treatment of the relationship of the bishop to both the presbyterate and to the papacy, as well as its theology of "priesthood."[29] It also discussed the minor orders, the subdiaconate and diaconate, as well as sequential ordination. The doctrinal teaching on the *cursus honorum* is found in the second chapter:

> Cum autem divina res sit tam sancti sacerdotii ministerium, consentaneum fuit, quo dignius et maiori cum veneratione exerceri posset, ut in ecclesiae ordinatissima dispositione plures et diversi essent ministrorum ordines, qui sacerdotio ex officio deservirent, ita distributi, ut, qui iam clericali tonsura insigniti essent, per minores ad maiores ascenderent. Nam non solum de sacerdotibus, sed et de diaconis sacrae litterae apertam mentionem faciunt et, quae maxime in illorum ordinatione attendenda sunt, gravissimis verbis docent; et ab ipso ecclesiae initio sequentium ordinum nomina atque uniuscuiusque eorum propria ministeria, subdiaconi scilicet, acolythi, exorcistae, lectoris et ostiarii in usu fuisse cognoscuntur, quamvis non pari gradu. Nam subdiaconatus ad maiores ordines a patribus et sacris conciliis refertur, in quibus et de aliis inferioribus frequentissime legimus.[30]

---

[29] Osborne, *Priesthood*, pp. 250, ff.

[30] Norman P. Tanner, ed., *Decrees of the Ecumenical Councils* vol. 2 (Georgetown: Georgetown University Press, 1990), p. 742.

The target of this chapter is not specifically the practice of sequential ordination, but rather a defense of the major and minor orders.[31] Nonetheless,
the inherited medieval sequence of grades, and sequential movement
through them (. . . *per minores ad maiores ascenderent*) is clearly
affirmed. Not surprisingly, the Council proposed no change in the pattern
or structure of sequential ordination. Moreover, the grades themselves
were understood as having existed from the very beginning of the church
(*ad ipso ecclesiae initio*).

Similarly, the canons on the sacrament of order promulgated by the
twenty-third session affirm and strengthen the inherited pattern in response to the challenges posed by the Reformation and the need for reform
within the Roman Catholic Church itself. For example, against the Reformers who abolished the minor orders and (more than often) the major
orders, Canon 2 says:

> Si quis dixerit, praeter sacerdotium non esse in ecclesia catholica alios ordines, et
> maiores et minores, per quos velut per gradus quosdam in sacerdotium tendatur:
> a.s.[32]

Not only are the minor and major orders defended, but the practice of
sequential ordination "by steps" (*per gradus*) as well.

In terms of the reform of the clerical *cursus*, Canons 11–14 are significant too. Canon 11, dealing with the interstices, outlines the general purpose of progression through the minor orders, i.e. probation and
preparation:

> Minores ordines iis, qui saltem latinam linguam intelligant, per temporum intersti-
> tia, nisi aliud episcopo expedire magis videretur, conferantur, ut eo accuratius,
> quantum sit huius disciplinae pondus, possint edoceri; ac in unoquoque munere
> iuxta praescriptum episcopi se exerceant, idque in ea, cui adscripti erunt, ecclesia,
> nisi forte ex causa studiorum absint, atque ita de gradu in gradum ascendant, ut in
> eis cum aetate vitae meritum et doctrina maior accrescat. Quod et bonorum morum
> exemplum, et assiduum in ecclesia ministerium, atque maior erga presbyteros et
> superiores ordines reverentia, et crebrior, quam antea, corporis Christi communio
> maxime comprobabunt. Cumque hinc ad altiores gradus et sacratissima mysteria sit
> ingressus, nemo iis initietur, quem non scientiae spes maioribus ordininbus dignum
> ostendat. Hi vero non nisi post annum a susceptione postremi gradus minorum or-
> dinum ad sacros ordines promoveantur, nisi necessitas aut ecclesiae utilitas iudicio
> episcopi aliud exposcat.[33]

---

[31] Osborne notes that the refutation of Calvin's writings on the minor orders are the focus
of the second chapter of Session 23. Osborne, *Priesthood*, p. 255.

[32] Tanner, *Decrees*, vol. 2, p. 743.

[33] Tanner, *Decrees*, vol. 2, p. 748.

Similarly, Canon 12 deals with the ages of clerics in the major orders, and returns to the theme of testing and worthiness:

> Nullus in posterum ad subdiaconatus ordinem ante vigesimum secundum, ad diaconatus ante vigesimum tertium, ad presbyteratus ante vigesimum quintum aetatis suae annum promoveatur. Sciant tamen episcopi, non singulos in ea aetate constitutos debere ad hos ordines assumi, sed dignos dumtaxat et quorum probata vita senectus sit. Regulares quoque nec in minori aetate, nec sine diligenti episcopi examine ordinentur; privilegiis quibuscumque quoad hoc pentitus exclusis.[34]

Here, a significant shift from the medieval pattern the raising of the age of the subdeacon from eighteen to twenty-two years; deacons are ordained at twenty-three. The medieval allowance to ordain presbyters as early as twenty-five years, rather than thirty, has become normative.

Canon 13 outlines the qualities sought subdeacons and deacons. They should be of good reputation, educated and trained. The means for such probation and preparation is, once again, progression through the minor orders:

> Subdiaconi et diaconi ordinetur habentes bonum testimonium et in minoribus ordinibus iam probati, ac litteris et iis, quae ad ordinem exercendum pertinent, instructi, qui sperent, Deo auctore, se continere posse.... Promoti ad sacrum subdiaconatus ordinem, si per annum saltem in eo non sint versati, ad altiorem gradum, nisi aliud episcopo videatuir, ascendere non permittantur. Duo sacri ordines non eodem die, etiam regularibus, conferantur; privilegiis ac indultis, quibusvis concessis, non obstantibus quibuscumque.[35]

The interval between conferral of the subdiaconate and the diaconate is to be a year. The two orders are not to be conferred in a single day, even if privileges and indults have been granted, indicating that in practice the subdiaconate and the diaconate were being conferred on the same individuals on the same day.

Canon 14 deals with the qualities sought in candidates for the presbyterate, and like Canon 13, reflects the role of sequential ordination in this process:

> Qui pie et fideliter in ministeriis anteactis se gesserint, ad presbyteratus ordinem assumantur; bonum habeant testimonium, et hi sint, qui non modo in diaconatu ad minus annum integrum, nisi ob ecclesiae utilitatem ac neccessitatem aliud episcopo videretur, ministraverint, sed etiam ad populum docendum ea, quae scire omnibus necessarium est ad salutem, ac administranda sacramenta, diligenti examine praecedente, idonei comprobentur, atque ita pietate ac castis moribus conspicui, ut

[34] Tanner, *Decrees*, vol. 2, pp. 748–749.
[35] Tanner, *Decrees*, vol. 2, p. 749.

praeclarum bonorum operum exemplum et vitae monita ab eis possint exspectari....
Cum promotis per saltum, si non ministraverint, episcopus ex legitima causa possit
dispensare.[36]

Those to be "advanced" to the presbyterate will have conducted themselves devoutly and faithfully in the previous ministries. While an interval
of a full year is commended between ordination to the diaconate and presbyterate, for the "need and benefit of the church" this period may be shorted. A final dispensation is given in the last sentence of the canon: "For a
legitimate reason, the bishop may give a dispensation when there has been
a promotion "by a leap (*promotis per saltum*)" to those who will not have
served [in an order]." Presumably, this canon is intended for those
ordained prior to the Council. Although the only other order mentioned in
the canon is the diaconate, it is unclear for what orders the dispensation is
intended. Nevertheless, following the teaching of Aquinas and the late
medieval theologians, reception of the lower ministries appears to be a
canonical rather than a sacramental necessity for ordination to the presbyterate.

The treatment of the clerical *cursus* demonstrates Trent's concern for
the careful preparation of presbyters as part of the reform of clerical life.
Here, the council fathers reflect some of the concurrent concerns of John
Calvin, and the understanding of sequential ordination in the Anglican
Book of Common Prayer. These Tridentine canons need to be seen within
the context of the establishment of seminaries by the same session of the
Council (Canon 18).[37] Until well into the 1960s, the conferral of the lower
ministries (on the Ember days) followed the seminary timetable: tonsure
after the first year, the minor orders from doorkeeper to acolyte at the end
of the second year, the subdiaconate at the end of the third year, the diaconate during the autumn of the fourth year, and the presbyterate at the end
of the fourth year. As Kenan Osborne has observed: "Only with Vatican II
has there been any substantial change to the thrust which Trent gave to
these preparatory orders."[38] The Romano-Gallican sequence of grades was
maintained in the Roman Catholic Church until 1972.

---

[36] Turner, *Decrees*, vol. 2, p. 749.

[37] See John Tracy Ellis, "A Short History of Seminary Education: I—The Apostolic
Church to Trent," *Seminary Education in a Time of Crisis*, eds. James M. Lee and Louis
J. Putz (Notre Dame, Indiana: Fides, 1965), pp. 1–29.

[38] Osborne, *Priesthood*, p. 255.

The documents of the Second Vatican Council do not give a great deal of attention to the minor orders or to the process of sequential ordination. *Lumen gentium* deals with the diaconate in Chapter 29, but in no way describes it as a transitional office:

> . . . . For, strengthened by sacramental grace they are dedicated to the people of God, in conjunction with the bishop and his body of priests, in the service of the liturgy, of the Gospel and of works of charity.[39]

After a brief description of the duties of the deacon, the Constitution adds:

> Since, however, the laws and customs of the Latin Church in force today in many areas render it difficult to fulfil these functions, which are so extremely necessary for the life of the Church, it will be possible in the future to restore the diaconate as a proper and permanent rank of the hierarchy.[40]

This section effectively paved the way for the restored permanent diaconate, and ends the ubiquitous use of the diaconate as simply a last step towards the presbyterate: it has become an end in itself.

With the apostolic letter of Pope Paul VI, *Ministeria quaedem* of 15 August 1972 (attached to the new rites of ordination), the tonsure, the minor orders and the subdiaconate were effectively abolished.[41] The "ministries" of reader and acolyte, which were opened to lay people, replaced minor orders of the Romano-Gallican sequence. Only those who have been ordained as deacons are regarded as clerics, though candidates for the diaconate and the presbyterate were "to receive the ministries of lector and acolyte and must exercise them for a suitable length of time so as to be better fitted for the future service of the word and of the altar."[42] While the apostolic letter maintains principle of sequential ordination, the grades which were once held indispensable—especially the subdiaconate which was treated as a major order—were abrogated. Despite the anathemas attached to the canons on orders promulgated by Trent, Paul VI effectively "denies" them by discontinuing the minor orders and the subdiaconate. Thus, *Ministeria quaedem* marks a dramatic shift in the evolution of the *cursus honorum*. Hence, the twentieth century is one of continuing development and transition in the history of the *cursus honorum*.

---

[39] *Lumen gentium*, n. 29. Austin Flannery, O.P., ed., *Vatican II: The Conciliar and Post Conciliar Documents* (Northport, N.Y.: Costello, 1980), p. 387.

[40] *Lumen gentium*, n. 29. Flannery, *Vatican II*, p. 387.

[41] *Ministeria quaedem*, Flannery, *Vatican II*, pp. 427–432.

[42] *Ministeria quaedem*, n. 11. Flannery, *Vatican II*, p. 431.

The rites for ordination of deacons, presbyters and bishops were also promulgated on 15 August 1972. As noted in the Introduction to this study, the rites for the ordinations of deacons and presbyters contain no reference to sequential ordination.[43] The ordination of a bishop, however, indicates that the candidate is a presbyter.[44] This dramatic shift from the earlier rites was to accommodate, no doubt, the restored vision of the diaconate as a permanent office. Yet it reveals a different understanding of the relationship between orders of deacon and presbyter that remains at odds with the *cursus honorum*. The new Code of Canon Law unequivocally prescribes sequential ordination through the major orders.[45]

The principle of the *cursus honorum* appears to remain firmly in place in the Roman Catholic Church, the calls for its reassessment from Patrick McCaslin and Michael Lawler notwithstanding.[46] The apostolic letter *Ministeria quaedem*, however, ought to remind Roman Catholics that the *cursus honorum* is not beyond further reform.

4. "The Parameters of its Adaptation"

The purpose of this study of the origins and evolution of the *cursus honorum* has been to contribute to a question posed by advocates for the restoration of the diaconate, i.e. could the church permit direct ordination to the presbyterate? Does the history of sequential ordination "help us to decide what the essentials of that tradition are, and the parameters of its adaptation?"[47] The thesis of this study is that the *cursus honorum* arose fundamentally to serve a pastoral rather than a theological need, specifically the preparation and probation of the clergy. From the beginnings of the legislation in the fourth century through to the Gregorian reforms of the eleventh and to the Reformation and Counter-Reformation in the sixteenth

---

[43] *Rites*, vol, 2, pp. 49-69.

[44] At the presentation of the bishop-elect, the presenter says to the principal consecrator: "Most Reverend Father, the church of N. asks you to ordain this priest, N., for service as a bishop." *Rites*, vol II, p. 89.

[45] *Code of Canon Law*, Canons 377-§2, §4; 378-§1, pp. 138/139, 140/141; Canons 1031-§1, 1032-§1, §2, pp. 374/375.

[46] McCaslin and Lawler, *Sacrament of Service*, pp. 14, 123-124.

[47] *Cf.* Taft, *Liturgy*, p. xv.

century, preparation and probation seem to be the consistent rationale for the clerical *cursus* (albeit, perhaps more noticeable in the breach than in the observance). As a tradition, the *cursus honorum* has undergone centuries of development and adaptation, which have continued into the reforms of the post-Vatican II Roman Catholic Church. In the process, it has assumed an implicit and often explicit theological rationale, especially in the sequence of presbyter to bishop. This is exemplified in the eleventh century by the ordination of Archdeacon Hildebrand to the presbyterate prior to his episcopal ordination, by the twelfth-century episcopal consecration rites, and by the teaching of the thirteenth-century scholastic theologians. Yet the sacramental necessity of presbyteral ordination prior to episcopal ordination has no claim as a universal tradition of the church. It is not supported by early, patristic and early medieval texts and practice. Unless one is willing to posit that episcopal ordination rites such as *OR* XXXIV and *OR* XXXV are deficient, or that bishops such as Fabian, Athanasius, Ambrose, Nectarius, Leo the Great, Hilary, Gregory the Great, Theodore of Tarsus, Nicholas I and the like, were less than true bishops, then one must admit that sequential ordination from the presbyterate to the episcopate is essentially a canonical convention, and not a theological priority, regardless of the teaching of the scholastic theologians on the matter. In addition, the scholastic theologians held that ordination to the presbyterate without prior ordination to the lower orders, including the diaconate, was nonetheless a valid ordination, albeit illicit. History indicates countless presbyters who were never deacons; such clerics were nonetheless true presbyters.

The practice of ordaining people to more than one order, and the use of one sacred order as a form of preparation for another may be legitimately questioned. Regardless, it cannot be denied that serial or sequential ordination is an ancient practice. Although the earliest extant canonical prescription for the practice does not appear until the mid-fourth century, clearly it was known in the third century, and likely in the second. Though prior to the tenth and eleventh centuries, sequential ordination was been seldom uniform, and *per saltum* ordinations were not unknown, the practice unquestionably became standard. In short, from a historical point of view all one can say is that there is evidence for both direct and sequential ordination.

Simply citing historical evidence and precedent cannot resolve the current question, i.e. whether or not the church ought once again to modify the practice of sequential ordination. The texts surveyed from the fourth to the twelfth century indicate that the primary objective of sequential ordination has been to ensure proven and prepared leaders for the church. Hence, current questions about the parameters of the canonical adaptation of the *cursus honorum* ought to take these considerations into account, rather than simply points of sacramental theology or historical precedent.

Elementally, sequential ordination and the interstices are two sides of the same coin; one without the other defeats the purpose of both, i.e. probation and preparation. And so, without adequate intervals between the reception of one order and the next the *cursus honorum* is of little value in achieving its fundamental purpose. A valid question raised concerning the actual exercise of the *cursus honorum* in the West from the fifth century to the present, is whether sequential ordination without adequate intervals has ever genuinely fulfilled its purpose? For example, can the current sequence from deacon to presbyter—within a canonical interval ranging anywhere from a day and to a year—truly serve as a period of training and testing? Given the growing dissatisfaction of this practice, articulated especially by proponents for the restoration of the diaconate, the answer seems to be no. A six-month period in the diaconate, often in situations where a deacon is either the unsupervised pastor of a parish or some sort of "priest *manqué*" assistant in another, cannot possibly serve as an appropriate and satisfactory period of preparation and probation for the presbyterate, let alone an authentic exercise of the diaconate. If a bishop is unsure if a person is an appropriate or adequately prepared candidate for the presbyterate, the bishop ought perhaps to rethink the ordination of such an individual as a deacon.

The history of sequential ordination seems to offer two alternatives. The first is to retain sequential ordination, but return to the canonical interstices of the patristic and medieval church, i.e. five years in the diaconate prior to election and ordination as a presbyter. The restoration of the ancient interstice between the diaconate and the presbyterate would doubtlessly infuriate those who reject the practice of using one order in preparation for another; it could fall into the category of sheer antiquarianism and impracticality. On the other hand, a five year period would afford an opportunity for a more authentic exercise of diaconal ministry in which deacons may well discover their vocation lies in this order rather than in another. The church might then determine who is called out of the diaconate to the presbyterate, much the way it now calls certain presbyters to the episcopate.

The second alternative is to return to the equally ancient practice of ordaining candidates directly to the presbyterate, as long as the requirements of preparation and probation have been met elsewhere. In the contemporary church, the standards for selection, training and testing are met by institutions such diocesan candidates committees, canonical examinations, theological colleges and seminaries, psychological testing, the prior experience of candidates as lay people. . . rather than by the canonical requirement of a sequence of orders. If, as McCaslin and Lawler propose, the diaconate and the presbyterate are such dissimilar ministries, maybe some other sort of "internship" for the presbyterate (which would be neither ordained nor institutionalized) ought to be considered.[48] Following the direction of Barnett, McCaslin and Lawler, and others, conceivably the diaconate would truly be strengthened if it ceased to be a transitional stage for presbyteral candidates. Since pastoral and theological reasons for retaining sequential ordination become more and more enigmatic, and since the original intention of the practice is now met by other means, there may be compelling reasons for this second alternative, i.e. direct ordination.

Christian history in general—and the history of the *cursus honorum* in particular—demonstrate that canonical traditions and pastoral practices do change. There is no compelling reason to suppose that the practice of sequential ordination is past the point of further adaptation. The movement for the restoration of the diaconate elicits such a reconsideration. The church listens to many voices; it is hoped that the history of the *cursus honorum* may be one such voice as the church contemplates the issues surrounding the restoration of the diaconate.

---

[48] McCaslin and Lawler, *Sacrament*, pp. 123–124.

BIBLIOGRAPHY

Primary Contemporary Sources

Advisory Council for the Church's Ministry. *Deacons in the Church.* Westminster: Church Information Office, 1974.

The Anglican Church of Canada. *The Book of Alternative Services.* Toronto: The Anglican Book Centre, 1985.

——. *The Book of Common Prayer.* Cambridge: The University Press, 1962.

——. *Journal of the 32nd General Synod of the Anglican Church of Canada.* St. John's: Anglican Church of Canada, 1989.

Anglican Consultative Council—3: Trinidad, 23 March – 2 April 1976. Coventry: Coventry Printers, 1976.

The Anglican Provincial Synod of British Columbia. *Canons and Constitutions.* N.p.: n.p. 1985.

Canons et. Constitutions For the Government of the Protestant Episcopal Church In the United States of America Otherwise known as the Episcopal Church, Adopted in General Conventions 1789–1991. N.p.: n.p., 1991.

The Canons of the Church of England. 4th ed., 5th supp. London: Church House Publishing, 1991.

Canon Law Society of America. *Code of Canon Law: Latin-English Edition (Codex Iuris Canonici).* Washington: Canon Law Society of America, 1983.

The Church of England. *The Alternative Service Book.* London: Hodder et. Stoughton, 1980.

The Church of England in the Dominion of Canada. *The Book of Common Prayer.* Cambridge: The University Press, 1918.

The Church of England in Australia. *An Australian Prayer Book.* Sydney: Anglican Publishing House, 1985.

The Church of the Province of New Zealand. *A New Zealand Prayer Book.* Auckland: Collins, 1989.

The Church of the Province of Southern Africa. *An Anglican Prayer Book*. Cape Town: Collins, 1989.

Coleman, Roger, ed. *Resolutions of the Twelve Lambeth Conferences: 1867–1988*. Toronto: Anglican Book Centre, 1992.

Committee on Ministry. *A Plan to Restore the Diaconate in the Anglican Church of Canada*. Toronto: Anglican Book Centre, 1989.

Davidson, R.T. ed., *The Six Lambeth Conferences, 1867–1920*. London: SPCK, 1929.

The Episcopal Church. *The Book of Common Prayer*. New York: The Church Hymnal Corporation, 1979.

Evans, G. R., and J. Robert Wright, eds., *The Anglican Tradition: A Handbook of Sources*. London: SPCK, 1991.

The First Prayer Book of King Edward VI. London: Dent, 1952.

The General Synod [of the Church of England]. *Deacons in the Ministry of the Church*. Westminster: Church House Publishing, 1988.

——. *The Liturgical Ministry of Deacons: A Report by the Liturgical Commission. . .* London: n.p., 1977.

The Lambeth Conference, 1958. London: SPCK, 1958.

The Lambeth Conference, 1968. London: SPCK, 1968.

The Lambeth Conference, 1988. London: Church House Publishing, 1988.

The National Council of Catholic Bishops. *The Rites: Volume II*. New York: Pueblo, 1980.

Primary Historical Sources

D'Achery, Jean-Luc, ed. *Spicilegium sive Collectio Veterum Aliquot Scriptorum*. Paris: Montalant, 1793.

Alcuin. *Disputatio puerorum*. In J.-P. Migne, ed. *Patrologia Latina 101*. (Paris), 1863.

Alexander II, Pope. *Epistle 32*. In J.-P. Migne, ed. *Patrolgia Latina 146*. (Paris) 1884.

Amalarius of Metz. *Liber Officialis*. ed. J. Hanssens, *Amalarius episcopi Opera liturgica omnia*. vol. 2. *Studi e Testi 139*. Vatican: Biblioteca Apostolica Vaticana, 1948.

Ambrose of Milan. *De officiis ministrorum*. In J.-P. Migne, ed., *Patrologia Latina 16* (Paris) 1880.

———. *Epistle 59, To the Church at Vercelli.* (Letter 63 in the Benedictine enumeration.) In J.-P. Migne, ed., *Patrologia Latina* 16 (Paris) 1880. English in Sr. Mary Melchior Beyenka, *St. Ambrose Letters.* vol. 26 of *The Fathers of the Church.* New York: The Fathers of the Church Inc., 1954.

Ambrosiaster. *Ad Efesios.* In H.I. Vogels, ed., *Corpus Scriptorum Ecclesiasticorum Latinorum* 81/1. Vienna: Hoelder-Pichler-Tempsky, 1966.

Andrieu, Michel. *Les Ordines Romani du haut moyen age.* vols. 3 et. 4. Louvain: Spicilegium Sacrum Lovaniense, (vol.3) 1951, (vol.4) 1956.

———. *Le Pontifical Romain au Moyen-Age.* vols. 1,2,3. *Studi e Testi* 87. Vatican: Biblioteca Apostolica Vaticana, 1938 (v.1), 1940 (vv.2et.3).

Aquinas, Thomas. *Summa Theologiae.* Ed. De Rubeis, Billuart, and P. Faucher. Rome: Marietti, 1953.

Augustine of Hippo. *Sermo 335.* In J.-P. Migne ed., *Patrologia Latina* 39 (Paris) 1865. English in J. T. Lienhard, trans., *Ministry: Message of the Fathers to the Church.* vol. 8. Wilmington, Delaware: Michael Glazier, 1984.

Banting, H.M.J., ed. *Two Anglo-Saxon Pontificals* (The Egbert and the Sidney Sussex Pontificals). London: Henry Bradshaw Society, 1989.

Bastiaensen, A. A. R, ed. *Vita Di Cipriano. Vite Dei Santi* 3. Verona: Fondazione Lorenzo Valla Arnoldo Mondadori Editore, 1975.

Bede. *Collectaneum.* In J.-P. Migne, ed. *Patrologia Latina* 94. (Paris) 1862.

———. *Historia ecclesiastica gentis anglorum.* Ed. C. Plummer. Oxford: Clarendon Press, 1896.

Besse, Jean-Claude. *Collectio Anselmo dedicata: Étude et Texte. Histoire de Textes du Droit du Moyen-Age.* Paris: Librairies Techniques, 1960.

Botte, Dom Bernard, ed. *La Tradition Apostolique de Saint Hippolyte.* Münster/ Aschendorffsche, Verlagsbuchhandlung, 1963. English in Geoffrey Cuming, trans. and notes, *Hippolytus: A Text for Students.* Bramcote Notts.: Grove Books, 1976.

Breviarium Hipponense. In J.-P. Migne, ed. *Patrogia Latina* 84. (Paris) 1862.

Burchard of Worms. *Decretorum Libri XX.* In J.-P. Migne, ed. *Patrologia Latina* 140. (Paris) 1880.

Camelot, P. Th. ed. and comm. *Ignace d'Antioche, Lettres. Sources Chrétiennes* 10. Paris: Éditions du Cerf, 1944.

Canons of Hippolytus. In Hans Achelis, ed., *Die Ägyptische Kirchen-Ordung.* vol. 6. *Texte und Untersuchungen.* Liepzig: J.C. Hinrichs'sche Buchhandlung, 1891. English in Paul Bradshaw, *The Canons of Hippolytus.* Bramcote Notts.: Grove Books, 1987.

Celestine. *Epistle* 4. In J.-P. Migne, ed. *Patrologia Latina* 56. (Paris) 1865.

Chavasse, Antoine. *Le Sacramentaire Gélasien Vaticanus Reginensis 316.* Tournai: Desclée, 1958.

Chronica Casinense. In J.-P. Migne, ed. *Patrologia Latina* 173. (Paris) 1895; H. Hoffman, ed., *Die Chronik von Montecassino,* Monumenta Germaniae Historica *Scriptores,* vol. 34. Hannover: Hahnsche Buchhandlung, 1980.

Chronicon Hugonis. In J.-P. Migne, ed. *Patrologia Latina* 154. (Paris) 1881.

Chronicum integrum. In J.-P. Migne, *Patrologia Latina* 51. (Paris) 1861.

de Clercq, Charles, ed. *Concilia Galliae, A. 511—A. 695. Corpus Christianorum Series Latina* 148a. Turnhout: Brepols, 1963.

Collectio Avellana. In O. Guenther, ed., *Corpus Scriptorum Ecclesiasticorum Latinorum* 35 (Leipzig) 1895.

Coustant, P. ed., *Epistolae Romanorum Pontificum.* vol. 1. Paris: A.-V. Coustelier, 1721.

Cresconius. *Crisconii Episcopi Africani Breviarium Canonicum.* In. J.-P. Migne, ed., *Patrologia Latina* 88 (Paris) 1850.

Cyprian of Carthage. *Cyprianum Antoniano fratris s. (Epistle* 55). In W. Hartel, ed.,*Corpus Scriptorum Ecclesiasticorum Latinorum,* 3.2 (1871). English in J.T. Lienhard, *Ministry.* 1984.

——. *Cyprianus presbyteris et diaconibus item plebi universae s. (Epistle* 38). In W. Hartel, ed., *Corpus Scriptorum Ecclesiasticorum Latinorum,* 3/2. (1871). English in J.T. Lienhard, *Ministry.* 1984.

Deshusses, Jean. "Les Sacramentaires: Etat actuel de la recherche." *Archiv für Liturgiewissenschaft* 24 (1982).

——. ed. *Le Sacramentaire Grégorien.* 3 vols. *Spicilegium Friburgense* 16. Fribourg: Editions Universitaires Fribourg/Suisse, 1971, 1979, 1982.

Duchesne, L. ed. *Liber Pontificalis: Texte, Introduction, et Commentaire.* 2nd ed. 2 vols. Paris: Ernest Thorin, 1886.

Dumas, A., ed. *Liber Sacrementorum Gellonensis. Corpus Christianorum Series Latina* 159. Turnhout: Brepols, 1981.

Faustini et Marcellini presbyterorum patris Ursinus adversus Damasum libellus precum ad imperatores, Praefatio. In J.-P. Migne, *Patrologia Latina* 13. (Paris) 1845.

Fehr, Berhard, ed. *Die Hirtenbriefe Aelfrics in altenglisher und lateinischer Fassung.* Bibliothek der angelsächsischen Prosa 9. [reprint] Ed. Peter Clemoes. Darmstadt: Wissenschafliche Buchgesellschaft, 1966.

Feltoe, Charles L. *Sacramentarium Leonianum.* Cambridge: University Press, 1896.

Fornasari, M., ed. *Collectio canonum in V libris.* Corpus Christianorum Continuatio Mediavalis 6. Turnhout: Brepols, 1970.

Friedberg, Aemilius, ed. *Decretum Magistri Gratiani.* Liepzig: Bernhard Tachnitz, 1879.

Gelasius. *Fragmentum* 10. In Andreas Thiel, ed. *Epistolae Romanorum Pontificum Genuinae.* vol. 1. Braunsberg: Edward Peter, 1868.

——. *Epistle* 14. In Andreas Thiel, ed. *Epistolae Romanorum Pontificum Genuinae.* vol. 1. Braunsberg: Edward Peter, 1868; In J.-P. Migne, ed. *Patrologia Latina* 84. (Paris) 1862.

Gerard of Cambrai, *Acta synodi Atrebatensis.* In. J.-P. Migne, *Patrologia Latina* 142. (Paris) 1880.

Gesta Innoncenti papae. In J.-P. Migne, ed. *Patrologia Latina* 214. (Paris) 1890.

Gilchrist, John, ed. *Diversorum patrum sententiae sive Collectio in LXXIV titulos digesta.* Monumenta Iuris Canonici, Series B. Corpus Collectionum I. Vatican: Biblioteca Apostolica Vaticana, 1973. English in, John Gilchrist, trans., *The Collection in Seventy-four Titles: A Canon Law Manual of the Gregorian Reform.* Toronto: Pontifical Institute of Mediaeval Studies, 1980.

von Glanvell, Victor Wolf. *Die Kanonessammlung des Kardinals Deusdedit.* Paderborn: Druck und Verlag von Ferdinand Schöningh, 1905.

Gregory of Nazianzus. *Oration II: On his Flight.* In J.-P. Migne, *Patrologia Graeca* 35. (Paris) 1886. English in J.T. Lienhard. *Ministry.* 1984.

——. *Oration XV.* In J.-P. Migne, ed., *Patrologia Graeca* 35. (Paris) 1886.

——. *Oration XLVIII.* In J.-P. Migne, ed., *Patrologia Graeca* 36. (Paris) 1885. English in C.C. Brown and J.E. Swallows, trans. *Nicene and Post-Nicene Fathers.* vol. 7. New York: Christian Literature Association, 1894.

Gregory of Tours. *Historia francorum*. Ed. W. Arndt and Br. Krusch. Monumenta Germaniae Historica. *Scriptores Rerum Merovingicarum* I. Hannover: 1951.

Hartmann, L. M., ed. *Gregorii I Papae: Registrum Epistularum 2*. Monumenta Germaniae Historica, *Epistolarum Tomus II*. Berlin: Weidmann, 1899.

Hartmann, Wilfried, ed. *Die Konzilien der Karolingischer Teilreiche, 843-859*, Hanover: Hansche Buchhandlung, 1984.

Heiming, O., ed. *Liber Sacramentorum Augustodinensis. Corpus Christianorum Series Latina* 159b. Turnhout: Brepols, 1984.

Herbert of Bosham. *Vita Sancti Thomae, archiepiscopi et martyris*. Ed. J. C. Robertson. *Rerum Britannicarum Medii Aevi Scriptores*. Rolls Series. 67.3. London: Kraus Reprints, 1965.

Hincmar of Rheims. *Epistles* 29 and 39. In J.-P. Migne, ed. *Patrologia Latina* 126. (Paris) 1879.

Hinschius, Paul, ed., *Decretales Pseudo-Isidorianae*. Leipzig: Bernhard Tauchnitz, 1863.

Hooker, Richard. *Of the Laws of Ecclesiastical Polity* Books V and VII. Ed. W. Speed Hill and P. G Stanwood. Cambridge, MA: Harvard University Press, 1977, 1981.

Hormisdas. *Epistle 25*. In J.-P. Migne, ed. *Patrologia Latina* 63; Andreas Thiel, ed. *Epistolae Romanorum Pontificum Genuinae*. vol. 1. Braunsberg: Edward Peter, 1868.

Hugh of St. Victor. *De sacramentis*. In J.-P. Migne, ed. *Patrologia Latina* 176. (Paris) 1880.

Hurst, D., ed. *Baeda Venerabilis Opera. Corpus Christianorum Series Latina* 119a. Turnhout: Brepols, 1969.

Ignatius the Deacon. *Vita Tarasii archiepiscopi Constantinopolitani*. In J.-P. Migne, ed. *Patrologia Graeca* 98. (Paris) 1865.

Innocent I. *Epistle 37*. In J.-P. Migne *Patrogia Latina* 20. (Paris) 1845.

Irenaeus. *Adversus Haereses*. In J.-P. Migne, ed., *Patrologia Graeca* 7 (Paris) 1882. English in Alexander Roberts and James Donaldson, trans., *Ante-Nicene Christian Library*. vol. 1.1. Edinburgh: T.et. T. Clarke, 1867.

Isidore of Seville. *De ecclesiasticis officiis*. In J.-P. Migne, ed., *Patrologia Latina* 83 (Paris) 1862; Christopher M. Lawson, ed. *De ecclesiasticis officiis. Corpus Christianorum Series Latina* 133. Turnhout: Brepols, 1989.

——. *Origines.* In J.-P. Migne, ed., *Patrologia Latina* 82 (Paris) 1850; W. M. Lindsay, ed. *Isidori Hispalensis episcopi Etymologiae sive Originum libri XX.* vol. 1. Oxford: 1911.

Isidorus Mercator (Pseudo-Isidore). *Decreta.* in J.-P. Migne, ed., *Patrologia Latina* 130 (Paris) 1880.

Ivo of Chartres. *Decretum* et. *Panormia.* In J.-P. Migne, ed., *Patrologia Latina* 161/162 (Paris) 1889.

——. *Sermo II.* In J.-P. Migne, ed., *Patrologia Latina* 162 (Paris) 1889.

Jaubert, Annie, ed. and comm. *Clément de Rome, Épitre aux Corinthiens. Sources Chrétiennes* 167. Paris: Éditions du Cerf, 1971.

Jerome. *Epistola CXLVI, Ad Evangelum Presbyterum.* In I. Hilberg, ed. *Corpus Scriptorum Ecclesiasticorum Latinorum* 56 (1918). English in Joseph T. Lienhard, *Ministry: Message of the Fathers to the Church,* 8. Wilmington, Delaware: Michael Glazier, 1984.

John Chrysostom. *De Sacerdotio.* In J.-P. Migne, ed., *Patrologia Graeca* 48 (1862). English in Graham Neville, trans., *Saint John Chrysostom, Six Books on the Priesthood.* Crestwood, New York: St.Vladimir's Press, 1984.

John VIII, Pope. *Epistles* 171, 183, and 187. In J.-P. Migne, ed. *Patrologia Latina* 126. (Paris) 1879

Laurence of Liège. *Gesta Virdunensium episcoporum et abbatum.* In J.-P. Migne, ed. *Patrologia Latina* 204.

Leo the Great. *Epistles* 6 and 12. In J.-P. Migne, ed. *Patrologia Latina* 54. (Paris) 1881.

Liberatus the Deacon. *Breviarium in Causae Nestorianorum et Eutychianorum.* In J.-P. Migne, ed. *Patrologia Latina* 68. (Paris) 1866.

Lietzmann, D. Hans. *Das Sacramentarium Gregorianum.* Münster: Verlag der Aschendorffschen Verlagsbuchhandlung, 1921.

Mabillon, J., ed. *Annales Ordinis S. Benedicti.* Lucae: Typis Leonardo Venturini, 1739.

Mansi, Joannes Dominicus. *Sacrorum Conciliorum Nova, et Amplissima Collectio.* vols. 3, 16–22. Venice: Expensis Antonii Zatta, 1759, 1771–1778.

Martínez Díez, Gonzalo and Rodriguez, Felix, eds., *La Coleccíon Canónica Hispana, III, Concilios Griegos y Africanos.* Madrid: Edicianes Aldecoa, 1982.

Mohlberg, Leo Cunibert. ed., *Liber sacramentorum Romanae Aeclesiae ordinis anni circuli* (*Cod. Vat. Reg. lat. 316; Paris, B.N. 7193, 41/56*).

Rerum Ecclesiasticarum Documenta, Series Major Fontes 4. Rome: Herder, 1981.

———. ed. *Missale Francorum* (*Cod. Vat. Reg. lat. 257*). Reum Ecclesiasticarum Documenta, Series Major Fontes 2. Rome: Casa Editrice Herder, 1957.

———. ed. *Missale Gallicanum Vetus* (*Cod. Vat. Palat. lat. 493*). Reum Ecclesiasticarum Documenta, Series Major Fontes 3. Rome: Casa Editrice Herder, 1958.

———, *et al.* eds. *Sacramentarium Veronense*. Rerum Ecclesiasticarum Documenta, Series Major Fontes 1. Rome: Herder, 1956.

Monumenta Germaniae Historica. *Epistolae 6. Epistolae Karolini Aevi 4.* Berlin: Weidmanns, 1925.

Mordek, Hubert, ed., *Kirchenrecht und Reform im Frankenreich: Die Collectio Vetus Gallica die älteste systematische Kanonessammlung des fränkischen Gallien*. Beiträge zur Geschicte und Quellenkunde des Mittelalters I. Berlin: Walter de Gruyter, 1975.

Munier, C. *Concilia Africae, A 345–A. 525. Corpus Christianorum Series Latina* 149. Turnhout: Brepols, 1974.

———. *Concilia Galliae, A. 314–A. 506. Corpus Christianorum Series Latina* 148. Turnhout: Brepols, 1963.

———. *Les Statuta Ecclesiae Antiqua*. Paris: Presse Universitaires de France, 1960.

Niketas-David Paphilagon. *Vita S. Ignatii*. In J.-P. Migne, ed. *Patrologia Graeca* 105. (Paris) n.d.

Paulinus. *Vita S. Ambrosii*. In J.-P. Migne, ed., *Patrologia Latina* 14 (1882). English in Sr. Mary Simplicia Kaniecka, trans. and ed., *Vita Sancti Ambrosii a Paulino eius Notario*. Washington: Catholic University of America, 1928.

Pautigny, Louis, ed. *Apologies*. Paris: Alphonse Picard et Fils, 1904. English in Thomas B. Falls, trans. *Writings of Justin Martyr. The Fathers of the Church.* vol. 6. New York: Christian Heritage, 1948.

Pelagius. *Epistle 5*. In Monumenta Germaniae Historica. *Epistolae 3, Merowingi et. Karolini 1*. Berlin: Weidmann, 1892; A. Theiner, ed. *Disquisitiones Criticae in Praecipuas Canonum et Decretalium*. Rome: Collegio Urbano, 1836; Paul Ewald, ed. *Neus Archiv. Gesellschaft für ältere deutsche Geschickskunde* 5. Hannover: Hahn'sche Buchhandlung, 1880.

———. *Epistle 23*. In Paul Ewald, ed. *Neus Archiv. Gesellschaft für ältere deutsche Geschichtsskunde* 5. Hannover: Hahn'sche Buchhandlung,

1880; Thiel, Andreas, ed. *Epistolae Romanorum Pontificum Genuinae* 1. Braunsberg: Edward Peter, 1868.

Pellegrino, Michele, ed. *Paolino di Milano, Vita di S. Ambrogio: Introdizione, testo critico et note.* Rome: Editrice Studium, 1961.

Perels, Ernst, ed. *Bonizo: Liber de vita christiana.* Berlin: Weidmannsche Buchhandlung, 1930.

Philosophumena. In J.-P. Migne, ed., *Patrologia Graeca* 16/III (Paris) 1863.

Pontius. *Vita S. Cypriani.* In J.-P. Migne, ed., *Patrologia Latina* 3 (Paris) 1886.

PP Collegii S. Bonaventurae. *Magistri Petri Lombardi Parisiensis episcopi Sententiae in IV libris distinctae.* Grottaferrata: 1981.

Pseudo-Alcuin. *Liber de divinis officiis.* In J.-P. Migne, ed., *Patrologia Latina* 101 (Paris) 1863.

Pseudo-Isidore. *Decretalium collectio.* In J.-P. Migne, ed. *Patrologia Latina* 130 (Paris) 1880; Paul Hinschius, ed., *Decretales Pseudo-Isidorianae.* Leipzig: Bernhard Tauchnitz, 1863.

Pseudo-Jerome. *De VII ordinibus ecclesiae.* In J.-P. Migne, ed., *Patrologia Latina* 30 (Paris) 1846. A. W. Kalff, ed. *Ps.-Hieronymi de septem ordinibus ecclesiae.* Würzburg: 1935.

Rahmani, I. E. ed. *Testamentum Domini Nostri Jesu Christi.* Hildesheim: Georg Olms, 1968.

Rhabanus Maurus. *De clericorum institutione.* In J.-P. Migne, ed., *Patrologia Latina* 107 (Paris) 1864. A. Knoepfler, ed. *Rabani Mauri De clericorum institutioni libri tres.* Veröffentlichungen aus dem Kirchen historischen Seminar München 5. Munich: J. J. Lentner'schen Buchandlung, 1900.

Refoulé, R. F. and P. de Labriolle, eds. and comm. *Tertullian: Traité de la prescription contre les Hérétiques. Sources Chrétiennes* 46. Paris: Éditions du Cerf, 1957.

Regino of Prüm. *De Synodalibus causis et Disciplinis Ecclesiasticis.* F.G.A. Wasserschleben, ed., Leipzig: Englemann, 1840.

Rousseau, A. and L. Doutreleau, eds. and comm. *Irénée de Lyons, Contre les Hérésies, Livre III. Sources Chrétiennes* 211.2. (Paris) 1974. English in A. Roberts and W. T. Rambaut, trans. *The Writings of Irenaeus* 5, *The Ante-Nicene Christian Library* 5. Edinburgh: T. and T. Clarke, 1884.

——. *Irénée de Lyons, Contres les Hérésies, Livre IV. Sources Chrétiennes* 100. (Paris) 1965. English in A. Roberts and W. T. Rambaut, trans.

The Writings of Irenaeus 5, *The Ante-Nicene Christian Library* 5. Edinburgh: T. and T. Clarke, 1884.

Rordorf, Willy, and André Tuillier, eds. *La Doctrine des Douze Apôtres (Didaché)*. *Sources Chrétiennes* 248. Paris: Éditions du Cerf, 1978.

Rotgerus of Triers. *Acta* of the Council of Rome (769). Wolfenbüttel, Herzog-August-Bibliothek. MS Helmst. 454.

Saint-Roch, P., ed. *Liber Sacramentorum Engolismensis. Corpus Christianorum Series Latina.* 159c. Turnhout: Brepols, 1987.

Schwartz, Eduard, ed. *Die Kirkengeschicte, Eusebius Werke* 2.1. *Die griechischen christlichen Schriftsteller der ersten drei Jahrhunderts.* Leipzig: J. C. Hinrichs'sche Buchhandlung, 1903. English in G. A. Williamson, trans. *Eusebius: the History of the Church from Christ to Constantine.* 2nd ed. London: Penguin Books, 1989.

Siricius. *Epistola I, Siricius Himerio Tarrconensi.* In J.-P. Migne, *Patrologia Latina* 13 (Paris) 1845. English in J.T. Lienhard. *Ministry.* 1984.

Socrates. *Historica Ecclesiastia.* In J.-P. Migne, *Patrologia Graeca* 67 (Paris) 1864. English in Charles D. Hartranft, trans., *Nicene and Post-Nicene Fathers.* vol. 2. New York: Christian Literature Association, 1892.

La Société Historique et Archéologique de la Charente. *Le Sacramentaire Gélasien d'Angoulême.* Angoulême: Ministère de l'Instruction Publique, n.d.

Sozomen. *Historia Ecclesiastica.* In J.-P. Migne, *Patrologia Graeca* 67 (Paris) 1864. English in Charles D. Hartranft, trans., *Nicene and Post-Nicene Fathers.* vol.2. New York: Christian Literature Association, 1892.

Tanner, Norman P., trans. et. ed., *Decrees of the Ecumenical Councils.* vol. 1. Georgetown: Sheed and Ward, Georgetown University Press, 1990.

Tertullian. *De praescriptione haereticorum.* Ed. A. Kroymann. *Corpus Scriptorum Ecclesiasticorum Latinorum* 70. (Vienna) 1942. English in J.T. Lienhard. *Ministry.* 1984.

——. *Liber de baptismo.* Eds. A. Reifferscheid and G. Wissowa. *Corpus Scriptorum Ecclesiasticorum Latinorum* 20.1. (Vienna) 1890. English in J.T. Lienhard. *Ministry.* 1984.

Thaner, Fridericus, ed. *Anselmi episcopi Lucensis Collectio Canonum una cum Collectione minore iussu instituti Savigniani.* Oeniponte: Librariae Academicae Wagneriane, 1906.

Theiner, A. ed. *Disquisitiones Criticae in Praecipuas Canonum et Decretalium*. Rome: Collegio Urbano, 1836.

Theodore the Lector. *Ecclesiastical History*. In J.-P. Migne, ed. *Patrologia Graeca* 86.1. (Paris) 1865.

Theodoret. *Historica Ecclesiastica*. In J.-P. Migne, ed., *Patrologia Graeca* 82. English in Blomfield Jackson, trans., *Nicene and Post-Nicene Fathers*. vol. 3. New York: Christian Literature Association, 1892.

Thiel, Andreas, ed. *Epistolae Romanorum Pontificum Genuinae* 1. Braunsberg: Edward Peter, 1868.

Turner, Cuthbert Hamilton, ed., *Ecclesiae Occidentalis Monumenta Iuris Antiquissima*. 2 vols. Oxford: Clarendon Press, 1899.

Urban II. *Epistle* 263. In J.-P. Migne, ed. *Patrologia Latina* 151. (Paris) 1881.

Vives, José, ed., *Concillios Visigóticos e Hispano-Romanos*. Madrid: Consejo Superior de Investigaciones científicas Instituto Enrique Florez: 1963.

Vogel, Cyrille. *Le Pontifical Romano-Germanique du dixième siècle*. vol. 1. Vatican: Biblioteca Apostolica Vaticana, 1963.

Vööbus, Arthur. ed. and trans. *The Didascalia Apostolorum in Syriac*. *Corpus Scriptorum Christianorum Orientalium* 176. Louvain: 1979

Wasserschleben, F. G. A., ed. *Regionis Abbatis Prumiensis: Libri duo de synodalibus causis et disciplinis ecclesiasticus*. Leipzig: Englemann, 1840.

Wasserschleben, Hermann, ed., *Die Irische Kanonensammlung*. Leipzig: Neudruck der 2. Auflage, 1885. Aalen: Scientia Verlag, 1966.

Watterich, J.M. *Pontificum Romanorum*. vol. 2. Leipzig: Neudruck der Ausgabe, 1862. Aalen: Scientia Verlag, 1966.

Weiland, L., ed. *Constitutiones et Acta Publica Imporatorum et Regnum*. vol. 1. *Monumenta Germaniae Historica*. Hannover: Impensis Bibliopolii Hahniani, 1893.

Werminghoff, A., ed. *Concilia Aevi Karolini*. 2 vols. *Monumenta Germaniae Historica*. Hannover et. Leipzig: Unveränderter Nachdruck, 1979.

Wilson, H. A., ed. *The Gelasian Sacramentary*. Oxford: 1894.

———, ed. *The Gregorian Sacramentary under Charles the Great*. Henry Bradshaw Society, vol. 49. London: Henry Bradshaw Society, 1915.

Zacharias, Pope. *Epistle* 13. In J.-P. Migne, ed. *Patrologia Latina* 89. (Paris) 1850.

Zosimus, Pope. *Epistles* 7 and 9. In J.-P. Migne, ed. *Patrologia Latina* 20. (Paris) 1845.

Secondary Sources

Abba, R. "Priests and Levites", *The Interpreter's Dictionary of the Bible.* vol. 3. Nashville: Abingdon Press, 1986. pp. 876–889.

Alexander, J. Neil. "A Call to Adventure: Seven Propositions on Ministry." *This Sacred History: Anglican Reflections for John Booty.* Ed. Donald S. Armentrout. Cambridge, MA.: Cowley Publications, 1990. pp. 21–30.

Alexander, Paul J. *The Patriarch Nicephorus of Constantinople.* Oxford: Clarendon Press, 1958.

Amann, E. *The Church of the Early Centuries.* London: Sands et. Co., 1930.

Andrieu, Michel. "La carrière ecclésiastique des papes et les documents liturgiques du moyen âge," *Revue des sciences religieuses* 21 (1947). pp. 90–120.

——. "Les ordres mineurs dans l'ancien rite romain", *Révue des sciences réligiieuses* 5 (1925). pp. 232–274.

——. "Le sacre épiscopal d'après Hincmar de Reims." *Revue d'histoire ecclésiastique.* 48 (1953). pp. 22–74.

Audet, Jean-Paul. *La Didaché: Instructions des Apôtres.* Paris: Librairie LeCoffre, 1958.

Babut, E. Ch. *La plus ancienne décrétale.* Diss. Faculté des Lettres de l'Université de Paris. Paris: Société Nouvelle de Librairie et d'Édition, 1904.

Balfour, Ian S. "The Relationship of Man to God, from Conception to Conversion, in the Writings of Tertullian." Diss. U of Edinburgh, 1980.

Barnard, L. W. *Justin Martyr: His Life and Thought.* Cambridge: The University Press, 1967.

Barnett, James. *The Diaconate: A Full and Equal Order.* New York: Seabury, 1981.

——."'Direct ordination and catholic order'." *Diakoneo* 12.5 (Novemeber, 1990), pp. 1–2.

Bavaud, Georges. "Le Document de Lima sur le ministère." *Nova et Vetera*, 59 (1984). pp. 93–102.

Benko, Stephen. "Vocabulary of Latin Terms." *Early Church History: The Roman Empire as the Setting of Primitive Christianity*. Ed. Stephen Benko and John O'Rourke. London: Oliphants, 1971. pp. 292–294.

Berthouzoz, Roger. *Liberté et Grâce suivant la théologie d'Irénée de Lyons*. Fribourg: Éditions Universitaires, 1980.

Bévenot, Maurice. "Tertullian's Thought about `Priesthood'." *Corona Gratiarum*. vol. 1. Brugges: Sint Pietersabdj, 1975. pp. 125–137.

Black, Matthew, ed. *Peake's Commentary on the Bible*. London: Thomas Nelson and Sons, 1962.

Bligh, John. "Deacons in the Latin Western Church since the Fourth Century", *Theology* 58 (1955). pp. 421–429.

Blunt, John Henry. *The Book of Church Law*. London: Rivingtons, 1872.

Botte, Dom Bernard. "Le rituel d'ordination des Statuta Ecclesiae Antiqua", *Recherches de Théologie ancienne et médiévale* 11 (1939). pp. 223–241.

Bowe, Barbara. *A Church in Crisis: Ecclesiology and Paraenesis in Clement of Rome*. Minneapolis: Fortress Press, 1988.

Bradshaw, Paul. *The Anglican Ordinal*. London: SPCK, 1971.

——. "Ordination." *Essays on Hippolytus*. Ed. Geoffrey Cuming. Bramcote Notts.: Grove Books, 1978. pp. 33–38.

——. *Ordination Rites of the Ancient Churches of East and West*. New York: Pueblo Publishing Company, 1990.

——. *The Search for the Origins of Christian Worship*. New York: Oxford University Press, 1992.

Brent, A. "History and Eschatological Mysticism in Ignatius of Antioch." *Ephemerides Theologicae Lovaniensis* 65.4 (1989). pp. 309–329.

Bright, William. *The Canons of the First Four General Councils of Nicaea, Constantinople, Ephesus, and Chalcedon*. Oxford: Clarendon Press: 1892.

Brown, Peter. *Augustine of Hippo: A Biography*. London: Faber and Faber, 1975.

Brown, Raymond E. *Priest and Bishop: Biblical Reflections*. New York: Paulist Press, 1970.

Brown, Raymond E. *et al.*, eds. *The Jerome Biblical Commentary*. Englewood Cliffs, New Jersey: Prentice Hall, 1968.

——. *The New Jerome Biblical Commentary.*Englewood Cliffs, New Jersey: Prentice Hall, 1990.

Bruce, F.F. *The International Bible Commentary.* Grand Rapids Michigan: Marshal Pickering/Zondervan, 1986.

Camelot, P. T. "Photius." *Catholicisme hier-aujourd'hui-demain.* vol. 11. Ed. G. Mathon *et al.* Paris: Letouzey, 1988. pp. 230 ff.

Cancouët, Michel, et. Violle, Bernard. *Les Diacres.* Paris: Desclée, 1990.

Chadwick, Henry. *The Early Church.* London: Penguin Books, 1981.

Clarke, G.W. trans. and ed., *The Letters of St. Cyprian of Carthage.* vol. 3. *Ancient Christian Writers.* vol. 46. New York: Newman Press, 1986.

Clarke, Lowther W.K. *The Concise Bible Commentary.* London: SPCK, 1952.

La Commission Episcopale de Liturgie et de Pastorale Sacramentelle. *Le Rôle des diacres dans l'action liturgique.* France: La Commission Episcopale de Liturgie et de Pastorale Sacramentelle, 1986.

Congar, Y., "Faits, problèmes, et réflections à propos du pouvoir d'ordre et des rapports entre le presbytérat et l'épiscopat" *La Maison Dieu* 14 (1948). pp. 107–128.

Coquin, M. "Le sort des «Statuta Ecclesiae antiqua» dans les Collections canonique jusqu'a la «Concordia» de Gratian." *Rechereches de Théologie Ancienne et Médiévale* 28 (1961). pp. 193–224.

Cross, F.L. and E.A. Livingstone, eds., *The Oxford Dictionary of the Christian Church.* 2nd ed., revised. Oxford: Oxford University Press, 1990.

Davies, J.G. "Deacons, Deaconesses and the Minor Orders in the Patristic Period." *Journal of Ecclesiastical History,* 14 (1963). pp. 1–5.

Davis, Raymond. *The Book of the Pontiffs.* Liverpool: Liverpool University Press, 1989.

Dekker, E., and A. Gaar, eds. *Clavis Patrum Latinorum.* 2nd ed. Bruges: C. Beyaert, 1961.

Deanesly, Margaret. *A History of the Medieval Church: 590–1500.* London: Methuen et. Co., 1979.

Dix, Dom Gregory. "The Ministry in the early Church c. A.D. 90–410." *The Apostolic Ministry.* Ed. Kenneth E. Kirk. London: Hodder et. Stoughton, 1957, pp. 183–303.

Dorris, Tom. "Deacons seek direct ordination." *The Episcopalian,* August, 1991.

Donovan, Daniel. "The Levitical Priesthood and the Ministry of the New Testament." Diss. Münster, 1970.

——. *What are they saying about the Ministerial Priesthood.* New York: Paulist Press, 1992.

Duchesne, Louis. *Origines du Culte Chrétien.* 2nd ed. Paris: A. Fontemoing, 1898.

Dudden, F. Homes. *Gregory the Great: His Place in History and Thought.* 2 vols. London: Longmans, Green, and Co., 1905.

——. *The Life and Times of Ambrose.* Oxford: Clarendon Press, 1953.

Dvornik, Francis. *The Photian Schism: History and Legend.* Cambridge: The University Press, 1948.

Ellard, Gerald. *Ordination Anointings in the Western Church before 1000 AD.* Cambridge MA: The Mediaeval Academy of America, 1933.

Faivre, Alexandre. "La Documentation canonico-liturgique de l'église ancienne." *Revue des sciences religieuses,* 54 (1980). pp. 204–215.

——. *The Emergence of the Laity in the Early Church.* Trans. David Smith. New York: Paulist Press, 1990.

——. *Naissance d'une Hiérarchie: Les premières étapes du cursus clerical. Théologie Historique* 40. Paris: Éditions Beauchesne, 1977.

Fedwick, P. J. "The Function of the *proestos* in the Earliest Christian *koinonia.*" *Recherches de théologie ancienne et médiévale* 48 (1981). pp. 5–13.

Ferguson, Everett, ed. *Encyclopedia of Early Christianity.* New York: Garland Publishing Inc., 1990.

Fischer, Balthasar. "Esquisse Historique sur les Ordres Mineurs." *Maison Dieu* 61. (1960). pp. 58–69.

——. "Hat Ambrosius von Mailand in der Woche zwischen seiner Taufe und seiner Bischofskonsekration andere Weihe empfangen?" *Kyriakon* 2. [Festschrift Johannes Quasten] Ed. P. Granfield and J. A. Jungmann. Muenster: Verlag Aschendorff, 1970. pp. 527–531.

Fransen, G. "The Tradition in Medieval Canon Law", *The Sacrament of Holy Orders.* Collegeville, Minnesota: The Liturgical Press, 1962. pp. 202–218.

Frend, W.H.C. *The Early Church.* Philadelphia: Fortress Press, 1987.

——. *The Rise of Christianity.* Philadelphia: Fortress Press, 1984.

Frere, W.H. "Early Forms of Ordination." *Essays on the Early History of the Church and the Ministry.* Ed. H. B. Swete. London: MacMillan, 1918, pp. 263–311.

Fuller, Reginald, ed. *A New Catholic Commentary on Holy Scripture.* New York: Thomas Nelson Publishers, 1969.

Gager, John G. "Religion and Social Class in the Early Roman Empire." *Early Church History: The Roman Empire as the Setting of Primitive Christianity.* Eds. Stephen Benko and John J. O'Rourke. London: Oliphants, 1972. pp. 99–120.

Gannon, John Mark. *The Interstices Required for Promotion to Orders.* Diss. Catholic University of America. The Catholic University of America Canon Law Studies, 196. Washington: The Catholic University of America Press, 1944.

Gaudemet, J. *La formation du droit canonique médiévale.* London: Variorum Reprints, 1980.

——. *L'Église dans l'Empire Romain (IVe–Ve Siècles).* Paris: Sirey, 1958.

——. *La formation du droit séculier et du droit de l'église aux IVe et. Ve siècles.* Paris: Sirey, 1957.

——. "Holy Orders in Early Conciliar Legislation", in *The Sacrament of Orders.* Collegeville, Minnesota: The Liturgical Press, 1962. pp. 182–201.

Geerlings, Wilhelm. *Traditio Apostolica Apostolische Überlieferung.* Fontes Christiani 1. Freiburg/Br.: Herder, 1989.

Gerostegios, Asterios. *St. Photius the Great.* Belmont, MA: Institute for Byzantine and Modern Greek Studies, 1980.

"Getting Our Orders Straight: A Defect of Intention", *Diakoneo*, X.1 (January, 1988) p. 1.

Goffart, Walter. *The Le Mans Forgeries.* Cambridge MA: Harvard University Press, 1966.

Gore, Charles. *The Church and the Ministry.* London: Longman, Green, and Co., 1919.

Grant, R. M. and H. H. Graham, trans. and comm. *The Apostolic Fathers.* vol. 2. New York: Thomas Nelson and Sons, 1965.

Gryson, R. "Les degrés du clergé et leurs dénominations chez saint Ambroise de Milan". *Revue Bénédictine* 76 (1966). pp. 119–127.

Gy, P. M. "Notes on the Early Terminology of Christian Priesthood." *The Sacrament of Orders.* Collegeville, Minnesota: The Liturgical Press, 1962. pp. 98–115.

Halleux, André de. *Les Ministères aux origines de l'église.* Paris: Cerf, 1971.

Hanson, Anthony Tyrrell. *Beyond Anglicanism.* London: Darton, Longman, et. Todd, 1965.

Hanson, Richard. *Christian Priesthood Examined.* London: Lutterworth Press, 1979.

Harris, R.V. *An Historical Introduction to the Canon Law of the Anglican Church of Canada*. Toronto: Anglican Book Centre, 1965.

Hatchett, Marion. *Commentary on the American Prayer Book*. USA: Seabury, 1980.

Hefele, C. J. *Histoire des Conciles*. vol. 16. Paris: Letouzay et Ané, 1907.

Hergenröther, J. *Photius, Patriarch von Konstantinopel*. Regensberg: Georg Joseph Manz, 1867.

Herron, Thomas J. "The Most Probable Date of the First Epistle of Clement to the Corinthians." *Studia Patristica* 21 (1989). pp. 106–121.

Hess, Hamilton. *The Canons of the Council of Sardica, A. D. 343*. Oxford: Clarendon Press, 1958.

Hocedez, E. "Une découverte théologique". *Nouvelle revue théologique* 51 (1924). pp. 332–340.

Hollis, Michael. *The Significance of South India*. London: Lutterworth Press, 1966.

Holmes, Urban T. *The Future Shape of Ministry*. New York: Seabury Press, 1971.

Holy Orders: The Ordination of Bishops, Priests, and Deacons. Alexandria, VA: Associated Parishes, Inc., 1991.

Hope, D.M. *The Leonine Sacramentary: A Reassessment of its Nature and Purpose*. Oxford: Oxford University Press, 1971.

Jaffé, P. *Regesta pontificum Romanorum ab condita ecclesia ad annum post Christum natum MCXCVIII*. Ed. G. Wattenbach. 2nd ed., 2 vols. Leipzig: Veit and Coup, 1885, 1888.

Jalland, T.G. "The Doctrine of the Parity of Ministers." *The Apostolic Ministry*. Ed. Kenneth E. Kirk. London: Hodder et. Stoughton, 1957, pp. 305–349.

Jedin, Hubert, and Dolan, John. eds. *History of the Church*. 3 vols. Trans. Anselm Biggs. New York: Crossroad, 1980–1987.

Jefford, Clayton N. *The Sayings of Jesus in the Teaching of the Twelve Apostles*. Leiden: E. J. Brill, 1989.

——. "Presbyters in the Community of the *Didache*." *Studia Patristica* 21 (1989). pp. 122–128.

Jeffers, James S. *Conflict at Rome: Social Order and Hierarchy in Early Christianity*. Minneapolis: Fortress Press, 1991.

Jilek, August. "Bischof und Presbyterium." *Zeitschrift für katholische Theologie* 106 (1984), pp. 376– 401.

Jones, A.H.M. "The Roman Civil Service (Clerical and Sub-Clerical Grades)." *The Journal of Roman Studies* 39 (1949). pp. 38–55.

Jones, James L. "The Roman Army." *Early Church History: The Roman Empire as the Setting of Primitive Christianity*. Ed. Stephen Benko and John O'Rourke. London: Oliphants, 1971. pp. 187–217.

Jounel, P. "Ordinations." *The Sacraments. The Church at Prayer*. vol. 3. Ed. A. G. Martimort. Collegeville, Minnesota: The Liturgical Press, 1988. pp. 139–180.

Kazhdan, Alexander P., gen. ed. *The Oxford Dictionary of Byzantium*. New York: Oxford University Press, 1991.

Kelly, J.N.D. *Early Christian Doctrines*. New York: Harper et. Row, 1978.

———. *Jerome: His Life, Writings, and Controversies*. Westminster, Maryland: Christian Classics, 1980.

———. *The Oxford Dictionary of Popes*. Oxford: Oxford University Press. 1988.

King, Charles B. Jr. "A Confusing Proposal," Letter. *The Living Church* (July 19, 1992), pp. 10–12.

Knowles, David. *The Middle Ages, The Christian Centuries* 2. New York: McGraw-Hill, 1968.

———. *Thomas Becket*. London: Adam and Chalres Black, 1970.

Kraft, R. A., trans, et. comm. *Barnabas and the Didache, The Apostolic Fathers* 4. New York: Thomas Nelson and Sons, 1965.

Lafontaine, P.H. *Les conditions positives de l'accession aux ordres dans la première législation ecclésiastique (300–492)*. Diss. U of Ottawa, 1963. Ottawa: Éditions de l'Université d'Ottawa, 1963.

Leclerq, Henri. "Ordinations irrégulières." *Dictionaire d'Archéologie Chrétienne et de Liturgie*. vol. 12.2. Paris: Librairie Letouzay et Ané, 1936. pp. 2391–2401.

Legg, Arnold H. "Bishops in the Church of South India", in *Bishops*. London: Faith Press, 1961, pp. 116–124.

———. "The Diaconate in the Church of South India." *The Diaconate Now*. Ed. Richard Nolan Washington: Corpus Books, 1968, pp. 125–142.

Lemaire, André. *Les Ministères aux origines de l'église*. Paris: Éditions du Cerf, 1971.

Lienhard, Joseph T., *Ministry. Message of the Fathers of the Church*. vol. 8. Gen. ed. Thomas Halton, Wilmington, Delaware: Michael Galzier, Inc. 1984.

Lietzman, Hans. *A History of the Early Church*. 2 vols. London: Lutterworth Press, 1961.

Llewellyn, Peter. *Rome in the Dark Ages*. London: Faber and Faber, 1970.

Luttenberger, Gerard H. "The Decline of Presbyteral Collegiality and the Growth of the Individualization of the Priesthood (4th–5th Centuries)". *Recherches de théologie ancienne et médiévale* 48 (1981). pp. 14–58.

——. "The Priest as a Member of a Ministerial College: The Development of the Church's Ministerial Structure from 96 to c.300 A.D.". *Recherches de théologie ancienne at médiévale* 43 (1976), pp. 5–63.

Maassen, Friedrich. *Die Geschichte der Quellen und der Literatur des canonischen Rechts im Abendlande biz zum Ausgange des Mittelalters*. vol. I. Graz: Verlag von Leuschner und Lubsensky, 1870.

MacMullen, Ramsay. *Christianizing the Roman Empire (AD 100–400)*. New Haven: Yale University Press, 1984.

Macquarrie, John. *Principles of Christian Theology*. 2nd ed. New York: Charles Scribner's Sons, 1977.

McCue, James W. "Bishops, Presbyters and Priests in Ignatius of Antioch." *Theological Studies* 28 (1967). pp. 828–834.

McDevitt, A. "The Episcopate as an Order and Sacrament on the Eve of the High Scholastic Period." *Franciscan Studies* 20 (1968). pp. 96–148.

Maier, Harry O. *The Social Setting of the Ministry as Reflected in the Writings of Hermas, Clement and Ignatius*. Waterloo: Wilfrid Laurier Press, 1991.

Mays, James L., ed., *The Harper's Bible Commentary*. San Francisco: Harper et. Row, 1988.

Mitchell, Leonel L. "Direct ordination to the presbyterate." *Open* 38.4 (Winter, 1993), pp. 7–10.

Molland, Einar. "Irenaeus of Lugdunum and the Apostolic Succession." *Journal of Ecclesiastical History* 1 (1950). pp. 12–28.

Moore, Peter, ed. *Bishops: But What Kind?*. London: SPCK, 1982.

Mühlenburg, Ekkehard. "Les débuts de la biographie chrétienne." *Revue de théologie et de philosophie*. 122 (1990). pp. 517–529.

Munier, Charles. "False Decretals to Gratian: Canon Law, History Of." *New Catholic Encyclopedia* 3. New York: McGraw-Hill Book Company, 1967. pp. 39–41.

Neill, Stephen. "The Historic Episcopate." *Bishops*. London: Faith Press, 1961, pp. 41–50.

Niederwimmer, Kurt. *Die Didache*. Göttingen: Vanderhoek und Ruprecht, 1989.

Osborne, Kenan B. *Priesthood: A History of the Ordained Ministry in the Roman Catholic Church*. New York: Paulist Press, 1988.

Pagé, Jean-Guy. *Prêtre: un métier sans avenir?*. Montreal: Éditions Paulines, 1989.

Paredi, Angelo. *Saint Ambrose, His Life and Times*. Notre Dame, Indiana: University of Notre Dame Press, 1964.

Plater, Ormonde. "Blizzard of papers on direct ordination." *Diakoneo* 15.3 (Easter, 1993), p. 12.

——. "Direct ordination: the historical evidence." *Open* 37.4 (Winter, 1992): pp. 1–2.

——. *Many Servants: An Introduction to Deacons*. Cambridge, MA: Cowley Publications, 1991.

Porter, H. B. Jr. *The Ordination Prayers of the Ancient Western Churches*. London: SPCK, 1967.

Powell, Douglas. "Ordo Presbyterii." *Journal of Theological Studies* 26 (1975), pp. 290–328.

Power, David. *Ministers of Christ and his Church*. London: Geoffrey Chapman, 1963.

Puniet, Dom Pierre de. *The Roman Pontifical: A History and Commentary*. London: Longmans, Green, and Co., 1937.

Ratcliffe, E. C. "'Apostolic Tradition': Questions Concerning the Appointment of the Bishop." *Liturgical Studies*. Ed. A. H. Couratin and D. H. Tripp. London: SPCK, 1976, pp. 156–160.

Reed, J. Sanders. *The Bishop's Blue Book*. New York: James Pott et. Co., 1894.

Reicke, Bo. "Deacons in the New Testament and the Early Church". *The Ministry of Deacons*. Geneva: World Council of Churches, 1965.

Renard, Hubert. *Diaconat et Solidarité*. France: Éditions Salvator, 1990.

Reynolds, Roger E. "An Early Medieval Tract on the Diaconate", *Harvard Theological Review* 72 (1979). pp. 97–100.

——. "'At Sixes and Sevens'—and Eights and Nines: The Sacred Mathematics of Sacred Orders in the Early Middle Ages." *Speculum* 54.4 (1979). pp. 669–684.

——. "The *De Officiis VII Gradum*: Its Origins amd Early Medieval Development", *Mediaeval Studies* 34 (1972). pp. 113–151.

——. "A Florilegium on the Ecclesiastical Grades in CLM 19414: Testimony to Ninth-Century Clerical Instruction", *Harvard Theological Review* 63 (1970). pp. 235–259.

——. "Image and Text: The Liturgy of Clerical Ordination in Early Medieval Art." *Gesta* 22.1 (1983). pp. 27–38.

——. "The `Isidorian' *Epistula ad Leudefredum*: An Early Medieval Epitome of the Clerical Duties", *Mediaeval Studies* 41 (1979). pp. 252–326.

——. "Law: Canon, to Gratian." *Dictionary of the Middle Ages.* Ed. Joseph R. Strayer. New York: Charles Scribner's Sons, 1986. pp. 395–413.

——. "Marginalia on a Tenth-century Tract on the Ecclesiastical Officers." *Law, Church, and Society: Essays in Honor of Stephen Kuttner.* Eds. K. Pennington and R. Sommerville. University of Pennsylvania Press: 1977. pp. 115–129.

——. *The Ordinals of Christ from their Origins to the Twelfth Century.* Beiträge zur Geschichte und Quellenkunde des Mittelalters 7, Berlin-New York: 1978.

——. "The Ordination Rite in Medieval Spain: Hispanic Roman, and Hybrid." *Santiago, Saint-Denis, and Saint Peter: The Reception of the Roman Liturgy in Léon-Castille in 1080.* Ed. Bernard F. Reilly. New York: Fordham University Press, 1985. pp. 131–155.

——. "Patristic `Presbyterianism' in the Early Medieval Theology of Sacred Orders." *Mediaeval Studies* 45 (1983). pp. 311–342.

——. "The Portrait of the Ecclesiastical Officers in the *Raganaldus Sacramentary* and its Liturgico-Canonical Significance". *Speculum* 46.3 (1971). pp. 432–442.

——. "The Pseudo-Hieronymian *De Septem Ordinibus Ecclesiae*", *Revue Bénédictine* 80 (1970). pp. 238–252.

——. "The Ritual of Clerical Ordination of the *Sacramentarium Gelasianum Saec. VIII*: Early Evidence from Southern Italy." *Rituels: Mélanges offerts au Père Gy op.* Ed. Paul De Clerck and Eric Palazzo. Paris: Éditions du Cerf, 1991.

——. "Sacred Orders in the Early Middle Ages: Shifts in the Theology of the Lower and Higher Ecclesiastical Orders from Late Antiquity through the Early Middle Ages Reflected in the Ordinals of Christ and Related Literature." Diss. Harvard University, 1968.

Richter, Klemens. "Zum Ritus der Bischofsordination in der `Apostolischen Überlieferung' Hippolyts von Rom und davon abhängingen Schriften." *Archiv für Liturgiewissenschraft*, 17–18 (1975–1976), pp. 7–51.

Schaefer, Mary M., and Henderson, J. Frank. *The Catholic Priesthood: A Liturgically Based Theology of the Presbyteral Office. Canadian Studies in Liturgy* 4. Ottawa: Canadian Conference of Catholic Bishops, 1990.

Scherman, Katherine. *The Birth of France: Warriors, Bishops and Long-haired Kings*. New York: Random House, 1987.

Schillebeeckx, Edward. *Ministry: Leadership in the Community of Jesus Christ*. New York: Cross Roads, 1985.

Schoedel, William R. *Ignatius of Antioch: A Commentary on the Letters of Ignatius of Antioch*. Philadelphia: Fortress Press, 1985.

Schöllgen, Georg. *Didache: Zwölf-Apostel-Lehre*. Freiburg: Herder, 1991.

Seckl, Emil. "The Pseudo-Isidorian Decretal and other Forgeries." *The New Schaff-Herzog Religious Encyclopedia*. vol. 9. Gen. ed. S. M. Jackson. New York: Funk and Wagnells, 1911. pp. 343–350.

Segelberg, E. "The Ordination Prayers in Hippolytus." *Studia Patristica*, 13 (1975). pp. 397–408.

Shepherd, Massey. "Elders in the New Testament", *The Interpreters Dictionary of the Bible*. vol. 1. Nashville: Abingdon Press, 1986. pp. 73–75.

——. "Ministry, Christian", *The Interpreters Dictionary of the Bible*. vol. 3. Nashville: Abingdon Press, 1986. pp. 368–392.

Simpson, W.J. Sparrow. *South Indian Schemes*. London: SPCK, 1930.

Stam, J.E. *Episcopacy in the Apostolic Tradition of Hippolytus*. Basel: Friedrich Reinhardt, 1969.

Strayer, Joseph R., gen. ed. *The Dictionary of the Middle Ages*. New York: Charles Scribner's Sons, 1982.

Stuchbery, Ian. Letter. *Anglican Journal* 118.8 (October, 1992), p. 8.

——. Letter. *Diakoneo* 15.5 (All Saints, 1992), p. 59.

Sultana, Joseph M. "The Authenticity of the Mono-Episcopate in the Ignatian Letters vis-à-vis Recent Critics." Diss. University of St. Michael's College, 1983.

Swete, H.B. ed. *Essays on the Early History of the Church and the Ministry*. London: MacMillan, 1918.

Sykes, Norman. *The Church of England and the non-episcopal Churches in the sixteenth and seventeenth centuries*. London: SPCK, 1949.

——. *Old Priest and New Presbyter*. Cambridge: University Press, 1956.

Symonds, R.P. "Deacons in the Early Church." *Theology* 58 (1955). pp. 408–414.

Taft, Robert. *The Liturgy of the Hours in East and West.* Collegeville: The Liturgical Press, 1986.

Tavard, George H. *A Theology for Ministry, Theology and Life Series* 6. Wilmington Delaware: Michael Glazier, Inc., 1983.

Taylor, J. "The Post-Reformation Episcopacy in England." *The Ministry of the Church.* Ed. Stephen Neil. London: Canterbury Press, 1947, pp. 75–87.

Telfer, W. "Episcopal Succession in Egypt." *Journal of Ecclesiastical History* 3.1 (1952).

Till, B.D. "Episcopacy in the Works of the Elizabethan and Caroline Divines." *The Historic Episcopate.* Ed. Kenneth Carey. Westminster: Dacre Press, 1954, pp. 63–83.

Tixeront, J. *Holy Orders and Ordination: A Study in the History of Dogma.* London: Herder, 1928.

Toporoski, Richard. "Ambrose." *The Dictionary of the Middle Ages.* vol. 1. Gen. ed. Joseph R Strayer. New York: Charles Scribner's Sons, 1982. pp. 230 ff.

Tuillier, André. "La doctrine des apôtres et la hiérarchie dans l'église primitive." *Studia Patristica* 18.3 (1989). pp. 229–262.

Turner, C. H. "The Organization of the Church." *The Cambridge Medieval History.* vol. 1. Cambridge: The University Press, 1911, pp. 143–182.

Vilela, Albano. "Le Presbyterium selon saint Ignace d'Antioche." *Bulletin de littérature ecclésiastique* 74 (1973). pp. 161–186.

Vogel, Cyrille. *Medieval Liturgy: An Introduction to the Sources.* Eds. and Trans. William Storey and Niels Rasmussen. Washington: The Pastoral Press, 1986.

——. *Ordinations Inconsistantes et Caractère Inamissible.* Torino: Bottega D'Erasmo, 1978.

Webster, John. "Ministry and Priesthood." *The Study of Anglicanism.* Eds. Stephen Sykes and John Booty. London: SPCK, 1988, pp. 285–296.

Weil, Louis. "Should the Episcopal Church Permit Direct Ordination." Unpublished essay, 1993.

White, Despina Stratoudaki. *Patriarch Photios of Constantinople: His Life, Scholarly Contributions, and Correspondence Together with a Translation of Fifty-two of His Letters.* Brookline, MA: Holy Cross Orthodox Press, 1981.

Wiesen, David S. *St. Jerome as a Satirist: A Study in Christian Latin Thought and Letters*. Ithica, NY: Cornell University Press, 1964.

Wild, Robert A. "The Pastoral Epistles." *The New Jerome Biblical Commentary*. Eds. R. Brown, J. Fitzmeyer, R. Murphy. Englewood Cliffs, New Jersey: Prentice Hall, 1990.

Williams, George H. "The Ministry of the Ante-Nicene Church (c. 125–325)", in H. Richard Niehbur et. Daniel D. Williams, eds., *The Ministry in Historical Perspectives*. New York: Harper Brothers, 1956. pp. 60–81.

Willis, G. G. *Essays in Early Roman Liturgy*. London: SPCK, 1964.

Woollcombe, K.J. "The Ministry and Order of the Church in the Works of the Fathers." *The Historic Episcopate*. Ed. Kenneth Carey. Westminster: Dacre Press, 1954.

Wortman, Julie A. "Diocese redefining roles of deacons, priests." *Episcopal Life*. May, 1991. pp. 1, 9.

——. "Deacons' revival brings servant ministry to fore." *Episcopal Life*. June, 1991. p. 7.

Wright, J. Robert. "Richard Hooker and the Doctrine of Cumulative or Sequential Orders." *Sewanee Theological Review* 36.2 (Easter, 1993). pp. 246–251.

——. "Sequential or Cumulative Orders vs. Direct Ordination."*Anglican Theological Review*. 75.2 (Spring, 1993). pp. 246–251.

Zimmermann, Harald. *Papstabsetzungen des Mittelalters*. Köln: Hermann Böhlaus Nachf, 1968.

Patristic Studies

This is a series of monographs designed to provide access to research at the cutting-edge of current Patristic Studies. Particular attention will be given to the development of Christian theology during the first five centuries of the Church and to the different types of Biblical interpretation which the Fathers used. Each study will engage with modern discussion of the theme being treated, but will also break new ground in original textual research. In exceptional cases, a volume may consist of the critical edition of a text, with notes and references, as well as translation. Revised doctoral dissertations may also be published, though the main focus of the series will be on more mature research and reflection. Each volume will be about 250–300 pages (100,000–120,000 words) long, with a full bibliography and index.

Inquiries and manuscripts should be directed to:

Peter Lang Publishing
Acquisitions Department
516 N. Charles Street, 2nd Floor
Baltimore, MD 21201

To order other books in this series, please contact our Customer Service Department at:

(800) 770-LANG (within the U.S.)
(212) 647-7706 (outside the U.S.)
(212) 647-7707 FAX

or browse online by series at:

www.peterlang.com